Frommer's 96

Boston

by Lisa Legarde

Macmillan • USA

About the Author

Lisa Legarde was born in New Orleans and graduated from Wellesley College with a B.A. in English. She has traveled extensively in Europe and North America and has covered Boston for *Frommer's New England* as well. She is currently at work on a walking tour guide to the city.

Macmillan Travel

A Simon & Schuster Macmillan Company
1633 Broadway
New York, NY 10019

ISBN: 0–02–860876–3
ISSN: 0899–322X

Editor: Margaret Bowen
Production Editor: Amy DeAngelis
Map Editor: Douglas Stallings
Design by Michele Laseau
Digital cartography by Ortelius Design and Jim Moore

Special Sales

Bulk purchases (10[+] copies) of Frommer's travel guides are available to corporations at special discounts. The Special Sales Department can produce custom editions to be used as premiums and/or for sales promotion to suit individual needs. Existing editions can be produced with custom cover imprints such as a corporate logo. For more information write to Special Sales, Simon & Schuster, 8th floor, 1633 Broadway, New York, NY 10019.

Manufactured in the United States of America.

Contents

6 Dining 81

7 What to See & Do in Boston 124

List of Maps

An Invitation to the Reader

In researching this book, I discovered many wonderful places. I'm sure you'll find others. Please tell us about them, so I can share the information with your fellow travelers in upcoming editions. If you were disappointed with a recommendation, I'd love to know that, too. Please write to:

Lisa Legarde
Frommer's Boston '96
Macmillan Travel
1633 Broadway
New York, NY 10019

An Additional Note

Please be advised that travel information is subject to change at any time—and this is especially true of prices. We therefore suggest that you write or call ahead for confirmation when making your travel plans. The authors, editors, and publisher cannot be held responsible for the experiences of readers when traveling. Your safety is important to us, however, so we encourage you to stay alert and be aware of your surroundings. Keep a close eye on cameras, purses, and wallets, all favorite targets of thieves and pickpockets.

What the Symbols Mean

✪ **Frommer's Favorites**

Hotels, restaurants, attractions, and entertainment you should not miss.

$ **Super-Special Values**

Hotels and restaurants that offer great value for your money.

The following abbreviations are used for credit cards:

AE American Express
CB Carte Blanche
DC Diners Club
DISC Discover
ER enRoute
EU Eurocard
JCB Japan Credit Bank
MC MasterCard
V Visa

1

Introducing Boston

More than anything else, it is the lure of history that draws visitors to Boston. From all over the country and the world they come to follow the path of Paul Revere, to visit the shrines where such "long-haired radicals" as John Hancock and Samuel Adams incited the colonists to revolution, and to pay homage to the one city that is, perhaps more than any other, the birthplace of the United States.

But there is a lot more about Boston to enchant and excite the visitor than the memories and monuments of the past, important as they are. Boston is very much a metropolis of the 1990s, a unique town that combines big-city excitement and sophistication with a pace that is positively relaxing. Boston has long prided itself on being the "Athens of America," and the city vibrates with cultural vitality. Bostonians are justly proud of the Boston Symphony Orchestra, the Museum of Fine Arts, Harvard University, and the Massachusetts Institute of Technology (the latter two located just across the Charles River in Cambridge). Schools, colleges, medical centers, and research and cultural institutions abound, and as a result Boston draws bright young people from all over the world.

The past still lives and is cherished in this modern city. Centuries-old meetinghouses sit side by side with modern towers that are part of contemporary "New Boston." Boston has some of the best hotels in America; scores of exciting restaurants—both Old World and daringly new in approach—many of which serve the best seafood in the country; a host of attractions and amusements for children; a vast number of museums, parks, flower gardens, and an aquarium; and a shopping scene that is irresistible. Boston has its Back Bay Brahmins and its students, the "old money" of Louisburg Square and the working people of Roxbury, South Boston, and the South End. It is a fascinating mix of people as various as the descendants of *Mayflower* stock, the Italians and eastern European Jews who came to work in the city's factories and mills at the turn of the century; and the African Americans, Hispanics, Asians, and, most prominently, Irish who have given Boston a full share of both raffish history and glory.

Boston itself has a population of 574,300, but as the hub of the Greater Boston area, which numbers some 4 million people spread out in 83 cities and towns, its importance is far reaching. The most diversified city in New England, it is the home of major computer,

Boston Orientation

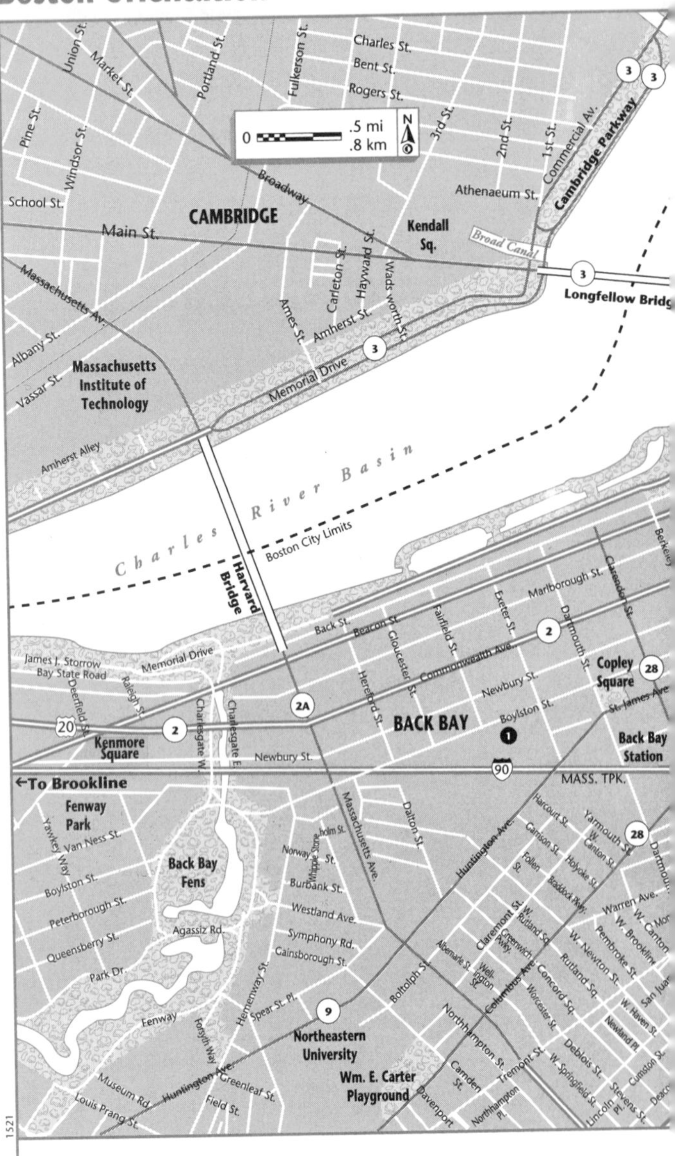

VISITOR CENTERS:

Boston Common Visitor Information Center ❷
Prudential Visitor Center ❶
Visitor Center ❸

1521

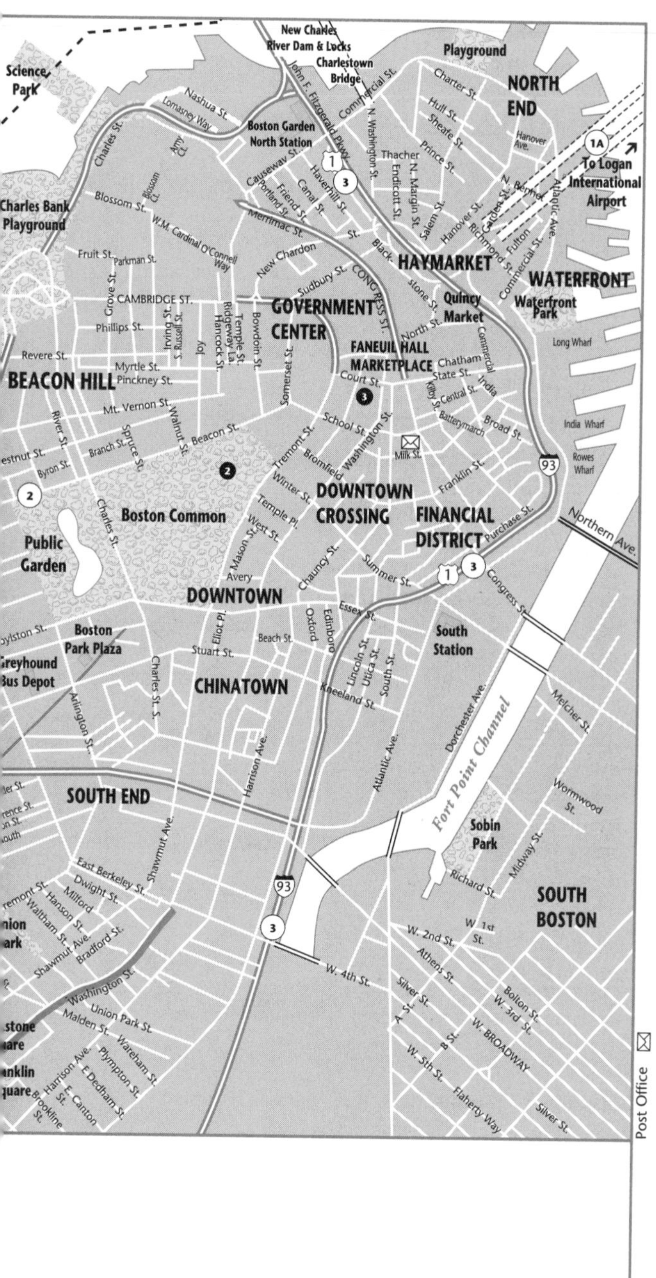

Science Park
New Charles River Dam & Locks
Charlestown Bridge
Playground
NORTH END
Boston Garden North Station
To Logan International Airport
Charles Bank Playground
HAYMARKET
WATERFRONT
Waterfront Park
Quincy Market
GOVERNMENT CENTER
FANEUIL HALL MARKETPLACE
BEACON HILL
Boston Common
DOWNTOWN CROSSING
FINANCIAL DISTRICT
Public Garden
DOWNTOWN
Boston Park Plaza
South Station
Greyhound Bus Depot
CHINATOWN
Fort Point Channel
SOUTH END
Sobin Park
SOUTH BOSTON
Long Wharf
India Wharf
Rowes Wharf
Northern Ave.

Post Office ⊠

banking, and insurance industries. Yet Boston is a particularly pleasant walking city—fruit and flower stands add color to street corners in the downtown shopping area and around Copley Square. Newbury, Charles, and Boylston streets are lined with inviting shops, antiques stores, and galleries.

Best of all for the traveler, Boston is ideally situated to be the starting point for a wide variety of New England holidays. Within Massachusetts alone you can, within an hour, drive to the North Shore resort towns of Salem, Marblehead, Essex, Newburyport, Gloucester, and Rockport, each filled with more than its share of historical and contemporary interest. Plymouth is only an hour's drive to the south; another 30 minutes on the highway will take you to Cape Cod. Turn west and Sturbridge Village, a re-creation of a 19th-century rural village, is just about 90 minutes away.

1 Frommer's Favorite Boston Experiences

- **Springtime in the Public Garden.** Take time to smell the flowers—tulips, pansies, and flowering trees and shrubs. Ride the swan boats, feed the ducks, bring a sandwich and have lunch. Relax away from the bustle of the city.
- **Shopping at the Nostalgia Factory.** You won't believe your eyes when you walk into the Nostalgia Factory, located on Newbury Street. Collectors of the odd and unique will lose themselves for hours here as they browse through vintage postcards, political pins, advertisements, and old posters. There's a gallery attached, in which you'll learn a thing or two about this country's recent history and social attitudes.
- **A Nighttime View from the Top.** From a perch high up in the Hancock Tower of the Prudential Center, view the city in its nighttime glamour, a panorama of light all across town, from the Charles River to Boston Harbor.
- **Friday or Saturday Afternoon at the Haymarket.** Whether you're in the market for fresh produce or not, the Haymarket is an experience you shouldn't miss. In addition to fruits and vegetables, there are some great shops for buying meats and cheeses here on Blackstone Street between North and Hanover streets. At the end of the day on Saturday you might even walk away with a bargain or two.
- **An Evening at Boston Pops.** The music at Symphony Hall is light and sparkling, like the champagne that is served. Pleasant music and great fun, especially on Old Timer's Night when everyone joins in the Sing-Along.
- **An Afternoon at The Sports Museum of New England.** Sports enthusiasts will love visiting this museum, with its incredible collection of sports memorabilia that includes bats, balls, jerseys, life-size statues, and shoes of New England sports greats.
- **A Visit to Faneuil Hall Marketplace and the Waterfront.** Soak up the ocean breezes, walk along the waterfront, get some good-

ies at the food stalls, and watch the street performers at the marketplace—it's great fun at any time of day.

- **Sea Cliffs on the Atlantic.** A trip to the rocky coastline north of the city in Marblehead and Rockport will be well worth your efforts. Climb the rocky cliffs along the shore and look at the sea, watch the sailboats, and admire the luxurious cabin cruisers.
- **A Few Hours at the Samuel Adams Brewery.** Learn how this famous Boston beer is made, right at the brewery. You'll get a guided tour and will enjoy free tastings of the lager.
- **A Holiday Visit to the Isabella Stewart Gardner Museum.** In December, the museum's garden courtyard is massed with brilliant poinsettias and the skylit atrium is ablaze with color.
- **A Meal at No-Name.** It doesn't look like much; you'll sit at communal tables with people you've never seen before, and it's filled to the bursting point with locals, businesspeople, and tourists, but don't let that stop you. The fish served here is excellent. No-Name is located at $15^1/_2$ Fish Pier.
- **Secondhand Book Shopping.** In my opinion, the best place to shop for secondhand books is at Avenue Victor Hugo on Newbury Street. On a rainy day you'll have no qualms about spending hours digging through the well-selected stock.
- **A Trip to the Children's Museum.** If you've got kids in tow, there's no better place to take them than the Children's Museum. It's one of the best in the country, and it features multicultural interactive, educational exhibits.
- **A Walk Down Hanover Street.** Hanover Street is the center of Boston's Little Italy, and it's a real treat to walk along enjoying the people and sights of this colorful neighborhood.
- **Shopping on Newbury Street.** Don't miss a visit to this wonderful boutique-lined thoroughfare. It's a great place to pick up some unique clothing and accessories. It's also a pleasant place to do some window shopping.

2 A Look at the Past

HISTORY

First settled in 1630 by members of the Massachusetts Bay Company, Boston was named for the hometown of many of the Puritans who had come to these shores seeking both fortune and religious freedom. The population increased rapidly, and in two years it became the capital of Massachusetts. Thanks to its excellent location on Massachusetts Bay, Boston quickly became an important shipbuilding, fishing, and trading center. Early in the history of the New World, the British began pressing for laws to restrict the colonies' trading activities, which were cutting into

Dateline

- **1614** Capt. John Smith explores the Boston area, names the Charles River, and calls the area "a paradise."
- **1624** William Blackstone settles on the Shawmut Peninsula

continues

(Boston) with a collection of 200 books and his Brahma bull.

- 1630 John Winthrop leads settlers to present-day Charlestown in June, and in September the settlement is named Boston in honor of the English hometown of many Puritans; on October 19, 108 voters attend the first Boston town meeting.
- 1632 Boston becomes the capital of Massachusetts.
- 1635 Boston Latin School, America's first public school, opens.
- 1636 Harvard College founded to educate young men for the ministry.
- 1638 America's first printing press established in Cambridge.
- 1639 America's first post office established in home of Richard Fairbank.
- 1682 A free school, ordered to provide for teaching children to write and "cipher," becomes the basis

continues

their own profits. First was the Revenue Act of 1764, imposing duties on sugar, silk, and wine. The Stamp Act, which taxed commercial and legal documents, newspapers, and playing cards, followed the next year. Outraged colonists refused to buy British goods, and Boston mobs ransacked the home of Gov. Thomas Hutchinson. Other Bostonians demonstrated peacefully, but rallied around the cry, "No taxation without representation!"

The Stamp Act was repealed in 1766, but another inflammatory law followed—the Townshend Acts, which taxed, among other things, the colonists' favorite drink, tea. Colonial anger soon erupted into riots, and in 1768 two British regiments were sent to occupy Boston and restore order. Tensions quickly mounted between the redcoats and colonists and broke into violence in 1770 with the Boston Massacre. Five colonists were killed, and the revolt had its first martyrs. The British Parliament repealed the Townshend Acts, except for the tax on tea. In 1773 the Tea Act called for the colonies to be flooded with cheap tea to tempt Bostonians who were drinking smuggled tea. But when British ships loaded with tea arrived in Boston Harbor, Boston's activist Sons of Liberty, disguised as Indians, boarded the ships on the night of December 16, 1773, and dumped the chests of tea into the harbor. The "Indians" included Samuel Adams and John Hancock, and the Boston Tea Party became immortalized as one of history's great acts of chutzpah.

In an effort to crush revolutionary uprisings, the British sent 700 soldiers to destroy an arms depot in Concord. Forewarned by Paul Revere and William Dawes, the Minutemen were ready, and "the shot heard round the world" was fired at the Battle of Lexington and Concord on April 19, 1775. The Battle of Bunker Hill (actually fought on Breed's Hill) on the Charlestown peninsula followed on June 17, 1775. And though the British won the battle, their losses were so great that they finally abandoned the city on March 17, 1776. On July 4, 1776, the Declaration of Independence was adopted by the Continental Congress. Although many Bostonians fought in the six-year war that followed, no further battles were fought in Boston.

When the war ended, Bostonians turned to commerce. Fortunes were made from the sea on codfish exports and whale by-products—you may have heard Boston's upper classes referred to as a "codfish aristocracy." Entrepreneurs sent ships to the Far East to trade in silks, spices, tea, and porcelain. Nearby Salem became a major port of China trade, and merchants from both towns competed for riches and political power. The influential merchant families became known as Boston Brahmins. They set the standards for the town's intellectual and cultural life, and their many business enterprises provided the fortunes that financed Boston's fine art and architecture, including the homes on Beacon Hill.

Boston's 19th-century cultural bloom encompassed many things: The city became a haven for intellectuals, many renowned cultural institutions were founded, and the city resounded with strong voices speaking out on politics and freedom. William Lloyd Garrison published the *Liberator* newspaper, a powerful voice in the abolitionist movement. Boston became an important stop on the Underground Railroad, the secret network developed by the abolitionists to smuggle slaves into Canada. Thousands of immigrants from Ireland, victims of the potato famine, settled in Boston and eventually changed the character of the city. Discriminated against by the old Bostonians at first, they eventually won political power and are still a strong influence in government.

As its population grew over the years, Boston needed more land, and an ingenious plan was executed that created both land and some sorely needed jobs. Early Boston had developed around three hills surrounded by ocean and swamp. Between 1799 and 1835 the hills were shorn and their tops used to extend the shoreline. A giant reclamation project started in 1856 filled in the mudflats of the back bay with gravel transported from Needham in railway trains, creating Commonwealth Avenue and other streets of the present Back Bay. By the turn of the century Boston had tripled its size with landfill. In addition to Back Bay, other areas built on reclaimed land are South Boston and East Boston.

After World War II, Boston's economy went into decline. Many of its textile, shoe, and glass mills closed, and its port activity slowed. With the advent of advanced technology, its economy revived, and Boston has become a leader in computer technology, medicine, insurance, and finance. And it still maintains its century-old

for the public school system.

- **1704** America's first newspaper, the *Boston News Letter,* published.
- **1721** First shots for smallpox given. Inoculations advocated by Dr. Zabdiel Boylston and Cotton Mather.
- **1764** Taxation without representation is denounced in reaction to the Sugar Act.
- **1770** On March 5, five colonists are killed outside the Old State House in the Boston Massacre.
- **1773** Boston Tea Party. On December 16, 342 chests of tea are dumped into Boston Harbor by colonists dressed as Indians.
- **1775** Paul Revere and William Dawes spread the word that the British are about to attack Concord and Lexington the night of April 18. The next day the "shot heard round the world" is fired there. The Battle of Bunker Hill is fought on June 17. The British win but suffer heavy casualties.
- **1776** British evacuate Boston by ship.

continues

- **1790** China trade helps build fortunes for Bostonians.
- **1825** First city census lists 58,277 people.
- **1831** William Lloyd Garrison publishes the first issue of the *Liberator,* a newspaper dedicated to emancipation.
- **1872** The Great Fire burns 65 acres and 770 buildings.
- **1878** Girls Latin School opens.
- **1895** Boston Public Library opens.
- **1897** First Boston Marathon is run.
- **1897** The first subway in America opens—a 1.7-mile stretch from Boylston Street to Park Street.
- **1918** Red Sox celebrate their victory in the World Series; a championship drought (of 78 years!) begins.
- **1942** A fire in the Coconut Grove nightclub kills 491 people.
- **1946** John F. Kennedy elected to Congress from Boston's First Congressional District.

continues

prominence as a center for higher learning with its prestigious colleges and research and development facilities.

3 Famous Bostonians

Judge Louis Dembitz Brandeis (1856–1941) The first Jewish judge to be appointed to the Supreme Court, Brandeis was a public advocate for consumers and labor unions. A graduate of Harvard Law School, he had a successful practice in Boston before his appointment to the court. He was instrumental in establishing savings bank life insurance and the Federal Trade Commission. Brandeis University in nearby Waltham, Massachusetts, is named for him.

Charles Bulfinch (1763–1844) Bulfinch gave Boston part of its distinctive look with his Federal style of architecture. His legacies include the Massachusetts State House, St. Stephen's Church in the North End, Massachusetts Hall at Harvard, and many Beacon Hill mansions in his trademark red brick and granite. An early advocate of urban planning, he favored laying out streets in grid patterns accented with small green ovals. He also designed the U.S. Capitol in Washington, D.C.

Sarah Caldwell (b. 1929) Caldwell founded the Opera Company of Boston in 1957 and brought first-rate opera back to the city. As stage director and operatic conductor she continues to demonstrate that a woman can excel in these areas.

Julia Child (b. 1912) This French chef made a name for herself on Boston's public television station and helped the city gain a reputation as a center of great gastronomical fare. She still lives in Cambridge.

James Michael Curley (1874–1958) Perhaps Boston's most colorful and notorious political figure, he was elected mayor four times, governor once, and U.S. congressman once, and served time in federal prison for fraud. Yet he was one of Boston's most beloved politicians because he brought jobs and prosperity to his constituents; they in turn repaid him at election time. There are two bronze likenesses of Curley near Dock Square—one standing, and one seated on a bench. There's room to sit beside the latter and talk politics.

Dorothea Dix (1802–87) An early investigative reporter, she persuaded the Massachusetts State Legislature to improve conditions for the mentally ill in state hospitals. She then mounted a national campaign on behalf of the mentally ill and managed to influence 15 other states and Canada to improve treatment in state hospitals.

Mary Baker Eddy (1821–1910) The founder of Christian Science, Eddy developed her beliefs over many years by studying the New Testament and healing herself of many illnesses through prayer. She believed her book *Science and Health with Key to the Scriptures* was divinely inspired. The Mother Church Building, one of Boston's most imposing structures, was built in 1894; an extension was added in 1904. Mrs. Eddy founded the *Christian Science Monitor* in 1908.

Ralph Waldo Emerson (1803–82) Philosopher, poet, essayist, and leader of the transcendental movement, Emerson was born in Boston, but in later years moved to Concord. He studied at Harvard and entered the ministry, where he won fame as a preacher; in the 1830s he turned to transcendentalism. He was also at the center of a group of literary intellectuals that included Thoreau, Hawthorne, Holmes, Alcott, Longfellow, Lowell, and Whittier. Known as the Saturday Club, they met for seven-course meals and discussion at the Parker House.

- **1957** Boston Celtics win first of 16 NBA championships.
- **1960** John F. Kennedy elected 35th president of the United States.
- **1966** Edward Brooke becomes the first black elected to the U.S. Senate in the 20th century.
- **1976** The restored Faneuil Hall Marketplace opens.
- **1990** The Women's Heritage Trail, celebrating 20 women who have been influential in Boston and the nation, is established.

William Lloyd Garrison (1805–79) An early leader in the antislavery movement and the publisher of the weekly newspaper the *Liberator,* he faced great opposition, and at one point a mob dragged him through the streets of the city. Eventually he was honored by President Abraham Lincoln and others for his fight to abolish slavery.

John Hancock (1737–93) One of the reasons Paul Revere rode to Lexington was to warn Hancock and Sam Adams that the British were *coming for them!* Mostly known for being the first signer of the Declaration of Independence and the president of the Continental Congress, Hancock played a major political role in his own state. He was governor of Massachusetts in 1780, and mayor of Boston for nine terms, dying in office. A wealthy businessman, he contributed much to the economic development of the city.

John F. Kennedy (1917–63) The 35th president of the United States and educated at Harvard, Kennedy captained a small navy gunboat in World War II. He served as both a congressman and senator in Washington, D.C., before he was elected president in 1960. The youngest man and first Catholic to hold the highest political office in the land, JFK was a liberal Democrat who had many admirers and enemies. He was assassinated in Dallas, Texas, in 1963. The Kennedy

Library in Dorchester and the Kennedy School of Government at Harvard in Cambridge are memorials to his life and accomplishments.

Frederick Law Olmsted (1822–1903) Olmsted coined the term "landscape architect" to describe his work creating city gardens and green spaces. He believed they contributed to one's psychological well-being. Olmsted brought beauty to Boston with the Emerald Necklace, a 7-mile-long ribbon of interconnected parks stretching from the Boston Common to Franklin Park and including the Public Garden, the Commonwealth Avenue mall, the Charles River Esplanade, the Back Bay Fens, and the Arnold Arboretum.

Paul Revere (1735–1818) Mainly remembered for his ride to Lexington and Concord, made famous by Longfellow in the "Landlord's Tale" from *Tales of the Wayside Inn,* he was also a printer and engraver, a dentist, a gold- and silversmith, and a manufacturer of bells. His home in the North End is now a museum open to the public.

4 Art & Architecture

ART

In the 19th century several famous artists made their reputations in Boston. John Singer Sargent painted portraits of many Bostonians, including the famous one of Isabella Stewart Gardner in a form-fitting black dress now featured in the Gardner Museum. Childe Hassam, born in Boston, memorialized his native city with impressionist-style paintings such as his famous depiction of Boston Commons. Winslow Homer, a late 19th-century painter who favored nautical and coastal scenes, is another Boston native.

Today many Boston artists have their studios and lofts in the Fort Point Channel area in South Boston, a neighborhood that has been compared to New York's SoHo. The Fort Point Arts Community at 249 A Street is a central clearinghouse for artists. The influence of art has been so strong in this area that many galleries have opened on South Street near South Station, some even relocating from famed Newbury Street. (The largest concentration of art galleries in Boston is still on Newbury Street.) For a comprehensive listing, pick up a *Gallery Guide,* available at most galleries.

Art covers more than just paintings and sculpture. It encompasses crafts, and contemporary crafts in all media can be found at the Society of Arts and Crafts, 175 Newbury Street, and at its satellite shop at 101 Arch Street in downtown Boston. Incidentally, Paul Revere is one of the country's most famous artisans. A renowned silversmith, he designed the silver/pewter bowl known as the "Revere bowl," which is still a favorite today for its simplicity of style. It is sold in fine shops and is often presented to visiting dignitaries.

Another form of art is stained glass. The Church of the Covenant at the corner of Berkeley and Newbury streets has the largest collection of Tiffany ecclesiastical stained-glass windows in the world. Trinity Church also has a famous stained-glass window by John La Farge.

Beantown Politics

Boston has produced some of the most prominent politicians in our history. From revolutionary leader Samuel Adams to President John F. Kennedy and presidential nominee Michael Dukakis, Bostonians have helped to shape the nation. And on the local level, Boston politics has almost always been characterized by vibrant and colorful leadership. At first the Brahmins governed the city, but by the late 1880s the influx of Irish immigrants created a new locus of political power, and Irish politicians became prominent. The first Irish mayor was elected in 1885; in 1910 John F. Fitzgerald ("Honey Fitz") became mayor and founder of the political dynasty that led to the presidency of his grandson, John Fitzgerald Kennedy. (Honey Fitz's daughter Rose was JFK's mother.)

Another flamboyant politician defeated Fitzgerald in 1913 and went on to become a political legend. James Michael Curley served as mayor of Boston four times over four decades. He spent part of his last mayoral term in a federal penitentiary convicted of fraud until President Truman pardoned him. In between terms as mayor of Boston, he served as governor of Massachusetts, and was once a U.S. congressman. Other well-known Boston politicians include former Speakers of the House John W. McCormack and Tip O'Neill, as well as Sen. Edward "Ted" Kennedy. To this day, Bostonians almost invariably elect a Democrat for mayor and other city offices.

ARCHITECTURE

Boston encompasses three and a half centuries of architecture in an area of about three miles. From Paul Revere's colonial home to the glass-walled John Hancock Tower, from Bulfinch's golden-domed State House to H. H. Richardson's Trinity Church, there is an abundance of outstanding architecture in Boston. And it is all so accessible! You will find a number of restored colonial buildings as you walk the Freedom Trail.

Charles Bulfinch, one of the greatest architects of the early 19th century, perfected the Federal style of architecture, and his brick mansions still stand on Beacon Hill. The home at 141 Cambridge Street that he designed in 1795 for the mayor of Boston is open to the public for tours. Bulfinch's crowning achievement is the "new" State House, completed in 1797 and located at the top of Beacon Street across from the Boston Common. Its famous gilded dome was first made of wood, then covered in copper by Paul Revere, and finally gilded in 1874.

The most interesting buildings in Boston for architecture buffs are the Victorian mansions in the Back Bay area. Most of them are still in use today, either as residences, businesses, or schools. The facades are elaborate and the interiors lavish. Many are museums or public buildings that are open for tours.

Architect I. M. Pei took Boston's architecture into the 20th century with designs for the Government Center and the Christian Science Center. The John Hancock Tower, with its glass facade, and the Kennedy Library are also among his works. Art deco values can be seen in the United Shoe Machinery Building, with its shiny gold-colored tile roof, at the corner of Federal and High Streets, and in the Hatch Memorial Shell on the Esplanade, where the Boston Pops Orchestra holds summer concerts.

Faneuil Hall Marketplace combines the old and the new. Designed in 1826 in Greek-revival style by Alexander Parris, it was long a Boston landmark known as Quincy Market, but by the 1970s it was showing signs of years of neglect. In 1976 it was renovated and renamed Faneuil Hall Marketplace, becoming the first of the festival markets that are appearing in cities throughout the country.

5 Boston Cuisine

SEAFOOD Early Bostonians made their living from the sea. Since fishing was so important, one of the local merchants presented the legislature with a codfish carved in pine (now known as the "Sacred Cod") to remind state representatives of the impact the fishing industry had on the Massachusetts economy. Today *les fruits de mer,* including cod, remain an important part of the local economy and cuisine. Chefs and owners of the city's best restaurants are at the docks before dawn to make purchases for the lunch and dinner menus from their favorite purveyors.

Cod is a large (it can grow up to six feet in length), white flaky fish that can be prepared in a variety of ways. In Boston restaurants you'll often find it cut into smaller pieces (fillets) and fried, broiled, poached, and even roasted. Scrod is a fillet of cod, haddock, or pollock, all of which are white fish. Other fishes you might see on menus around Boston are tuna, bluefish, flounder, tilefish (another white fish), and striped bass. Monkfish—an incredibly ugly, but very tasty fish—is nicknamed *crapaud* (toad) or *diable de mer* (sea devil) by the French. Due to its hideousness, it is always served without the head.

In Boston, lobster is a favorite crustacean. I prefer it boiled and served with drawn butter, but you can also get it stuffed, broiled, baked, in a pie, in a salad (if you can find a lobster salad with black olives, tomatoes, and a vinaigrette, order it), served Newburg style (lobster meat cut into large pieces, cooked in butter, simmered in wine, mixed into a cream and egg yolk sauce, and served in timbales or over hot toast). Another nice lobster dish is lobster thermidor (boiled lobster broken into small pieces, cooked with mushrooms, butter, mustard, paprika, parsley, sherry, and cream sauce, and served in the shell). If you head to the city's ethnic neighborhoods you'll see that lobster hasn't escaped their menus, either.

Of course, a trip to Boston wouldn't be complete without having some clams. There are basically two types of clams—soft-shell and hard-shell. Soft-shell clams are most often served steamed, while the hard-shell are served in a variety of ways. Before we get to that, you should know that hard-shell clams, or quahogs (co-hogs) are divided into three categories: littlenecks (the smallest in size), cherrystones (medium size), and large (chowder) clams. Littlenecks and cherrystones are both excellent served raw with a dash of Tabasco and lemon juice. My favorite, however, is fried clams. If you order fried clams almost everywhere else in the country, you'll get a plate full of once-frozen, breaded, deep-fried, chewy clam strips, but in Boston, and other places around New England, you get the whole clam, belly and all, fried in a light batter and served with an enormous side of french fries. When they're done right, they just melt in your mouth—there's nothing hard or chewy about them.

If you get a chance, you should also try a New England clambake, which is a huge pot full of clams, corn, potatoes, sausage or chicken, and sometimes lobster that have been steamed to perfection. Real clambakes were traditionally done over an open fire of wood and hot stones at the beach, but nowadays most people do the cooking right on their stoves at home.

The clam chowder you'll find in Boston, known as New England clam chowder, is made with large, hard-shell clams cut into pieces, potatoes, salt pork, milk, and cream. It's a thick soup that should in no way be confused with the tomato-based Manhattan clam chowder.

Scallops, shrimp, and mussels are also abundant off the shores of nearby towns.

BAKED BEANS AND OTHER OLD-TIME FAVORITES

Probably the most famous of Boston dishes is those dark, sweet Boston baked beans. I'm not talking about the kind you get in a can, either. Real Boston baked beans are of the homemade variety. The beans used are either dried pea beans or navy beans that have been soaked in water overnight. After that they're simmered until the skins pop open, and then the real fun begins. You take those cooked beans and put them in a bean pot (or Crock-Pot) with some salt pork, dry mustard, brown sugar, molasses, and a little bit of boiling water. Then you cook them slowly for about eight hours. Once you've had them you'll never want to eat the kind that come in a can again. In Boston, baked beans are most often served with brown bread, a heavy, slow-cooked bread made with whole wheat flour, rye flour, cornmeal, molasses, and buttermilk. Some people put raisins in it. It's delicious either way. Cornbread is also a Boston favorite.

As far as desserts go, there are a couple of old-time specialties that still grace some menus and are worth trying. Apple pandowdy, a simple, but traditional dish, is basically apple pie cooked in a shallow baking dish. The crust is less fussy than crust used on a regular apple pie because it's made with biscuit dough. Apple pandowdy is usually served hot with a pudding sauce, or whipped cream flavored with nutmeg. Indian pudding is a heavy, slow-cooked "pudding" made with cornmeal, scalded and cold milk, and molasses. It's baked for three hours and served with a hard sauce, whipped cream, or ice cream.

There are a few things you should know before heading into the nearest ice cream parlor (which you should do at least once while in Boston because you'll find some of the country's best ice cream).

A milk shake in Boston (and other parts of New England) is not made with ice cream; it's just milk and flavored syrup shaken until well mixed. If you want it with ice cream you should ask for a frappé. A chocolate ice cream soda is made with vanilla ice cream and chocolate syrup. If you want chocolate ice cream you have to ask for it. After you've ordered ice cream in a dish, you'll probably be asked if you want jimmies. Those are chocolate sprinkles to the rest of us.

DRINK Notwithstanding Massachusetts' old blue laws and Puritan history, you can buy alcoholic drinks almost anytime in Boston; on Sunday morning, however, no purchases can be made before noon. Beer is the favorite drink, but wine is becoming increasingly popular. Samuel Adams lager is brewed in Boston, and wines are produced in Nashoba Valley near Concord.

2

Planning a Trip to Boston

This chapter is devoted to the where, when, and how of your trip—the advance-planning issues required to get it together and take it on the road.

After deciding where to go, most people have two fundamental questions: What will it cost? and How do I get there? This chapter will answer both of those questions and resolve other important issues, such as when to go and where to obtain more information about Boston and its environs.

1 Visitor Information & Money

VISITOR INFORMATION

As soon as you know you're going to Boston, check the following two sources: The **Greater Boston Convention and Visitors Bureau** (Prudential Tower, Box 490, Suite 400, Boston, MA 02199; ☎ **617/536-4100** or 800/888-5515 outside MA; fax 617/424-7664) offers a free travel planner, a comprehensive guidebook ($4.95), and a *Kids Love Boston* guidebook. If you're looking for up-to-date information on attractions, performing arts and nightlife, galleries, and travel services, call **Boston by Phone** (☎ **800/374-7400**) from anywhere in the United States. The **Massachusetts Office of Travel and Tourism** (13th floor, 100 Cambridge St., Boston, MA 02202; ☎ **617/727-3201** or 800/447-6277; fax 617/727-6525) will send a free getaway guide that includes an attractions guide, map, seasonal calendar, and lodgings guide. If you're looking for information specific to Cambridge, contact **Cambridge Discovery, Inc.** (P.O. Box 1987, Cambridge, MA 02238; ☎ **617/497-1630**).

In addition to the information centers listed above, it is possible to gather Boston information on the internet. A good place to start is: http://www.city.net/countries/united_states/massachusetts/boston; or http://www.city.net/countries/united_states/massachusetts/cambridge. Once you get there you'll find everything from useful telephone numbers to transportation information to sports and recreation clubs to maps and politics. You'll also find connections to other on-line sources that deal specifically with Boston and Cambridge.

MONEY

Boston tends to be an expensive city. But with advance planning using this book, you can choose where to save and where to spend. You could save on lodgings by staying at a bed-and-breakfast inn and then you could splurge on the best restaurants; or you could spend most of your money on luxury hotels and then eat take-out food for picnics. Or you could enjoy free concerts and lectures and then spend your money on a shopping spree.You get the idea. Whatever you decide to do, you're going to need some cash while you're on the road.

Traveler's checks are as good as cash and can be replaced if they are lost or stolen. However, some establishments restrict the amount they will accept or cash, so purchase some in small denominations for convenience. And for your protection, make a list of the serial numbers and keep it separate from the checks in case you need to replace them.

If you prefer not to carry too much cash at one time, there are Automated Teller Machines (ATMs) all over Boston. Most are located at banks, shopping malls, and supermarkets. Call your ATM network

What Things Cost in Boston	U.S. $
Taxi from airport to downtown Boston	16.00–22.00
Bus from airport to downtown Boston	8.00
MBTA subway token	.85
Double at the Four Seasons Hotel (deluxe)	300.00–460.00
Double at Boston Park Plaza Hotel & Towers (moderate)	155.00–245.00
Double at Chandler Inn Hotel (budget)	89.00
Lunch for one at Zuma's Tex-Mex Café (moderate)	6.95–17.95
Lunch for one at Samuel Adams Brewhouse (budget)	5.95–9.50
Dinner for one, without wine, at Aujourd'hui (deluxe)	26.00–35.50
Dinner for one, without wine, at Rocco's (moderate)	9.00–24.00
Dinner for one, without wine, at Jimbo's Fish Shanty (budget)	6.00–16.00
Glass of beer	2.75–4.00
Coca-Cola	1.00
Cup of coffee	1.00
Roll of ASA 100 Kodacolor film, 36 exposures	6.75–7.75
Admission to the Museum of Fine Arts, Boston	8.00
Movie ticket	7.00–7.50
Theater ticket	30.00–90.00

before you leave home to check out its Boston locations. Cirrus (☎ **800/424-7787**) and PLUS Global ATM Locator Service (☎ **800/843-7587**) are international networks that connect with most other ATM institutions. They can supply you with directories listing locations of machines.

2 When to Go

Boston attracts large numbers of visitors year-round because there's always something happening, but you probably won't have too much trouble securing a room during your stay. If you want to avoid huge crowds, try not to travel during one of the major citywide events (listed below). You should also avoid trying to get rooms near colleges at graduation time (early June). Hotel rates are usually lower during the winter, but go up in the summer and fall.

CLIMATE

New England has never been known for ideal weather. Winters can be cold and snowy, and summers are often hot and sticky, with temperatures soaring into the 80s and 90s during July and August. Spring is usually mild and beautiful; fall is crisp and clear, with the kind of Octobers that the poets used to write about. But it can be hot in fall and breezy in summer, cool in spring and warm in January, so be prepared for anything.

Once in Boston, you can check the weather by looking up at the lights on the old John Hancock Insurance Company in Back Bay. (The new Hancock building is the glass-paneled one.) A steady blue light means clear; flashing blue, cloudy; steady red, rain; flashing red, snow—except during the summer, when flashing red means the Red Sox game has been canceled.

Boston's Average Temperatures & Rainfall

	Jan	Feb	Mar	Apr	May	June	July	Aug	Sept	Oct	Nov	Dec
Temp (°F)	30	31	38	49	59	68	74	72	65	55	45	34
Rain (inches)	4.0	3.7	4.1	3.7	3.5	2.9	2.7	3.7	3.4	3.4	4.2	4.9

BOSTON CALENDAR OF EVENTS

January

- **Chinese New Year,** Chinatown. Dragon parade, fireworks, and many festive parties. Special programs at Children's Museum. Date of festivities determined by Chinese lunar calendar; may fall any time between January 21 and February 19.
- **Martin Luther King, Jr., Birthday Celebration.** Various locations citywide. Third Monday of the month.

February

- **Boston Festival,** Public Garden, Boston Common, and Faneuil Hall Marketplace. A celebration of winter, with ice-skating, sledding, and ice sculpture. Held throughout the month, with special programs scheduled for Valentine's Day and the winter school vacation, which usually occurs during the third week of the month.

March

- **St. Patrick's Day/Evacuation Day Parade,** South Boston. Parade in celebration of the city's Irish heritage and of the day the British abandoned Boston in 1776. March 17.
- **New England Spring Flower Show,** Bayside Expo Center, Dorchester. Annual harbinger of spring presented by the Horticultural Society. Third week of the month.

April

✪ **Patriot's Day.** An annual celebration of the beginning of the American War of Independence. The day's events begin with "Paul Revere" and "William Dawes" riding to Lexington and Concord to warn the patriots that the British are coming; later, a mock battle in full uniform is fought at Lexington and then Concord. There is also a reenactment of the hanging of the lanterns in Boston's Old North Church.

Where: Lexington Green, Concord North Bridge, Old North Church. **When:** Patriot's Day is April 19, but the holiday is celebrated on the third Monday of the month, which is a state holiday in Massachusetts. **How:** Contact the Lexington Visitors Center (1875 Massachusetts Ave., Lexington, MA 02173; ☎ **617/862-1450**).

- **Boston Marathon,** from Hopkinton, Massachusetts, to Boston. This world-class marathon attracts the world's top distance runners. The race begins at noon on the third Monday of the month.

May

- **Greater Boston Kite Festival,** Franklin Park. A fun event that sends hundreds of kites, from the modest diamond-shaped kind to outlandish flying machines, into the skies. Midmonth.
- **Lilac Sunday,** Arnold Arboretum, Jamaica Plain. The only day of the year that picnicking is permitted at the arboretum. From sunrise to sunset everyone enjoys the fragrance and beauty of the more than 400 varieties of lilacs in bloom. Usually held on the third Sunday of the month.

June

- **Bunker Hill Weekend,** Charlestown Navy Yard. An 18th-century historic military encampment with activities that include maneuvers, open-fire cooking, cleaning and mending of clothing and equipment, and a parade commemorating the Battle of Bunker Hill, which the patriots lost. Usually held on the second weekend of June; Bunker Hill Day is June 17.
- **Boston Dairy Festival,** Boston Common. Once a year, cows return to Boston Common, where they grazed in centuries past. Milking contests, dairy foods, ice-cream festival, and children's activities. First week in June.

July

✪ **Boston Harborfest.** Boston's annual Fourth of July celebration of the harbor's illustrious maritime history. Events include concerts, guided tours, cruises, fireworks, the Boston Chowderfest, and the annual turnaround of the USS *Constitution.* The week is literally packed with activities. Call or write the address below for a detailed schedule of events.

Where: Sites along Boston Harbor and the Harbor Islands. **When:** First week in July. **How:** Contact Boston Harborfest (45 School St., Boston, MA 02108-3204; ☎ 617/227-1528 or fax 617/227-1886).

- **Boston Pops Concert and Fireworks Display,** Hatch Memorial Shell at the Esplanade. Program includes the *1812 Overture* with the actual—and deafening—firing of cannon. July 4.

August

- **Salem's Heritage Days,** Salem. A week-long event with programs highlighting Salem's multicultural heritage. Third week in August.

September

- **Art Newbury Street,** on Newbury Street from the Public Garden to Massachusetts Avenue. Open-house time for the galleries on this fashionable street, which is closed to traffic for the event. There are musical groups and other free entertainment. Late September.

October

✪ **Head of the Charles Regatta.** College crew teams from across the country participate in this very popular race, which has become something of an annual gathering for preppy America. Crowds line the Charles River in Cambridge to cheer their favorites, eat, and have fun.

Where: Along the Charles River. **When:** Late October. **How:** You can watch from either the Boston or Cambridge side; the many bridges spanning the river also make good perches.

November

- **Thanksgiving Celebration,** Plymouth. Thanksgiving feast at Plimoth Plantation, the re-creation of the Pilgrims' first settlement. There's a walk, in costume, to church and a special dinner in town. Thanksgiving Day.

December

- **Boston Tea Party Reenactment,** at the Tea Party Ship and Museum, Congress Street Bridge. To celebrate one of history's great moments of political rebellion. Mid-December.

✪ **First Night.** Boston is perhaps unrivaled on this night, as events are held throughout the city to celebrate the New Year. Parades, ice sculptures, and both indoor and outdoor entertainment. At midnight, there is a spectacular fireworks display over the harbor.

Where: Back Bay and the waterfront. **When:** December 31; late afternoon for the children's parade and through the night for the revelry. **How:** Contact First Night Citywide at **617/542-1399.**

3 Tips for Special Travelers

FOR TRAVELERS WITH DISABILITIES Boston, like all other U.S. cities, has taken the required steps to provide access for the disabled. Hotels must provide rooms for the handicapped, museums and street curbs have ramps for wheelchairs. The Americans with Disabilities Act (ADA), effective in 1992, requires all forms of public transportation to provide special services to persons with disabilities. All MBTA buses have lifts or kneelers (call **800/LIFT-BUS** for more information). While some bus routes are wheelchair accessible at all times, you might have to make a reservation as much as a day in advance for others. Some taxis are now equipped to handle wheelchairs—call individual taxi services to find out if they're available. In addition, there is now an Airport Handicap Van (☎ **617/561-1769**). For reduced fares in public transportation, persons with disabilities can obtain an MBTA Transportation Access Pass (TAP) from the Downtown Crossing Station during the week from 8:30am to 4:15pm. For more information call **617/722-5438** in advance of your trip. A TAP will cost you $3, and it's valid for five years. (*Note:* Although Boston has made progress, some wheelchair-dependent travelers have recently reported difficulty negotiating curbs and buses. You should do some research before you leave home.) An excellent source of information for the disabled is the **Information Center for Individuals with Disabilities** (Fort Point Pl., 27-43 Wormwood St., 1st floor, Boston, MA 02210; ☎ **617/727-5540** or 800/462-5015, voice or TDD; the phone for the hearing impaired is **TDD 617/727-5236.** Hours are 8:30am to 4:30pm. They also publish helpful fact sheets. The **Massachusetts Coalition for Citizens with Disabilities** (20 Park Plaza, Suite 603, Boston, MA 02116; ☎ **617/482-1336** or 800/TRY-MCCD, voice or TDD) is also helpful.

FOR GAY MEN & LESBIANS The **Gay and Lesbian Helpline** offers information (☎ **617/267-9001**) Monday through Friday from 4 to 11pm and Sunday 6 to 11pm. The phone number for **Boston Alliance of Gay and Lesbian Youth** (BAGLY) is **800/422-2459.** ***In Publications*** (258 Shawmut Ave., Boston, MA 02118; ☎ **617/426-8246**), New England's largest gay and lesbian weekly newspaper, lists upcoming events, news, and features.

FOR SENIORS Boston offers many discounts to seniors. Hotels, restaurants, museums, and movie theaters try to woo them with special deals. Discounts are usually offered in restaurants and theaters only at off-peak times, but museums and other attractions offer reduced rates at all times. Seniors can ride the MBTA subways for 20¢ (85¢ for others). Local bus fares for seniors are 15¢. On zoned and express buses and on the commuter rail the senior citizen fare is half the regular fare.

On the commuter rail all you need as proof of age is a valid driver's license or passport, but for the subway and buses you have to have an MBTA senior citizen card. You can purchase the senior citizen card for 50¢ at the Downtown Crossing Station weekdays from 8:30am to 4:15pm. Call **617/722-5438** in advance of your trip.

A Golden Age Passport will give you free lifetime admission to all recreation areas run by the federal government, including parks and monuments.

If you're planning a trip to Boston, you might want to contact **Elderhostel, Inc.** (75 Federal St., Boston, MA 02116; ☎ **617/426-8056**) for information on its programs for those 60 and older. Generally participants live in a college dorm, take courses at the college in the morning, and enjoy the area they're visiting in the afternoon.

FOR FAMILIES Children (usually under 17) can stay free in their parents' hotel room, when using existing bedding. And many hotels have package deals for families that offer a suite or breakfast for the kids, plus discount coupons for museums and restaurants. The **Greater Boston Convention and Visitors Bureau** (☎ **617/536-4100**) has a brochure listing family-friendly hotel packages and special discounts. Give them a call, or write to them at Prudential Tower, Box 490, Suite 400, Boston, MA 02199.

FOR STUDENTS Boston is a great place for students. Restaurants, museums, theaters, concert halls, and other places usually offer discounts for college and high school students with valid IDs. During the summer months students can rent rooms in college dorms on some of the campuses. Check with the schools for information. Visiting students might check the bulletin boards at Boston University, Harvard, and MIT; many events will be open to them. The *Boston Phoenix* also lists a number of activities for students in its weekly edition.

4 Getting There

BY PLANE

The major domestic carriers flying into Boston's **Logan International Airport** are American, Continental, Delta, Northwest, TWA, USAir, and United. Most of the major international carriers also fly into Boston.

Logan airport is only about 10 minutes from downtown via taxi, limousine, or subway (the MBTA Blue Line). There is also a water shuttle to Rowes Wharf on Atlantic Avenue.

FINDING THE BEST AIRFARE To get the best price, you need to shop around. Fares are constantly changing; they vary from airline to airline and even from day to day at the same airline. Try to schedule your travel for weekdays during the busy summer season and avoid major holiday periods when fares go up. In general, the lowest fares are economy (also known as tourist) or APEX—the former has no restrictions, while the latter (an Advance Purchase Excursion fare) requires you to reserve and pay for the ticket 7, 14, 21, or 30 days in advance and stay for a minimum number of days. APEX fares are usually nonrefundable, and there is a charge for changing dates. However, the savings are considerable. Knowing all this, get on the phone, call your travel agent, who has reliable sources of competitive price data on all the airlines and knows which categories are available on which lines, or call several airlines yourself. Though these days most airlines try to have the same fares as their competitors, one or two will occasionally offer lower fares to compete for more passengers, so check and keep checking all the airlines as far in advance of your trip as possible. If you're a member of the on-line service America On Line (AOL), go to keyword "travel" and look for EasySabre. There you can look up all available flights and fares to Boston for the dates you intend to travel. You can also make reservations though this service.

OTHER GOOD VALUE CHOICES A charter flight can be a good option if you choose the company carefully. Tour operators book a block of seats and then offer them at substantial reductions. However, you must book and pay in advance, and usually you can't make any changes. You may lose your full payment or have to pay a penalty if you cancel. Investigate to make sure you have a reliable company that won't cancel or close shop before the flight. Airlines sometimes supply tickets to conventional agencies or charters at sharply reduced prices during a slow period. Organizations that resell them are known as "bucket shops." Some are reliable; others may not be. It is best to check with the Better Business Bureau. On standby you wait at the airport for an empty seat on your flight. After all reserved seats are accounted for, you can board at great savings. If not, you go home and try again, or book a regular flight.

LOGAN INTERNATIONAL AIRPORT Boston's Logan International Airport may be the most accessible of any in the country, situated as it is just 3 miles across the harbor from the downtown area. Access to the city is by cab, bus, and subway via underwater tunnels, or by boat. The **subway** is fast and cheap—seven minutes (to Government Center) and 85¢. Free **shuttle buses** run from each terminal to Airport Station on the MBTA Blue Line from 5:30am to 1am every day of the year. From there you can go to the State Street or Government Center stops.

Some hotels have their own **limos**; ask about these when you make your reservations. A **cab** from the airport to downtown costs between $16 and $22. (See "Getting Around," below, for more information on taxis in Boston.) The ride into town may take anywhere from 10 minutes to a half hour, depending on traffic backups in the tunnel or on the John F. Fitzgerald Expressway.

For a quick ride to Rowes Wharf on Atlantic Avenue (perfect for the Boston Harbor Hotel, Marriott Long Wharf, or for getting a cab elsewhere) in just seven minutes, dock to dock, try the **Airport Water Shuttle.** Courtesy buses from the terminals connect with the weather-protected, heated boats, which sail every 15 minutes from 6am to 8pm on weekdays and every half hour beginning at noon on Sundays and national holidays (except Thanksgiving Day, Christmas, New Year's Day, and Independence Day). There is no service on Saturday.

One-way fares are $8 for adults and children 12 and up, and $4 for senior citizens; children under 12 free.

If you're headed for the suburbs, look for the **Share-A-Cab booths** at each terminal and save up to half the fare. Limo and bus service north, south, and west of the city is available, usually by prearrangement. Call **Carey Limousine Boston** (☎ **617/623-8700**) or **Stagecoach Executive Sedan Services, Inc.** (☎ **617/723-9393** or 800/922-9500).

If you'd rather avoid all the hassles of securing public transportation and have opted to rent a car, the following rental agencies offer shuttle service from the airport to their offices: **Avis** (☎ **800/331-1212**); **Budget** (☎ **800/527-0700**); **Hertz** (☎ **800/654-3131**); **National** (☎ **800/227-7368**); or **Thrifty** (☎ **800/367-2277**).

FLYING WITH FILM AND LAPTOPS Traveling with electronic devices and film (whether exposed or not) is often thought to be a problem. X-ray machines won't affect film up to ASA 400, but you might want to request a visual check anyway. Ditto for laptops. As this book goes to press, a visual check for computers is standard practice in most airports. Most airports have X-ray machines that purport not to do damage to computer memory; however, I still insist that they do the visual check. You'll have to turn it on for them, so make sure your batteries are charged up. You'll be allowed to use your computer in flight, but not during take-off and landing because of possible interference with cockpit controls. In many cases, airport security guards will also ask you to turn on electronic devices (including camcorders and personal stereos) to prove that they are what they appear to be, so make sure batteries are charged and working for these items as well.

BY CAR

Driving to Boston is not difficult. The major highways leading to and from Boston are I-95/Route 128, which connects Boston to highways in Connecticut and New York; I-90, the Massachusetts Turnpike, an east-west toll road that links up with the New York Thruway; I-93/U.S. 1, extending north to Canada and leading to the Northeast Expressway, which enters downtown Boston; and I-93/Route 3, the Southeast Expressway, which connects Boston with the south, including Cape Cod.

The Massachusetts Turnpike ("Mass Pike") has a number of extensions that go through the center of the city and connect with the Central Artery (the John F. Fitzgerald Expressway), which is linked to the Northeast Expressway. If you want to avoid Central Artery construction, exit at Prudential Center in the Back Bay. The Southeast Expressway is a busy commuter route, so try to avoid it at rush hour.

The approach to Cambridge is either Storrow Drive or Memorial Drive, one on each side of the Charles. The exit at Larz Andersen Bridge and John F. Kennedy Street leads to Harvard Square, if you turn right.

Since Boston is 208 miles from New York, the driving time is about 4½ hours. The 992-mile drive from Chicago to Boston should take around 21 hours; from Washington, D.C., it takes about 8 hours to cover the 468 miles.

A word of caution about driving in the city: The face of Boston is being changed by the "Big Dig," a construction project that is relocating the Central Artery (the John F. Fitzgerald Expressway) underground. A third harbor tunnel, to connect Boston with Logan International Airport, is also in the works. The delays may be long and the detours confusing, although the planners promise a minimum of traffic backup. It would be best to avoid the Central Artery by choosing alternate routes.

Once you've reached your hotel, leave your car in the garage and walk or use public transportation. You're best off saving the car for trips to the suburbs, the North Shore, or Plymouth; if you must drive in town, ask your hotel's concierge to route you around the construction area.

BY TRAIN

There are three rail centers in Boston—**South Station** on Atlantic Avenue, **Back Bay Station** at 145 Dartmouth Street, and **North Station** on Causeway Street. **Amtrak** (☎ **482-3660**) has arrival and departure points at South Station and Back Bay Station. At South Station take the Red Line to Park Street, the central hub of the **MBTA** (☎ **617/722-3200** weekdays), from which you can make connections to the Blue and Green lines. The Orange Line connects Back Bay station with Park Street and other points. The MBTA operates trains to Ipswich, Rockport, and Fitchburg from North Station, and commuter lines to points south of Boston from South Station.

Amtrak (☎ **800/USA-RAIL**) runs to Boston's South Station from New York, with stops at Route 128 and Back Bay. Express trains make the trip in 4 hours; others take about 4½ to 5 hours or longer. Fares range from $80 to $120 round trip for reserved express service. If you're coming from Washington, D.C., count on 8½ hours; round-trip Metroliner costs $238; regular, unreserved train fares run from $110 to $160 round trip. Traveling time from Chicago is 22 hours (sleepers available), and the fares range from $128 to $198 round trip. All of these fares are subject to change. Please note that Amtrak fares vary—there are regular quoted fares as well as discounted fares, which are available when passenger sales are slow. Always remember to ask for the discounted rate.

If you'd been to South Station in the past, you might hesitate before taking the train to Boston; however, since its recent renovation it's become a popular meeting spot for Bostonians who aren't even catching a train. The tables around the food stalls are quite busy at breakfast and lunch. There's a glass-walled concourse, terrazzo floors, and an imposing coffered ceiling.

It's interesting to note that the one-ton clock above the main entrance is the only remaining hand-wound tower clock in New England. It is wound once a week from a small room behind the 14-foot-diameter clock face.

BY BUS

If you're arriving by **Greyhound** (☎ **800/231-2222**), **Plymouth & Brockton** (☎ **508/746-0378** or 800/433-7800), **Vermont Transit** (☎ **800/451-3292**), or **Brush Hill** (☎ **617/986-6100**) bus lines, you'll disembark at South Station, where you can take the subway (Red Line) or a commuter rail to your final destination. **American Eagle** (☎ **617/426-7838**), **Peter Pan** (☎ **617/426-7838** or 800/343-9999), and **Concord Trailways** (☎ **617/426-7838**) arrive at the Peter Pan Terminal, 555 Atlantic Avenue, a short walk from South Station, where you can get the subway or a commuter rail.

Sample fares and times on Greyhound to Boston from other major cities are as follows: From New York, $48 round trip, 4 to 5 hours. From Washington, D.C., $80 round trip, 11 hours. From Chicago, $210 round trip, 24 to 27 hours. These fares are all subject to change. Greyhound will occasionally discount tickets purchased several weeks in advance.

3

For Foreign Visitors

Although American fads and fashions have spread across Europe and other parts of the world so that America may seem like familiar territory before your arrival, there are still many peculiarities and uniquely American situations that any foreign visitor will encounter.

1 Preparing for Your Trip

ENTRY REQUIREMENTS

DOCUMENT REGULATIONS Canadian citizens may enter the United States without visas; they need only proof of Canadian residence.

Citizens of the U.K., New Zealand, Japan, and most western European countries traveling with valid passports may not need a visa for fewer than 90 days of holiday or business travel to the United States, providing that they hold a round-trip or return ticket and enter the United States on an airline or cruise line participating in the visa waiver program. (Note that citizens of these visa-exempt countries who first enter the United States may then visit Mexico, Canada, Bermuda, and/or the Caribbean islands and then reenter the United States, by any mode of transportation, without needing a visa. Further information is available from any U.S. embassy or consulate.)

Citizens of countries other than those stipulated above, including citizens of Australia, must have two documents: a valid passport, with an expiration date at least six months later than the scheduled end of the visit to the United States; and a tourist visa, available without charge from the nearest U.S. consulate. To obtain a visa, the traveler must submit a completed application form (either in person or by mail) with a 1½-by-½ inch-square photo and demonstrate binding ties to the residence abroad.

Usually you can obtain a visa at once or within 24 hours, but it may take longer during the summer rush from June to August. If you cannot go in person, contact the nearest U.S. embassy or consulate for directions on applying by mail. Your travel agent or airline office may also be able to provide you with visa applications and instructions. The U.S. consulate or embassy that issues your visa will determine whether you will be issued a multiple- or single-entry visa and any restrictions regarding the length of your stay.

MEDICAL REQUIREMENTS No inoculations are needed to enter the United States unless you are coming from, or have stopped over in, areas known to be suffering from epidemics, particularly cholera or yellow fever.

If you have a disease requiring treatment with medications containing narcotics or drugs requiring a syringe, carry a valid signed prescription from your physician to allay any suspicions that you are smuggling drugs.

CUSTOMS REQUIREMENTS Every adult visitor may bring in, free of duty: 1 liter of wine or hard liquor; 200 cigarettes or 100 cigars (but no cigars from Cuba) or 3 pounds of smoking tobacco; and $100 worth of gifts. These exemptions are offered to travelers who spend at least 72 hours in the United States and who have not claimed them within the preceding six months. It is altogether forbidden to bring into the country foodstuffs (particularly cheese, fruit, cooked meats, and canned goods) and plants (vegetables, seeds, tropical plants, and so on). Foreign tourists may bring in or take out up to $10,000 in U.S. or foreign currency with no formalities; larger sums must be declared to Customs on entering or leaving.

INSURANCE

There is no national health system in the United States. Because the cost of medical care is extremely high, I strongly advise every traveler to secure health coverage before setting out.

You may want to take out a comprehensive travel policy that covers (for a relatively low premium) sickness or injury costs (medical, surgical, and hospital); loss or theft of your baggage; trip-cancellation costs; guarantee of bail in case you are arrested; costs of accident, repatriation, or death. Such packages (for example, "Europe Assistance" in Europe) are sold by automobile clubs at attractive rates, as well as by insurance companies and travel agencies.

MONEY

CURRENCY & EXCHANGE The U.S. monetary system has a decimal base: one American dollar ($1) = 100 cents (100¢).

Dollar bills commonly come in $1 (a "buck"), $5, $10, $20, $50, and $100 denominations (the last two are not welcome when paying for small purchases and are not accepted in taxis or at subway ticket booths). There are also $2 bills (seldom encountered).

There are six denominations of coins: 1¢ (one cent or a "penny"), 5¢ (five cents or a "nickel"), 10¢ (ten cents or a "dime"), 25¢ (twenty-five cents or a "quarter"), 50¢ (fifty cents or a "half dollar"), and the rare $1 piece.

TRAVELER'S CHECKS Traveler's checks denominated in U.S. dollars are readily accepted at most hotels, motels, restaurants, and large stores. But the best place to change traveler's checks is at a bank. Do not bring traveler's checks denominated in other currencies.

CREDIT CARDS The method of payment most widely used is the credit card: VISA (BarclayCard in Britain), MasterCard (EuroCard in Europe, Access in Britain, Chargex in Canada), American Express,

Diners Club, Discover, and Carte Blanche. You can save yourself trouble by using "plastic money" rather than cash or traveler's checks in most hotels, motels, restaurants, and retail stores (a growing number of food and liquor stores now accept credit cards). You must have a credit card to rent a car. It can also be used as proof of identity (often carrying more weight than a passport), or as a "cash card," enabling you to draw money from banks that accept them.

Note: The "foreign-exchange bureaus" so common in Europe are rare even at airports in the United States, and nonexistent outside major cities. Try to avoid having to change foreign money, or traveler's checks denominated other than in U.S. dollars, at a small-town bank, or even a branch in a big city; in fact, leave any currency other than U.S. dollars at home—it may prove a greater nuisance to you than it's worth.

SAFETY

GENERAL While tourist areas are generally safe, crime is on the increase everywhere, and U.S. urban areas tend to be less safe than those in Europe or Japan. Visitors should always stay alert. This is particularly true of large U.S. cities. It is wise to ask the city's or area's tourist office if you're in doubt about which neighborhoods are safe. Avoid deserted areas, especially at night. Don't go into any part of the city at night unless there is an event that attracts crowds—for example, Boston's concerts in the parks. Generally speaking, you can feel safe in areas where there are many people and many open establishments.

Avoid carrying valuables with you on the street, and don't display expensive cameras or electronic equipment. Hold on to your pocketbook, and place your billfold in an inside pocket. In theaters, restaurants, and other public places, keep your possessions in sight.

Remember also that hotels are open to the public, and in a large hotel security may not be able to screen everyone entering. Always lock your room door—don't assume that once inside your hotel you are automatically safe and no longer need be aware of your surroundings.

DRIVING Question your rental agency about personal safety, or ask for a brochure of traveler safety tips when you pick up your car. Obtain written directions, or a map with the route clearly marked, from the agency showing how to get to your destination. And, if possible, arrive and depart during daylight hours.

Recently more and more crime in all U.S. cities has involved cars and drivers, most notably, what is called "carjacking." If you drive off a highway into a doubtful neighborhood, leave the area as quickly as possible. If you have an accident, even on the highway, stay in your car with the doors locked until you assess the situation or until the police arrive. If you are bumped from behind on the street or are involved in a minor accident with no injuries and the situation appears to be suspicious, motion to the other driver to follow you to the nearest police precinct, well-lighted service station, or all-night store. *Never* get out of your car in such situations.

If you see someone on the road who indicates a need for help, do *not* stop. Take note of the location, drive on to a well-lighted area, and telephone the police by dialing **911.**

Park in well-lighted, well-traveled areas if possible. Always keep your car doors locked, whether attended or unattended. Look around you before you get out of your car, and never leave any packages or valuables in sight. If someone attempts to rob you or steal your car, do *not* try to resist the thief/carjacker—report the incident to the police department immediately.

You may wish to contact the Greater Boston Convention and Visitors Bureau before you arrive. They can provide you with a safety brochure.

2 Getting to the U.S.

Travelers from overseas can take advantage of the **APEX (Advance Purchase Excursion) fares** offered by all the major U.S. and European carriers. Aside from these, attractive values are offered by **Icelandair** on flights from Luxembourg to New York and by **Virgin Atlantic Airways** from London to New York/Newark.

Some large American airlines (for example, TWA, American Airlines, Northwest, United, and Delta) offer travelers on their transatlantic or transpacific flights special discount tickets under the name **Visit USA,** allowing travel between any U.S. destinations at minimum rates. They are not on sale in the United States, and must, therefore, be purchased before you leave your foreign point of departure. This system is the best, easiest, and fastest way to see the United States at low cost. You should obtain information well in advance from your travel agent or the office of the airline concerned, since the conditions attached to these discount tickets can be changed without advance notice.

The visitor arriving by air, no matter what the port of entry, should cultivate patience and resignation before setting foot on U.S. soil. Getting through Immigration control may take as long as two hours on some days, especially summer weekends. Add the time it takes to clear Customs and you'll see that you should make very generous allowance for delay in planning connections between international and domestic flights—an average of two to three hours at least.

In contrast, travelers arriving by car or by rail from Canada will find border-crossing formalities streamlined to the vanishing point. And air travelers from Canada, Bermuda, and some places in the Caribbean can sometimes go through Customs and Immigration at the point of departure, which is much quicker and less painful.

For further information about travel to and arrival in Boston, see "Getting There" in Chapter 2.

3 Getting Around the U.S.

International visitors can buy a USA Railpass, good for 15 or 30 days of unlimited travel on Amtrak. The pass is available through many foreign travel agents. Prices in 1995 for a 15-day pass were $229 off-peak and $344 peak; a 30-day pass costs $339 off-peak and $425 peak. (With a foreign passport, you can also buy passes at some Amtrak offices in the United States, including locations in San Francisco,

Los Angeles, Chicago, New York, Miami, Boston, and Washington, D.C.) Reservations are generally required and should be made for each part of your trip as early as possible.

Visitors should be aware of the limitations of long-distance rail travel in the United States. With a few notable exceptions (for instance, the Northeast Corridor line between Boston and Washington, D.C.), service is rarely up to European standards: delays are common, routes are limited and often infrequently served, and fares are rarely significantly lower than discount airfares. Thus, cross-country train travel should be approached with caution.

The cheapest way to travel in the United States is by bus. **Greyhound,** the nation's nationwide bus line, offers an Ameripass for unlimited travel for 7 days (for $259), 15 days (for $459), and 30 days (for $559). Bus travel in the United States can be both slow and uncomfortable, so this option is not for everyone.

FAST FACTS: For the Foreign Traveler

Automobile Organizations Auto clubs will supply maps, suggested routes, guidebooks, accident and bail-bond insurance, and emergency road service. The major auto club in the United States, with 955 offices nationwide, is the **American Automobile Association (AAA).** Members of some foreign auto clubs have reciprocal arrangements with the AAA and enjoy its services at no charge. If you belong to an auto club, inquire about AAA reciprocity before you leave. The AAA can provide you with an **International Driving Permit** validating your foreign license. You may be able to join the AAA even if you are not a member of a reciprocal club. To inquire, call 800/222-4357. In addition, some automobile rental agencies now provide these services, so you should inquire about their availability when you rent your car.

Business Hours See "Fast Facts: Boston" in Chapter 4.

Climate See Chapter 2, Section 2.

Currency Exchange You will find currency-exchange services in major airports with international service. Elsewhere, they may be quite difficult to come by. In Boston, a reliable choice is **Thomas Cook Currency Services, Inc.** (160 Franklin St., Boston, MA; ☎ **617/426-0016**), which has been in business since 1841 and offers a wide range of services. There is also an office in Cambridge at 39 JFK Street (☎ **617/868-6605**). They sell commission-free foreign and U.S. traveler's checks, drafts, and wire transfers; they also do check collections (including Eurochecks). Their rates are competitive and service excellent. Other places in Boston at which to change money are the **Boston Bank of Commerce,** 133 Federal Street (☎ **617/457-4400**); **Ruesch International,** 45 Milk Street (☎ **617/482-8600**); **BayBank,** 1414 Massachusetts Avenue (☎ **617/556-6050**); and **Shawmut Bank,** One Federal Street (☎ **617/292-3964**).

Drinking Laws The legal drinking age in Boston is 21.

Electric Current The U.S. uses 110–120 volts, 60 cycles, compared to 220–240 volts, 50 cycles, as in most of Europe. Besides a 100-volt converter, small appliances of non-American manufacture, such as hairdryers or shavers, will require a plug adapter, with two flat, parallel pins.

Embassies/Consulates All embassies are located in the national capital, Washington, D.C.; some consulates are located in major cities, and most nations have a mission to the United Nations in New York City.

Listed here are the embassies and New York or Boston consulates of the major English-speaking countries—Australia, Canada, Ireland, New Zealand, and Britain. If you are from another country, you can get the telephone number of your embassy by calling "Information" in Washington, D.C. (☎ **202/555-1212**).

The **Australian embassy** is at 1601 Massachusetts Avenue NW, Washington, DC 20036 (☎ **202/797-3000**). The **consulate in New York** is located at the International Building, 630 Fifth Avenue, Suite 420, New York, NY 10111 (☎ **212/408-8400**). The **consulate in Los Angeles** is located at 611 N. Larchmont, Los Angeles, CA 90004 (☎ **213/469-4300**).

The **Canadian embassy** is at 501 Pennsylvania Avenue NW, Washington, DC 20001 (☎ **202/682-1740**). The **consulate in New York** is located at 1251 Avenue of the Americas, New York, NY 10020 (☎ **212/596-1600**); the **consulate in Boston** is at 3 Copley Place, Suite 400, Boston, MA 02116 (☎ **617/262-3760**). A third **consulate, in Los Angeles,** is located at 300 Santa Grand Avenue, Suite 1000, Los Angeles, CA 90071 (☎ **213/346-2700**).

The **Irish embassy** is at 2234 Massachusetts Avenue NW, Washington, DC 20008 (☎ **202/462-3939**). The **consulate in New York** is located at 345 Park Avenue, 17th floor, New York, NY 10022 (☎ **212/319-2555**). The **consulate in San Francisco** is located at 655 Montgomery Street, Suite 930, San Francisco, CA 94111 (☎ **415/392-4214**).

The **New Zealand Embassy** is at 37 Observatory Circle NW, Washington, DC 20008 (☎ **202/328-4800**). The **consulate in New York** is located at 780 3rd Avenue, Suite 1904, New York, NY 10017-2024 (☎ **212/832-4038**). The **consulate in Los Angeles** is located at 12400 Wilshire Boulevard, Suite 1150, Los Angeles, CA 90025 (☎ **310/207-1605**).

The **British embassy** is at 3100 Massachusetts Avenue NW, Washington, DC 20008 (☎ **202/462-1340**). The **consulate in Boston** is located at 600 Atlantic Avenue, Federal Reserve Plaza, 25th floor, Boston, MA 02210 (☎ **617/248-9555**). The **consulate in New York** is located at 845 Third Avenue, New York, NY 10022 (☎ **212/745-0200**). The **consulate in Los Angeles** is located at 11766 Wilshire Boulevard, Suite 400, Los Angeles, CA 90025 (☎ **310/477-3322**).

Emergencies Call **911** for fire, police, and ambulance. If you encounter such travelers' problems as sickness, accident, or lost or stolen baggage, call the **Travelers Aid Society,** an organization that specializes in helping distressed travelers, whether American or foreign. In Boston the number is 617/542-7286 (they are open Monday through Friday from 8:30am to 4:30pm).

Gasoline [Petrol] One U.S. gallon equals 3.75 liters, while 1.2 U.S. gallons equal one Imperial gallon. You'll notice there are several grades (and price levels) of gasoline available at most gas stations. And you'll also notice that their names change from company to company. Unleaded gas with the highest octane is the most expensive. Each gas company has a different name for the various levels of octane, but most fall into the "regular," "super," and "plus" categories (most rental cars take the least expensive "regular" unleaded).

Holidays On the following legal national holidays, banks, government offices, post offices, and many stores, restaurants, and museums are closed: January 1 (New Year's Day), third Monday in January (Martin Luther King Day), third Monday in February (Presidents' Day, Washington's Birthday), last Monday in May (Memorial Day), July 4 (Independence Day), first Monday in September (Labor Day), second Monday in October (Columbus Day), November 11 (Veterans Day/Armistice Day), fourth Thursday in November (Thanksgiving Day), and December 25 (Christmas Day).

Finally, the Tuesday following the first Monday in November is Election Day, and is a legal holiday in presidential election years.

Legal Aid The well-meaning foreign tourist will probably never become involved with the American legal system. However, there are a few things you should know just in case. If you are pulled up for a minor infraction (for example, of the highway code, such as speeding), never attempt to pay the fine directly to a police officer; you may wind up arrested on the much more serious charge of attempted bribery. Pay fines by mail, or directly into the hands of the clerk of the court. If accused of a more serious offense, it's wise to say and do nothing before consulting a lawyer. Under U.S. law, an arrested person is allowed one telephone call to a party of his or her choice. Call your embassy or consulate.

Mail If you want your mail to follow you on your vacation and you aren't sure of your address, your mail can be sent to you, in your name, **c/o General Delivery** at the McCormack Post Office (☎ **617/654-5684**). The addressee must pick it up in person and produce proof of identity (driver's license, credit card, passport, etc.).

Generally to be found at intersections, mailboxes are blue with a red-and-white stripe and carry the inscription U.S. MAIL. If your mail is addressed to a U.S. destination, don't forget to add the five-figure postal code, or ZIP (Zone Improvement Plan) Code, after the two-letter abbreviation of the state to which the mail is addressed (MA for Massachusetts).

Newspapers/Magazines National newspapers include the *New York Times, USA Today,* and the *Wall Street Journal.* National news weeklies include *Newsweek, Time,* and *U.S. News & World Report.* The major newspapers in Boston are the *Boston Globe* and *Boston Herald.*

Radio/Television Audiovisual media, with four coast-to-coast networks—ABC, CBS, NBC, and Fox—joined in recent years by the Public Broadcasting System (PBS) and the cable network CNN, play a major part in American life. In big cities, televiewers have a choice of a few dozen channels (including basic cable), most of them transmitting 24 hours a day, without counting the pay-TV channels showing recent movies or sports events. For the major stations in Boston, see "Fast Facts: Boston," Chapter 4.

Safety See "Safety" in "Preparing for Your Trip," above.

Taxes In the United States there is no VAT (value-added tax) or other indirect tax at a national level. Every state, and each city in it, is allowed to levy its own local tax on all purchases, including hotel and restaurant checks, airline tickets, and so on.

Telephone/Telegraph/Telex The telephone system in the United States is run by private corporations, so rates, especially for long-distance service, can vary widely—even on calls made from public telephones. Local calls in the United States usually cost 25¢.

Generally, hotel surcharges on long-distance and local calls are astronomical. You are usually better off using a **public pay telephone**, which you will find clearly marked in most public buildings and private establishments as well as on the street. Outside metropolitan areas, public telephones are more difficult to find. Stores and gas stations are your best bet.

Most long-distance and international calls can be dialed directly from any phone. For calls to Canada and other parts of the United States, dial 1 followed by the area code and the seven-digit number. For international calls, dial 011 followed by the country code, city code, and the telephone number of the person you wish to call.

For **reversed-charge** or **collect calls,** and for **person-to-person calls,** dial 0 (zero, not the letter "O") followed by the area code and number you want; an operator will then come on the line and you should specify that you are calling collect, or person to person, or both. If your operator-assisted call is international, ask for the overseas operator.

For local directory assistance ("Information"), dial 411; for long-distance information dial 1, then the appropriate area code and 555-1212.

Like the telephone system, **telegraph** and **telex** services are provided by private corporations like ITT, MCI, and above all Western Union. You can bring your telegram in to the nearest Western Union office (there are hundreds across the country), or dictate it over the phone (a toll-free call, **800/325-6000**). You can also telegraph money, or have it telegraphed to you very quickly over the Western Union system.

Telephone Directory There are two kinds of telephone directories available to you. The general directory is the so-called **white pages,** in which private and business subscribers are listed in alphabetical order. The inside front cover lists the emergency number for police, fire, and ambulance, and other vital numbers (like the Coast Guard, poison-control center, crime victims hotline, and so on). The first few pages are devoted to community-service numbers, including a guide to long-distance and international calling, complete with country codes and area codes.

The second directory, printed on yellow paper (hence its name**, yellow pages**), lists all local services, businesses, and industries by type of activity, with an index at the back. The listings cover not only such obvious items as automobile repairs by make of car, or drugstores (pharmacies), often by geographical location, but also restaurants by type of cuisine and geographical location, bookstores by special subject and/or language, places of worship by religious denomination, and other information that the tourist might otherwise not readily find. The yellow pages also include city plans or detailed area maps, often showing postal ZIP Codes and public transportation routes.

Time The United States is divided into four time zones (six, if Alaska and Hawaii are included). From east to west, these are: Eastern Standard Time (EST), Central Standard Time (CST), Mountain Standard Time (MST), Pacific Standard Time (PST), Alaska Standard Time (AST), and Hawaii Standard Time (HST). Always keep changing time zones in mind if you are traveling (or even telephoning) long distances in the United States. For example, noon in New York City (EST) is 11am in Chicago (CST), 10am in Denver (MST), 9am in Los Angeles (PST), 8am in Anchorage (AST), and 7am in Honolulu (HST).

Daylight Saving Time This is in effect from the first Sunday in April through the last Saturday in October (actually, the change is made at 2am on Sunday) except in Arizona, Hawaii, part of Indiana, and Puerto Rico. Daylight Saving Time moves the clock one hour ahead of standard time.

Tipping This is part of the American way of life, based on the principle that you should pay for any special service you receive. Here are some rules of thumb: bartenders: 10% to 15%; bellhops: at least 50¢ per piece, $2 to $3 for a lot of baggage; cab drivers: 15% of the fare; cafeterias, fast-food restaurants: no tip; chambermaids: $1 a day; checkroom attendants (restaurants, theaters): $1 per garment; cinemas, movies, theaters: no tip; doormen (hotels or restaurants): not obligatory; gas station attendants: no tip; hairdressers: 15% to 20%; redcaps (airport and railroad station): at least 50¢ per piece, $2 to $3 for a lot of baggage; restaurants, nightclubs: 15% to 20%

of the check; sleeping-car porters: $2 to $3 per night to your attendant; valet parking attendants: $1.

Toilets Foreign visitors often complain that public toilets are hard to find in most U.S. cities. True, there are none on the streets, but the visitor can usually find one in a bar, restaurant, hotel, museum, department store, or service station—and it will probably be clean (although the last mentioned sometimes leaves much to be desired). Note, however, a growing practice in some restaurants and bars of displaying a sign saying toilets are for the use of patrons only. You can ignore this sign, or better yet, avoid arguments by paying for a cup of coffee or soft drink, which will qualify you as a patron. The cleanliness of toilets at railroad stations and bus depots may be open to question. Some public places are equipped with pay toilets, which require you to insert one or more coins into a slot on the door before it will open.

THE AMERICAN SYSTEM OF MEASUREMENTS

Length

1 inch (in.)			=	2.54cm				
1 foot (ft.)	=	12 in.	=	30.48cm	=	.305m		
1 yard (yd.)	=	3 ft.			=	.915m		
1 mile	=	5,280 ft.					=	1.609km

To convert miles to kilometers, multiply the number of miles by 1.61 (for example, 50 mi. × 1.61 = 80.5km). Note that this conversion can be used to convert speeds from miles per hour (m.p.h.) to kilometers per hour (kmph).

To convert kilometers to miles, multiply the number of kilometers by .62 (example, 25km × .62 = 15.5 mi.). Note that this same conversion can be used to convert speeds from kilometers per hour to miles per hour.

Capacity

1 fluid ounce (fl. oz.)			=	.03 liters		
1 pint	=	16 fl. oz.	=	.47 liters		
1 quart	=	2 pints	=	.94 liters		
1 gallon (gal.)	=	4 quarts	=	3.79 liters	=	.83 Imperial gal.

To convert U.S. gallons to liters, multiply the number of gallons by 3.79 (example, 12 gal. × 3.79 = 45.48 liters).

To convert U.S. gallons to Imperial gallons, multiply the number of U.S. gallons by .83 (example, 12 U.S. gal. × .83 = 9.95 Imperial gal.).

To convert liters to U.S. gallons, multiply the number of liters by .26 (example, 50 liters × .26 = 13 U.S. gal.).

To convert Imperial gallons to U.S. gallons, multiply the number of Imperial gallons by 1.2 (example, 8 Imperial gal. × 1.2 = 9.6 U.S. gal.).

Weight

1 ounce (oz.)			=	28.35g				
1 pound (lb.)	=	16 oz.	=	453.6g	=	.45kg		
1 ton	=	2,000 lb.			=	907kg	=	.91 metric tons

To convert pounds to kilograms, multiply the number of pounds by .45 (example, 90 lb. × .45 = 40.5kg).

To convert kilograms to pounds, multiply the number of kilos by 2.2 (example, 75kg × 2.2 = 165 lb.).

Area

1 acre			=	.41ha		
1 square mile	=	640 acres	=	2.59ha	=	2.6km

To convert square miles to square kilometers, multiply the number of square miles by 2.6 (example, 80 sq. mi. × 2.6 = 208km).

To convert hectares to acres, multiply the number of hectares by 2.47 (example, 20ha × 2.47 = 49.4 acres).

To convert square kilometers to square miles, multiply the number of square kilometers by .39 (example, 150km × .39 = 58.5 sq. mi.).

Temperature

To convert degrees Fahrenheit to degrees Celsius, subtract 32 from °F, multiply by 5, then divide by 9 (example, 85°F – 32 × 5 ÷ 9 = 29.4°C).

To convert degrees Celsius to degrees Fahrenheit, multiply °C by 9, divide by 5, and add 32 (example, 20°C × 9 ÷ 5 + 32 = 68°F).

4

Getting to Know Boston

Boston is an easy city to negotiate once you get the "lay of the land." Contrary to the general impression, Boston's streets were not built on existing cattle paths. The settlers carefully copied the procedures used in England for laying out streets (which, come to think of it, were probably based on following cattle paths). I'll orient you with some views from above, then show you how to get around on ground level.

1 Orientation

VISITOR INFORMATION

Before you start walking around town, stop by one of Boston's visitor information centers for free maps, folders, weekly listings of special exhibits, and a schedule of visiting hours and fees at the historic shrines.

The **National Park Service Visitor Center,** at 15 State Street (☎ **617/242-5642**), right next to the Old State House and the State Street "T" station, is a good place to start your tour of historic Boston. The audiovisual show, "The Freedom Trail," provides basic information on 16 historic sites, and the knowledgeable uniformed park rangers are eager to help. In warm weather they give free guided tours of the Freedom Trail. There are special ramps for the disabled, comfortable chairs for relaxing, and restrooms. (Their map of Boston even designates public restrooms.) Open daily from 9am to 5pm except Thanksgiving Day, Christmas, and New Year's Day.

The **Boston Common Information Center,** at 146 Tremont Street on the Common, is open Monday to Saturday from 8:30am to 5pm and Sunday from 9am to 5pm, and there you can get maps and brochures. To guide you, there's a red-brick line in the sidewalks from the Common to the end of the Freedom Trail.

And the **Greater Boston Convention and Visitors Bureau, Inc.,** at Prudential Plaza (☎ **617/536-4100**), is open from 8:30am to 5:30pm Monday through Friday, offering the latest information on goings-on about town.

In Cambridge stop by or call the **Cambridge Discovery Inc.,** located at Harvard Street and Peabody Street in Harvard Square (☎ **617/497-1630**). It's open Monday to Saturday 9am to 6pm and Sunday 1 to 5pm.

PUBLICATIONS After you arrive, you'll want to pick up a copy of *Where* magazine, available at most hotels throughout the city. It will give you up-to-date information regarding shopping, nightlife, attractions, and what's currently being shown in museums and galleries around the city. On Thursdays the *Boston Globe* publishes a special insert called "Calendar" that will tell you the current goings-on around town. If you miss the Thursday *Globe,* pick up the *Boston Herald* on Friday; it has a similar insert called "Scene." The *Boston Phoenix* is also published every Friday. The *Tab* is a free publication (you can usually pick it up at street corners) that will give you neighborhood-specific events information. *Boston Magazine* is a monthly publication.

CITY LAYOUT

BIRD'S-EYE VIEWS My favorite way to survey any new city is from above, and Boston offers three skyscraper observation points: the John Hancock Tower, the Prudential Center Skywalk, and the Air-Traffic Control Tower at Logan Airport. If you're arriving by jet, try **Logan Tower** for your first look at the city, the harbor, and the beaches you'll be touring later. Take the elevator in the center of the parking garage to the 16th floor, where you can listen to piped-in control-tower talk while you enjoy the view. There's no admission charge, and it's open from 9am to 6pm (summer hours until 9pm). Or try the picture-window lounge, one floor up, where you can watch the planes, the ships, and the city traffic from 3pm to midnight Sunday through Thursday and noon to 2am on Friday and Saturday.

A popular high point in Boston is the **observatory** at the John Hancock Tower at Copley Square (☎ **617/572-6429**). Take the "T" to Copley Station, then walk one block to the Hancock building, where elevators whiz you up 60 floors in 30 seconds. Admission is $3.50 for adults and $2.75 for children ages 5 to 15 and senior citizens; this includes access to five exhibits (including a Boston 1775 diorama) and a light-and-sound show about Boston's role in the American Revolution. There are also five new interactive computer exhibits that will test your knowledge of the city of Boston. New telescopes and binoculars allow you to zoom in on points of interest hundreds of feet away. There is also a gift shop on the premises. Hours are 9am to 11pm Monday through Saturday and noon to 11pm on Sunday (May to October), and noon to 11pm on Sunday from November to April. The ticket office closes at 10:15pm, and the observatory shuts down at 11pm.

The **Prudential Center Skywalk,** on the 50th floor of the Prudential Tower, 800 Boylston Street (☎ **617/236-3318**), offers the only 360° view of Boston and beyond. From the enclosed observation deck you can, with the help of one of the coin-operated telescopes, see for miles, even as far as the mountaintops of southern New Hampshire or south to Cape Cod. The Skywalk hours are Monday through Saturday from 10am to 10pm and Sunday from noon to 10pm. Admission is $3.50 for adults and $2.75 for senior citizens and children ages 5 to 15. On the 52nd floor the view can be enjoyed with food and drink at the Top of the Hub Restaurant and Lounge.

From any of these towers you can observe the general layout of Boston, described below.

From the John Hancock Tower, face the ocean and you'll see the wharves from which Boston's fishing fleet and merchant ships used to sail. They still bear names such as India Wharf and Commercial Wharf, but now accommodate luxury apartments, marinas, hotels, restaurants, and urban-renewal projects. In front of you is the New England Aquarium, which you must visit later, and across the harbor, the airport and the North Shore beaches. As you turn counterclockwise, you see the Mystic River Bridge leading out of the city to the north. (Since Boston was established on a peninsula, it is connected by bridges and tunnels to surrounding areas.) To the left of the bridge is Bunker Hill Monument; to the right is the site of the Charlestown Navy Yard (now decommissioned and home to luxury apartments), where the USS *Constitution* (Old Ironsides) is docked. Now, look across the panorama of Boston—the Old State House, wedged in between the skyscrapers of the banks and insurance companies; the new Waterfront Park; the Faneuil Hall Marketplace and Faneuil Hall; City Hall; and in the distance, the golden dome of the State House. In the center is a long stretch of green (in season) that marks Boston Common, the Public Garden, and the tree-shaded expanse of Commonwealth Avenue. To the right of Commonwealth Avenue is the Charles River, which separates Boston from Cambridge. The park area bordering it is the Esplanade, where locals sunbathe and jog and the Boston Pops and other orchestras and dance groups perform at the Hatch Memorial Shell. To the left is the vast complex of apartments, hotels, upscale shops, and restaurants known as Copley Place and the Prudential Center. And in between is Back Bay, with the art galleries and boutiques of Newbury Street, the Boston Public Library, the Romanesque Trinity Church, and Old South Church at Copley Square. Beyond is the Christian Science Center, with its beautiful reflecting pool; Kenmore Square; Fenway Park; and in the distance the Blue Hills (where there is winter skiing).

MAIN ARTERIES & STREETS Because it seems to be the relative center of everything, I'll begin with **Boston Common,** the oldest people's park in the United States, dating back to the 1630s.

Standing at the Visitor's Information Center on the Common you're at **Tremont Street,** a busy shopping center. Across the Common is **Beacon Street,** with the gold-domed State House designed by Charles Bulfinch. This is also the start of **Beacon Hill,** with **Louisburg Square,** the last outpost of the proper Bostonians, at the top. **Charles Street,** with boutiques and antiques, is at the bottom. Between them are rows of steep little streets, stretching back toward the Massachusetts General Hospital.

Park Street forms the right-hand side of the Common (the Park Street subway is here) and then gives way to the rest of Tremont Street, which leads to Government Center, Faneuil Hall Marketplace, and the waterfront. Beyond that area is the North End.

Boylston Street runs along the left side of the Common and leads to the Public Garden, the Back Bay area, Copley Place, the Prudential Center, John B. Hynes Convention Center, and the Christian Science Center. **Massachusetts Avenue,** behind the convention center, divides this area from the cultural and educational zone on the other side, which includes Symphony Hall; the Museum of Fine Arts, Boston; the Isabella Stewart Gardner Museum; Northeastern University; and Simmons College. Boston University is beyond Kenmore Square.

If you're still standing at the Visitor's Information Center, behind you is the shopping district—Downtown Crossing, with Filene's department store and Filene's Basement—and Chinatown. (See Chapter 7 for more complete descriptions.)

Remember, there is no real pattern to Boston's streets. They just happened. You only need to be aware of the general arrangement, and if you get lost, well, sometimes you'll discover the most interesting shops and restaurants along the way.

FINDING AN ADDRESS Because of the way the streets are laid out, there's just no easy way to find an address in Boston. You'll need landmarks, subway stops, the neighborhood, and perhaps the color of the building. Your best bet is a friendly and knowledgeable pedestrian.

STREET MAPS Free maps of downtown Boston and the rapid transit lines are available at visitor information centers. The **Prudential Life Insurance Company** (800 Boylston St.; ☎ **617/236-3318**) has a neighborhood map of Boston, which it distributes at the Skywalk viewing platform, open Monday through Saturday, 10am to 10pm, and Sunday from noon to 10pm. It's helpful for walking trips of Beacon Hill, North End, Chinatown, South End, Charlestown, and Harvard Square. And if you write to the **Greater Boston Convention and Visitors Bureau** (P.O. Box 490, Boston, MA 02199), they will send you a visitor information kit that includes a city/subway/Freedom Trail map. Enclose $4.95 check or money order.

The Metropolitan District Commission (MDC) has an excellent map of the reservations, parks, and recreation areas in Greater Boston. It tells where to find salt- and freshwater beaches, swimming and wading pools, picnic areas, foot trails and bridge paths, playgrounds, tennis and golf courses, fresh- and saltwater fishing, bicycle paths, and outdoor ice-skating rinks. Write to the MDC at 20 Somerset Street, Boston, MA 02108 (c/o Public Information Office), for a copy. Please enclose a self-addressed, stamped business-sized envelope.

I also like using Gousha's Boston Fast Map, available at virtually any bookstore in Boston. A fun map to use while you're in town or just to purchase as a souvenir is MapEasy Inc.'s GuideMap to Boston; it's a hand-drawn map of Boston's major areas.

NEIGHBORHOODS IN BRIEF

The North End Between downtown and the waterfront, the North End is one of the city's oldest sections, and it's where many immigrants first settled. Now primarily Italian American, there's an abundance of Italian groceries, meat markets, restaurants, and coffee and pastry shops. In July and August street festivals to honor patron saints draw throngs of Bostonians. Two stops on the Freedom Trail are here: Paul Revere's House and the Old North Church.

Faneuil Hall Marketplace/Waterfront/Haymarket Squeezed together near the North End, these neighborhoods are prime tourist attractions. Haymarket, just off the Central Artery, is the site of the famous pushcart open-air food market, where Bostonians and suburbanites shop for excellent produce among other things. Faneuil Hall Marketplace, bounded by the Central Artery, Government Center, and the waterfront, is fun as well as historically important; it encompasses the restored market buildings that now house restaurants, take-out food stalls, shops, and Faneuil Hall itself. The waterfront on Atlantic Avenue was once home to warehouses and docks for the busy China trade. Now there are condos, shops, and offices, as well as some noteworthy restaurants. Also on the waterfront are the New England Aquarium, harbor cruise ships, and whale-watching boats.

Government Center This area is a showcase of modern architecture in Old Boston. Flanked by Beacon Hill and Faneuil Hall Marketplace, it is home to state and federal office towers and to Boston's City Hall.

Financial District Bounded by State, Milk, Devonshire, and Water streets, the financial district is the banking, insurance, and legal center of the city. Several impressive office towers now loom over the old Custom House, which was once famous for its observation deck tower.

Beacon Hill The dominant feature on Beacon Hill is the Massachusetts State House, with its famous Charles Bulfinch–designed golden dome. Bounded by Government Center, Boston Common, and Charles Street, it is now an exclusive residential section with a European ambience, Federal-style architecture, and some old cobblestone streets.

Downtown Crossing Just down a bit from the Common on Washington Street between Bromfield and West streets is Downtown Crossing, the city's downtown shopping district. This is a pedestrian mall, home to a Filene's department store, a Jordan Marsh department store, and a Filene's Basement store.

Chinatown A small area located off the Southeast Expressway, only a few blocks from Downtown Crossing, Chinatown is packed with Chinese and Vietnamese restaurants, groceries, and curio shops. The fourth largest Chinatown in the United States, it has more than 8,000 residents.

Back Bay A busy residential, shopping, and business area, Back Bay was literally the back of the bay a century ago. Since the bay was filled in, it has become one of the city's prime areas. Bounded by the Charles River and the Public Garden, Massachusetts Avenue and Shawmut Avenue, it boasts many Boston landmarks, including Trinity Church, the Boston Public Library, the John Hancock Tower, the Copley Place shopping center, the Prudential Center, and the Hynes Convention Center. Famed Commonwealth Avenue and Newbury Street are major thoroughfares in the Back Bay. This is also where you'll find the Swan Boats in the Public Garden and the Bull & Finch Pub in the Hampshire House on Beacon Street, the inspiration for the television show *Cheers.*

Huntington Avenue At its beginning near Copley Square, Huntington Avenue is nothing more than just another street, but once past the

Prudential Center (it runs parallel to Boylston Street), it grows in importance. The Christian Science Center, Symphony Hall (at the corner of Huntington and Massachusetts Avenues), Northeastern University, and the Museum of Fine Arts all have Huntington Avenue addresses.

The South End The area on the upper end of Tremont Street has some lovely restored Victorian homes, art galleries, boutiques, and some of the choicest bistros in town. Don't confuse this neighborhood with South Boston, a residential neighborhood known for its St. Patrick's Day Parade.

Kenmore Square This part of the city is best known for Fenway Park, home of the city's beloved Red Sox baseball team. Commonwealth Avenue, Beacon Street, and Brookline Avenue intersect here, and just a few blocks beyond the square on Commonwealth Avenue is Boston University, with shops, restaurants, movies, and clubs bustling with students.

Charlestown This is where you'll find the Bunker Hill Monument and the USS *Constitution* (Old Ironsides). It's on the tip of the Boston peninsula, reached by bridges, and is largely a residential neighborhood with a strong sense of community.

2 Getting Around

BY PUBLIC TRANSPORTATION

DISCOUNT PASSES The Boston Visitor Passport is one of the best deals in town. You get unlimited travel for a one-, three-, or seven-day period on all subway lines and local buses and Zones 1A and 1B of the Commuter Rail system, plus more than $35 worth of discounts on museums, restaurants, and entertainment! The cost is $5 for one day, $9 for three days, and $18 for seven days. Just show the passport to the collector or driver and you're on your way. They may be purchased at North Station, South Station, Back Bay Station, at Airport, Government Center, Harvard, and Riverside "T" stations, as well as the information center at Boston Common, and in Quincy Market. Your hotel might also be able to provide you with the Visitor Passport, so be sure to ask. If you'd like to get it in advance of your trip, call 617/722-5218.

BY SUBWAY Other than your feet, the subways are the most practical means of transportation in Boston.

The MBTA stands for the **Massachusetts Bay Transport Authority.** It is universally called the "T" for short, and it runs the city's subways, trolleys, and buses. There are about 25 special phone numbers, but if you find the list confusing, call the general offices at **617/722-3200.**

The "T" has its own symbol, the letter T in a circle. You can't miss it. This is the oldest subway system in the country, and some frazzled commuters complain that the system is still using the original 1897 trains. But the system is being modernized. If you avoid the rush hours, a subway ride is not at all traumatic; during off-peak hours, you'll be

Boston MBTA Rapid Transit Lines

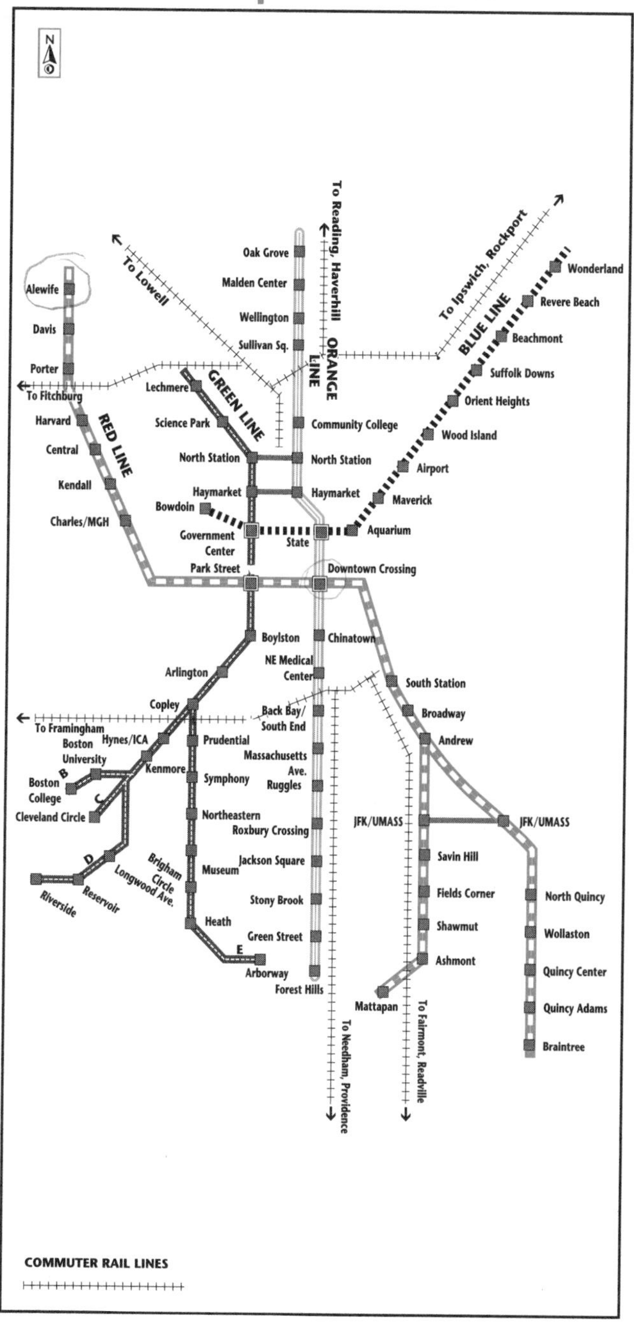

1522

able to get a seat *and* an unobstructed look at the murals adorning the station walls in the historic districts. The scenes include both Boston's past and the parks and buildings you'll see when you emerge onto the street. Above the roar of the trains you might be able to hear the music of local artists, who perform on the station platforms from 7 to 10am and 4 to 7pm—they make the commute a bit more pleasant!

Route and fare information and timetables are available at the Park Street subway station (under the Common), which is the center of the system. Each line is shown on subway maps in color—Blue, Red, Green, and Orange. The inbound sign refers to trains heading toward downtown Boston, while outbound refers to those heading away from downtown.

Fares are now 85¢ (by token) for underground (rapid transit) lines, and extra for some surface line extensions. You can also purchase tokens at the MBTA's token vending machines. You'll find them at the Airport station (Blue Line), Back Bay (Orange Line), Prudential (Green Line), and South Station (Red Line). For specific information on the subway system call **617/722-3200** Monday through Friday from 6:30am to 11pm, Saturday and Sunday 8am to 6pm.

Most stations have escalators for at least one flight of stairs, but not for the two flights you find at many stations. Elevators are also available in some areas. To find out where they are, call **Elevator Update Line** at **617/451-0027**, or the **Office for Transportation Access** at **617/722-5123** (TDD for the hearing impaired, **617/722-5415**) 8:30am to 5pm weekdays or 800/392-6099, nights, weekends, and holidays. Morning service on the "T" starts about 5am in some areas, and the lines close down between 12:30 and 1am. Be sure to check time schedules, available at Park Street, so you won't be stranded. (For specific information about wheelchair access, see "Tips for the Disabled" in Chapter 2.)

BY BUS/TRAM Trolleys and buses, also run by the MBTA, provide crosstown service and service to the suburbs. The local bus fare is 60¢; express buses are $1.50 and up. Trolley fare is based on zones and exact change is required. Call the central numbers listed above for route and schedule information. There are lift buses for the disabled. For information, call **800/LIFT-BUS.**

BY TAXI

Taxis in Boston are expensive and not always easy to find. But when you do get one, this is the fare arrangement: the first one-quarter of a mile costs $1.50, with a charge of 27¢ for each additional one-eighth of a mile. "Wait time" is extra; and there is a charge for tolls for the tunnel, turnpike, or bridges. Don't accept a flat rate within the city—check the meter. However, fares to outlying districts and the suburbs usually have a flat rate.

Boston's taxi drivers may be among the most literate in the country—many students work their way through college by driving a cab. They're probably the best dressed, too, since Boston has a "dress code" for the drivers—they must wear shirts, be clean, and keep their beards (if they have one) neatly trimmed! Most of the cabbies, no matter what their backgrounds, are full of opinions, ranging from politics to hotels, restaurants, highway construction, and talk-show hosts.

To call ahead for a cab, try **Checker Taxi** (☎ **617/536-7000**), **Town Taxi** (☎ **617/536-5000**), or **Independent Taxi Operators Association (ITOA)** (☎ **617/426-8700**).

BY CAR

As noted above, cars are not practical in Boston. Once you're in town and your car is safely deposited at a hotel garage, stick to the subways, taxis, or walking.

However, for some purposes you just can't beat the freedom of a personal car—for example, if you decide to take any of the excursions to small-town Massachusetts listed in Chapter 11. Below you'll find some helpful information for driving in and around Boston.

RENTALS If you've decided you'd like to have a car, you can find offices of all of the major car-rental firms both in Boston and at Logan Airport. If you've rented a car to drive to Boston and plan to fly home, check carefully about return facilities. Some of the smaller firms don't want to accept out-of-state cars or will levy drop-off charges. Have your rental agency call ahead to confirm the arrangements.

Here are some numbers so you can make arrangements before leaving home: **Avis** (☎ **800/331-1212**), **Budget** (☎ **800/527-0700**), **Dollar** (☎ **800/421-6868**), **Hertz** (☎ **800/654-3131**), **National** (☎ **800/227-7368**), and **Thrifty** (☎ **800/367-2277**).

If you've made a last minute decision to rent, call the following local numbers. The agencies have several offices in the city, and when you call, ask for the one nearest your hotel: Avis (☎ **561-3500**), Budget (☎ **787-8200**), Dollar (☎ **523-5098** or 723-8312), Hertz (☎ **569-7272**), National (☎ **569-6700**), and Thrifty (☎ **569-6500**).

The rates for the major companies are high, so you might prefer one of the smaller rental agencies or a local auto dealership. Consult the yellow pages of the phone book.

When you go to pick up your car, be sure you have a valid driver's license (you must be 21 or over) and a credit card. Without a credit card you must leave a large cash deposit. And before you sign the contract, read it carefully. Know what your obligations are (for example, returning the car with a full tank, or paying the company to refill it).

It's necessary to have adequate car insurance; your rental fee does not include it. But that doesn't mean you have to purchase expensive supplements. Your own auto insurance might cover you for damage to a rental car. Check with your insurance agent. Also check with your credit card company. It may provide coverage on car rentals. Otherwise be prepared to pay for Collision Damage Waiver or Loss Damage Waiver. Without coverage you could be liable for the full retail price of the car if it is damaged or stolen. In addition, if you're under 25 years of age you may be required to pay an additional daily fee.

PARKING If you're a motorist staying at one of the motels on the outskirts of town, it will be easier to leave the car in the lot and come into town by public transportation. Driving can be confusing, since the streets have no logical numerical or alphabetical order and one-way streets and construction sites can appear unexpectedly. Parking garages are expensive; on-street spaces are hard to find; and the meter maids are always on the job to ticket drivers who violate the no-parking, no-standing, and resident-only signs, or those who allow their meters to lapse. I almost certainly get a ticket every time I park in downtown Boston. Read the hieroglyphics on the meter carefully. In some areas parking is allowed only at certain hours; in others there is no charge after 6pm or on Sunday and holidays. Rates vary in different sections of the city (usually $1 an hour downtown), so have a supply of quarters and dimes ready. (Time limits vary from 30 minutes to one or two hours.) Even though garages and parking lots are expensive, they're cheaper than a $50 fine or towing charge.

Boston's two largest garages are hidden underground at the Prudential Center and Boston Common. The garage at the "Pru" has entrances on Boylston Street, Huntington Avenue, the Sheraton Boston Hotel & Towers, and near Lord & Taylor and Saks Fifth Avenue. At the Boston Common Garage on Charles Street, round-trip bus service to the other side of the Common and back is included in the fee.

Rates keep rising and I hesitate to give any definite prices, since they're likely to change from the time you drive in to the time you drive out. City-owned garages such as the Boston Common Garage usually have the lowest prices. The garage and parking lot near Government Center and the Haymarket pushcart area have good deals. If you park before 8am and are out by 6pm, you get a special rate; after that you pay hourly rates. Figure $3 to $6 an hour at Lafayette Place Garage on Chauncy Street, Dock Square at Faneuil Hall Marketplace, and at garages at the Transportation Building at Park Plaza, the New England Aquarium, Copley Place, the Prudential Center, the John Hancock Building, and near Symphony Hall.

In an innovative twist Boston has replaced a parking garage with a park. But the city didn't tear down the garage; it just lowered it underground and topped it with a beautiful public park, cafe, and fountains. The garage is at Zero Post Office Square, bounded by Milk, Pearl, Franklin, and Congress Streets, across the street from Hotel Le Meridien, and near Faneuil Hall Marketplace and the New England Aquarium. It is open 24 hours with entrances on Pearl and Congress streets and is safe and easy to use.

DRIVING RULES/TOLLS Boston has a one-way toll structure for the Mystic River Bridge and Callahan Tunnel. You pay a double fee entering Boston from the north (50¢ when crossing the bridge, $1 through the tunnel), and pay nothing when leaving the city. There are toll booths on the Massachusetts Turnpike extension from Newton into Boston.

Drivers in Boston can make a right turn on a red light when traffic permits, unless there is a posted sign forbidding it.

For a short time there was a mandatory seat belt law in Boston, but now adults can choose to buckle up or not. Infants and toddlers must be strapped into car seats, and young children must use seat belts. And that is the law.

BY BICYCLE

Yes, Boston does have bicycle trails. There are more than 50 miles of marked bike paths, including the 17-mile Esplanade loop around the Charles River. A convenient place to rent a bike is **Earth Bikes,** at 35 Huntington Avenue, near Copley Square and the Green Line Copley Square subway station (☎ **617/267-4733**). They have several types of new bikes, including mountain bikes, Urban Cruisers, and bicycles built for two; they also carry cycling accessories. Rentals start at $12 for a half day and include free use of helmets and complimentary maps. Earth Bikes is open from April to October, 10am to 7pm, Thursday through Monday. For hours on Tuesday, Wednesday, or rainy days, please call. A deposit (cash or by American Express, Visa, or MasterCard) is required, as is a driver's license or passport.

There are other rental shops listed in the yellow pages for Boston and Cambridge.

FAST FACTS: Boston

Airport See "Arriving" in Chapter 2.

American Express The company has several **travel service** offices in the Boston area. The main office is at 1 Court Street (☎ **617/723-8400**), close to the Government Center MBTA stop. There is also an office in Cambridge near Harvard Square at 44 Brattle Street (☎ **617/661-0005**). To report a lost or stolen American Express charge card, call **800/528-4800**; to report lost or stolen American Express traveler's checks, call **800/221-7282.**

Area Code When you're dialing from out of state, use area code **617** or **508** (check individual listings). For some calls beyond the metropolitan area you must dial "1," followed by the phone number. Since the state is divided into zones, you may have to use an area code for an adjoining city. For example, nearby Salem is 1–508; and all telephones in Plymouth and Cape Cod are also reached by dialing 1–508.

Babysitters Many of the hotels can arrange for babysitters. Ask the concierge.

Banking Hours Most in-town banks are open Monday to Friday 9am to 3pm. Away from the center of town, many banks are open until 5pm, or even 8 or 9pm on Thursday and Friday; most are open Saturday 9am to noon or later. Be prepared to use an ATM if you need cash after the banks close.

Business Hours Standard business hours are 9am to 5pm. Some retail stores are open until 7pm or 9pm. Most retail establishments are open Sunday afternoon.

Car Rentals See "Getting Around" in this chapter.

Climate See "When to Go" in Chapter 2.

Dentists Dentists are listed in the yellow pages of the phone book by specialty. And there are some who offer 24-hour emergency service. You can also call some of the area dental colleges for references.

Doctors Most Boston hospitals have physician referral services. Among them are: **Beth Israel Hospital Physician Referral** (☎ **617/735-5356**), **Massachusetts General Hospital Physician Referral Service** (☎ **617/726-5800**), and **New England Deaconess Hospital Physician Referral Service** (☎ **617/732-8006**). The latter operates 24 hours a day. There are also many local walk-in medical centers staffed by qualified physicians where you can get help. Check with the concierge at your hotel, or again, look for listings in the phone book.

Drugstores When you need a prescription filled and it's after 5pm, try **CVS Pharmacy** (Porter Square Shopping Center, Massachusetts Ave., Cambridge; ☎ **617/876-5519**). It's right next to the MBTA's Porter Square stop. Or try **Phillips Drug Co.,** at 155 Charles Street, off the Charles Street MBTA stop in Boston (☎ **617/523-1028**). They both have 24-hour pharmacies open seven days a week. Sometimes a hospital emergency room can fill your prescription at the hospital's pharmacy.

Emergencies Call **911** for fire, ambulance, or to summon the Boston/Cambridge police. For the state police, call **617/523-1212.** You can reach the Poison Information Center at **617/232-2120.** No coins are needed at pay phones for 911 calls.

Eyeglasses Many opticians promise new glasses in an hour's time for certain prescriptions and same-day service for most others. Among them is **Eye World,** 481 Washington Street at Downtown Crossing (☎ **617/357-9747**), and at Copley Square (699 Boylston St.; ☎ **617/437-1070**). Many others are listed in the phone book.

Hospitals Boston has some of the best hospitals in the country. Let's hope you won't need their care during your visit, but here are some names for reference: **Beth Israel Hospital** (330 Brookline Ave.; ☎ **617/735-2000,** or for emergency 617/735-3337); **Brigham and Women's Hospital** (75 Francis St.; ☎ **617/732-5500**); **Boston Evening Medical Center** (314 Commonwealth Ave.; ☎ **617/267-7171**); **Cambridge Hospital** (1493 Cambridge St.; (☎ **617/498-1000**, or for emergency 617/498-1429); **Children's Hospital** (300 Longwood Ave.; ☎ **617/735-6000,** or for emergency services 617/735-6611); **Massachusetts Eye and Ear Infirmary** (243 Charles St.; ☎ **617/523-7900**); and **Massachusetts General Hospital** (55 Fruit St.; ☎ **617/726-2000,** or 617/726-3375 for children).

Hotlines **AIDS Hotline** (☎ **617/424-5916**), **Massachusetts Poison Control System** (☎ **617/232-2120**), **Rape Crisis** (☎ **617/492-7273**), **Suicide Hotline Samaritans** (☎ **617/247-0220**). If you're having a personal crisis, call **617/244-4350.**

Information See "Visitor Information" in this chapter.

Laundry/Dry Cleaning Usually your hotel can take care of this for you. Or ask for the nearest cleaner or Laundromat.

Libraries The main branch of the Boston Public Library is at Copley Square. It is worth a visit even if you're not looking for a book.

Liquor Laws Liquor is sold only in licensed package stores. It cannot be sold to anyone under 21 in stores, bars, or restaurants. Liquor stores are closed on Sundays, but alcohol may be served in restaurants after noon on Sunday. A valid ID is needed. Some suburban Boston towns are "dry." *Note:* If you've just turned 21 or you look young, you may have trouble getting served in Boston and surrounding towns.

Lost Property If you've lost something on the "T," call **Lost and Found** (☎ **617/722-5533,** 722-5221, or 722-5403, depending on the line you were riding); if you lost it in a cab, call the cab company or the **Boston Police Department's Hackney Carriage Unit** (☎ **617/536-3200**).

Money See "Visitor Information and Money" in Chapter 2.

Newspapers/Magazines Boston has two daily newspapers: The *Boston Globe* and the tabloid-style *Boston Herald.* They both have information about what's going on in town. The *Boston Phoenix,* a weekly, does a good job of in-depth reporting on Boston and is hip to everything happening in town in the fields of art, theater, music, and dance. *Boston Magazine,* published monthly, has good features on politicians and names in the news.

Photographic Needs Film can be purchased at any drugstore. For photographic supplies try **Lechmere** at the Cambridgeside Galleria near Kendall Square (☎ **617/491-2000**) or **Bromfield Camera Co., Inc.,** at 10 Bromfield Street (☎ **617/426-5230**). You can get one-hour or same-day color processing at many places in the city.

Police See "Emergencies," above.

Post Office The McCormack State Post Office Building at Post Office Square (☎ **617/654-5684**; subway: State Street) is a conveniently located office in downtown Boston. For general postal information, call **617/451-9922.** Collection times are marked inside the mail-slot door on the big blue collection boxes.

Radio Local radio stations include: WEEI (sports), 590 AM; WRKO (talk and sports, Red Sox games), 680 AM; WGBH (public radio, classical music, and jazz), 89.7; WCRB (classical music), 102.5; WBUR (public radio news, classical music), 90.9; WSSH (soft rock), 99.5 FM; WBCN (rock), 104.1 FM; WODS (oldies), 103.3 FM; and WPLM (big band), 99.1.

Religious Services Consult the telephone directory under churches, synagogues, etc. The Saturday newspaper editions run a listing of Sunday services.

Restrooms The best ones are in hotels, department stores, and public buildings. Restaurants try to limit the use of their restrooms to customers, but if you ask nicely they may allow you to use them. To avoid conflict, you can always become a customer and just buy a cup of coffee. Some public places are equipped with pay toilets, usually costing 10¢.

Safety On the whole, Boston is a safe city for walking, but there are some areas to avoid at night: Tremont Street from Stuart Street to Boylston Street; and Boylston Street where it crosses the "Combat Zone" at Washington Street. With the construction of new office buildings and the renovation of existing properties, the zone is shrinking. As "adult entertainment" is squeezed out, this will probably become a choice area in the future. Until then, do your strolling during daylight hours. Always keep a close eye on your possessions, and be particularly careful with cameras, purses, and wallets, all favorite targets of thieves and pickpockets.

Shoe Repairs **Filene's Basement** (☎ **617/348-7974**) is a good bet. And if you have another pair of shoes with you, you can shop while you wait.

Taxes Taxes are levied on almost everything, it seems. The lodging tax for your room is 9.7%; 5% for restaurant meals and take-out foods; and 10% for gasoline. The general sales tax is 5% on all items except food, clothing (up to a value of $175), prescription drugs, fuel for heating, and newspapers. There is also a tax on alcohol based on alcoholic content.

Taxis See "Getting Around" in this chapter.

Telegrams/Telex For **Western Union,** dial 800/325-6000.

Television TV stations include: Channel 2 (WGBH), public television; Channel 4 (WBZ), NBC; Channel 5 (WCVB), ABC; Channel 7 (WHDH), CBS; Channel 38 (WSBK), sports and movies. Cable TV is available throughout Boston and the suburbs.

Transit Info For information on service and schedules, call the MBTA at 617/722-3200.

Useful Telephone Numbers You can reach the **Travelers Aid Society** at **617/542-7286.** Other sources of assistance include the **Convention and Visitors Bureau** (☎ **617/536-4100**) and the **Disabled Information Center** (☎ **617/727-5540**). **Directory assistance** can be reached at **411,** and you can call **617/654-5083** for **postal information.** For the correct **time,** call **617/637-8687.**

Weather To get the weather report, dial **617/936-1234.**

5

Accommodations

Where to stay in Boston? That depends upon your taste and the style in which you're accustomed to traveling. Boston offers an excellent range of accommodations—from luxury hotels in the finest European manner to the gracious style of "Old Boston" and the sleek modernity of new hotels.

You shouldn't have much trouble getting a room in Boston, but it's always advisable to reserve ahead. Reservations are imperative during the spring and fall when conventions descend upon the city, as well as during the popular summer vacation months of July and August. Most hotels do not charge for children sharing rooms with their parents, and some offer special rates for students with ID cards and senior citizens. Just ask. Parking is available at most hotels (usually for a fee) and motels, while others have arrangements with nearby garages.

The **Greater Boston Convention and Visitors Bureau** (see "Visitor Information and Money" in Chapter 2) publishes a free travel-planning guide, a comprehensive guidebook, and another guide called *Kids Love Boston;* all three are helpful in finding accommodations that will suit your needs and can offer substantial savings. To get the kit in advance of your trip, send $4.95 and a request for the Visitor Information Kit to the Greater Boston Convention & Visitors Bureau, Inc., Prudential Tower, P.O. Box 990468, Dept. TPO, Boston, MA 02199-0468. Also contact the **Massachusetts Tourism Office** (100 Cambridge St., Boston, MA 02202; ☎ **617/727-3201** or 800/447-MASS; fax 617/727-6525); they have a free bed-and-breakfast guide listing guest houses, arranged by region and town, across the state; a "vacation kit" that includes an attractions guide, map, seasonal calendar, and lodgings guide; and other publications on vacations in Massachusetts.

There is a 9.7% tax on all hotel rooms (5.7% for the state, 4% for the city). Not all suburban cities have imposed a local tax, so you may have to pay only the 5.7% state tax in some towns.

To help you choose a Boston hotel, recommendations are divided into categories by location and then by price; within these categories the hotels are listed alphabetically. I've concentrated on those hotels that are convenient to historic areas and transportation, those that provide special touches of luxury or service, and those that offer good value for the money. The listings you'll find here cover Boston, Cambridge, and several suburbs on the rim of the city. I've also listed resort hotels with easy access to the city and points of interest.

Each hotel is grouped into one of four price categories on the basis of the lowest-priced double room offered. Allowing for some inevitable overlapping, the categories are as follows: *Very Expensive,* $200 and up per night; *Expensive,* $175 and up per night; *Moderate,* $100 and up per night; and *Budget,* under $80 per night. The budget category includes some fine guest houses. And note that many hotels offer weekend package deals that can knock prices down a category or two.

BED & BREAKFASTS In Boston, good budget hotels are often difficult to find. Bed-and-breakfast accommodations offered in the home of a local family are usually more comfortable, cleaner, and as inexpensive as a budget hotel, and in most cases breakfast is thrown in as part of the rate. To find a suitable bed-and-breakfast, you might want to contact the following organizations:

Bed and Breakfast Associates (P.O. Box 57166, Babson Park Branch, Boston, MA 02157; ☎ **617/449-5302** or 800/347-5088; fax 617/449-5958). This reservation service lists 150 bed-and-breakfasts and inns in the metropolitan Boston area and throughout eastern Massachusetts, including the North Shore, South Shore, and Cape Cod. They also arrange long-term lodging and list furnished apartments and house-sharing opportunities. A member of the B&B National Network, they can also help arrange reservations elsewhere in the United States and in Canada.

A Bed and Breakfast Agency of Boston (47 Commercial Wharf, Boston, MA 02110; ☎ **617/720-3540** or 800/CITY-BNB; fax 617/523-5761; residents of the United Kingdom, call 0800/89-5128). Offers accommodations in historic homes (including Federal and Victorian town houses) and in waterfront lofts in Boston and Cambridge; nightly, weekly, monthly, and special winter rates are available. Their listings include 155 rooms with 60 suites and furnished studios and condos, all within walking distance of downtown. Trolley Tour discounts are available to visitors who rent rooms through A Bed and Breakfast Agency of Boston.

New England Bed and Breakfast (P.O. Box 9100, Newton, MA 02159; ☎ **617/244-2112** or 498-9819). Offers home accommodations in the suburbs that are a short drive from Boston but within walking distance to public transportation. They have residences for nonsmokers, and will make an appropriate match if you have allergies.

Host Homes of Boston (P.O. Box 117, Waban Branch, Boston, MA 02168; ☎ **617/244-1308**; fax 617/244-5156). Lists 50 host homes with clean, comfortable accommodations offering personalized hospitality. Many hosts speak foreign languages and all provide breakfast. A two-night minimum stay is required.

If you're headed for the Cape, Nantucket, or Martha's Vineyard, try one of the following bed-and-breakfast referral agencies:

Bed & Breakfast Marblehead & North Shore/Greater Boston & Cape Cod (P.O. Box 35, Newtonville, MA 02160; ☎ **617/964-1606** or 800/832-2632 outside Massachusetts; fax 617/332-8572). They will match you up with well-selected, carefully inspected accommodations in Cape Cod, Greater Boston, and areas north of Boston.

Bed & Breakfast Cape Cod/Nantucket/Martha's Vineyard (P.O. Box 341, West Hyannisport, MA 02672-0341; ☎ **508/775-2772**; fax 508/775-2884; E-mail gnuk90a@prodigy.com). If you contact this agency early enough, they'll send you a free brochure listing homes and inns all over Cape Cod, Martha's Vineyard, and Nantucket. Selections include historic sea captain's homes, country inns, and host homes. There are more than 90 from which to choose, and they range in price from $55 to $185.

1 Best Bets

- **Best Historic Hotel.** The Omni Parker House is the oldest continually operating hotel in the United States, and it's permeated with a sense of history. It was the meeting place of the legendary Saturday Club (whose members were Nathaniel Hawthorne, Ralph Waldo Emerson, and Henry Wadsworth Longfellow, among others) beginning around 1855.
- **Best for Business Travelers.** The Hotel Le Meridien, located in the heart of the financial district, has a full service business center with currency exchange, as well as a great health club. And, so you'll know what to wear without leaving the hotel, a weather report is delivered to your room every evening.
- **Best for Families.** The Boston Park Plaza Hotel & Towers offers great family services. Kids are treated to Red Sox Sundaes and free gifts, and there's a story hour complete with milk and cookies. Movie screenings are given for the whole family.
- **Best Service.** Without a doubt, the hotel offering the best service in Boston is the Four Seasons. Standards are high here, and the friendly and efficient staff will take care of your every need—and then some.
- **Best Moderately Priced Hotel.** The all-suite Eliot Hotel is a lovely little European-style hostelry with beautifully appointed rooms and Italian marble bathrooms, and it's easily affordable for those on a modest budget.
- **Best Hotel Pool.** The enormous Sheraton Boston Hotel & Towers is a little impersonal due to its size, but it does have a great indoor/outdoor pool.
- **Best Views.** There are several hotels that offer superb panoramas of Boston. The Boston Harbor Hotel has the most spectacular view—especially from its harborfront suites.

2 Downtown

The downtown area extends from Atlantic Avenue to Washington Street. I've included hotels on the waterfront, along the Freedom Trail, the financial district, and the downtown shopping area.

Boston Accommodations

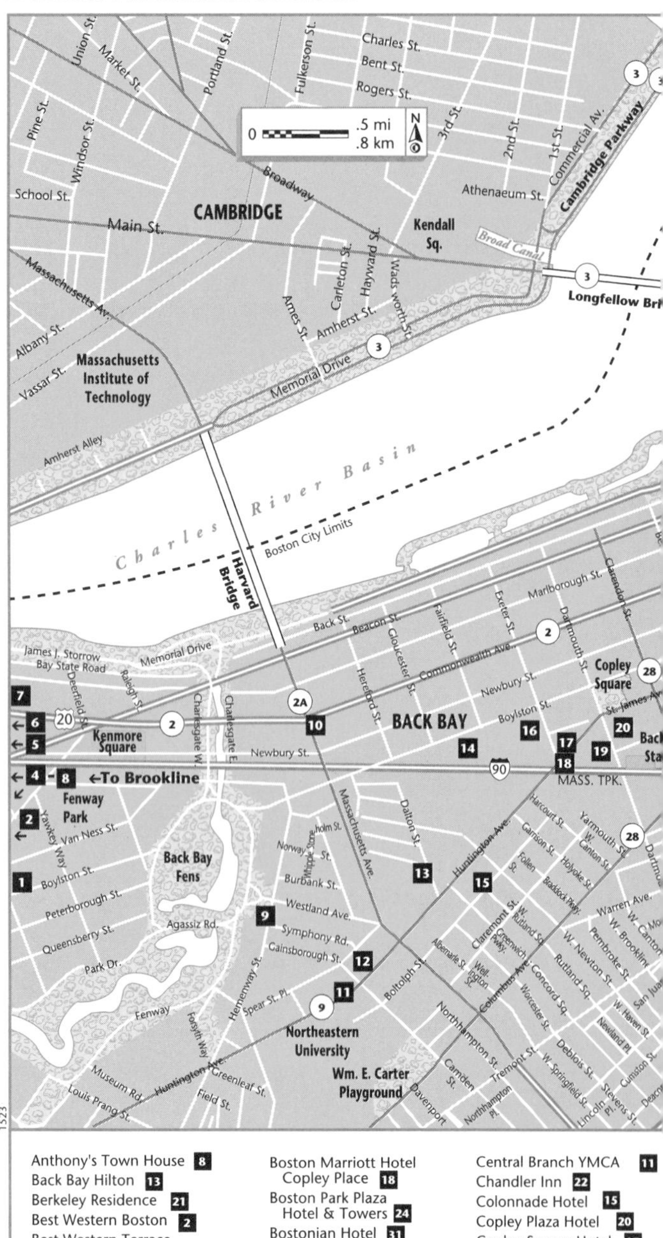

Anthony's Town House 8
Back Bay Hilton 13
Berkeley Residence 21
Best Western Boston 2
Best Western Terrace Motor Lodge 6
Boston Harbor Hotel 33
Boston Marriott Hotel Copley Place 18
Boston Park Plaza Hotel & Towers 24
Bostonian Hotel 31
Bostonian International Hostel 9
Central Branch YMCA 11
Chandler Inn 22
Colonnade Hotel 15
Copley Plaza Hotel 20
Copley Square Hotel 17
Eliot Hotel 10
57 Park Plaza Hotel 25

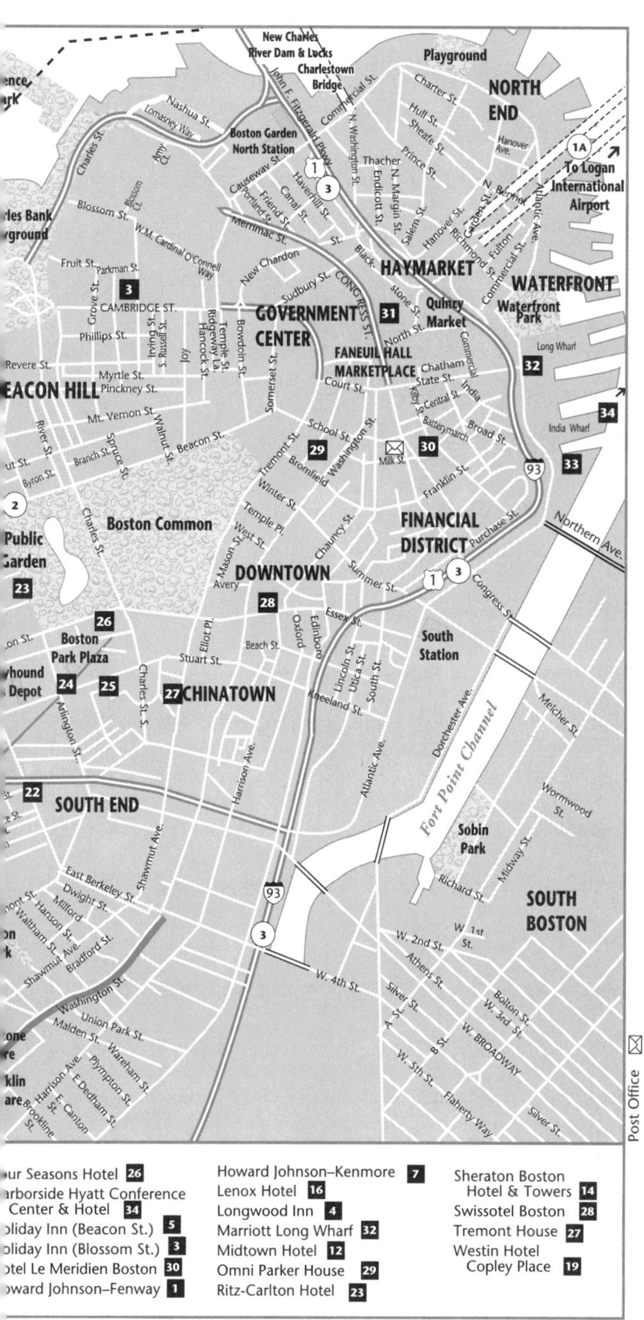

New Charles River Dam & Locks
Charlestown Bridge
Playground
NORTH END
1A
To Logan International Airport
Boston Garden North Station
John F. Fitzgerald Pkwy.
Commercial St.
Charter St.
Hull St.
Sheafe St.
Prince St.
Hanover Ave.
Nashua St.
Lomasney Way
Charles St.
Amy Ct.
Causeway St.
N. Washington St.
Thacher
Endicott St.
N. Margin St.
Salem St.
Hanover St.
Garden St.
N. Bennet
Atlantic Ave.
Richmond St.
Fulton
Commercial St.
Haverhill St.
Canal St.
Friend St.
Portland St.
Merrimac St.
Blossom St.
Blossom Ct.
W.M. Cardinal O'Connell Way
Fruit St.
Parkman St.
Grove St.
CAMBRIDGE ST.
New Chardon
Sudbury St.
CONGRESS ST.
Blackstone St.
HAYMARKET
WATERFRONT
Waterfront Park
Quincy Market
GOVERNMENT CENTER
Phillips St.
Irving St.
S. Russell St.
Joy
Hancock St.
Ridgeway La.
Temple St.
Bowdoin St.
Somerset St.
North St.
FANEUIL HALL MARKETPLACE
Chatham
State St.
Commercial
India
Long Wharf
Court St.
Kilby St.
Central St.
Revere St.
Myrtle St.
Pinckney St.
Mt. Vernon St.
Walnut St.
River St.
Branch St.
Spruce St.
Beacon St.
Byron St.
School St.
Tremont St.
Bromfield
Washington St.
Milk St.
Batterymarch
Broad St.
India Wharf
Franklin St.
Winter St.
Temple Pl.
West St.
Mason St.
Chauncy St.
Boston Common
FINANCIAL DISTRICT
Purchase St.
Northern Ave.
Summer St.
Congress St.
Avery
DOWNTOWN
Essex St.
Oxford
Edinboro
Charles St.
Boston Park Plaza
Eliot Pl.
Beach St.
Stuart St.
Lincoln St.
Utica St.
South St.
South Station
CHINATOWN
Charles St. S.
Kneeland St.
Arlington St.
Harrison Ave.
Atlantic Ave.
Dorchester Ave.
Fort Point Channel
Melcher St.
SOUTH END
Wormwood St.
Sobin Park
Shawmut Ave.
Midway St.
East Berkeley St.
Dwight St.
Milford
Hanson St.
Waltham St.
Shawmut Ave.
Bradford St.
Richard St.
SOUTH BOSTON
W. 1st St.
W. 2nd St.
Athens St.
W. 4th St.
Silver St.
Bolton St.
W. 3rd St.
Washington St.
Union Park St.
Malden St.
Wareham St.
Plympton St.
Harrison Ave.
E. Dedham St.
E. Canton St.
Brookline St.
A St.
B St.
W. BROADWAY
W. 5th St.
Flaherty Way
Silver St.
Post Office
Boston
1
2
3
93
3
22
23
24
25
26
27
28
29
30
31
32
33
34
ur Seasons Hotel 26
arborside Hyatt Conference Center & Hotel 34
oliday Inn (Beacon St.) 5
oliday Inn (Blossom St.) 3
otel Le Meridien Boston 30
oward Johnson–Fenway 1
Howard Johnson–Kenmore 7
Lenox Hotel 16
Longwood Inn 4
Marriott Long Wharf 32
Midtown Hotel 12
Omni Parker House 29
Ritz-Carlton Hotel 23
Sheraton Boston Hotel & Towers 14
Swissotel Boston 28
Tremont House 27
Westin Hotel Copley Place 19

VERY EXPENSIVE

✪ Boston Harbor Hotel

70 Rowes Wharf (entrance on Atlantic Ave.), Boston, MA 02110. ☎ **617/439-7000** or 800/752-7077. Fax 617/330-9450. 230 rms, 26 suites. A/C MINIBAR TV TEL. $200–$385 single or double; from $350 suite. Extra person $50. Weekend packages available. AE, DC, DISC, MC, V. Self-parking $21 weekdays; valet parking $23 daily. MBTA: Aquarium (Blue Line) or South Station (Red Line).

To reach Boston's waterfront luxury hotel, you can be conventional and drive *or* you can make a grand entrance by sailing (in just seven minutes) across the harbor from Logan Airport to the hotel's on-site ferry pavilion (see below for details).

Conveniently located adjacent to the financial district, the hotel is within walking distance of Faneuil Hall Marketplace, the New England Aquarium, and Downtown Crossing. A magnificent central archway topped by a copper-domed observatory accents this traditional red-brick building. A museum-quality art collection of more than 100 paintings, drawings, and prints enhances the public spaces of the hotel.

Guest rooms have a view either of the harbor or the Boston skyline, and all have operable windows so you can enjoy the fresh ocean air. Each is a luxurious bed- and living-room combination, decorated in green and yellow or rose and blue, with mahogany furnishings that include armoire, desk, and comfortable chairs. Suites are even more elegant, with floral draperies and bed coverings; a few have private terraces. Standard guest room amenities include hairdryers, bathrobes, umbrellas, slippers, and minibars.

If you come by plane and want to take the Water Shuttle, take the free bus at your terminal to the shuttle. It leaves every 15 minutes from 6am to 8pm, Monday through Friday, and every 30 minutes from 12:15 to 7:45pm, Saturdays and Sundays. (You can also take the ferry back to the airport.) One-way fare is $8 for adults and $3 for children under 12.

Dining/Entertainment: Rowes Wharf Restaurant serves fresh seafood and American cuisine, while the Harborview Lounge is the place for afternoon tea and evening cocktails. Both offer magnificent views of the harbor. The Rowes Wharf Bar serving cocktails and light fare is open from 11:30am to midnight. Seasonal dining is also available outdoors in the Rowes Wharf Cafe (open May to September).

Services: 24-hour room service, twice-daily maid service, concierge, shoeshine, baby-sitting. Pets are welcome.

Facilities: Three floors for nonsmokers, 18 rooms for disabled guests, gift shop, fully equipped and professionally staffed business center. Guests may use facilities of Rowes Wharf Health Club and Spa, which includes whirlpool; sauna, steam, and exercise rooms; 60-foot lap pool; and a salon for facials, massage, pedicures, and manicures. (Spa hours are from 6am to 9pm Monday through Friday and 8am to 8pm on Saturday and Sunday.) There is a $10 charge for use of the exercise room on weekdays only. Aerobic and swim clothes may be purchased.

The Bostonian Hotel

40 North St., Boston, MA 02109. ☎ **617/523-3600** or 800/343-0922. Fax 617/523-2454. 152 rms, 11 suites. A/C MINIBAR TV TEL. $205–$265 single; $245–$285

double; $295–$335 honeymoon/executive; $450–$725 suite. Children under 12 stay free in parents' room. Extra person $20. Special weekend rates and other packages available. AE, DC, JCB, MC, V. Parking $20. MBTA: Government Center (Green Line) or Haymarket (Green or Orange Line).

With flower-decked balconies, this picture-postcard, red-brick building overlooks Faneuil Hall Marketplace. Though small in comparison with some of Boston's other hotels, it's big in charm and has all the amenities expected at a top-rate hostelry.

Located in Dock Square, a site that was part of the waterfront in colonial days, the Bostonian has two wings—one dates from 1824, and the other, an old warehouse building, from 1890. One wing is furnished in a contemporary style, the other more traditionally. The interior structure is a pleasant agglomeration of architectural styles, and public spaces are subtly decorated with artworks on loan from the Bostonian Society. Light colors and floral patterns dominate in bed covers, draperies, and upholstery. All the rooms are furnished with armoires and tables, and a significant number have French doors that open onto private balconies. Some suites have double vanities and separate dressing areas (terrycloth robes are provided). All rooms have VCRs in stereo, and a 26-inch TV tucked into the armoire. Additionally, rooms are outfitted with in-room safes and two-line phones with dataport. Bathrooms are equipped with hairdryers, heat lamps, and both overhead and European-style hand-held shower sprays. If you are a light sleeper or want to sleep late in the morning, you might prefer a room facing away from the bustle of the market, since marketplace activity begins almost at dawn.

Dining/Entertainment: On the fourth-floor rooftop is the glass-enclosed Seasons Restaurant, one of Boston's finest (see Chapter 6).

Services: Evening turndown, shoeshine, limousine service to Logan airport, newspaper delivery, 24-hour room and concierge services.

Facilities: Complimentary health club privileges at the nearby Sky Club.

Harborside Hyatt Conference Center & Hotel

101 Harborside Dr., Boston, MA 02129. ☎ **617/568-1234** or 800/233-1284. Fax 617/568-6080. 270 rms. A/C TV TEL. $195 single or double. AE, CB, DC, DISC, MC, V. Parking $7 maximum for overnight guests. Directions: Follow the signs to the grounds of Logan International Airport and take Harborside Dr.

The Harborside Hyatt has a waterfront location and unobstructed views of the city's harbor and skyline. The architecture is striking; anchoring one end of the building is a lighthouse whose light is controlled by the Logan Airport control tower so it doesn't interfere with runway lights. Inside, fiber-optic stars change color in the skydome ceiling in the reception area. Public spaces are accented with nautical memorabilia, and the first-class guest rooms have all the amenities you'd expect from a deluxe hotel, plus such extras as irons and ironing boards in each room, luxury baths, fine wood furnishings, and excellent views.

Dining/Entertainment: The hotel's restaurant serves breakfast, lunch, and dinner. Floor-to-ceiling windows allow for spectacular views.

Services: The water taxi to Rowes Wharf from the hotel dock; 24-hour airport shuttle service.

Facilities: Health club with indoor lap pool.

✪ Hotel Le Meridien

250 Franklin St. (at Post Office Sq.), Boston, MA 02110. ☎ **617/451-1900** or 800/543-4300. Fax 617/423-2844. 326 rms, 22 suites. A/C MINIBAR TV TEL. $215–$235 single; $235–$260 double; $450 suite. Extra bed $20. Weekend rates from $125 per night, including free use of pool and health club plus parking. AE, CB, DC, MC, V. Parking $17. MBTA: State St. (Blue Line).

Located in the old Federal Reserve Bank building, which was designed by R. Clipston Sturgis in 1922 to resemble a 16th-century Roman palazzo, Hotel Le Meridien is an historic landmark. Incorporated into its design are some of the bank's elegant architectural details, like the original grand marble staircase that leads to the dining areas. Two murals by N. C. Wyeth grace the walls of the bar, and ornately carved marble fireplaces and floor-to-ceiling arched windows take you back in time.

While the Meridien is especially convenient for business travelers, it is also a good location for vacationers due to its close proximity to major attractions. First and foremost, though, it's a great place for anyone who wants to be pampered. One guest room is not identical to the next here. In fact, there are 153 different room configurations, including dramatic loft suites with first-floor living room, a bedroom in the loft area, and bathrooms on both levels. A glass mansard roof was later added to the structure, and as such a number of rooms have glass walls and extraordinary views. *Note:* At press time, the Hotel Le Meridien was undergoing a $5.5 million renovation to its guest rooms. It should be completed before the beginning of 1996.

Dining/Entertainment: A historic coffered, gold-leafed ceiling tops the elegant Julien restaurant and bar. A six-story glass atrium creates a perennial garden court for the Café Fleuri, which serves breakfast, lunch, dinner, a seasonal Saturday "Chocolate Bar Buffet," and Sunday jazz brunch. La Terrasse is the hotel's seasonal outdoor cafe.

Services: 24-hour room service and concierge; laundry and dry cleaning service; daily weather report.

Facilities: Indoor swimming pool, health club. Full service business center. Two floors for nonsmokers, 15 rooms for the disabled.

Marriott Long Wharf

296 State St., Boston, MA 02109. ☎ **617/227-0800** or 800/228-9290. Fax 617/227-2867. 402 rms, 12 suites. A/C TV TEL. $220–$269 single or double. Extra person free. Weekend packages from $189 single or double; $450–$490 suite. AE, DC, DISC, MC, V. Parking $22. MBTA: Aquarium (Blue Line).

Pointing out to sea like an ocean liner, the Marriott Long Wharf stands on the waterfront, just across the harbor from Logan International Airport. The multitiered brick hotel is something of a tourist attraction itself, with a 50-foot-wide public walkway on the lower level. At the entrance an escalator, embellished by a pyramid-shaped glass-and-steel structure, leads to the second-floor lobby. *Note:* A Rufus Porter harbor scene, one of the few remaining original frescoes painted by the

19th-century artist, dominates the lobby wall near the escalator. Although the locale is not identified, it is thought to be Boston Harbor in the early 1800s. It's well worth seeing, even if you're not a hotel guest.

Most rooms have views of the wharves—either Long Wharf and the aquarium or Mercantile Wharf and Waterfront Park. Rooms are large and decors vary, but all have a radio, in-room movies, and a choice of either king-size or double beds. Floral-printed quilted spreads add color accents, and a round table and chairs are arranged for viewing the waterfront scene below.

If you like little extras like fresh flowers in your room; complimentary continental breakfast, cocktails, and hors d'oeuvres served in a private lounge; more private exercise facilities; and a game room, book a room on the seventh-floor Concierge Level.

Dining/Entertainment: The atrium-style Palm Garden, a cafe and lounge used for Sunday brunch, is crowned with a magnificent 420-foot ceiling mural; Waves Bar & Grill is trendy and popular; Oceana Restaurant features a 180° expanse of glass wall fronting the harbor.

Services: Concierge.

Facilities: Business center, indoor swimming pool with an outdoor terrace, exercise room, saunas, whirlpools, game room, 18 rooms with special facilities for the handicapped.

Omni Parker House

60 School St., Boston, MA 02108. ☎ **617/227-8600** or 800/THE-OMNI. Fax 617/742-5729. 535 rms, 12 suites, A/C TV TEL. $165–$295 single; $185–$325 double; $260 minisuite; $295–$600 large and elegant suite. Children under 16 stay free in parents' room. Weekend packages available. AE, CB, DC, DISC, MC, V. Valet parking $22; self-parking $15. MBTA: Government Center (Green Line) or Park St. (Red Line).

Located right on the historic Freedom Trail, this establishment is the oldest continuously operating hotel in America. Over the years guests have included the Divine Sarah Bernhardt, Isabella Stewart Gardner, Alexander Graham Bell, Emerson, Hawthorne, Longfellow, Dickens, Willa Cather, Malcolm X, and General Ulysses S. Grant among others. In the 19th century, the Parker House also served as a meeting place for a literary salon known as the Saturday Club. The elegance of this member of the Omni Hotel chain continues to attract political leaders (like Michael Dukakis, Paul Tsongas, and Bill Clinton) and other notables. This is not, however, the hotel of choice for the Hollywood crowd. Public spaces are comfortably furnished in 19th-century style. Walls are covered with American oak (original to the hotel), and doors are accented with burnished bronze. Renovations have restored the elegance that made it a favorite hostelry in the days of Emerson. Guest rooms vary in shape and size, and some bathrooms are equipped with showers only, but accommodations are comfortable and pleasantly decorated. Rooms have views of the old City Hall or the new Government Center.

Dining/Entertainment: Parker's Restaurant serves superb food (including the famous Parker rolls, which were invented here) in gracious style. Parker's Bar is on the site of the Saturday Club of 1860s fame. On the lower level of the hotel is the Last Hurrah Bar & Grill, a favorite of the local politicians and a busy, late-evening spot for drinks and dancing.

Services: Room service until 11pm, concierge, secretarial service.

Facilities: Rooms for nonsmokers and the disabled; use of nearby health club.

EXPENSIVE

Holiday Inn

5 Blossom St., Boston, MA 02114. ☎ **617/742-7630** or 800/HOLIDAY. Fax 617/742-4192. 303 rms, 2 suites. A/C TV TEL. $199 single or double. $15 for rollaway. Extra person $20. Children under 18 stay free in parents' room. 10% senior discount with AARP card. Weekend and corporate packages available. AE, DC, DISC, JCB, MC, V. Parking $16 in covered lot adjacent to hotel.

Nestled at the base of Beacon Hill, near the Charles River, is this appealing modern hotel, which is part of a plaza complex that includes a variety of shops. As you would expect at a Holiday Inn, the rooms have modern, functional furniture and simple decor. All furnishings are new, as this Holiday Inn has recently completed a $10 million renovation of all guest rooms and public spaces. Each room has a picture-window view of the city.

Dining/Entertainment: Foster's Bar & Grill Restaurant serves breakfast, lunch, and dinner.

Services: In-room coffee/tea service on executive floor, complimentary *USA Today* newspaper delivered to your door.

Facilities: Rooms for nonsmokers, coin-op launderette, outdoor pool, small exercise room.

Swissôtel Boston (The Lafayette)

1 Avenue de Lafayette, Boston, MA 02111. ☎ **617/451-2600** or 800/621-9200. Fax 617/451-0054. 45 rms, 46 suites. A/C MINIBAR TV TEL. $225–$290 single or double. $370–$2,500 suite or Swiss Butler Executive Level. Children under 18 stay free in parents' room. Extra person $25. Weekend packages available. AE, CB, DC, DISC, JCB, MC, V. Valet parking $19 weekdays, $5 weekends. MBTA: Downtown Crossing (Red Line).

The plain-looking exterior of this hotel, which rises 22 stories above the busy Downtown Crossing shopping center, is deceiving. Guests arriving at the concourse entrance are whisked by private elevator to an elegant lobby worlds away from the bustle below. Designed in classic European style, the hotel is decorated with both antique and contemporary furnishings, and elegant touches like Waterford crystal chandeliers and imported marble columns.

Guest rooms are grouped around four atriums, each with semiprivate lobbies, creating the effect of several small hotels within the hotel. Each room features a sitting area with desk, settee, and king- or twin-size beds. The suites have either L-shaped rooms with sitting areas or living rooms with connecting bedrooms. All rooms have three telephones with dataports. A special feature is the Executive Level, where guests are pampered from check-in to express checkout. A Swiss

Butler on this level performs traditional butler functions, acts as a private concierge, and even runs errands at no extra charge above the room rate.

Dining/Entertainment: Café Suisse serves breakfast, lunch, dinner, and a Sunday brunch featuring both Swiss and American favorites. The Lobby Lounge, located in the atrium lobby, offers cocktails and light meals.

Services: 24-hour room service, valet service, same-day dry cleaning, and turndown.

Facilities: Health club, exercise room, saunas, 52-foot-long indoor swimming pool, sun terrace, high-tech business center. Six floors for nonsmokers.

3 Back Bay

Many of Boston's hotels are clustered in the upscale Back Bay. The streets of this elegant district are lined with fine shops, restaurants, and old mansions, as well as more modern high-rises. For your convenience I've divided the listings in this area into two sections, the first including hotels near the Boston Common/Public Garden/Theater District areas, and the second including those closer to the Copley Square/Convention Center/Massachusetts Avenue landmarks. The first group is closer to downtown Boston.

BOSTON COMMON/PUBLIC GARDEN/THEATER DISTRICT

VERY EXPENSIVE

✪ Four Seasons Hotel

200 Boylston St., Boston, MA 01226. ☎ **617/338-4400** or 800/332-3442. Fax 617/426-7199. 288 rms, 80 suites. A/C MINIBAR TV TEL. $260–$420 single; $300–$460 double; from $650 one-bedroom suite; from $1,100 two-bedroom suite. Weekend packages available. AE, CB, DC, MC, V. Valet Parking $22. MBTA: Arlington St. (Green Line).

The elegant Four Seasons Hotel, overlooking the Public Garden and Beacon Hill, is a small, brick-and-glass hotel that has earned an impressive reputation since it opened in 1985. Newly refurbished, the 288 guest rooms and 80 suites harmonize with the Old World charm of Boston and the simplicity that marks today's architectural styles. Each room is elegantly appointed and has a unique view of the city. Beds are large and comfortable, and breakfronts conceal the 19-inch remote-control TV and refrigerated minibar. The suites range from Four Seasons Executive Suites, which have enlarged alcove areas for entertaining or business meetings, to luxurious one-, two-, and three-bedroom deluxe suites, which are the utmost in elegance, privacy, and comfort. All rooms have bay windows that open, as well as individual climate control, three two-line phones with computer and fax capability, hairdryers, and terrycloth bathrobes. Children receive bedtime snacks and toys. Small pets are accepted and receive the royal treatment with a special pet menu and amenities.

Dining/Entertainment: The elegant restaurant Aujourd'hui, one of Boston's best (see Chapter 6 for full listing), serves fine French cuisine;

the Bristol Lounge is open for lunch, afternoon tea, dinner, and breakfast on Sunday. The Bristol features live entertainment nightly.

Services: Twice-daily maid service, complimentary overnight shoeshine, complimentary limousine service to downtown Boston addresses, 24-hour valet and room service (with hot meals available at any hour), individual safe-deposit boxes, and an attentive concierge. For those who lose luggage en route, the staff of the Four Seasons will purchase new items and will provide you with a full set of toiletries and other necessary items.

Facilities: Indoor swimming pool and whirlpool with a view of the Public Garden; health spa with weight machines, StairMasters, treadmills, private masseuse, and sauna. (The pool and spa are shared with residents of the condominiums that occupy upper floors of the hotel.) Five no-smoking floors, rooms for the disabled.

Ritz-Carlton Hotel

15 Arlington St., Boston, MA 02117. ☎ **617/536-5700** or 800/241-3333. Fax 617/536-1335. 278 rms, 48 suites. A/C MINIBAR TV TEL. $230–$330 single; $270–$370 double; $500–$2,000 one-bedroom suite, $720–$2,100 two-bedroom suite. Ritz Carlton Club $565–$795 one-bedroom suite, $830–$1,175 two-bedroom suite. Weekend packages available. AE, CB, DC, DISC, ER, JCB, MC, V. Valet parking $20. MBTA: Arlington St. (Green Line).

Overlooking the Boston Public Garden in Back Bay, the Ritz-Carlton has a tradition of gracious service and charm that has made it famous for more than a half century, attracting both the "proper Bostonian" and the celebrated guest. The service and attention to detail are legendary. The hotel has the highest staff-to-guest ratio in the city, including white-gloved elevator operators.

The guest rooms have classic French provincial furnishings accented with imported floral fabrics and crystal chandeliers. Each room has a refrigerator, well-stocked honor bar, color TV concealed in an armoire, clock radio, message phone, and individual climate-control unit. The bathrooms are finished in Vermont marble, and soft terrycloth bathrobes are provided. Fresh flowers are provided in all suites. All the guest room closets lock, and all the windows open. Each of the suites has a wood-burning fireplace.

The rooms on the 14th and 15th floors have a panoramic view of Boston Public Garden and the city. Guests on those floors are also invited to relax in the Ritz-Carlton Club, a pleasant lounge, open from 7am to 11pm, serving complimentary breakfast, afternoon tea, hors d'oeuvres, and after-dinner sweets.

Dining/Entertainment: The superb Dining Room is described in Chapter 6, and the popular Ritz Bar, located off the street-floor lobby, is covered in Chapter 10. The second-floor Lounge is famous for afternoon tea, and evenings from 5:30pm until midnight cigar and pipe smokers can relax there over cognac, rare cordials, caviar, and desserts. The Café is open for breakfast, lunch, and dinner from 7am to midnight. The Roof, located on the 17th floor, offers a splendid view of the city. Diners will enjoy their meals outdoors (seasonally) while listening to the sounds of the Ritz-Carlton Orchestra and vocalist.

Services: Concierge, complimentary shoeshine, twice-daily maid service, nightly bed turndown, morning newspaper. Room-service pantries operate on each floor 24 hours a day.

Facilities: In-room safes; flower shop; hair salon; Fitness Center with eight-station Universal machine, exercise bicycles, computerized treadmill, weights, sauna, and massage room; use of pool in nearby Le Pli Health Spa.

MODERATE

$ Boston Park Plaza Hotel & Towers

64 Arlington St. (at Park Plaza), Boston, MA 02116. ☎ **617/426-2000** or 800/225-2008. Fax 617/426-1708. 960 rms. A/C TV TEL. Main hotel $155–$215 single or double; Towers $195–$245 single or double; $375–$1,500 suite. Extra person $20. Senior discounts and special packages available. Children stay free in parents' room. AE, DC, MC, V. Valet parking $18. MBTA: Arlington St. (Green Line).

Built as the great Statler Hilton in 1927, the hotel is proud of its history, but it's equally proud of its renovations. The lovely old features—such as the spacious lobby with its crystal chandelier, gilt trim, and red-carpeted corridors—have been retained, but the rooms have been updated with modern comforts. Room size and decor vary greatly. The top-floor Towers offer extra services and a hospitality suite serving continental breakfast, evening hors d'oeuvres, and cocktails. The hotel's location is central—just a block from Boston Common and the Public Garden, and about the same distance from the theater district.

Note: The Park Plaza Hotel and Towers has initiated an environmental policy that is a model for the industry. All nonbiodegradable products have been eliminated from guest rooms, recycling programs are in effect, and stationery and forms are printed on dioxin-free recycled paper. A "Green Team" of hotel employees is attempting to conserve energy and water and to eliminate hazardous waste.

Dining/Entertainment: Guests enjoy dining in the Cafe Rouge bistro, serving continental cuisine; Boston's famous Legal Sea Food restaurant; the Captains Bar; Cafe Eurosia; and Swans Court in the Grand Lobby.

Services: 24-hour room service, concierge, shoeshine.

Facilities: Health club, travel agency, hairdresser, kids' video/game room, foreign currency exchange, Amtrak and airline ticket offices, gift shop, pharmacy, beauty salon, and smoke-free floors.

57 Park Plaza Hotel—Howard Johnson

200 Stuart St. (at Park Sq.), Boston, MA 02116. ☎ **617/482-1800** or 800/HOTEL-57. Fax 617/451-2750. 350 rms, 10 suites. A/C TV TEL. $25–$145 single; $140–$155 double; suite $140–155 single, $130–$165 double; $120–$165 minisuite. Extra person or cot $15. Children under 18 stay free in parents' room. Cribs free. Weekend and family packages available. AE, DC, MC, V. Free parking indoors and with direct access to your floor. MBTA: Boylston St. (Green Line).

Don't let the middlebrow Howard Johnson name fool you. This place may not sound glamorous, but its rooms are actually quite nice.

Each pastel-colored room has a private balcony with a commanding view of the city, king-size beds or two double beds, a sitting area, and a shower-bath combination. Also available are minisuites with one king-size bed and a parlor area with sofa, table, and chairs.

You can swim year-round in the seventh-floor pool or take a free sauna. This centrally located downtown hotel is part of a complex that includes the 57 Restaurant and two cinemas.

$ Tremont House

275 Tremont St., Boston, MA 02116. ☎ **617/426-1400** or 800/331-9998. Fax 617/482-6730. 281 rms, 34 suites. A/C TV TEL. $115–$130 single; $130–$145 double; $170–$270 suite. Extra person $15. AE, CB, DC, DISC, ER, MC, V. Parking $15 in nearby garage or lot. MBTA: Boylston St. (Green Line).

The star of Boston's theater district is the Tremont House. It's located in the heart of the district, across from the Wang Center for the Performing Arts.

Built in 1925, this 15-story brick building was formerly the landmark Hotel Bradford. It has been completely renovated to preserve its traditional Boston style. The original gold-leaf decorations and crafted ceilings in the lobby and ballrooms have been restored, the original marble walls and columns refurbished, and elegant, sparkling-new chandeliers installed.

Since Tremont House is geared to travelers on a modest budget, its guest rooms are affordable and furnishings are modern. There are three top-of-the-line units that feature kitchenettes with a range, sink, and refrigerator—great for families who want to eat in. Four floors are reserved for nonsmokers, and there are 14 equal-access rooms.

If you'd like an evening of dancing without leaving the hotel, try the Roxy nightclub, featuring Top 40s hits and international music; or the NYC Juke Box Club for the beat of the nineties Thursday, Friday, and Saturday. Broadway's Restaurant & Bar serves a casual pub-style menu at breakfast, lunch, and dinner.

COPLEY SQUARE/CONVENTION CENTER/ MASSACHUSETTS AVENUE

VERY EXPENSIVE

Copley Plaza Hotel—A Wyndham Hotel

138 St. James Ave., Boston, MA 02116. ☎ **617/267-5300** or 800/WYNDHAM. Fax 617/247-6681. 373 rms, 61 suites. A/C MINIBAR TV TEL. $220–$270 single; $245–$295 double; $395–$1,400 suite. Extra person $20. AE, CB, DC, JCB, MC, V. Valet parking $22. MBTA: Copley Sq. (Green Line) or Back Bay (Orange Line).

Built in 1912, The Copley Plaza—A Wyndham Hotel, the "Grand Dame of Boston," is located on Copley Square in the historic Back Bay. The Renaissance Revival Copley Plaza has been synonymous with elegance since it opened. Renowned for its opulent decorative features like crystal chandeliers, majestic Italian marble columns, gilded vaulted ceilings, mirrored walls, and mosaic tile floors, the hotel has hosted royalty, statesmen, and celebrities, and every United States president since William Howard Taft took a room here. Newly renovated guest rooms and suites reflect the elegance of the hotel's public spaces and are furnished with reproduction antiques. Additional in-room features include coffeemakers, phones with computer dataports, and in-room movies. Bathrooms are equipped with hairdryers, heat lamps, and baskets filled with fine soap, shampoo, and bubble bath. After you settle into your room you can obtain a walking tour that focuses on the hotel's art, architecture, and history from the concierge.

Dining/Entertainment: The Copley Plaza Hotel features outstanding dining and drinking facilities: the Plaza Dining Room (see Chapter 6), offering classic American cuisine; the Library Bar; the Plaza Bar, serving light meals and featuring live entertainment; Copley's Restaurant (breakfast, lunch, afternoon tea, and dinner); andCopley'sBar.

Services: 24-hour room service, twice-daily maid service, in-lobby shoeshine, concierge.

Facilities: Fitness center; guests can use the nearby Le Pli Spa (with pool and sauna) at the Heritage without charge; four floors are reserved for nonsmokers. Rooms for disabled available.

EXPENSIVE

Boston Back Bay Hilton

40 Dalton St., Boston, MA 02115. ☎ **617/236-1100** or 800/HILTONS. Fax 617/267-8893. 330 rms and suites. A/C TV TEL. $135 single; $145 double. Extra person $20. AE, CB, DC, DISC, MC, V. Parking $15. MBTA: Prudential (Green Line, E train).

Located near the Prudential Center and the Hynes Convention Center just one block from Exit 22 off the Massachusetts Turnpike, the rooms at the Boston Back Bay Hilton were renovated in 1993, many in Southwest style. All rooms have either one king-size or two double beds. The hotel's unique triangular shape and soundproofing in the rooms helps keep the level of street noise down. Small pets are welcome. The Back Bay Hilton caters to the business traveler.

Dining/Entertainment: Boodles Restaurant is known for grilled specialties. Boodles Bar has a great selection of American specialty beers, and the Rendezvous Lounge is open for continental breakfast, cocktails, and light meals.

Services: Room service, business services, currency exchange.

Facilities: Indoor pool, sun deck, fully equipped fitness center. No-smoking rooms available.

Boston Marriott Hotel/Copley Place

110 Huntington Ave., Boston, MA 02116. ☎ **617/236-5800** or 800/228-9290. Fax 617/236–5885. 1,139 rms, 77 suites. A/C TV TEL. $190–$210 single; $210–$230 double; $250–$1,100 suite. Senior discounts. Children stay free in parents' room. AE, DC, DISC, ER, JCB, MC, V. Valet parking $21; self-parking $17. MBTA: Prudential (Green Line, E train).

Opening directly into Copley Place, this hotel's gorgeous lobby features a four-story-long chandelier, Italian marble floors, full-size trees, and a waterfall. Guest rooms with Queen Anne-style mahogany furniture, including armchairs or an ottoman, and a desk and table, echo the finery of the Marriott's lobby. Rooms are equipped with full-length mirrors, hairdryers, and ironing boards. Ultrasuites feature individual whirlpool baths. One suite even holds a grand piano. A glass walkway with gazebo-style turrets connects the Marriott with the Prudential Center. No need to cross busy Huntington Avenue!

Dining/Entertainment: Gourmeli's and Bello Mondo are the hotel's two Italian restaurants, and Champions Sports Bar is a comfortable place to watch sporting events and enjoy light meals. Sunday brunch, with entertainment, is served in the Terrace Lounge.

Services: 24-hour room service, concierge, full-service business center with fax machines and personal computers and dataports for personal computers or fax machines.

Facilities: Heated indoor pool, saunas, whirlpool, exercise room, no-smoking rooms, rooms for the disabled.

The Colonnade Hotel

120 Huntington Ave., Boston, MA 02116. ☎ **617/424-7000** or 800/962-3030. Fax 617/424-1717. 288 rms, 15 suites. A/C MINIBAR TV TEL. Standard $195 single, $240 double; superior $255 single, $250 double; deluxe $245 single, $270 double. Suites $450–$1,400. Children under 12 stay free in parents' room. AE, CB, DC, MC, V. Parking $20. MBTA: Prudential or Symphony (Green Line).

Located in the historic Back Bay, across from the Prudential Shopping Center, the Colonnade is one of Boston's finest. The hotel's contemporary European atmosphere is enhanced by a friendly, professional staff whose members give every guest personalized VIP service. The rooms in this independent family-owned hotel either feature contemporary oak furnishings and are decorated in coppery autumn colors with dark accents or contain mahogany furnishings against a rose-colored backdrop. The newly designed suites have dining rooms and sitting areas decorated in a "residential motif." Marble baths have pedestal sinks, bathrobes, and hairdryers.

Dining/Entertainment: The Cafe Promenade, open daily from 7am to 11pm, features seasonal menus, as well as gourmet pizzas in a bistro setting. Every Friday and Saturday night you'll find dinner and dancing with the Winiker Swing Orchestra in Zachary's Bar.

Services: 24-hour room service, concierge, nightly turndown, multilingual staff, Hertz car rental in the lobby.

Facilities: Seasonal "rooftop resort" with pool and fitness room.

✪ Eliot Hotel

370 Commonwealth Ave., Boston, MA 02215. ☎ **617/267-1607** or 800/44-ELIOT. Fax 617/536-9114. 16 rms, 78 suites. A/C MINIBAR TV TEL. $165–$185 single; $175–$195 double; $185–$205 suite for one, $195–$215 suite for two. Children under 12 stay free in parents' room. All rates include continental breakfast. AE, DC, MC, V. Valet parking $18.

In a parklike setting on Commonwealth Avenue, the Eliot is located adjacent to the Harvard Club. The stunning portico, sparkling 5-foot-wide imported crystal chandelier in the lobby, and richly upholstered period furnishings are an elegant introduction to the nine-story European suite hotel. Spacious suites are furnished with traditional English-style chintz fabrics, authentic botanical prints, and antique furnishings. French doors separate the living and bedrooms, and modern conveniences, such as Italian marble baths, dual-line telephones, two TVs, and coffeemakers are standard in all the suites. Many also have ice makers, a microwave, and a well-stocked refrigerator.

Dining/Entertainment: Breakfast is served in the Charles Eliot Room, where guests enjoy classical music and the *Wall Street Journal.*

Services: Concierge; room service available.

Facilities: Smoke-free floor, rooms for the disabled, safe-deposit boxes.

The Lenox Hotel

710 Boylston St., Boston MA 02116. ☎ **617/536-5300** or 800/225-7676. Fax 617/267-1237. 214 rms, 3 suites. A/C TV TEL. $160–$235 single; $180–$235 double. Executive corner room with wood-burning fireplace $250; suite with wood-burning fireplace $400. Extra person $20. Children under 18 stay free in parents' room. Cots $20. Cribs free. Corporate and weekend packages available. AE, CB, DC, DISC, ER, JCB, MC, V. Parking $20. MBTA: Copley Sq. (Green Line).

From the grandfather clock in the lobby to the wood-burning fireplaces in the corner rooms, the Lenox has a charm that makes it unique among Boston hotels. Located on Boylston Street near the Copley Place and Prudential shopping centers, it reflects its turn-of-the-century beginnings (it was built in 1900) and the personal touches of a family-run inn. The high-ceilinged rooms have separate sitting areas that have been recently redecorated with Chippendale-style furnishings. Despite such signs of luxury as hand-carved gilt moldings, this is an affordable hotel with rooms in moderate, superior, and deluxe categories. All have in-room fax machines and modem hookups; many rooms have marble baths.

Dining/Entertainment: The Upstairs Grille and the Samuel Adams Brewhouse serve meals. Diamond Jim's Piano Bar is a sing-along lounge.

Services: Nightly turndown service, *USA Today* delivered to room, room service.

Facilities: 100 smoke-free rooms, rooms for the disabled, wheelchair lift to the lobby, kids' channel on TV, exercise room.

Sheraton Boston Hotel & Towers

Prudential Center, 39 Dalton St., Boston, MA 02199. ☎ **617/236-2000** or 800/325-3535. Fax 617/236-6061. 1,187 rms, 85 suites. A/C MINIBAR TV TEL. $190 single; $220 double; suites from $255. Children under 17 stay free in parents' room. Students, faculty, and retired persons with IDs receive a 25% discount, depending on availability. AE, CB, DC, DISC, ER, JCB, MC, V. Parking $16. MBTA: Prudential (Green Line, E train).

With its three top-rated restaurants and attractive rooms, this hotel is one of the most popular in the city. It is actually two hotels in one—the original Sheraton and the luxurious Sheraton Towers, with private elevators to the top floors of the hotel. The complex is connected directly to the Hynes Convention Center.

The rooms are decorated with traditional furnishings in mahogany and cherrywood and accented with floral drapes and bedspreads. Many of the suites have an extra phone in the bathroom, a wet bar, and a refrigerator.

Guests who stay on the Club Level will enjoy free local calls and no access charges on long distance calls as well as complimentary breakfasts and evening hors d'oeuvres (both are served in the Club Level Lounge). In-room amenities on the Club Level include a desk, phone with dataport, morning newspaper, coffeemaker, and iron.

The Sheraton Towers, located on the 26th floor of the hotel, features private check-in, an elegant atmosphere accented by antiques, and a wonderful view from the lounge, where Towers guests can enjoy complimentary breakfast, afternoon tea, and late-day hors d'oeuvres and beverages. Luxury touches in the Tower rooms include Egyptian cotton sheets, goose-down comforters, plush bathrobes, electric blankets, a "valet hanger" for suits, shoe trees, and phones in the bathroom (some even have a wall-mounted TV). Guests staying on this floor have their own personal butler.

Dining/Entertainment: Open for breakfast, lunch, and dinner, the Mass. Bay Company features an eclectic seasonal menu. A Steak in the Neighborhood offers dining in a casual atmosphere. Serving breakfast, lunch, and dinner, the menu suits all tastes and offers over 70 different beers.

Services: 24-hour room service.

Facilities: Tropical domed pool pavilion with Jacuzzi, Universal, and other fitness equipment; special accommodations for the disabled; no-smoking rooms.

Westin Hotel

10 Huntington Ave., Boston, MA 02116. ☎ **617/262-9600** or 800/228-3000. Fax 617/424-7483. 800 rms, 46 suites. A/C MINIBAR TV TEL. $149–$210 single; $169–$250 double; $285–$1,500 suite. Extra person $20; $30 on Executive Club Level. Weekend packages available. AE, CB, DC, DISC, ER, JCB, MC, V. Valet parking $21. MBTA: Copley Sq. (Green Line).

Dominating the busy corner at Dartmouth Street and Huntington Avenue, this 36-story hotel is a concrete-and-glass marvel at the gateway to Copley Place, Boston's shopping mecca. You're greeted by two-story-high twin waterfalls cascading into flower-banked pools at the glass pedestrian entrance opposite the Boston Public Library. Moving staircases carry guests between the falls to the Grand Lobby.

The guest rooms are spacious and airy with excellent views from the large bay windows—you might request a view of downtown Boston, the airport and harbor, or the Charles River and Cambridge when making reservations. Furnishings are oak or mahogany. Each room has an in-room safe. This is a chain hotel, so guest rooms are standard throughout.

Dining/Entertainment: Three restaurants and three bars offer a variety of dining experiences: Ten Huntington is a casual bar serving light meals. Seafood is the specialty of Turner Fisheries, which has an oyster bar and greenhouse-style lounge and features live jazz nightly. The Brasserie, an informal dining room by the waterfall, is open for breakfast and lunch. The Lobby Lounge is a relaxing spot for drinks and conversation.

Services: Valet service, 24-hour room service, bilingual concierge. Among hotel employees, 15 languages are spoken.

Facilities: Health club, pool, no-smoking rooms. Forty rooms are designed for the disabled; these adjoin regular rooms to accommodate guests who may be traveling with the disabled person.

MODERATE

Copley Square Hotel

47 Huntington Ave., Boston, MA 02116. ☎ **617/536-9000** or 800/225-7062. Fax 617/236-0351. 143 rms, 12 suites. A/C TV TEL. $115–$155 single; $135–$175 double; $250 suite. Children under 17 stay free in parents' room. AE, DISC, ER, JCB, MC, V. Parking available in adjacent lot for $16. MBTA: Copley Sq. (Green Line).

Although it was built in 1891 and is located in the shadow of the megahotels near Copley Place and the Prudential Center, the Copley Square Hotel, with attractively decorated rooms, good value, and excellent service, is definitely not overshadowed by the "superstars." Each of the rooms at the Copley Square Hotel has two double beds, a queen-size or king-size bed, and a unique layout. All rooms are equipped with hairdryers, coffee/tea makers, in-room safes, and phones with modem hookups and guest voice mail. The hotel's owners, the Saunders family, have instituted an environmental policy based on the Native American saying "We have not inherited the earth from our ancestors; we are borrowing it from our children." The hotel staff participates in energy and water conservation and waste reduction and recycling. Environmentally sound products are supplied in the guest rooms and are used throughout the hotel.

Dining/Entertainment: Pop's Place serves breakfast. The Original Sports Saloon, with menu items named for sports personalities, serves lunch and dinner. Café Budapest, one of Boston's finest restaurants (see Chapter 6), is located in the adjacent lower lobby.

Services: 24-hour currency exchange.

Facilities: No-smoking rooms.

Midtown Hotel

220 Huntington Ave., Boston, MA 02115. ☎ **617/262-1000** or 800/343-1177. Fax 617/262-8739. 159 rms. A/C TV TEL. $99–$134 single; $109–$144 double. Extra person $10. Children stay free in parents' room. 10% senior discount with AARP card; government employees' discount subject to availability. AE, DC, MC, V. Free parking. MBTA: Prudential (Green Line, E train).

This hotel is located within Boston's cultural belt. Stay here and you'll be within easy walking distance of Symphony Hall, the Boston Museum of Fine Arts, the Christian Science Center, and Copley Square. The large rooms are modern and attractive. Tables of Content, an American bistro, is open 7am to 9pm. There is a heated outdoor pool.

BUDGET

Berkeley Residence YWCA

40 Berkeley St., Boston, MA 02116. ☎ **617/482-8850.** Fax 617/482-9692. 200 rms (none with bath). $32 single; $46 double; $54 triple. Long-term stay (4-week minimum) $127 per week, including breakfast and dinner daily. JCB, MC, V. Parking $14 in public lot one block away. MBTA: Arlington St. (Green Line) and Back Bay (Orange Line).

This pleasant, well-located hotel/residence for women offers a dining room, patio garden, pianos, a library, and laundry facilities. Passes are available to the pool and exercise room at the nearby Boston YWCA.

Central Branch YMCA

316 Huntington Ave., Boston, MA 02115. ☎ **617/536-7800.** 67–150 rms, depending on season (none with bath). TV. $39 single; $56 double. AE, DISC, MC, V. All rates include breakfast. Parking in nearby lots or on street. MBTA: Northeastern (Green Line, E train).

You'll find the Central Branch Y located about 10 minutes from downtown, near Symphony Hall and the Boston Museum of Fine Arts. Offering attractive and modern accommodations with a TV in each room, this hostelry now accepts both men and women 18 years of age and over. Rooms have maid service and rates include the use of a pool, gym, weight room, fitness center, and indoor track. There is also a cafeteria on the premises. Luggage and an ID are required for check-in. The Y offers rooms for singles, couples, and families. Call for reservations.

Chandler Inn Hotel

26 Chandler St., Boston, MA 02116. ☎ **617/482-3450** or 800/842-3450. Fax 617/542-3428. 56 rms. TV TEL. Nov–Apr $59 single, $69 double; May–Oct $79 single, $89 double. Children under 12 stay free in parents' room. All rates include continental breakfast. AE, CB, DC, DISC, MC, V. Parking available in nearby garages. MBTA: Back Bay/South End (Orange Line).

The Chandler Inn Hotel, on the edge of Back Bay at the corner of Chandler and Berkeley streets, is a no-frills hotel with newly refurbished guest rooms. Each room has a private bath/shower. It's near the Boston Center for the Arts in the revitalized, diverse neighborhood of the South End, and is just a short walk to the shopping areas of Newbury Street, Copley Place, or Downtown Crossing. The Back Bay (Amtrak) and Greyhound Bus stations are just a few blocks away. It's a practical choice if you're seeking value.

Hostelling International–Boston

12 Hemenway St., Boston, MA 02115. ☎ **617/536-9455.** Fax 617/424-6558. 190 beds. $15 per bed for members; $18 per bed for nonmembers. JCB, MC, V. MBTA: Hynes/ICA (Green Line, B, C, or D train).

Located near Symphony Hall, this hostel can accommodate 200 people. There are two dine-in kitchens, 19 bathrooms, and a large common room. You bring your own "sheet sleeping sack" or rent one (no sleeping bags permitted). To get a bed during the summer season you must be a member of Hostelling International–American Youth Hostels. For information and a membership application write to Hostelling International–American Youth Hostels, Dept. 481, 733 15th Street, NW, #840, Washington, DC 20005, or call **202/783-6161** or 800/444-6111.

4 Kenmore Square & Environs

Hotels in this area are located near Fenway Park, the hospitals at the Longwood Avenue Medical Complex, and several colleges and

Family-Friendly Hotels

Boston Park Plaza Hotel & Towers *(see p. 63)* The "Cub Club" can make life a joy for parents. The kids get a coupon book, Red Sox Sundaes, environmental gifts, and Swan Boat rides. They can play in Benny's Den video-game room or go to a story hour hosted by celebrity storytellers, where they're served milk and cookies. Picnic lunches/suppers, family movies, and bedtime snacks are also available. And there's a big bag of peanuts for feeding the ducks and swans in the Public Garden. Special family rates with free parking.

Ritz-Carlton Hotel *(see p. 62)* This hotel pampers the kids with a video library, games and toys, child snacks, and beverages, all served up in a "Junior Presidential Suite," designed by Fred Fiandaca. These lucky guests get a stuffed "Carlton the Lion," too. The Ritz also has occasional special weekends for young ladies and gentlemen, including "A Weekend of Social Savvy" and "The Junior Chef Debut." At Christmas there's a "Nutcracker Suite" package.

Four Seasons Hotel *(see p. 61)* Kids (and their parents) love the pool and spa and the executive suite, where they can get children's videos for the VCR, milk and cookies delivered by room service, child-size bathrobes, and any needed child accessories. The concierge has food packets for the ducks and squirrels in the Public Garden.

Charles Hotel *(see p. 74)* Kids adore family swim time at Le Pli Spa, which adjoins the hotel. The Harvard Square scavenger hunt is fun, and so is the room service menu, which includes pepperoni pizza. The snack bars are stocked with juice, milk, and cookies. If the kids want to read a special book (remember, this is Cambridge), they can order it from nearby Barillari Books and the concierge staff will deliver it to their room in 15 minutes.

Royal Sonesta Hotel *(see p. 76)* Summerfest features supervised children's programs (5 to 12 years), with complimentary use of bicycles, Polaroid cameras, health club, indoor/outdoor pool, boat rides along the Charles River, and unlimited ice cream!

museums. Some are in Boston, some in Brookline—this area is where the dividing line between the two cities falls.

Expensive

Doubletree Guest Suites Hotel

400 Soldiers Field Rd., Boston, MA 02134. ☎ **617/783-0090** or 800/222-TREE. Fax 617/783-0897. 310 rms. A/C MINIBAR TV TEL. $159–$209 single or double. Extra person $20. Children under 18 stay free in parents' room. Weekend packages from $99 per night. AE, CB, DC, DISC, ER, JCB, MC, V. Parking $12 Sun–Thurs, free Fri–Sat.

This hotel has one of the best deals in town—two-bedroom suites for the price charged by many hotels for a single unit. In fact, all rooms are suites with a living room, bedroom, and bath. Some floors are reserved for nonsmoking guests, and there are suites on each floor for the handicapped.

The suites are situated around a 15-story sunlit atrium and can be reached via glass elevators. Rooms are large, and most bedrooms have king-size beds and a writing desk. Living rooms feature full-size sofa beds, dining table, and an additional TV. Telephones are located in the bedroom, living room, and bath. Each room has a fully stocked honor bar and refrigerator large enough to stash away food and drinks for breakfast and lunch.

Dining/Entertainment: Scullers Grille and Scullers Lounge offer full-service meals from 6:30am to 11pm. Scullers Jazz Cabaret has nightly shows in the lounge at 8:30 and 10:30pm.

Services: Complimentary round-trip van service to downtown Boston and Cambridge is available.

Facilities: Indoor swimming pool, whirlpool, sauna, and exercise room.

MODERATE

Best Western Boston

342 Longwood Ave., Boston, MA 02115. ☎ **617/731-4700** or 800/528-1234. Fax 617/731-6273. TDD 617/731-9088, for the hearing impaired. 152 rms, 14 kitchenette suites. AC TV TEL. $99–$159 single or double. Children under 17 stay free in parents' room. AE, CB, DISC, ER, MC, V. Parking $14 with in/out privileges. MBTA: Kenmore Sq. (Green Line, B, C, or D train); from there take bus to Longwood Ave.

Located in the heart of a large medical complex, including the Beth Israel, Brigham and Women's, New England Deaconess, and Children's hospitals, as well as the Dana Farber Cancer Institute and the Joslin Clinic, this Best Western is a good base for those with business at the hospitals as well as tourists, since it's near museums, colleges, and Fenway Park. With a bus stop at the door, downtown Boston is only minutes away.

The guest units are quite large—each has a sitting area.Three quarters of the hotel is nonsmoking, and facilities include a restaurant and lounge. Since the hotel adjoins a business complex—the Longwood Galleria—there's access to a food court, retail stores, and a fitness center that hotel guests may use at a small fee.

Holiday Inn

1200 Beacon St., Brookline, MA 02146. ☎ **617/277-1200** or 800/HOLIDAY. Fax 617/734-6991. 208 rms. A/C TV TEL. $90–$155 single; $100–$170 double; $150–$190 suite. Extra person $10. Children under 18 stay free in parents' room. AE, DC, DISC, JCB, MC, V. Free parking. MBTA: Take Green Line, C train; stops at hotel.

Just 10 minutes from downtown via subway, this sparkling hotel is built around a colorful atrium with a garden lounge, putting green, sun deck, and a 40-foot swimming pool plus whirlpool. Rooms are furnished in either pecan, walnut, or oak finish. An entire floor is designated for nonsmokers, and 10 rooms are equipped for handicapped guests. There's the popular Café on the Green and two lounges.

Howard Johnson Hotel—Kenmore

575 Commonwealth Ave., Boston, MA 02215. ☎ **617/267-3100.** 179 rms. A/C TV TEL. $95–$145 single; $100–$160 double. Extra cot $10. Children under 18 stay free in parents' room. Senior discount. AE, CB, DC, DISC, ER, JCB, MC, V. Free parking. MBTA: Blandford St. (Green Line, B train).

Practically on the Boston University campus, this hotel is a great choice—it's located just a few subway stops from downtown, near Kenmore Square and Fenway Park and across the Charles River from the MIT campus. You can spot it easily by its glass-enclosed elevator, which goes to the rooftop lounge and provides a good view of the area. The indoor swimming pool and skylighted sun deck on the roof are open year-round from 11am to 9pm.

Howard Johnson Lodge Fenway

1271 Boylston St., Boston, MA 02215. ☎ **617/267-8300** or 800/654-2000. Fax 617/267-8300, ext. 151. 94 rms. A/C TV TEL. $75–$113 single; $85–$123 double. Extra person $10. Senior discount and special family packages. Children under 18 stay free in parents' room. AE, CB, DC, DISC, ER, JCB, MC, V. Free parking. MBTA: Kenmore Sq. (Green Line, B, C, or D train).

Red Sox fans take note: There's no hotel in Boston closer to Fenway Park than this one. Besides being adjacent to the park (you might even catch a home run ball hit over the left-field fence), this hotel is convenient to the Back Bay colleges, the Boston Museum of Fine Arts, and the Isabella Stewart Gardner Museum. There's an outdoor pool, open 9am to 7pm, and the Italian restaurant, Pranzàre Ristorante. Some rooms are outfitted with a microwave oven and a refrigerator.

BUDGET

Anthony's Town House

1085 Beacon St., Brookline, MA 02146. ☎ **617/566-3972.** 12 rms (none with bath). A/C TV. $35–$75 single or double. Extra person $10. Special weekly rates available. No credit cards. Free on-site parking. MBTA: Green Line, C train to Hawes St. stop (two beyond Kenmore Sq.).

Located one mile from Boston's Kenmore Square, this turn-of-the-century restored four-story brownstone town house is listed in the Historic Register and is just a 10-minute subway ride from the center of town. Each of the floors has three rooms and a shared bath with enclosed shower. All are decorated with Queen Anne– and Victorian-style furnishings, and the large front rooms have bay windows and comfortable lounge chairs. *Note:* Room prices listed above cover all seasons. Rates during most of the year are generally on the higher end.

Longwood Inn

123 Longwood Ave., Brookline, MA 02146. ☎ **617/566-8615.** 22 rms (17 with bath). May 1–Oct 31 $53–$63 single, $59–$69 double; Nov 1–Apr 30 $43–$53 single, $46–$56 double. 1-bedroom apt (sleeps four plus) $370 week. No credit cards. Free parking. MBTA: Longwood Ave. (Green Line, D train).

Located in a residential area near the Boston-Brookline border (just three blocks from Boston), this large Victorian guesthouse offers comfortable accommodations at modest rates. Guests can use the fully equipped kitchen and the coin-operated washer and dryer. There is a common dining room and TV lounge, and telephones are in the lobby. Guests also have access to the tennis courts, running track, and children's playground located near the inn. Public transportation is easily accessible, and the inn offers special long-term rates.

5 Cambridge

You simply can't visit Boston without spending time in Cambridge. It's just five minutes away across the Charles River and is a treasure trove of historical sites, museums, bookstores, ethnic and elegant restaurants, and fine hotels. And, of course, it's the home of Harvard University and MIT. If you choose to stay in Cambridge, you'll be just a short ride on the Red Line from Boston. You can also use shuttle services provided by hotels located some distance from subway stations.

VERY EXPENSIVE

✪ Charles Hotel

1 Bennett St., Cambridge, MA 02138. ☎ **617/864-1200** or 800/882-1818. Fax 617/864-5715. 296 rms, 44 suites. A/C MINIBAR TV TEL. 209–$239 single; $239–$259 double; $325–$1,400 suite. Children under 18 stay free in parents' room. Weekend packages available. AE, CB, DC, DISC, ER, JCB, MC, V. Parking $16. MBTA: Harvard Sq. (Red Line).

In Charles Square, the upscale shopping, dining, and office complex just a stone's throw away from Harvard's halls of ivy, this hotel creates a special niche of its own with its award-winning jazz bar, European-style Le Pli Day Spa, the city's only four-star restaurant, and distinctive guest rooms. Antique blue-and-white New England quilts, handcrafted between 1865 and 1885, hang in the Charles's great oak staircase as well as at the entrance to each guest-room floor.

The updated country style of the guest rooms is bright and airy, with custom-designed adaptations of early American Shaker pieces. The light wood tones of the armoires, apothecary chests, and four-poster beds are accented with homespun fabrics. Bathrooms are equipped with hairdryers, scales, and terrycloth robes. All rooms have large windows that can be opened, and are equipped with dataports. A novel service includes a tie-in with the nearby Words Worth discount bookstore. A Charles staffer will purchase books for you and even have them gift-wrapped. The tab is added to your bill.

There are five great weekend packages, including a workout weekend for two with a full day of pampering at the spa for about $500. In addition there is a $1,000 spa weekend with spa and salon treatments and gourmet low-calorie meals.

Dining/Entertainment: The new Henrietta's Table serves breakfast, lunch, dinner, and Sunday buffet brunch. The highly acclaimed Rialto emphasizes French, Italian, and Spanish cuisine by award-winning chef Jody Adams (see recommendation in Chapter 6).

Services: 24-hour room service, twice-daily maid service, evening turndown with bottle of iced mineral water. Pets can be accommodated.

Facilities: Glass-enclosed pool, Jacuzzi, sun terrace, and exercise room at the new Well Bridge Health and Fitness Center. Beauty treatments are available at Le Pli Day Spa. Facilities for teleconferencing. Seven floors for nonsmokers, 13 rooms for the disabled, rooms with special amenities for women travelers.

EXPENSIVE

Hyatt Regency Cambridge

575 Memorial Dr., Cambridge, MA 02139. ☎ **617/492-1234** or 800/233-1234. Fax 617/491-6906. 469 rms. A/C MINIBAR TV TEL. $109–$239 single or double. Suites $400–$575. Extra person $20. Children under 17 stay free in parents' room. Weekend packages available. AE, DC, DISC, ER, JCB, MC, V. Parking $18.

Nicknamed "the pyramid on the Charles," this hotel has a magnificent towering, terraced exterior. Inside, well-appointed guest rooms surround a 16-story atrium complete with diamond-shaped glass elevators, fountains, trees, and balconies. Families are especially welcome here. There are special reduced room rates for parents who choose to have their children sleep in a different room, and there are also adult's and children's bicycles available for guest use.

The Hyatt Regency is convenient for those visiting colleges, since it's halfway between Harvard and MIT and across the bridge from Boston University.

Dining/Entertainment: Jonah's Seafood Cafe, open to the atrium on one side and to a view of the river on the other, serves breakfast, lunch, or Sunday brunch. On the rooftop, the revolving, glass-enclosed Spinnaker restaurant serves lunch and dinner. Brunch is served on Sunday. Drinks are served until 1am weekdays and 2am on Friday and Saturday. The Pally Sadoe Sports Bar features billiard tables, dartboards, board games, and sports TV.

Services: Concierge; shuttle service to points of interest (there's no public transportation nearby); babysitting; currency exchange; laundry/valet service; room service; car rental service.

Facilities: 15 rooms for the disabled; nonsmoking floor; junior Olympic-size swimming pool; full health club with steam room, sauna, and whirlpool.

The Inn At Harvard

1201 Massachusetts Ave., Cambridge, MA 02138. ☎ **617/491-2222** or 800/458-5886. Fax 617/491-6520. 112 rms, 1 suite. A/C TV TEL. $155–$249 single or double; $450 presidential suite. Extra person $10. Children stay free in parents' room. Senior discount and special packages available. AE, CB, DC, MC, V. Parking $18. MBTA: Harvard Sq. (Red Line).

The Inn at Harvard, located on the campus of Harvard University at the intersection of Massachusetts Avenue and Quincy Street at Harvard Square, is a rather impersonal structure of red-brick Georgian-style architecture that seems a bit out of place here among the ivy-covered walls of the university. Enter through the four-story, glass-roofed atrium, where you'll find a library stocked with current periodicals, newspapers, and Harvard Press publications, and a small, upscale restaurant serving breakfast and dinner. (Guests can use the adjacent Faculty Club for lunch.)

Guest rooms are decorated in subdued sand-colored tones, and each room has a lounge chair or two armchairs around a table, windows that open, and an original painting from the Fogg Art Museum. Some have dormer windows and window seats. There are two phones with voice mail in each room, and one phone has computer modem hookups. All rooms have night-lights.

Dining/Entertainment: The atrium restaurant serves seasonal New England fare.

Services: Business services with fax, courier, typing, copying, and package receiving and shipping; complimentary newspaper delivery; free shoeshine; room service.

Facilities: Two smoke-free floors; six wheelchair-accessible rooms; safe-deposit boxes; backgammon and chess tables in the atrium library.

Royal Sonesta Hotel

5 Cambridge Pkwy., Cambridge, MA 02142. ☎ **617/491-3600** or 800/766-3782. Fax 617/661-5956. 400 rms, 28 suites. A/C MINIBAR TV TEL. $165–$215 single; $185–$235 double; $275–$635 suite. Children under 18 stay free in parents' room. AE, CB, DC, DISC, ER, JCB, MC, V. Parking $15. MBTA: Lechmere (Green Line; 10-minute walk).

Although it's technically in Cambridge, this hotel is still very close to Boston—closer, in fact, than it is to Harvard Square; it's near Longfellow Bridge, MIT, and the Boston Museum of Science, and the new CambridgeSide Galleria (filled with shops and restaurants and housing the New England Sports Museum) is located directly across the street. Original contemporary artwork (including work by Andy Warhol and Frank Stella) is displayed throughout the public spaces, as well as in some guest rooms. Most rooms have a lovely view of the Charles River or the city. If you get a room with a river view, you'll be able to see the gold dome of the Massachusetts State House. Everything is custom designed, with decorator furnishings, living-room and bedroom combinations, and luxurious bathrooms. Each room is equipped with an in-room safe. The hotel has seasonal promotions, like free ice cream during the summer, with special rates, giveaways for children, and fun events for adults.

Dining/Entertainment: Davio's restaurant serves breakfast, lunch, and dinner and has an outdoor patio overlooking the Charles River that's great for warm-weather dining. The Gallery Cafe is a more casual eatery.

Services: Room service (Sun–Thurs 6am–1am, Fri–Sat 6am–2am), baby-sitting service, secretarial services, courtesy van service to Boston and Cambridge.

Facilities: Business-class rooms with personal computer, fax machine, and multiline phones; rooms for nonsmokers and the disabled; health facility with a heated pool that has a retractable roof.

Sheraton Commander Hotel Cambridge

16 Garden St., Cambridge, MA 02138. ☎ **617/547-4800** or 800/325-3535. Fax 617/868-8322. 176 rms. A/C MINIBAR TV TEL. $135–$185 single; $135–$195 double; $225–$375 suite. Extra person $20. Children under 18 stay free in parents' room. AE, CB, DC, DISC, JCB, MC, V. Free parking. MBTA: Harvard Sq. (Red Line).

Located in the most interesting and historic district of Cambridge, this hotel, located across the Common from Harvard University, opened in 1927. It stands only a few feet from the elm where, on July 3, 1775, Gen. George Washington took command of the American troops (there's an imposing statue of the first U.S. president in the front courtyard of the hotel), and for years it has been the hotel of choice for this country's politicians. In fact, in 1952 the Sheraton Commander hosted John F. Kennedy.

The hotel successfully captures the spirit of old New England with its charming colonial decor, which begins in the lobby and extends to the guest rooms. Each unique room features electronic locks, in-room coffeemakers, and guest voice mail. The Club Level offers additional amenities and a private lounge.

Dining/Entertainment: The 16 Garden Street Restaurant serves breakfast, lunch, dinner, and, on Sunday, a splendid brunch. The 16 Garden St. Café serves lighter fare throughout the afternoon and evening.

Services: Room service, concierge, limited business services.

Facilities: Fitness center, sun deck.

Moderate

Harvard Manor House

110 Mt. Auburn St., Cambridge, MA 02138. ☎ **617/864-5200** or 800/458-5886. Fax 617/864-2409. 72 rms. A/C TV TEL. $95–$160 single or double. Children 16 and under stay free in parents' room. Corporate, AAA, and AARP rates available. AE, DC, ER, MC, V. Parking $10. MBTA: Harvard Sq. (Red Line).

Now under the management of Doubletree Hotels Corporation, the Harvard Manor House, a six-story brick structure overlooking Harvard Square just one block from the Charles River, is a great place from which to watch the square's street festivals. The rooms are pleasant and clean and the atmosphere is comfortable and unpretentious. Business travelers who prefer the personalized service of a small hotel will enjoy the convenience of on-premises fax and copy services. There's same-day laundry service and a complimentary daily newspaper as well.

Howard Johnson Hotel Cambridge

777 Memorial Dr., Cambridge, MA 02139. ☎ **617/492-7777** or 800/654-2000. Fax 617/492-7777, ext. 1799. 205 rms. A/C TV TEL. $78–$135 single; $88–$145 double. Extra person $10; no charge for cribs. Children under 18 stay free in parents' room. Senior discounts available with AARP card. AE, CB, DC, DISC, ER, JCB, MC, V. Free parking.

An attractive, modern motel with a swimming pool and sun deck, this Howard Johnson is well situated near the major Boston college campuses and just a 10-minute drive from downtown Boston.

Each of the bedrooms has a picture window, giving visitors (in most rooms) a panoramic view of the Boston skyline. Rooms are large, with modern furnishings, and some have a private balcony. Prices vary with the size of the room, the floor, and the view.

Also at the hotel is the Bisuteki Japanese Steak House, where dinners are prepared at your table in the hibachi style of "firebowl" cooking.

BUDGET

A Cambridge House Bed & Breakfast Inn

2218 Massachusetts Ave., Cambridge, MA 02140. ☎ **617/491-6300** or 800/232-9989 in U.S. and Canada, 800/96-2079 in the United Kingdom. Fax 617/868-2848. 16 rms (13 with bath). A/C TV TEL. $79–$165 single, $99–$225 double. Extra person $30. All rates include breakfast. AE, DISC, MC, V. Free parking. MBTA: Porter Sq. (Red Line).

A Cambridge House is a beautifully restored 1892 colonial home listed in the National Register of Historic Places. Each room is warmly decorated with Waverly fabrics and antiques. Most of the rooms have fireplaces and four-poster canopy beds covered with Fieldcrest linens and plush down comforters. Complimentary beverages and freshly baked pastries are served by the fireplace in the library or parlor. And a full breakfast, also complimentary, prepared by a professionally trained chef, is offered every morning. There's something different each day—omelets, crêpes, waffles, or fresh fruit. Every evening complimentary wine and cheese are also offered.

6 Highway High Spots

Sometimes you can find great accommodations just off the main highway. Here are three near Boston—two in Dorchester at Exit 13 of the Southeast Expressway, close to the Kennedy Library; the third on the opposite side of Boston at Exit 27A of Route 128.

$ Susse Chalet Boston Inn

900 Morrissey Blvd., Boston, MA 02122. ☎ **617-287-9200** or 800/258-1980. Fax 617/282-2365. 106 rms. A/C TV TEL. $56.70–$71.70 single; $61.70–$78.70 double. Extra person $3. AE, CB, DC, MC, V. Free parking.

Under the same management as the Susse Chalet Boston Lodge (see below), this attractive inn also has high standards and low prices. It's a four-story building with large guest rooms, including no-smoking rooms and rooms for the disabled. All double-bedded rooms have a reclining chair, and each room is equipped with a mini-refrigerator. A suite on the second floor has three skylights, two windows, two double beds that can be folded into a wall niche, a sofa bed, and a wet bar. It's a good choice for a large family of up to six people. The current rate is between $100 and $125.

There is a seasonal outdoor swimming pool, and coin-operated washers and dryers are available for guest use. Just across the lot is Boston Bowl, a popular recreational facility with 10 pocket billiard tables, 20 candlepin lanes, 30 tenpin lanes, and a video-game room, open 24 hours. The adjoining Swiss House Restaurant is open for breakfast, lunch, and dinner.

Susse Chalet Boston Lodge

800 Morrissey Blvd., Boston, MA 02122. ☎ **617/287-9100** or 800/258-1980. Fax 617/265-9287. 175 rms. A/C TV TEL. $51.70–$69.70 single; $58.70–$76.70 double. Extra person $3. AE, CB, DC, MC, V. Free parking.

This balconied chalet-style motor lodge has three floors of rooms. The single-bedded room is the same size as the double, and each room is equipped with a mini-refrigerator. An outdoor swimming pool is available for guest use in the warmer months. The facilities in the adjacent Susse Chalet Boston Inn (see above) are also available to Motor Lodge guests.

Westin Waltham

70 3rd Ave., Waltham, MA 02154. ☎ **617/290-5600** or 800/228-3000. Fax 617/290-5626. 346 rms, 33 suites. A/C MINIBAR TV TEL. $119–$175 single; $129–$185 double. Extra person $10. Children stay free in parents' room. Weekend packages and senior and AAA discounts available. AE, CB, DC, DISC, ER, JCB, MC, V. Free parking.

It's easy to spot the Westin from the highway—it's a drum-shaped building with a 90-foot-long Palladian glass and metal facade, dominating a hilltop above Route 128. Rising behind the rounded entrance is an eight-floor tower whose guest rooms are decorated with light-colored fabrics and rich woods. All rooms have two telephones, hair-dryers, ironing boards and irons, business-size desks, message retrieval, express checkout service via in-room cable TV, and windows that open. The executive floor has more amenities: a private lounge that serves a complimentary continental breakfast, hors d'oeuvres, and beverages; a telescope for viewing the area near the Cambridge Reservoir; and Executive Suites with VCRs, scales, and two-line telephones. Boston is about a 25-minute drive, and Lexington and Concord are about 15 minutes away. The Westin is a convenient locale for day trips north on Route 128 to Rockport and Gloucester or southwest to Sturbridge Village.

Dining/Entertainment: The Vineyard Café, with a panoramic view of the Cambridge Reservoir, serves breakfast, lunch, and dinner and features "theme" menus each month.The Lobby Lounge offers jazz entertainment in the evenings, and Circuits is the hotel's pub and nightclub.

Services: Hourly airport shuttle service ($10 per person), currency exchange, multilingual staff, 24-hour room service, concierge.

Facilities: Business center; four smoke-free floors; 13 rooms for the disabled; health club with indoor pool, whirlpool, sauna, and fitness room.

7 Nearby Resorts

If you've always wanted to visit Boston but your heart's set on a resort vacation, check this trio of resort hotels within a half-hour drive of the city, each offering complete vacation packages.

Colonial Hilton

Walnut Street, Lynnfield, MA 01940. ☎ **617/245-9300** or 800/HILTONS. Fax 617/245-0842. 280 rms. A/C TV TEL. $109–$139 single or double. Extra person $10. Children stay free in parents' room. Senior discounts and special packages available. AE, DC, DISC, MC, V. Free parking.

Just off I-95 in Lynnfield, this 220-acre luxury resort hotel offers an 18-hole golf course, indoor and outdoor tennis courts, racquetball courts, indoor basketball court, an Olympic-size swimming pool, and health club. The largest and most luxurious rooms are in the tower.

On a hilltop overlooking the golf course is the top-rated Colonial Restaurant, specializing in prime rib; there's also another casual dining restaurant. Rooms are available for nonsmokers and the disabled.

Stouffer Renaissance Bedford Hotel

44 Middlesex Tpk., Bedford, MA 01730. ☎ **617/275-5500** or 800/HOTELS-1. Fax 617/275-8956. 286 rms. A/C TV TEL. Sun–Thurs $150–$170 single, $160–$180 double; Fri–Sat $79 single, $99 double. Children stay free in parents' room. Senior discounts and weekend packages available. AE, CB, DC, DISC, JCB, MC, V. Free parking. Directions: Head 3 miles north of I-95 on the Middlesex Turnpike.

Near Lexington's historical section, this Stouffer hotel is located amid the headquarters of many leading corporations. In a welcome change from the tower style of many hotels, this one looks like a country resort with its scenic pine-wooded setting. The two-level rambling structure has a fitness center, indoor pool, whirlpool, sauna, and indoor and outdoor tennis courts. A fine restaurant and lounge are conveniently located in the hotel.

There is a choice of king-size or twin beds. Eleven rooms have special facilities for the handicapped, and rooms are available for nonsmokers. Several suites have sofas and conference tables for meetings, and all rooms have in-room movies and a digital alarm clock. Complimentary morning paper and coffee are brought to your room with your wake-up call; there is also complimentary shoeshine and 24-hour room service.

Tara's Ferncroft Conference Resort

50 Ferncroft Rd., Danvers, MA 01923. ☎ **508/777-2500** or 800/THE-TARA. Fax 508/750-7991. 367 rms, 17 suites. A/C TV TEL. $109–$129 single; $129–$149 double; $175–$550 suite. Extra person $15. Children under 18 stay free in parents' room. Weekend packages available. 20% senior discount for AARP members. AE, CB, DC, DISC, MC, V. Free parking.

This is the perfect spot for a golfing vacation. The 18-hole championship course was designed by Robert Trent Jones, and the rooms located high above Route 1 North have a view of either the golf course or the surrounding countryside. Since it's only a half-hour from Boston, about 20 minutes to Gloucester and Rockport, and even closer to Salem, it's the perfect anchor for sightseeing on the North Shore.

All rooms have a sofa, desk, heat controls, coffeemaker, and either double or king-size beds. Special amenities include an electric shoeshine buffer and a large vanity mirror with salon-style makeup lights in the bedroom. A number of rooms at the top of the Tara offer additional amenities and are priced slightly higher. There are also smoke-free floors and 20 rooms for the disabled.

If golf isn't your game, other sports facilities are available, including tennis, racquetball, basketball, volleyball, horseshoes, an indoor and outdoor pool, and a health and fitness center with cardiovascular room, nautilus room, aerobic studio, sauna, and masseuse. Sports enthusiasts might also enjoy cross-country skiing, ice-skating, and sledding.

The Ferncroft Grille features steak and seafood specialties, and Bogey's Restaurant and Pub is the place to go for light fare.

6

Dining

Seafood is one of Boston's greatest culinary strengths—no seafood lover would dispute the excellence of the Ipswich clams, Atlantic lobsters, Wellfleet oysters, mussels, cod, haddock, and flounder that have won the city acclaim. The waters off Massachusetts have provided Bostonians with fresh fish and shellfish for centuries. The old, cherished recipes for steamed clams in drawn butter, for fish chowder, and for Boston scrod are still yours to enjoy.

Besides restaurants serving New England-style seafood, Boston is also home to dining establishments offering all kinds of cuisines. Throughout the city you'll be practically tripping over little restaurants that serve Indian, Middle Eastern, Mexican, Russian, and Brazilian food.

To simplify your dining selections, I've categorized the restaurants based on their price range and their cuisine. *Very Expensive* includes those restaurants charging $18 to $35 per main course; *Expensive* refers to those pricing main courses at $12 to $20; and *Moderate* covers those with a tab of $8 to $12 per main course. However, if you order wine, appetizers, soups, salad, dessert, and coffee, the prices in each category may rise substantially. In the top restaurants, dinner for two may come to more than $125. The *Budget* category includes restaurants charging around $8 for a meal. Look in Cambridge (with its huge population of students) and to the ethnic restaurants for the best values. And there are always the fast-food places and the "fancy" fast-food places in Faneuil Hall Marketplace.

It's always best to phone ahead and make reservations, particularly for dinner, and at the better restaurants for lunch, too.

1 Best Bets

- **Best Spot for a Romantic Dinner.** The brass-accented dining room at the Bay Tower Room is consistently voted by the readers of *Boston Magazine* the most romantic in town. You'll dine on the 33rd floor at candlelit tables, all of which have a lovely view.
- **Best View.** You can't get a better view than the one you'll find 52 stories high at Top of the Hub. With three walls of glass, the restaurant and lounge offer a panoramic view of Boston. Come before sunset and linger over your meal until dark—this way you'll see the city two ways.

- **Best Barbecue.** Anyone who grew up south of the Mason-Dixon line knows how difficult it is to find good barbecue in the Northeast. The Original Sports Saloon has been successful at providing Boston diners with the best barbecue in town for almost five years. If you're up for a picnic, you can even get this award-winning barbecue in convenient takeout packages.
- **Best French Cuisine.** At Maison Robert the atmosphere is as impressive as the food. You won't find better French cuisine anywhere in the city—in fact, when visiting French chefs come to town, Maison Robert is their first choice.
- **Best Indian Cuisine.** For years, Kebab 'N' Curry was Boston's premiere Indian restaurant, but when its owners opened Bombay Club, they outdid themselves. The tandoori specialties are some of the best I've had.
- **Best Italian Cuisine.** In spite of its informal name, the upscale Mama Maria Ristorante offers the best Italian cuisine in Boston. The seafood pasta specialties are among my favorites.
- **Best Seafood.** Legal Sea Food is the place to go for fresh seafood. If you love New England clam chowder, Legal Sea Food offers one of the best I've ever had. There are several locations throughout the city.
- **Best Southwestern Cuisine.** For those of you who find traditional southwestern cuisine just a little boring, head for the Cottonwood Cafe, where chefs blend Mexican, Spanish, Native American, and French cuisines (among others) to create a new and improved version of the cuisine that swept the nation a few years back.
- **Best Vietnamese Cuisine.** Pho Pasteur, now at several locations throughout Boston, consistently offers the city's best Vietnamese food and is well worth a visit for both the uninitiated and the veteran.
- **Best Pizza.** Pizza in its purest form (thin crust, tomato sauce, and a variety of traditional toppings) has suddenly become difficult to find. Often when you do happen upon this endangered dish, it just doesn't measure up. Not so at The European, which, in my opinion, offers the best pizza in Boston.
- **Best Afternoon Tea.** Afternoon tea at the Ritz-Carlton is an elegant and traditional affair. A harpist plays quietly in the background while diners enjoy scones and Devonshire cream (among other treats).
- **Best Live Music.** House of Blues has started popping up in other major cities around the country, but the very first one to open was in Cambridge, and it truly does offer the best live music. The stage has hosted all the big names in blues as well as lesser known artists, and the show is always worth sticking around for, no matter who's playing when you're there.

2 Restaurants by Cuisine

AMERICAN

The Bay Tower, Faneuil Hall Marketplace
Boodles, Back Bay (E)
The Capital Grille, Back Bay (E)
Cornucopia on the Wharf, on the Waterfront (E)
Dakota's, Downtown Crossing (E)
Durgin-Park Inc., Faneuil Hall Marketplace (M)
57 Restaurant, Theater District (E)
The Harvest, Cambridge (VE)
Jacob Wirth Company, Theater District (M)
L'Espalier, Back Bay (VE)
Locke-Ober, Downtown Crossing (VE)
The Original Sports Saloon, Copley Square (B)
Rowes Wharf Restaurant, on the Waterfront (VE)
Union Oyster House, Faneuil Hall Marketplace (M)
Wursthaus, Cambridge (B)

BARBECUE

The Original Sports Saloon, Copley Square (B)

CANTONESE

Chau Chow, Chinatown (M)
Imperial Seafood, Chinatown (M)

CARIBBEAN

Green Street Grill, Cambridge (M)

CHINESE

Buddha's Delight, Chinatown (B)
Golden Palace Restaurant and Teahouse, Chinatown (M)
Ocean Wealth, Chinatown (M)

CONTINENTAL

Parker's Restaurant, Government Center (VE)
Plaza Dining Room, Copley Square (VE)
St. Botolph Restaurant, Back Bay (E)
Top of the Hub, Back Bay (E)
Upstairs at the Pudding, Cambridge (VE)

DELI

Rubin's, Brookline (M)
S&S Deli and Restaurant, Cambridge (M)

ECLECTIC

Biba Food Hall, Public Garden (E)
The Blue Room, Cambridge (E)
Hamersley's Bistro, South End (M)
Icarus, South End (M)
Olives, Charlestown (E)
Les Zygomates, Financial District (M)

FRENCH

Du Barry Restaurant Français, Copley Square (E)
Julien, Near Faneuil Hall (VE)
Rialto, Cambridge (E)
Ritz-Carlton Dining Room, Public Garden (VE)

GERMAN

Jacob Wirth Company, Theater District (M)
Wursthaus, Cambridge (B)

GREEK

Paramount Steak House, Beacon Hill (B)

HUNGARIAN

Café Budapest, Copley Square (VE)

Indian

Bombay Club, Cambridge (M)
Passage to India, Cambridge (B)

International

Aujourd'hui, Public Garden (VE)
Café Jaffa, Back Bay (M)
Dakota's, Downtown Crossing (E)
House of Blues, Cambridge (M)
Seasons, Faneuil Hall Marketplace (VE)
Tapas, Cambridge (M)
West Street Grill, Beacon Hill (M)

Italian

Botolph's on Tremont, South End (M)
Daily Catch, on the Waterfront (M)
Davio's, Copley Square (E)
The European, the North End (B)
Felicia's, the North End (E)
Galleria Umberto, the North End (B)
La Groceria, Cambridge (M)
La Piccola Venezia, the North End (B)
Mamma Maria Ristorante, the North End (E)
Pagliuca's, the North End (B)
Rialto, Cambridge (E)
Ristorante Marino, Cambridge (M)
Ristorante Toscano, Beacon Hill (E)
Rocco's, Theater District (E)
Spinnaker Italia, Cambridge (M)
Upstairs at the Pudding, Cambridge (M)
Vinny Testa's, Brookline (E)

Japanese

Sakura-Bana, Financial District (M)
Tatsukichi-Boston, Faneuil Hall Marketplace (M)

Kosher

Milk Street Cafe, Financial District (B)
Rubin's, Brookline (M)

Mexican

Casa Romero, Back Bay (E)
Sol Azteca, Brookline (E)

Middle Eastern

Algiers Coffeehouse, Cambridge (B)

New England

Henrietta's Table, Cambridge (M)
Upstairs at the Grille (M)

Portuguese

Casa Portugal, Cambridge (M)

Seafood

Anthony's Pier 4, on the Waterfront (E)
Daily Catch, on the Waterfront (M)
East Coast Grill, Cambridge (M)
Jimbo's Fish Shanty, on the Waterfront (B)
Jimmy's Harborside Restaurant, on the Waterfront (E)
Legal Sea Food, Back Bay (E)
Mass. Bay Co., Back Bay (E)
Rowes Wharf Restaurant, on the Waterfront (VE)
Skipjack, Back Bay (M)
Turner Fisheries, Back Bay (M)
Union Oyster House, Faneuil Hall Marketplace (M)

Southern

East Coast Grill, Cambridge (M)

Southwestern

Border Café, Cambridge (M)
Cottonwood Café, Cambridge (E)

SPANISH

Dalí, Cambridge (M)
Rialto, Cambridge (E)

TEX-MEX

Zuma's Tex-Mex Cafe, Faneuil Hall Marketplace, (B)

THAI

Bangkok Cuisine, Back Bay (M)

VEGETARIAN

Buddha's Delight, Chinatown (B)
Country Life Vegetarian Buffet, Financial District (B)
Milk Street Cafe, Financial District (B)

VIETNAMESE

Buddha's Delight, Chinatown (B)
Pho Pasteur, Chinatown (B)

3 On the Waterfront

Natives and tourists alike expect to be served the very best fresh fish in Boston area restaurants. And they're not disappointed. Each restaurant has buyers at the piers at daybreak bidding for the finest fish of the day.

VERY EXPENSIVE

✪ Rowes Wharf Restaurant

In the Boston Harbor Hotel, Rowes Wharf on Atlantic Ave. ☎ **617/439-3995.** Reservations recommended. Main courses $8.25–$16.75 at lunch, $18.75–$31 at dinner. Breakfast $2–$12.75. AE, DC, DISC, MC, V. Breakfast daily 6:30–11am; lunch daily 11:30am–2pm; dinner daily 5:30–10pm. Sun brunch 11am–2:30pm. MBTA: Aquarium (Blue Line). SEAFOOD/AMERICAN.

Back in the 1920s and 1930s, ferryboats plied Boston Harbor bringing North Shore residents to the terminal at Rowes Wharf, from which they made their way into the city. Today the crowds are still coming to Rowes Wharf, but now to this restaurant on the site of the old terminal. (The ferries are long gone, but there is a water shuttle from the airport.)

The view from the enormous picture windows is of the harbor and the boats. Inside, the ambience is relaxed and comfortable, with several dining areas. Chef Daniel Bruce creates masterpieces with fish and has a wonderful way with sauces. Boston's famous scrod is presented with an almond-crusted topping in a curry-laced sauce. Steamed Maine lobster is served with a lime-chili sauce, and there is an herb-rubbed grilled partridge fricassee. The crab cakes are delectable. Appetizers include Northeast oysters on the half shell. Desserts vary with the inspiration of the chef. On the lunch menu several items are prepared low in sodium, cholesterol, and calories.

EXPENSIVE

Anthony's Pier 4

140 Northern Ave. ☎ **617/423-6363.** Reservations recommended. Main courses $9.95–$24.95 at lunch, $13.95–$29.95 at dinner. AE, CB, DC, MC, V. Mon–Sat 11:30am–11pm, Sun and holidays 12:30–10:30pm. Closed Christmas Day. MBTA: South Station (Red Line). SEAFOOD.

This is one of the most outstanding restaurants in New England, and it has won the Business Executive's Dining Award first prize as

Boston Dining

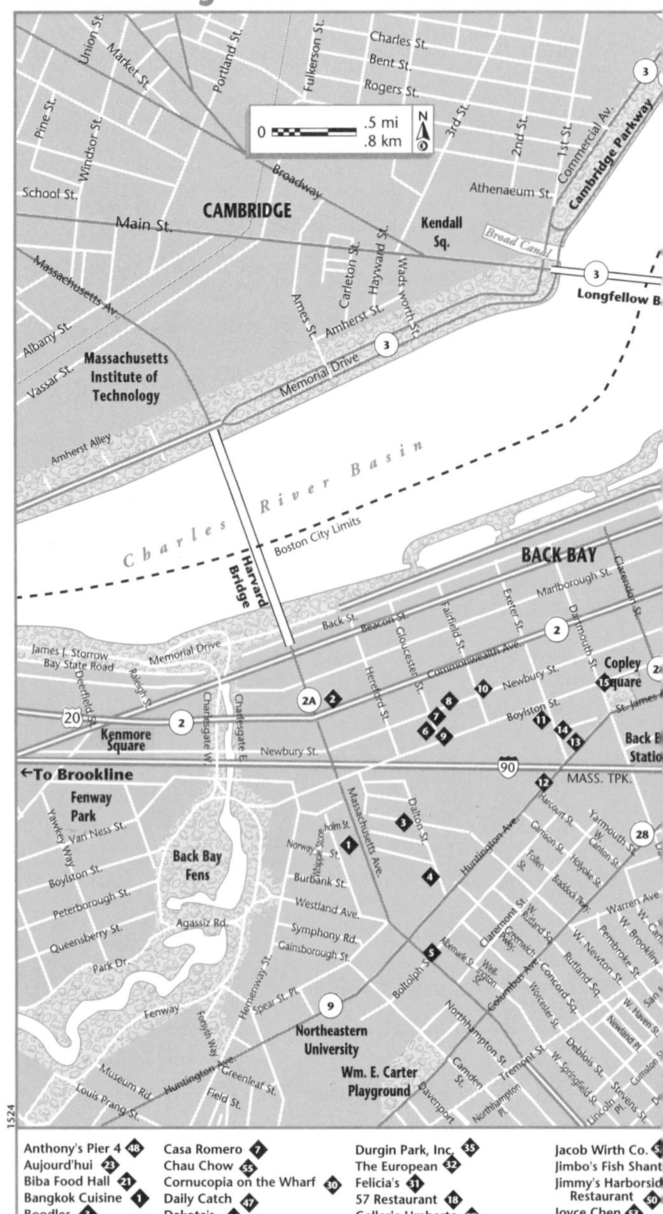

- Anthony's Pier 4 48
- Aujourd'hui 23
- Biba Food Hall 21
- Bangkok Cuisine 1
- Boodles 3
- Buddha's Delight 51
- Cafe Budapest 14
- Cafe Jaffa 6
- The Capital Grille 2
- Casa Romero 7
- Chau Chow 55
- Cornucopia on the Wharf 30
- Daily Catch 47
- Dakota's 46
- David's Restaurant 54
- Davio's 8
- Du Barry Restaurant Francais 10
- Durgin Park, Inc. 35
- The European 32
- Felicia's 31
- 57 Restaurant 18
- Galleria Umberto 27
- Golden Palace Restaurant and Teahouse 59
- Hammersley's 17
- Imperial Seafood 57
- Jacob Wirth Co. 5
- Jimbo's Fish Shant
- Jimmy's Harborsid Restaurant 50
- Joyce Chen 53
- Julien 42
- L'Espalier 9
- La Piccolo Venezia
- Legal Sea Food 20

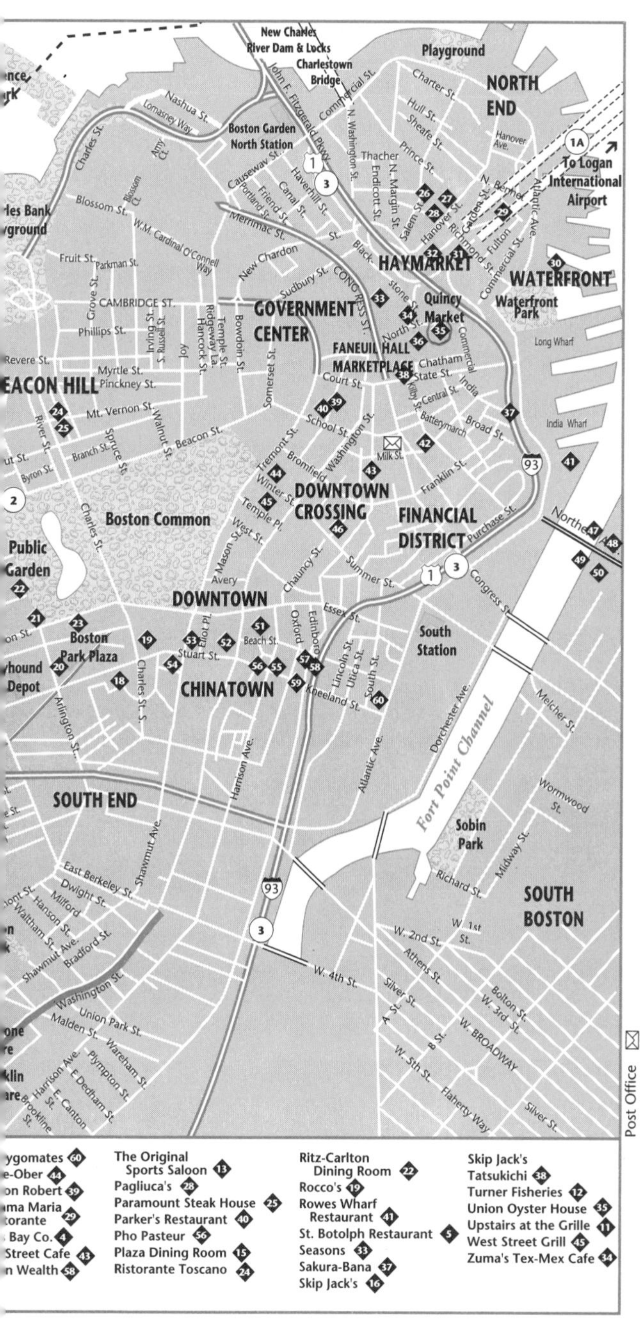
New Charles River Dam & Locks
Charlestown Bridge
Playground
NORTH END
To Logan International Airport
Boston Garden North Station
HAYMARKET
WATERFRONT
Waterfront Park
GOVERNMENT CENTER
Quincy Market
FANEUIL HALL MARKETPLACE
BEACON HILL
DOWNTOWN CROSSING
FINANCIAL DISTRICT
Boston Common
Public Garden
DOWNTOWN
Boston Park Plaza
CHINATOWN
South Station
Fort Point Channel
SOUTH END
Sobin Park
SOUTH BOSTON
Long Wharf
India Wharf
Charles St.
Nashua St.
Lomasney Way
Commercial St.
John F. Fitzgerald Pkwy.
N. Washington St.
Charter St.
Hull St.
Sheafe St.
Prince St.
Hanover Ave.
Thacher
Endicott St.
N. Margin St.
Salem St.
Hanover St.
Richmond St.
Garden St.
N. Bennet
Atlantic Ave.
Fulton
Causeway St.
Friend St.
Canal St.
Haverhill St.
Portland St.
Merrimac St.
Blossom St.
Blossom Ct.
Amy Ct.
W.M. Cardinal O'Connell Way
New Chardon
Sudbury St.
Congress St.
Blackstone St.
North St.
Fruit St.
Parkman St.
Grove St.
CAMBRIDGE ST.
Phillips St.
Irving St.
S. Russell St.
Joy
Ridgeway La.
Hancock St.
Temple St.
Bowdoin St.
Somerset St.
Revere St.
Myrtle St.
Pinckney St.
Mt. Vernon St.
Court St.
Chatham
State St.
Kilby St.
Central St.
India
Broad St.
Batterymarch
School St.
Washington St.
Milk St.
River St.
Branch St.
Spruce St.
Walnut St.
Beacon St.
Byron St.
Tremont St.
Bromfield
Winter St.
Temple Pl.
West St.
Mason St.
Avery
Franklin St.
Purchase St.
Northern Ave.
Chauncy St.
Summer St.
Congress St.
Essex St.
Eliot Pl.
Beach St.
Oxford
Edinboro
Stuart St.
Lincoln St.
Utica St.
South St.
Kneeland St.
Charles St. S.
Arlington St.
Harrison Ave.
Atlantic Ave.
Dorchester Ave.
Melcher St.
Wormwood St.
Midway St.
Richard St.
W. 1st St.
W. 2nd St.
Athens St.
W. 4th St.
Silver St.
A St.
B St.
Bolton St.
W. 3rd St.
W. BROADWAY
W. 5th St.
Flaherty Way
Shawmut Ave.
East Berkeley St.
Dwight St.
Milford
Hanson St.
Waltham St.
Bradford St.
Washington St.
Union Park St.
Malden St.
Wareham St.
Plympton St.
E. Dedham St.
E. Canton St.
Harrison Ave.
Brookline St.
Post Office
...ygomates 60
...e-Ober 44
...on Robert 39
...ma Maria ...torante 29
... Bay Co. 4
... Street Cafe 43
...n Wealth 58
The Original Sports Saloon 13
Pagliuca's 28
Paramount Steak House 25
Parker's Restaurant 40
Pho Pasteur 56
Plaza Dining Room 15
Ristorante Toscano 24
Ritz-Carlton Dining Room 22
Rocco's 19
Rowes Wharf Restaurant 41
St. Botolph Restaurant 5
Seasons 33
Sakura-Bana 37
Skip Jack's 16
Skip Jack's
Tatsukichi 38
Turner Fisheries 12
Union Oyster House 35
Upstairs at the Grille 11
West Street Grill 45
Zuma's Tex-Mex Cafe 34

America's most popular restaurant for many years. Dramatically situated at the end of a pier, the restaurant's waterfront walls are made of glass, allowing clear views of incoming sea vessels.

To start, you're served marinated mushrooms and relishes, then hot popovers. There are, of course, a number of other appetizers, including oysters Rockefeller (some of the best I've tasted), and an excellent clam chowder. Among the featured dishes are fresh New England seafood, Dover sole from the English Channel (flown over especially for Anthony's), and roast beef. This is also a good place to try a traditional clambake. Some of my favorite desserts are the Grand Marnier soufflé and the baked Alaska. It's best to drive to this restaurant; there is free parking on the wharf. Jackets are requested for men at dinner.

Cornucopia on the Wharf

100 Atlantic Ave. ☎ **617/367-0300.** Reservations recommended at dinner. Main courses $13.50–$23.95. AE, MC, V. Daily lunch 11:30am–2:30pm; dinner 5:30–10:30pm. Patio open daily 11:30am–9:30pm. MBTA: Aquarium (Blue Line). AMERICAN REGIONAL.

If you're spending the morning or afternoon at the Aquarium, Cornucopia on the Wharf is an excellent spot for lunch. The modern interior is dominated by hand-painted columns and a large bar. Picture windows allow diners clear views of neighboring wharves and the harbor. The menu is short, offering such favorites as broiled scrod with roasted garlic mashed potatoes, and braised leeks with almond brown butter. The grilled swordfish niçoise with tomatoes, haricots verts (green beans), olives, grilled potato, and roasted red onion is also a good choice. A good entrée at lunch might be the codfish cakes with baked beans and Boston brown bread. Along with each dish, the chef's wine recommendation is listed on the menu. For dessert you must try the chocolate mousse in a chocolate meringue cage with cinnamon anglaise.

Jimmy's Harborside Restaurant

242 Northern Ave. ☎ **617/423-1000.** Reservations recommended. Main courses $10.95–$25.95. Children's menu $4.95–$6.95. AE, CB, DC, MC, V. Lunch Mon–Sat noon–4pm; dinner nightly 4–9:30pm. MBTA: South Station (Red Line). SEAFOOD.

This Boston landmark offers a fine view of the harbor and Logan Airport from both the main downstairs dining room and the sunny Merchant's Club on the upper level. If you come only once, try a shore dinner, perhaps broiled scallops à la Jimmy or succulent Atlantic lobster. Dinners include appetizer (order the creamy fish chowder with generous chunks of whitefish), salad, potato, dessert, and beverage. (A bowl of fish chowder à la carte makes a fine lunch.) Occasionally there are specialties not listed on the menu that only the regular diners ask for, such as the excellent and moderately priced gray sole—check to see if it is available. The à la carte menu includes prime ribs of beef, swordfish alla Teresa, and Jimmy's famous finnan haddie, a specialty of the house. Special dinners are available for children.

While you're waiting to be seated, you can enjoy delicious complimentary hors d'oeuvres in the lounge. It's best to drive to this restaurant.

MODERATE

Daily Catch

261 Northern Ave., on the Fish Pier. ☎ **617/338-3093.** Reservations not accepted. Main courses $10–$16.50. No credit cards. Sun–Thurs noon–10:30pm Fri–Sat noon–11pm. MBTA: South Station (Red Line). ITALIAN/SEAFOOD.

Sop up the flavor of the North End at the Fish Pier with seafood prepared Italian style. There's Sicilian-style calamari (squid), freshly shucked clams, mussels with a garlic flavored sauce, broiled and fried fish, and shellfish. Those who love calamari can find it here prepared eight different ways. If you've never tasted it before, try the fried version with linguine for a good introduction. And if you really want to try something different, order the squid ink pasta Alfredo. All food is prepared to order, and is served to diners right in the frying pans in which it was cooked.

The original Daily Catch is in the North End, 323 Hanover St. (☎ **617/523-8567**). A third Daily Catch (☎ **617/734-5696**) is located at 441 Harbor Street. The hours are the same for both as for the waterfront restaurant.

BUDGET

Jimbo's Fish Shanty

245 Northern Ave. ☎ **617/542-5600.** Main courses $6–$14. AE, DC, MC, V. Mon–Thurs 11:30am–9:30pm, Fri–Sat 11:30am–10pm, Sun noon–8pm. MBTA: South Station (Red Line). SEAFOOD.

When you first step into Jimbo's, you may not be sure if you're in a restaurant or a toy store on Christmas Eve. The crowd is elbow to elbow, and model trains circle endlessly overhead on tracks suspended from the ceiling. "Jimbo" is supposedly a retired hobo who converted an old grotto into a hobo shanty with a line of switchyard food. Bindlestiff (hobo) or not, you'll enjoy the stick food (skewers) threaded with fish or beef, the exceptionally fresh seafood, and the pasta dishes with varied sauces, including a lobster cream version. My favorite dessert is amaretto pie (a mocha ice cream, amaretto liqueur, and chocolate mousse concoction).

4 The North End

EXPENSIVE

Felicia's

145 Richmond St. ☎ **617/523-9885.** Reservations recommended. Main courses $7.95–$16.95. AE, CB, DC, MC, V. Mon–Sat 4:30–9:30pm, Sun 2–9:30pm. Closed: Easter, Thanksgiving, and Christmas. MBTA: Haymarket (Green or Orange Line). ITALIAN.

The most famous of the restaurants in Boston's North End ("Little Italy") is Felicia's, "located one flight up at 145 Richmond Street." One of the specialties here is chicken Verdicchio, boneless breast of chicken cooked with lemon, mushrooms, artichoke hearts, sautéed in Verdicchio white wine and served with spaghetti or salad. There's a complete dinner that includes the chicken or a veal scaloppine, plus shrimp marinara, fettuccine, salad, dessert, and coffee. Homemade cannelloni filled with scallops and crabmeat and served with a sauce of melted cheese is another favorite. The upstairs dining room has dark wooden booths, tables with red cloths, and colored wax-covered Chianti bottles. There's a fine selection of Italian wines, and Felicia's now offers "Early Bird Specials" starting at 4:30pm during the week and 2pm on Sunday.

Mamma Maria Ristorante

3 North Sq. ☎ **617/523-0077.** Reservations recommended. Main courses $7.50–$10.50 at lunch, $14.50–$25.75 at dinner. AE, DC, DISC, MC, V. Lunch Tues–Sat 11:30am–2:30pm; dinner Mon–Sat 5–10pm, Sun 5–10pm. MBTA: Haymarket (Green or Orange Line). ITALIAN.

If you enjoy northern Italian cooking and Mediterranean cuisine, try this upscale North End restaurant. Favorites include grilled lamb chops served with roasted red peppers and veal tenderloins with shiitake mushrooms. Appetizers include scampi alla Nizza, shrimp served with warm tomato pulp, basil, and virgin olive oil; and fichi alla San Lorenzo, a combination of figs, goat cheese, prosciutto, and herbed vinaigrette. The pasta dishes are especially delicious prepared with seafood—lobster, shrimp, calamari, scallops, or mussels. And a full order can be split to serve two as a first course.

Valet parking is available every evening, a wonderful bonus in the crowded North End.

Budget

The European

218 Hanover St. ☎ **617/523-5694.** Main courses $7.95–$13. AE, CB, DC, DISC, MC, V. Sun–Thurs 11am–11pm, Fri–Sat 11am–12:30am. MBTA: Haymarket (Green or Orange Line). SOUTHERN ITALIAN.

At the European you'll find reasonably priced complete dinners, a vast menu—which features some great pizzas—and fast service. It claims to be Boston's oldest Italian restaurant (since 1917), and it's my opinion that it serves the best (and possibly the biggest) pizza in town. Lines are usually long, but don't let that deter you; the dining rooms are cavernous. This is not the place to go for a romantic dinner, as it can get quite noisy, but that's part of the charm of the place. Look for the famous clock above the front door—it's been there since the restaurant opened in 1917.

Galleria Umberto

289 Hanover St. ☎ **617/227-5709.** Reservations not accepted. Pizza 70¢ per slice, calzones $2.10–$2.50, croquettes 80¢. No credit cards. Lunch Mon–Sat 11am–2pm. MBTA: Haymarket (Green or Orange Line). ITALIAN.

Galleria Umberto is a real bargain. And the food is good. Pizza is one of Umberto's most popular dishes, but you might like to try the arancini (a rice ball filled with gravy, ground beef, peas, and cheese). The calzones (ham and cheese, spinach, spinach and cheese, and spinach and sausage) are also tasty. Have a quick lunch and get on with your sightseeing.

Pagliuca's

14 Parmenter St. ☎ **617/367-1504.** Reservations not accepted. Main courses $5.50–$8.50. AE, MC, V. Sun–Thurs 11am–10:30pm, Fri–Sat 11am–11pm. MBTA: Haymarket (Green or Orange Line). ITALIAN.

This spot doles out southern Italian cooking the way Americans like it—great pastas with lots of garlicky tomato sauce and big chunks of Italian bread to mop it up, plus such specialties as cioppino, or chicken with peppers, onions, and potatoes.

La Piccola Venezia

63 Salem St. ☎ **617/523-9802.** Reservations not accepted. Main courses $4.95–$10.95. No credit cards. Daily 11:30am–10pm. MBTA: Haymarket (Green or Orange Line). ITALIAN.

This is a great place to eat well on a budget. The atmosphere is quite casual, and the decor is nothing much to look at, but the food, dished out in very large portions (whether it's spaghetti with meatballs or veal parmigiana) is always good. Order a pitcher of the house wine, settle back and listen to some live accordian music, and dig in.

5 Near Faneuil Hall/Government Center/Financial District

VERY EXPENSIVE

Julien

In the Hotel Le Meridien, 250 Franklin St. ☎ **617/451-1900.** Reservations recommended. Main courses $14.50–$18.75 at lunch, $26–$33 at dinner. AE, CB, DC, MC, V. Lunch Mon–Fri noon–2pm; dinner Mon–Thurs 6–10pm, Fri–Sun 6–10:30pm. MBTA: State St. (Blue Line). FRENCH.

For the height of luxury, consider Julien, where two original murals by noted artist N. C. Wyeth add to the beauty of the room. The seasonal menus in the French classic style are prepared by Charles Prentis, Julien chef de cuisine, in consultation with Michelin-starred French chefs who come to Boston several times a year. Specialties include terrine of fresh, homemade foie gras with truffles, and scallop salad on a bed of salted cod and garlic purée with caviar to start. The pan-seared sea bass fillet with Cajun spices served with a crab and red bean boullion is an excellent choice, as is the salmon soufflé. The roasted rack of lamb with a Dijon sabayon, served with olive- and thyme-flavored potatoes, is also quite good. The desserts are among the best in town. As in the finest restaurants of Paris, you are served a complimentary hors d'oeuvre before you order and petits fours and chocolates at the conclusion of your meal. The wines are carefully chosen from the best French, American, German, and Italian wineries and are priced from about $18 to $200 per bottle. Julien also offers daily specials at lunch, which include one soup, one appetizer, one pasta, one meat, and one fish.

The Business Lunch, a good deal, includes a soup or salad, a choice of entrées, and coffee or tea.

Note: The **Café Fleuri,** the atrium-style informal dining room in the Meridien, serves a delicious lunch from 11:30am to 2:30pm weekdays.

On Sunday a sumptuous buffet is served at 11am and 1:30pm and includes a sparkling wine cocktail as an aperitif. Prices are $36 for adults and $18 for children. Café Fleuri is open from 7am to late evening, serving breakfast, lunch, and dinner.

✪ Maison Robert

45 School St. ☎ **617/227-3370.** Reservations recommended. Main courses $9–$22 at lunch, $16–$30 at dinner. Le Café has a fixed-price menu (at either $17 or $23) as well as à la carte selections. AE, CB, DC, MC, V. Lunch Mon–Fri 11:30am–2pm; dinner Mon–Sat 5:30–10pm. MBTA: Government Center (Green Line) or Park St. (Red Line). INNOVATIVE FRENCH.

Maison Robert is one of the finest French restaurants anywhere. To be exact, two of the finest French restaurants—the elegantly formal Bonhomme Richard on the main floor and the cozy Le Café on the ground floor. When the great chefs of France come to Boston, they dine with Lucien Robert, a restaurateur of uncompromising standards.

Decorated in French Second Empire style, the Bonhomme Richard is a gracious dining room with crystal chandeliers and stunning fresh flower arrangements. Lunch and dinner are served in the classical French tradition. Start with the wonderful crab, corn, and mustard soufflé with a mango and lemon sauce, or a sautéed leek tart with saffron butter, sour cream, and caviar. As you proceed to the main course, you'll feast on the likes of French-cut rack of lamb with garlic sauce, and Dover sole pan-fried with butter and lemon. Desserts are excellent. I love the *profiteroles exotiques* (profiteroles filled with toasted coconut ice cream on a warm dark rum sauce) and the *dessert aux cinq chocolats* (white and dark frozen chocolate torte on a chocolate almond cake with Godiva chocolate sauce). The service is as superb as the food, and there is a well-selected wine list, which includes Sauternes and ports and liqueurs.

Le Café has a less formal environment and meals are less expensive, though they are thoroughly French in style and prepared with superb care. Paid valet parking is available for both restaurants.

If you're here in summer, get a table on the outdoor terrace next to the statue of Benjamin Franklin. This was the first outdoor statue in Puritan New England. There's jazz on the terrace in summer from 5:30 to 7:30pm.

Parker's Restaurant

In the Omni Parker House, 60 School St. ☎ **617/227-8600.** Reservations recommended, especially for brunch. Main courses $16–$28. Sun brunch $24. AE, CB, DC, DISC, MC, V. Lunch Mon–Fri 11:30am–2:15pm; Sun brunch 11:30am–2:30pm. MBTA: Government Center (Green Line) or Park St. (Red Line). CONTINENTAL.

In the era of Emerson and Longfellow, the Omni Parker House was *the* place in town—home to Boston's literati. This elegant dining spot, the hotel's main dining room, is still a bastion of haute cuisine. The original walnut-paneled walls are still there, providing an elegant backdrop for sparkling chandeliers and large paintings.

Roasted veal tenderloin with pasta, pesto, and shrimp and rack of lamb share honors with lobster and linguine. Other excellent choices include veal with wild mushrooms or duck breast with a raspberry

Boston Brunches

An excellent brunch is served at the **Ritz-Carlton Hotel** (15 Arlington St., ☎ **617/536-5700**) every Sunday in the beautiful main dining room. You can choose delicacies such as oysters on the half shell, caviar and blinis, gravlax, seafood mousse, sturgeon, assorted pâtés, soup, roast beef carved to order, lamb, pastas, crêpes, omelets to order, quiche, salads, and hot and cold vegetables. Later, it's on to the dessert table for pastries, fruit tarts, cakes, cheese, and fruit. Though it's a self-service buffet, there's a waiter to help you. Reservations are necessary and are taken for 10:45am to 2:30pm.

The Sunday brunch at **Aujourd'hui** in the Four Seasons Hotel (200 Boylston St.; ☎ **617/338-4400**) is a bountiful New England-style buffet served in a gracious dining room with a view of the Public Garden. Beautifully decorated serving tables are piled high with such goodies as pâtés, salads, smoked and steamed fish, roast sirloin, chicken, lobster, egg dishes, waffles, and a fabulous assortment of desserts. Sunday brunch is available from 11:30am to 2:30pm. Reservations are recommended.

Overlooking the harbor at Boston's historic waterfront, the **Rowes Wharf Restaurant** at the Boston Harbor Hotel (70 Atlantic Ave.; ☎ **617/439-7000**) offers a traditional American brunch buffet of both fresh and smoked seafood, carved prime rib and rack of lamb, seasonal garden salad, soused shrimp, and regional specialty items. Also featured are omelettes made to order, Belgian waffles, freshly baked pastries, and desserts. Brunch is served Sunday from 10:30am to 2:30pm. When you make reservations, be sure to ask for a table overlooking the harbor.

The most delightful place for Sunday brunch is the **Café Fleuri** at the Hotel Le Meridien (250 Franklin St.; ☎ **617/451-1900**). The setting is a magnificent garden court, light and airy, with lots of greenery. The food is just as elegant, with a hot and cold buffet befitting the Meridien's French background. The desserts are fabulous. Seatings are at 11am and 2pm. Reservations are accepted.

demiglaze. All entrées include vegetables and potatoes and, of course, the famous Parker House rolls.

The seasonal weekday luncheon menu is equally delicious and features salads, several seafood choices including Parker's famous clam chowder, and chicken, pork, and beef dishes. Valet parking is available at a cost of $10.

Seasons

In the Bostonian Hotel, at North and Blackstone sts. ☎ **617/523-3600.** Reservations recommended. Three-course meal $39. AE, CB, DC, JCB, MC, V. Dinner only, daily 6–10pm. MBTA: Government Center (Green Line) or Haymarket (Green or Orange Line). INTERNATIONAL.

Some restaurants trade off a great view for ordinary food, drink, and service, but Seasons has it all—superlative food, service, and setting. On the fourth floor of the Bostonian Hotel, the restaurant, which is reached by its own glass elevator, looks out on the panorama of Faneuil Hall Marketplace from its windowed walls. Orchids on the tables and a subdued color scheme create a luxurious setting.

Seasons features a wide variety of dishes prepared with a flair by executive chef Peter McCarthy, who has won raves from restaurant critics. The menu changes seasonally. Some of my favorites on a recent menu include the layered potato and smoked salmon croquette with caviar cream to start. My favorite salad is the arugula, plum, and feta salad served on a slice of tomato pizza.

Like the rest of the menu, the dessert menu is short, but all dishes are well executed. American wines are featured and include 50 different Chardonnays, 65 Cabernet Sauvignons, and some rare selections from the country's top wine producers. The service is impeccable, with attention given to all the little details. Valet parking is available.

MODERATE

The Bay Tower

60 State St. ☎ **617/723-1666.** Reservations recommended. Main courses $15–$36. AE, CB, DC, MC, V. Mon–Thurs 5:30–10pm, Fri–Sat 5:30–10:30pm. MBTA: State St. (Blue Line). AMERICAN.

This beautiful glass-walled room overlooks the spectacular panorama of Faneuil Hall Marketplace, the harbor, and the airport. Located on the 33rd floor of one of Boston's business towers, the restaurant has tables arranged in ascending tiers so that every diner shares the view. Candlelight casts a romantic glow.

The menu changes daily, but a recent one included appetizers such as Spinney Creek oysters with a green apple mignonette and crab and lobster ravioli. The grilled quail and the sesame-crusted tuna were both excellent main courses. Vegetarian and special dietary preparations are available on request. The dessert menu might include a white chocolate cheesecake or chocolate velour torte. A $9 cover is charged in the lounge after 9:30pm (on Friday and Saturday only dining room customers are exempt). Validated parking is available in the 60 State Street garage.

$ Durgin-Park Inc.

340 N. Market St. ☎ **617/227-2038** or 227-2877. Reservations not accepted. Main courses $4.95–$16.95, specials $15.90–$24.95. AE, MC, V. Lunch daily 11:30am–2:30pm; dinner Mon–Sat 2:30–10pm, Sun until 9pm. MBTA: Government Center (Green Line). AMERICAN.

One of the unwritten laws of Boston seems to be that you must not leave town without visiting Durgin-Park. And judging from the mobs of people (approximately 2,000 a day) always waiting in line to get into this restaurant in Faneuil Hall Marketplace, it's a law that's pretty well obeyed. Durgin-Park has been here forever, and it's now part of the chic new market area (which was built around it), though there's still nothing chic about Durgin-Park: the place is noisy and crowded, and you must share a long table with about 10 other patrons. But if you don't expect gracious service, are in a convivial mood, and think that exposed heating pipes are period pieces, then join the long lines (you'll brush elbows with politicians, butchers, and Back Bay society matrons here). The food is of the highest quality and portions are very large.

If you can, go for dinner (old Bostonese for the noontime meal) and order Poor Man's roast beef or Yankee pot roast. For supper try a tremendous slab of prime rib of beef with vegetables. All steaks and chops are broiled on an open fireplace over real wood charcoal. Seafood, including salmon, sole, haddock, shrimp, oysters, scallops, and lobster, is received twice daily and fish dinners are broiled to order. Be sure to try their clam chowder and Boston baked beans. The fish and chips here are excellent, as is the lobster stew. Homemade corn bread comes with every meal. For dessert I strongly recommend that venerable New England specialty, baked Indian pudding (a molasses and cornmeal concoction, slow-baked for hours and hours), luscious with ice cream.

If you're going for "dinner," beat the crowd by getting there before 11:30am. Otherwise, the long line may drive you to drink; happily, a stop at the Gaslight Pub downstairs permits you to wait in a shorter line before being seated upstairs. And on Sunday, when every other restaurant is serving a brunch of eggs and quiche, you can feast on full-course Durgin-Park dinners at their midday rates until 2:30pm.

Les Zygomates

129 South St. ☎ **617/542-5108.** Reservations recommended. Main courses $12–$20. AE, MC, V. Lunch Mon–Fri 11:30am–2:30pm; dinner Mon–Thurs 6–10:30pm, Fri–Sat 6–11:30pm. Subway: Red Line to JFK. ECLECTIC.

This brand-new, trendy bistro has already begun attracting throngs of fashionable young people. Over the bar are dozens of bottles of wine, all of which have been well selected and are reasonably priced. There's a great focus here on wine, and both the co-owner, Lorenzo Savona, and manager, Cat Silirie, are wine connoisseurs. Chef/co-owner Ian Just hails from Paris. The main dining room, with its brick walls and red banquettes, is tastefully decorated. As an appetizer, I tried the terrine of duck with prunes, which was very nicely done. For a main course, the roasted chicken breast stuffed with vermont goat cheese and served with a white wine tomato sauce was simple, but tasty. The desserts here aren't pretentious—a simple vanilla and chocolate mousse with a crème anglaise or a light sorbet in an edible bowl were a nice ending to a good meal.

Sakura-Bana

57 Broad St. ☎ **617/542-4311.** Reservations recommended. Main courses $8.75–$29. AE, DC, MC, V. Mon–Thurs 11:30am–2:30pm and 5–10pm; Fri 11:30am–2:30pm and 5–11pm; Sat 1–11pm, Sun 5–10pm. Closed first Sun each month. MBTA: State St. or Aquarium (Blue Line). JAPANESE.

Sakura-Bana means "cherry blossom" in Japanese. But this little restaurant in Boston's financial district is not a demure little cherry blossom. It's a lively, casual place serving traditional Japanese food and drink. There are Japanese hot dishes on the menu and the expected teriyaki, yakitori, and tempura; but the main attraction is the sushi bar. If you're staying nearby, the restaurant will deliver to your hotel room from 6 to 9:30pm any night except Friday and Saturday. If you're planning to dine at Sakura-Bana at lunch, try to get there early so you can get a table without having to wait too long.

Tatsukichi-Boston

189 State St. ☎ **617/720-2468.** Reservations recommended. Main courses $10–$20. AE, DC, DISC, JCB, MC, V. Restaurant lunch Mon–Fri 11:45–2:30pm; dinner Sun–Wed 5–10pm, Thurs–Sat 5–11pm; VIP karaoke lounge Mon–Thurs 7pm–1am, Fri–Sat 6pm–1am. MBTA: Aquarium or State St. (Blue Line). JAPANESE.

Located just one street over from the mélange of fast-food places at Faneuil Hall Marketplace, this award-winning restaurant is a favorite with the area's Japanese community as well as local fans of Japanese cuisine. Tatsukichi serves an extensive array of authentic Japanese dishes, including sukiyaki, shabu-shabu, udon-suki, and kushinage (fresh pieces of meat, seafood, vegetables, and fruit arranged on skewers, lightly battered, breaded, and quickly fried, served with Tatsukichi's own dipping sauces). There's a full sushi bar, as well as private tatami rooms. Japanese is spoken, and there is a karaoke lounge.

Union Oyster House

41 Union St., between Faneuil Hall and City Hall on the Freedom Trail. ☎ **617/227-2750.** Reservations recommended. Main courses $4.95–$10.50 at lunch, $12.95–$24.95 at dinner; lobster $21.95–$28.95. AE, CB, DC, DISC, MC, V. Sun–Thurs 11am–9:30pm, Fri–Sat 11am–10pm. Lunch served until 5pm Sun–Fri, until 6pm Sat. Union bar: 11am–3pm lunch, 3–11pm late-supper fare. Bar open until midnight. MBTA: Haymarket (Green or Orange Line). AMERICAN/SEAFOOD.

America's oldest restaurant in continuous service, Union Oyster House began serving oysters in 1826. At the crescent-shaped bar on the lower level, "where Daniel Webster drank many a toddy in his day," you can enjoy the Oyster House sampler, a mixed appetizer of about a dozen pieces each of oysters, clams, and scampi (Webster probably paid about 15¢ a dozen). The stalls and oyster bar are still "in their original positions."

The food is traditional New England. An oyster stew doused in fresh milk and country butter makes a good beginning. Follow that with a broiled or grilled dish such as scrod or salmon, or perhaps seafood primavera, a fried dish, or a grilled veal chop. A complete shore dinner with chowder, steamers, broiled lobster, salad, corn, and dessert is definitely something to write home about. Low-calorie menu selections, introduced in 1994, are popular here as well. For dessert, try traditional Boston gingerbread with whipped cream. Ask to be seated at John F. Kennedy's favorite booth, marked by a plaque dedicated to his memory.

Budget

Country Life Vegetarian Buffet

200 High St. ☎ **617/951-2534.** Buffet $7 lunch, $5–$8 dinner, $8.50 brunch. AE. Lunch Mon–Fri 11:30am–3pm; dinner Sun and Tues–Thurs 5–8pm. Sun brunch 10am–3pm. MBTA: Aquarium (Blue Line). VEGETARIAN.

No meat, chicken, fish, or dairy products are served in this restaurant. But what a great selection of grains, vegetables, fruits, and nuts! A hot entrée and a soup are featured each day along with two tremendous salad bars—one with fresh vegetables, tabbouleh, and tofu, and one with fresh fruits and nuts. The hot entrée and the soup change every day, and you can call their prerecorded daily menu line (☎ **617/951-2462**) to see what they're serving—perhaps oat burgers with home fries, macrobiotic dishes, Hawaiian barbecue, golden squash soup, or sweet and sour seitan. There are always two or three varieties of whole-grain bread, herbal tea, grain coffee, and spring water. Diners can make unlimited trips to the buffet tables. Desserts are extra. A great Sunday brunch is available. No alcohol is served. Herbal teas and fruit juice are popular, but soy milk and rice milk are also available.

$ Milk Street Cafe

50 Milk St. ☎ **617/542-2433** or 542-FOOD. Main courses $3–$6. No credit cards. Mon–Fri 7am–3pm. MBTA: State St. (Blue Line). KOSHER VEGETARIAN.

Right in the heart of Boston's financial district, at the corner of Devonshire and Milk streets, you can find fresh, homemade vegetarian fare. The restaurant is strictly kosher, but most customers are neither kosher nor vegetarian. They come for the good, fresh food, which includes two homemade vegetarian soups (one cream soup and one dairy free), salads, a hot entrée special, quiche, sandwiches, and salad plates. The veggie melts, Middle Eastern plates, and fruit and cheese platters are very popular. At breakfast there are scones, bagels, muffins, danish, fruit salad, and fresh-squeezed juices along with herbal teas and coffee.

There is a second Milk Street Cafe at Zero Post Office Square (☎ **617/350-7275**), open Monday to Thursday from 7am to 6pm (8pm in summer) and on Friday from 7am to 3pm. It is housed in a copper-roofed and glass-enclosed kiosk in Boston's newest park, which is lined with trees, bordered with flowers, and high-lighted by a fountain. The fixed-price Sunday brunch here, served from 10am to 2pm, is $14.95, or you can order à la carte. Within the glass pavilion, the cafe serves only vegetarian kosher food, but outside, during spring, summer, and fall, it maintains four food carts that sell glatt kosher deli, kosher hot dogs, pizza, and ice cream.

Zuma's Tex-Mex Café

7 N. Market St., Faneuil Hall Marketplace. ☎ **617/367-9114.** Main courses $4.97–$13.99. AE, CB, DC, DISC, MC, V. Mon–Thurs 11:30am–11pm, Fri–Sat 11:30am–midnight, Sun noon–10pm. MBTA: Government Center (Green Line) TEX-MEX.

Zuma's Tex-Mex Café is one of the hottest places in the Faneuil Hall Marketplace, not just as an "in" place but also literally—the southwestern cuisine is hot! Zuma's is on the lower level of the North Market; it's casual, friendly, and a mecca for high-energy people. The walls are blue and accented with a neon arch and small lights in the ceiling. The food is good, the servings generous, and the prices low. Some of the winners include chicken marinated in fresh citrus juices and tequila; burritos; a huge platter of South Texas barbecue ribs grilled over mesquite; and the firecrackers (jalapeño peppers stuffed with shrimp).

Taquitos, small tacos, are only a dollar each; the chimichangitas are also a bargain at $1.47. Owner Steve Immel boasts about the key lime pie, his famous margaritas (including a neon version), and his most popular dish, enchiladas verdes.

6 Downtown Crossing

VERY EXPENSIVE

Locke-Ober

3 Winter St. ☎ **617/542-1340.** Reservations required. Main courses $8–$22 at lunch, $17–$40 at dinner. AE, DC, MC, V. Lunch Mon–Fri 11:30am–3pm; dinner Fri 6–10:30pm, Sat 5:30–10:30pm, Sun 5:30–10pm. MBTA: Downtown Crossing (Red or Orange Line). AMERICAN.

This restaurant is a legend in town. Some Bostonians have lunch here every day at the same table and, even though there is a huge menu, choose the same classic favorites at each meal. Part of the attraction is the setting—the carved paneling, stained-glass windows, crystal chandeliers, and mammoth silver buffet covers on the long, mirrored downstairs bar, which dates from 1880. The upstairs dining room is the choice of those who prefer a clublike atmosphere.

But of course you've come for the food—rack of lamb, finnan haddie, Weiner schnitzel à la Holstein, lobster stew, and the greatest dish on the menu, lobster Savannah, Locke-Ober's star for decades. Portions are enormous, so you won't leave hungry and you won't feel ripped off by the restaurant's rather high prices. It might be difficult to choose from the dessert menu (it lists approximately 30 items), but I'd recommend the zabaglione.

EXPENSIVE

Dakota's

34 Sumner St. (at the 101 Arch Street building). ☎ **617/737-1777.** Reservations recommended. Main courses $7.95–$23.50. AE, DISC, MC, V. Lunch Mon–Fri 11:30am–3pm; dinner Mon–Sat 5:30–10pm. MBTA: Downtown Crossing (Red or Orange Line). CREATIVE AMERICAN/INTERNATIONAL.

Dakota's name doesn't refer to the state, but rather to the rich mahogany-colored granite used throughout the restaurant. The decor combines dark woods, white walls, and that granite, which looks like marble. Located in the heart of the downtown shopping district near Filene's and Jordan Marsh, the restaurant is just a few blocks from the financial district.

The menu offerings range from wood-grilled portobello mushrooms served with polenta and smoked onion salsa or warmed aged goat cheese with a touch of cayenne pepper and honey to start. My favorite main courses are the pan-seared golden trout with steamed purple and Yukon Gold potatoes, marinated green beans, and herb salad, and the grilled double pork chop served with banana leaf-steamed sweet potatoes, panang curry, and scented tomato relish. At lunch you can get soups and salads, grilled sandwiches (including a Dakota Burger), and Dakota's specials like poached salmon with ginger rice or five pepper chicken. There are also special "Light Fare" selections.

7 Chinatown

Many restaurants in Chinatown offer dim sum, the traditional Chinese midday meal featuring dozens of subtly seasoned dumplings, filled with meats and vegetables; steamed rolls; shrimp balls; spareribs; and items like thousand-layer cake (which isn't really cake but a stack of steamed crêpes with a dab of fruit). The waiter wheels a cart laden with tempting snack-sized morsels up to your table, and you order by pointing (unless you know Chinese). Each piece ranges from about 75¢ to $1.50. Since he comes back several times and everything looks so good, however, you can run up a high tab without even trying. When you're finished, the waiter figures the bill by counting the empty serving plates. Two excellent spots for dim sum are **Imperial Seafood,** at 70 Beach Street, and Golden Palace, at 14-20 Tyler Street (see the descriptions below).

Although there are Chinese restaurants almost everywhere, Chinatown itself comprises only a few densely crowded blocks around Beach Street and Harrison Avenue near the Southeast Expressway. Park in Chinatown's garage off the expressway, in the New England Medical Center garage on Harrison Avenue, or at the Lafayette Place shopping center. From there walk down Chauncy Street to Beach Street to Chinatown or take the "T" Orange Line to Chinatown and New England Medical Center.

Most Chinese restaurants are open every day, begin serving around 9am, and stay open till 3am or later. The menus are geared to American palates, but sometimes there's a second menu for Chinese patrons. Ask for it, or tell your waiter you want your meal Chinese style.

MODERATE

Buddha's Delight

5 Beach St. ☎ **617/451-2395.** Main courses $5.25–$10.95. No credit cards. Sun–Thurs 11am–10pm, Fri–Sat until 11pm. MBTA: Chinatown or New England Medical Center (Orange Line). VEGETARIAN VIETNAMESE/CHINESE.

They don't serve meat, poultry, dairy, or fish, but through the wizardry of the chef, tofu and gluten is fried and barbecued to taste like chicken, pork, beef, and even lobster. Cuong Van Tran learned the secrets of vegetarian cooking from Buddhist monks in a temple outside Los Angeles, California. The results are delicious, healthy, and inexpensive. Try the Vietnamese fried spring rolls and the Vietnamese "pizza" (similar to egg foo yong, but without the egg). If you're overwhelmed by the number of offerings on the menu, you should focus on the specialties of the house and the "Chow Fun" and "Stir Fried Noodles" sections of the menu.

Chau Chow

52 Beach St. ☎ **617/426-6266.** Reservations not accepted. Main courses $4.25–$26.50. No credit cards. Sun–Thurs 11am–2am, Fri–Sat 10am–4am. MBTA: Chinatown or New England Medical Center (Orange Line). CANTONESE.

With its unimpressive decor, this restaurant is one of Chinatown's most unassuming dining spots. Good food at reasonable prices explains this restaurant's popularity (and frequently long lines). Among the specialties are jumbo shrimp with ginger, scallions, and onions; Love Bird Fried Rice; shrimp and chicken in a cream and tomato sauce on a bed of fried rice; and sizzling flounder in a black bean sauce with onions and green pepper. The menu is heavy on seafood, but there are also traditional beef, chicken, and pork dishes among the offerings. Sauces here are not overpoweringly spicy, and the food is some of the freshest around.

Golden Palace Restaurant and Teahouse

20 Tyler St. ☎ **617/423-4565.** Main courses $4–$7 at lunch, $5–$12 at dinner. AE, MC, V. Daily 8:30am–11:30pm. MBTA: Chinatown or New England Medical Center (Orange Line). CHINESE.

The cuisine of Hong Kong is served at this enormous and ornate establishment. The food isn't the usual American-Chinese fare, a fact that hasn't escaped the local Chinese residents, whom you'll see dining here every day. Good bets are the fried pork chop Peking style and the shrimp dinners. The dim sum, served daily from 8:30am to 3pm, is one of the best in Boston. As a result, the place is packed with diners and dim sum carts at lunchtime. The lunch menu also offers some good, inexpensive items, but the real reason to make a trip to the Golden Palace Restaurant and Teahouse is for the dim sum.

Imperial Seafood

70 Beach St. ☎ **617/426-8439.** Reservations recommended. Main courses $4.25–$5.50 at lunch, $9.95–$14.95 at dinner; dim sum $1.25–$2.75 per piece. AE, DC, MC, V. Daily 8:30am–4am. Dim sum served daily 8:30am–3:30pm. MBTA: Chinatown or New England Medical Center (Orange Line); South Station (Red Line); Boylston (Green Line). CANTONESE.

This is my choice for good Cantonese food. Start with the imperial egg roll, stuffed with crabmeat, mushrooms, ham, scallions, chicken, and bamboo shoots, or the eight delights soup, a light broth filled with seafood. Among the restaurant's most popular entrées are braised duck and *char siu ding,* an enormous production with pork cubes, straw mushrooms, vegetables, and cashews. I could become addicted to the shrimp, baked in shells and served with green peppers and scallions. Dim sum at Imperial Seafood was on the "Best of Boston" list in 1994 and 1995.

Ocean Wealth

8 Tyler St. ☎ **617/423-1338.** Reservations recommended. Main courses $6.50–$16. AE, MC, V. Daily 11am–4am. MBTA: Chinatown or New England Medical Center (Orange Line). CHINESE.

As its name implies, this upscale restaurant's focus is on seafood. In fact, three large fish tanks are a major part of the decor. If you wish, the crabs, lobsters, fish, and eels are available for your dinner. Or choose from among the 200 dishes on the regular menu or the specialties on the shorter menu. (If you know the language, ask for the Chinese menu.) Try the lobster with vermicelli, garlic shrimp, roast duck with pan-fried noodles, or the eight delights with either tofu soup or noodle soup. If you're brave, you might try the eel served with a spicy black bean sauce. If you're wealthy, try the $100 shark's-fin soup.

Pho Pasteur

8 Kneeland Ave. ☎ **617/783-2060.** Menu items $3.75–$9. MC, V. Daily 8am–8pm. MBTA: Chinatown or New England Medical Center (Orange Line). VIETNAMESE.

The specialty here is meal-in-a-bowl soups—noodle beef soup, rice noodle chicken soup, and egg noodle beef and chicken soups. Other specialties include chicken, shrimp, or beef with lemongrass, and the seafood firepot. The response to the food at Pho Pasteur was so enthusiastic that owner Ha Nguyen opened a second restaurant, also Pho Pasteur, at 137 Brighton Avenue in Allston (☎ **617/783-2340**). The menu there includes lo mein and chow mein; rice with pork, chicken, beef, or shrimp; and noodles with fish balls. There are several special dinners at $9. Pho Pasteur in Allston stays open from 11am to 11pm Monday through Saturday and from 11am to 10pm on Sunday.

8 At the Public Garden/Beacon Hill

Very Expensive

✪ Aujourd'hui

In the Four Seasons Hotel, 200 Boylston St. ☎ **617/451-1392.** Reservations recommended (imperative on holidays). Main courses $16.50–$19.50 at lunch, $29–$39 at dinner; Sun buffet brunch $35. AE, CB, DC, MC, V. Breakfast daily 6:30–11am; lunch Mon–Fri 11:30am–2:30pm; dinner Sun–Thurs 6–10pm, Fri–Sat 6–11pm. Sun brunch 11:30am–2:30pm. MBTA: Arlington St. (Green Line). INTERNATIONAL.

You feel the luxury of this four-star restaurant the minute you ascend the grand staircase to reach the quietly elegant room with floor-to-ceiling windows overlooking the Public Garden. The well-spaced tables are beautifully set, and comfortable banquettes and chairs and floral bouquets provide muted color against the rich oak paneling.

The executive chef, Jamie Mammo, uses regional products and the freshest ingredients available; Aujourd'hui's wine list is one of the best in the country. Appetizers I tried include an excellent grilled portobello mushroom carpaccio and a wonderful ginger-cured tuna sashimi. Although the menu changes frequently, entrées might include a juniper-roasted venison chop with a sweet potato and turnip cake and cider-glazed chard; or grilled Atlantic salmon served with minted couscous and chicory salad. In addition, the crab cakes here are the best I've ever had. The dessert menu changes, but might include a wonderful fruit tart or an extremely decadent chocolate creation.

Ritz-Carlton Dining Room

15 Arlington St. ☎ **617/536-5700.** Reservations highly recommended. Main courses $28–$43. Grand buffet (Sun) $42. AE, CB, ER, DC, DISC, JCB, MC, V. Lunch Sat noon–2:30pm; dinner Sun–Thurs 5:30–10pm, Fri–Sat 5:30–11pm. Sun brunch 10:45am–2:30pm. MBTA: Arlington St. (Green Line). FRENCH.

A unique fame attends the magnificent second-floor restaurant of the elegant Ritz-Carlton Hotel overlooking the Boston Public Garden. Whether it's dinner under the soft lights of the crystal chandeliers with soft piano music or Sunday brunch, a meal here is a memorable experience.

The restaurant concentrates mostly on classics, such as a superb rack of lamb with thyme, broiled sirloin steak in a shallot sauce, and the Maine lobster "au whiskey." But it has also added innovative entrées and a "Cuisine Vitale" of light, low-calorie dishes, noted on the menu. These might include chicken consommé with julienne pancakes, broiled Atlantic swordfish with mangoes and a sweet-and-sour sauce, or broiled Boston scrod. Nearly 30 in all, the superb appetizers range from beluga caviar to escargots or baked clams with curry cream. There's a wonderful selection of desserts, including chocolate and Grand Marnier soufflés and a baked Alaska.

On Saturdays in the spring, the Ritz-Carlton Dining Room hosts a series of Fashion Luncheons showcasing the designs of local designers and established boutiques.

EXPENSIVE

Biba Food Hall

272 Boylston St. ☎ **617/426-7878.** Reservations recommended. Main courses $17–$34 at dinner. CB, DC, DISC, MC, V. Lunch Mon–Fri 11:30am–2pm, Sun 11:30am–2:30pm; dinner Sun–Thurs 5:30–9:30pm, Fri–Sat 5:30–10:30pm. Bar menu offered until 2am. MBTA: Arlington St. (Green Line). ECLECTIC.

Everyone in Boston loves Biba Food Hall. Lydia Shire is the dynamic chef extraordinaire who masterminded this vibrant restaurant and its unique dishes such as "chicken under pressure with a brick sauce." Located in the posh Heritage on the Garden across from the Public Garden, it is a stunning place decorated in bright geometric patterns based on Albanian kilim rug motifs. A grand spiral staircase with shiny red handrails leads to the second-floor dining room with its colorful murals and view of the Public Garden.

The food is as dynamic as the decor. Some of it is prepared in the brick wood-burning oven visible from the dining room or the tandoori oven used for roasting and baking. Everything is made on the premises, from bread and sausages to desserts. The menu is à la carte and is divided into food categories such as meat, fish, starch, legumes, offal, and sweets. You're wondering about offal? Well, it might include calves' brains, veal kidneys, tongue, or sweetbreads, prepared so that they actually taste delicious. Other favorites include lobster pizza; crab accented with scallions and ginger served on a bed of Asian noodles; and crisp-skinned haddock with square-cut spaghetti. The latest favorite desserts are stacked crème brûlée with apricot glaze and little angel-food cakes with mint ice cream and chocolate fudge sauce.

Although Biba is hyped as a glamorous international bistro, there is no dress code (you can even come in shorts), and the price range is wide so there is something on the menu for everyone. If you're up for trying a new cocktail, give Biba's Purple Martini a whirl. There is valet parking service.

Ristorante Toscano

41 Charles St. ☎ **617/723-4090.** Reservations recommended at dinner. Main courses $7–$12 at lunch, $16–$28 at dinner. AE. Lunch Mon–Sat 11:30am–2:30pm; dinner Mon–Thurs 5:30–9:30pm, Fri–Sat 5:30–10:30pm, Sun 5:30–10pm. MBTA: Charles St. (Red Line). NORTHERN ITALIAN.

The owners of this establishment call it a neighborhood restaurant, although it's not what I would consider a typical neighborhood eating place. But then the upscale Beacon Hill section (where it is located) is not a typical neighborhood, either. Toscano (named after Tuscany) is a warm, friendly place where the Florentine chef prepares authentic northern Italian cuisine, including two excellent veal dishes (*scaloppine toscano* and *lombata alla griglia*); an excellent tortellini with ham, cheese, and cream; and a pasta with wild mushroom sauce. In addition to the printed menu, which includes chicken, steak, and seafood dishes, there are daily specials recited by the waiters. If you opt for dessert the tiramisù (a lavish concoction of sponge cake with four kinds of cream, mascarpone cheese, espresso, and cognac) is good here. Valet parking is available.

MODERATE

West Street Grille

15 West St. ☎ **617/423-0300.** Reservations accepted. Main courses $9.50–$20.75. AE, DC, MC, V. Mon–Wed 11:30am–10pm, Sat 11:30am–midnight; bar menu 2:30–5:30pm. MBTA: Park St. (Red or Green Line). INTERNATIONAL.

The West Street Grille occupies the former site of Cornucopia, but it's an entirely different type of place. The main feature of the first-floor dining room is the mirrored, mahogany bar that attracts young professionals every evening (except Sunday). Banquettes are the seating arrangement of choice here—on the second floor they are made of dark wood and are strewn with throw pillows. The third-floor dining room is brighter and slightly less casual than those on the lower floors. To start your meal here I would recommend the marinated calamari salad made with lime juice, chipotle chilies, cilantro, and just a touch of tequila. Entrées might include a wonderful grilled tuna steak, a carpaccio sandwich, or the unusual oven-fried chicken in a cornflake crust (because it's oven fried, the chicken is not greasy, and the cornflake crust is much tastier than the breaded variety). The white bean and artichoke ragout is lovely. All dishes are beautifully presented, and there's also a long wine list. Daily specials are offered. The desserts here are better than many served in the pricier restaurants. Everyone is raving about the crème brûlée, which, surrounded by puff pastry and laced with vanilla, doesn't at all resemble the traditional dish of the same name.

BUDGET

Paramount Steak House

44 Charles St. ☎ **617/523-8832.** Meals $4–$9. No credit cards. Daily 7am–10pm. MBTA: Charles St. (Red Line). GREEK.

This small cafeteria rates big in the good Greek food department. A heaping souvlaki platter of barbecued lamb, rice pilaf, Greek salad, and bread runs about $7, and there are good chicken and beef dishes, spinach pie, and sandwiches. Paramount is a friendly place that attracts many of the Beacon Hill natives.

Family-Friendly Restaurants

The Bristol Lounge This place, located in the elegant Four Seasons Hotel (200 Boylston St.; ☎ **617/338-4400**), has a kids' menu featuring appetizers, main courses, desserts, and beverages. They can choose from such guaranteed favorites as a Fenway Frank, buttered "pasghetti," macaroni and cheese, and a peanut butter and jelly sandwich (at $4!). And to keep the kids busy, there are sticker fun books.

The Ground Round This chain has several locations around town; a good one is at 800 Boylston Street (☎ **617/247-0500**). All have free popcorn on the table, cartoons on a wall screen, video games, and crayons. On special days kids pay a penny a pound for their entrée. An added convenience for Mom and Dad—there are diaper-changing tables in the men's and ladies' restrooms.

Bertuccis A popular pizza chain with several restaurants around town—including one at the Faneuil Hall Marketplace—has a large chalkboard where kids can draw while waiting for their meal. There's more than just pizza available here; at the table kids can play with flour-coated dough and pretend to make a pizza. Try the location at 799 Main Street (☎ **617/661-8356**).

TGI Friday's At 26 Exeter Street (☎ **617/266-9040).** Once exclusively a singles place, it now caters to kids early in the evening. They get balloons, and a package of surprises wrapped in the restaurant's red and white paper. Crayons, a coloring book, peanut butter, and crackers are included.

Bennett Street Café At the Charles Hotel in Cambridge (☎ **617/864-1200**). There's a cup of crayons on every table, so the kids can create their own masterpieces on the paper tablecloths. Mom and Dad can use the crayons, too.

Serendipity 3 At Faneuil Hall Marketplace (☎ **617/523-2339**). Kids love to read the whimsical menu here and to eat such favorites as the foot-long chili hot dog, Tom Sawyer's potato skins, Ftaateeta's Toast, and the unforgettable frozen hot chocolate.

9 Back Bay

THEATER DISTRICT TO COPLEY SQUARE

VERY EXPENSIVE

Plaza Dining Room

In the Copley Plaza Hotel, Copley Sq. ☎ **617/267-5300,** ext 1638. Reservations recommended. Main courses $16–$28. AE, CB, DC, DISC, JCB, MC, V. Dinner only Tues–Thurs 6–10pm, Fri–Sat 5:30–10pm. MBTA: Copley Sq. (Green Line) or Back Bay (Orange Line). CONTINENTAL.

For many years this has been one of Boston's premiere dining rooms, with its Waterford crystal chandeliers, ornately sculpted vaulted ceilings, and dark woods. It is the place to dine in splendor.

The menu changes seasonally and always features classic continental cuisine (some with a creative contemporary twist), with recipes based on the freshest seasonal local ingredients. Most of the appetizers are so tempting it's difficult to choose. My two favorites, however, are the grilled Brie with sun-dried tomatoes (wrapped in grape leaves and served with baguettes) and the spicy and somewhat unusual Cajun scallops (served with creamed spinach and lime butter). Among the exceptionally presented main courses are the duck breast à l'orange served with sliced kiwi and papaya and topped with a Grand Marnier-peppercorn sauce (the kiwi and papaya, not traditionally served with this dish, are a wonderful accent to the light citrus flavor of the duck); tournedos of venison wrapped in apple-smoked bacon and served with a cranberry-walnut au jus; and the light but tasty seared tuna served over fresh stir-fry vegetables. Desserts are also splendid—from classic soufflés and tarte tatin to Tuip Royale Romanoff. The wine list is quite extensive, featuring about 180 different wines. The dress code is formal (a jacket and tie are required for men).

EXPENSIVE

57 Restaurant

200 Stuart St., at Park Plaza. ☎ **617/423-5700.** Reservations recommended. Main courses $14.55–$25.95. AE, DC, DISC, MC, V. Lunch daily 11:30am–3pm; dinner Mon–Sat 3–11pm, Sun noon–10pm. Lounge open till 2am. MBTA: Boylston St. or Arlington St. (Green Line). AMERICAN.

The 57 Restaurant still features the roast beef that made it famous during its heyday when it was located at 57 Carver Street. Now occupying an elegant rust-and-beige dining room next to the 57 Park Plaza Hotel, it continues to serve succulent ribs and steaks, including an excellent peppercorn sirloin and filet mignon. But there's more than steak on the menu; one of my favorites is the Athenian shore-style shrimp—a Greek-inspired classic with large Gulf shrimp sautéed with whole tomatoes and feta cheese. All entrées are served with potato, vegetable, and salad. Desserts are worth trying, especially the grasshopper pie, a crème de menthe chiffon concoction. There is two-hour validated parking in the adjacent "57" Garage.

Legal Sea Food

In the Boston Park Plaza Hotel & Towers, 35 Park Plaza. ☎ **617/426-4444.** Fax 617/426-3321. Reservations not accepted. Main courses $5.95–$12.95 at lunch, $13.95–$23.95 at dinner. AE, CB, DC, DISC, MC, V. Mon–Thurs 11am–10pm, Fri–Sat 11am–11pm. Sun noon–10pm. MBTA: Arlington St. (Green Line). SEAFOOD.

Legal Sea Food began as a small family fish market in Cambridge. Not long ago its owners opened a restaurant, which has since earned an international reputation for serving only top-quality fish and shellfish—broiled, baked, stir fried, grilled, fried, steamed, and in casserole. Today Legal Sea Food is Boston's best seafood restaurant. For dinner and lunch there is a vast "school" from which to choose: scrod, haddock, bluefish, trout, salmon, or more esoteric selections such as the world's ugliest fish—monkfish—tilefish, butterfish, and mako shark. Don't forget to try one of Legal's homemade ice creams for dessert. If you're health and calorie conscious, there are symbols on the menu to help you choose your meal.

Skipping a nautical decor, the dining room has mirrored walls and cushioned wicker chairs in soft neutral tones. The ceilings have an unusual baffle effect that adds nicely to the comfortable ambience. Legal also has two other branches in Boston (at Prudential Center and the Statler Building), as well as branches in Cambridge, Chestnut Hill, Burlington, Natick, and Worcester.

✪ Rocco's

5 S. Charles St. South. ☎ **617/723-6800.** Reservations recommended. Main courses $6.75–$11 at lunch, $9–$24 at dinner. AE, DC, DISC, MC, V. Lunch Mon–Fri 11:30am–2:30pm, Sat–Sun noon–3pm; dinner Sun–Wed 5:30–10pm, Thurs–Fri 5:30–11:30pm, Sat 5:30–11:30pm. MBTA: Arlington St. (Green Line). ITALIAN.

This is an exciting restaurant that owner Patrick Bowe calls "High Cafe." The dining room is lavishly decorated in rococo style (hence the name, Rocco's) with a hand-painted ceiling mural depicting such bacchanalian scenes as cherubs and satyrs. Paintings and sculptures (which are for sale) adorn the blue-and-white glazed walls, and two massive brass chandeliers hang from the 20-foot ceiling. Rocco's is serious about food and offers customers fine Italian cuisine prepared from the freshest choices in the marketplace. Choose a pasta as either an appetizer or the main dish—perhaps the spaghetti fra diavolo. Another good choice to start is the crisp, not rubbery, fried calamari. For your entrée, you might enjoy grilled quails San Leo or the Sicilian baked tuna. The roast chicken cacciatore is quite good as well. There is an excellent selection of wines sold by the bottle or glass plus a large list of beers. Also outstanding are the desserts.

MODERATE

Jacob Wirth Company

31 Stuart St. ☎ **617/338-8586.** Reservations recommended. Main courses $4.95–$13.50. AE, DC, DISC, MV. Mon–Thurs 11:30am–11pm, Fri–Sat 11:30am–midnight, Sun noon–6pm. MBTA: Boylston St. (Green Line). GERMAN/AMERICAN.

Located near the theater district and the New England Medical Center, this restaurant has been serving Bostonians for 127 years, and it's still going strong. The hearty German meals are all reasonably priced and at dinner include Wiener schnitzel, sauerbraten, mixed German grills, and bratwurst and knockwurst along with fish and prime ribs. There are daily blackboard specials besides the regular menu and a large selection of sandwiches. The restaurant features 18 beers on tap.

Skipjack

199 Clarendon St. ☎ **617/536-3500.** Reservations recommended. Main courses $10.95–$19.95 at dinner. AE, CB, DC, DISC, JCB, MC, V. Mon–Thurs and Sun 11am–10pm, Fri–Sat 11am–11pm. Sun brunch 11:30am–3pm. MBTA: Copley Sq. (Green Line). SEAFOOD.

Skipjack is a trendy spot specializing in fresh fish prepared in many styles. You could stock an aquarium with the exotic fish—including opah—from Hawaii, Florida, and the Caribbean plus the usual varieties and fresh shellfish. Order your selection plain grilled or Skipjack grilled; blackened, broiled, or teriyaki style; or just baked or fried. Try the tuna Provençale; the red snapper with ginger and lime sauce; or the seafood marinara complete with mussels, clams, squid, and scallops. Among the excellent appetizers are crab cakes and blackened tuna sashimi served Japanese style. If you love chocolate, don't leave without trying the chocolate bread pudding.

Skipjack tries to please everyone. There's a jazzy bar area, neon-lighted entrance, and multicolored walls, yet it's a nice family place in the afternoon or early evening. On Sunday there is live jazz during brunch hours. There are two Skipjacks locally (one is in Brookline), and Bostonians wouldn't mind having more. It's that good! There is also a take-out service. Call ahead (☎ **617/536-4949**) and order a sandwich or salad for a picnic lunch.

Turner Fisheries

In the Westin Hotel, 10 Huntington Ave., Copley Place. ☎ **617/424-7425.** Reservations recommended. Main courses $14–$26.95 at dinner. AE,CB, DC, DISC, MC, V. Mon–Sat 11am–11:30pm; Sun brunch 10:30am–2pm; Sun dinner until 11:30pm. MBTA: Copley Sq. (Green Line). SEAFOOD.

This restaurant is perhaps best known for winning the Boston Harborfest Chowderfest for several years in a row and being elevated to the Chowderfest Hall of Fame. But the chefs know that there's more to seafood than just chowder, and they serve some of the freshest fish in town, with the menu featuring each day's special catch. You will find everything from bouillabaisse to tea-smoked salmon to scrod in parchment to New England seafood pie; and you can request your choice pan fried, broiled, grilled, or blackened. All are served with a vegetable medley and red-skinned potato. The raw bar here is also a big draw. There are comfortable booths if you like privacy, and tables spaced beneath ceiling paddle fans if you like a breeze.

Upstairs at the Grille

710 Boylston St., in the Lenox Hotel. ☎ **617/421-4961**. Reservations recommended. Main courses $2.25–$11.25 at breakfast, $4.25–$10.50 at lunch, $9.50–$17.50 at dinner. AE, CB, DC, DISC, ER, JCB, MC, V. Daily 7am–11pm. Subway: Green line to Copley Sq. NEW ENGLAND.

The atmosphere at Upstairs at the Grille is a bit like that of an English pub, with dark wood paneling and fine paintings. The restaurant features a seasonal menu of hearty New England fare. Grilled specialties are cooked to order over a fire of hardwoods (some of which might be ash and mesquite), and you'll have a choice of specialty sauces (like wild mushroom demiglace, tomato basil sauce, or a citrus beurre blanc) as well as compound butters (such as lemon dill caper, pesto, and jalapeño-cranberry). If you'd rather have your meat broiled or baked, or your fish poached, your wish will be accommodated by the chef. There is a nicely chosen wine list.

COPLEY SQUARE TO MASSACHUSETTS AVENUE

VERY EXPENSIVE

Café Budapest

In the Copley Square Hotel, 90 Exeter St. ☎ **617/734-3388.** Reservations recommended. Main courses $8.50–$24 at lunch, $19.50–$33 at dinner. AE, MC, V. Lunch Mon–Sat noon–3pm; dinner Mon–Thurs 5–10:30pm, Fri–Sat 5pm–midnight, Sun 1–10:30pm. MBTA: Copley Sq. (Green Line). HUNGARIAN.

With its own mirrored entrance on Exeter Street, this beautiful restaurant has three dining rooms: the elegant Pink Room; the peasant-style Blue Room; and the wood-paneled main dining room, accented with stained glass, ruby goblets, and red leather chairs.

The Hungarian cuisine is among the best in town. If you're splurging, order a full-course dinner for two consisting of a mixed grill of filet mignon, Wiener schnitzel, pork chops, and other delights, topped off by a rich pastry and coffee. On the à la carte menu I recommend the beef Stroganoff, veal gulyás, and veal cutlet supreme. Whatever else you have, be sure to start with soup. The country-style soups are delicious, but I have a hard time passing up the iced, tart cherry soup with Hungarian burgundy wine. For dessert you must try Dobostorte or strudel, and Viennese coffee. Complete lunches, including entrée, soup, salad, dessert, tea or coffee, are available. A la carte entrées are available.

✪ L'Espalier

30 Gloucester St. ☎ **617/262-3023.** Reservations imperative. Fixed price. $62 for the four-course dinner menu and dessert; $72 for a dégustation menu consisting of hors d'oeuvres, two appetizers, two main courses, cheese course, and selection of desserts. AE, DISC, MC, V. Dinner Mon–Sat 6–10 pm. MBTA: Hynes/ICA (Green Line, B, C, or D train). CREATIVE AMERICAN.

L'Espalier offers superb cuisine in the elegance of a Beacon Hill town house. Chefs Frank and Catherine McClelland are the husband-and-wife team who have made this restaurant one of Boston's best. The breads, sorbets, ice creams, and desserts (many adapted from the family's heirloom cookbooks) are all made on the premises.The three dining rooms (reached by a wide spiral staircase) have intricate carvings on the walls, fireplaces, striking floral arrangements, and special lighting effects, all of which are playful accents to the restaurant's new contemporary decor.

The fixed-price menu features an appetizer, main course, and dessert. There are six choices in each category, the menu changing every week or so, but there is always a caviar selection, a hot or cold soup, fish, lamb, veal, beef, or venison. If they're on the menu, try the soft-shell crab tempura with grilled corn, almond, and wild mushroom salsa with a miso ginger sauce to start. Follow it with the excellent skillet-seared Maine salmon in amaranth crust with grilled trap squid, Vidalia onion, and red pepper salad, served in a wonderfully light lemon grass and green olive broth. Another good choice is the grilled rack and loin of lamb in a portobello-shallot crust with quinoa, fava bean, and tomato salad in a sorrel, mint, and Bordeaux au jus. Favorite desserts are the chocolate-hazelnut daquoise or the black currant soufflé.

If you have trouble making a decision, there is a dégustation menu. Other choices include an elegant vegetarian menu and an à la carte cheese tray (the Grand Fromage, with two local cheeses). The wine cellar is extensive, with 200 bottles, including an array of wines from Bordeaux and California.

EXPENSIVE

Boodles

In the Back Bay Hilton, 40 Dalton St. ☎ **617/BOODLES.** Reservations recommended. Main courses $6.75–$19.50. AE, CB, DC, DISC, MC, V. Lunch daily 11:30am–2:30pm; dinner nightly 5–11:30pm. MBTA: Prudential (Green Line, E train). AMERICAN.

If you ever thought that cooking over a grill just meant lighting a few coals and tossing on the meat, you'll be amazed at what the chefs at Boodles do. This British-style restaurant with a hunt club motif specializes in grilling aged steak, poultry, and fish. The menu is extensive, ranging from grilled pork tenderloin to grilled sirloin steak to lobster brochette and swordfish. There is also a nice selection of appetizers, salads, and soups (not everything is grilled). Two vegetables are included with the main course, plus a choice of sauces, butters, and savory condiments. At dinner you receive a complimentary crock of real Boston baked beans. Lunch includes burgers grilled on mesquite. Recently, Boodles Bar, offering over 90 microbrewed beers, was named the "Best Hotel Beer Bar in the United States," and a new offering at the restaurant is the nightly brewers dinner, which pairs two selected beers with a three-course gourmet dinner.

The Capital Grille

359 Newbury St. ☎ **617/262-8900.** Reservations recommended. Main courses $14.95–$25.95. AE, CB, DC, DISC, MC, V. Dinner only, Sun–Thurs 5–10pm, Fri–Sat 5–11pm. MBTA: Hynes/ICA (Green Line, B, C, or D train). AMERICAN.

Bostonians like a good steak house, and they've found one in this handsome New York–style establishment. The dining room has the feel of a private club with its leather furnishings and handcrafted woodwork. But not so private is the open kitchen, where you can watch the chefs prepare your meal or the glass-enclosed meat locker where beef—sirloin and porterhouse steaks, filet mignon, and prime rib—is being dry aged. To start, try the pan-fried calamari with hot cherry peppers or the light but appetizing crab and lobster cakes. Offerings from the grill include chicken, chops, swordfish, salmon, or lobster in addition to all the steaks listed above. Desserts are fairly simple, but they're all good. One of my favorites is the white chocolate mousse. The fresh strawberries in cream with brown sugar are also a great way to end a meal here. The wine cellar stocks more than 3,000 bottles of wine. Valet parking is available.

Casa Romero

30 Gloucester St. ☎ **617/536-4341.** Reservations recommended. Main courses $12–$20. AE, MC, V. Dinner only, Sun–Thurs 5–10pm, Fri–Sat 5–11pm. MBTA: Hynes/ICA (Green Line, B, C, or D train). MEXICAN.

Casa Romero, hidden away in an alley on the side of L'Espalier, features authentic Mexican cuisine with some spicy-hot presentations for the true aficionado and somewhat milder dishes for those not yet initiated into south-of-the-border cooking. Señor Romero or one of the waiters will be happy to describe the ingredients used in preparation. The specialties include a very good *mole poblano* (chicken in a spicy chocolate sauce), *camarones Veracruz* (giant shrimp sautéed in a spicy tomato sauce), and *puerco adobado* (pork tenderloin marinated with oranges and smoked peppers). The ambience at Casa Romero is handsome colonial Mexico: high-backed leather chairs, charming pottery, plentiful artwork, inlaid tiles, and fresh flowers. Summer evenings in the walled garden are delightful!

Davio's

269 Newbury St. ☎ **617/262-4810.** Reservations recommended. Main courses $9.95–$24.95. Pizzas $6.95–$8.50. AE, CB, DC, DISC, MC, V. Lunch Mon–Sat 11:30am–3pm; dinner Mon–Thurs and Sun 5–10pm, Fri–Sat 5–11pm; Sun brunch 11:30am–3pm. MBTA: Copley Sq. (Green Line). CREATIVE NORTHERN ITALIAN.

When a restaurant is booked to capacity on a Monday evening, you can be sure it has something special going for it: a top-notch kitchen, dedicated staff, or a pleasing atmosphere—or a combination of all three, like Davio's.

Davio's is comfortable; exposed brick walls, velvet drapes, brass fixtures, and soft music in the background set the scene. The enthusiastic young owner-chef, Steve DiFillipo, has created a continental menu with an Italian slant. Instead of the usual pastas with various red sauces, you might find veal scaloppine sautéed with a Marsala, garlic, and plum tomato sauce; roast pork loin with confettura of fig, shallot, and thyme with a purée of leeks and parsnips; or grilled red snapper with crab fritters and a tomato-chili pepper-honey glaze. There are usually three special entrées daily, plus a house pâté, homemade pasta, and a ravioli creation. There's also a soup of the day in addition to the always-available superb minestrone. Dessert choices include a white chocolate torte and an excellent mixed-fruit tart. Davio's has a fine selection of Italian, French, and California wines, including some rare and expensive old Italian vintages. Half bottles are also available. The restaurant offers valet parking. Davio's also has an upstairs cafe with an outside dining terrace in good weather. (Hours at the cafe are 11:30am to 3pm and 5 to 11pm).

Du Barry Restaurant Français

159 Newbury St. ☎ **617/262-2445.** Reservations recommended. Main courses $4.25–$20 at lunch, $12–$20 at dinner. AE, CB, DC, DISC, MC, V. Lunch Mon–Fri noon–2:30pm, Sat 12:30–3pm; dinner Mon–Sat 5:30–10pm, Sun 5:30–9:30pm. MBTA: Copley Sq. (Green Line). FRENCH.

Traditional French cuisine is Du Barry's specialty, and it can be enjoyed in the cozy dining room and, during the summer, in the private open garden and enclosed terrace. All the specialties from escargots to crêpes Suzette are made to order. Consider *coq au vin de bourgogne, chateaubriand sauce béarnaise,* or *brochette d'agneau grillé bordelaise,* with an authentic French onion soup gratinée as an appetizer. At lunch you can have the onion soup with a salad at $5, or choose from a range of other entrées including soft-shell crabs, frogs' legs, and sea scallops.

This is also a great place to brush up on your French. Teachers have been bringing their students here to practice their language skills for many years.

Mass. Bay Co.

In the Sheraton Boston Hotel & Towers, 39 Dalton St. ☎ **617/236-2000,** ext 4168. Reservations recommended. Main courses $7.95–$21.50 at lunch, $16.95–$28.95 at dinner. AE, DC, DISC, ER, JCB, MC, V. Breakfast 6:30–10am, lunch Mon–Fri 11:30am–2pm; dinner nightly 5:30–10:30pm. Lounge food daily 11:30–1am. MBTA: Prudential (Green Line, E train). INNOVATIVE SEAFOOD.

Sometimes when an old restaurant makes dramatic changes regular patrons are left feeling blindsided, but you'll be hard pressed to find someone with a complaint here. Chef Frederick Burkle's entirely new menu is garnering lots of praise. A simple but delicious appetizer is the crab cakes Jonah with jalapeño tartar sauce. They're contrasted by the elaborate tuna carpaccio on a warm Gorgonzola-potato cake with shaved fennel and fava bean salad. As a main course I would suggest the herb- and garlic-roasted free-range chicken served on an artichoke and peasant vegetable stew with pan au jus or the beautifully presented mustard-poached halibut on garlic mashed potatoes with roasted rope-cultured mussels and a pink peppercorn beurre blanc.

St. Botolph Restaurant

99 St. Botolph St. ☎ **617/266-3030.** Reservations recommended. Main courses $6.25–$12.75 at lunch, $14.95–$19.50 at dinner; brunch $15. Dinner daily 5:45–10:30pm; cafe menu Mon–Sat 11:30am–midnight, Sun 3pm–midnight; Sun brunch 11:30am–3pm. MBTA: Prudential (Green Line, E train). CONTINENTAL.

From the cafe menu try the grilled garlic shrimp with focaccia toast or the spinach and mushroom polenta with Gorgonzola cream to start. Sandwiches include the Botolph Burger with a choice of bacon, mushrooms, or cheese. There are several interesting grilled pizzas and pastas on the cafe menu.

The dinner menu changes monthly, but a recent one included, as an appetizer, grilled asparagus in lemon and garlic with roasted sweet peppers and shiitake caps. As an entrée you might enjoy the grilled center-cut pork chops with creamy herb polenta, stewed plum tomatoes, and Gorgonzola butter, or the Atlantic salmon rubbed with pesto in a lemon-thyme vinaigrette and served over cooked greens.

Top of the Hub

Prudential Center (between Boylston St. and Huntington Ave.). ☎ **617/536-1775.** Reservations recommended. Main courses $5.95–$13.50 at lunch, $15.25–$24.50 at dinner. Sun brunch $20. AE, DC, DISC, MC, V. Lunch Mon–Fri 11:30am–2:30pm, Sat noon–3pm; dinner Sun–Thurs 5:30–10pm, Fri–Sat 5:30–11pm, Sun brunch 10am–2:30pm. MBTA: Hynes/ICA (Green Line, B, C, or D train). CONTINENTAL.

For high-style dining—52 stories high—the Top of the Hub is a top choice. The view is spectacular; on a clear day you can see all of Boston below you from the three glass-walled sides of the restaurant and lounge. At night the twinkling lights from the city and airport, plus the starlight, create a special magic. I would suggest coming before sunset and lingering over your meal until dark—this way you get the best of both worlds.

The accent is on fresh seafood from the Boston fishing fleet, but there are some good meat dishes on the menu as well. Sample the mussel cream soup or the garlic bread with a tomato and leek salsa. Follow it with pan-roasted swordfish, poached North Atlantic salmon, or Eastern Shore shrimp and scallop cakes. The filet mignon is good; so is the rack of lamb. The lunch menu includes sandwiches, salads, and pastas, as well as seafood entrées. If it's on the dessert menu when you're there, try the key lime pie. The food isn't the best in Boston, but the view is great and service is friendly and efficient.

Reduced parking rates are available in the Prudential garage after 4pm weekdays and all day on Saturday and Sunday. When you make your reservation, ask for a table by the window.

MODERATE

Bangkok Cuisine

177A Massachusetts Ave. ☎ **617/262-5377.** Reservations not accepted. Main courses $4.75–$6.50 at lunch, $8–$13.50 at dinner. AE, DISC, MC, V. Lunch Mon–Sat 11:30am–3pm; dinner Mon–Thurs 5–10:30pm, Fri 5–11pm, Sat 3–11pm, Sun 4–10pm. MBTA: Hynes/ICA (Green Line, B, C, or D train). THAI.

Bangkok Cuisine was the first Thai restaurant in Boston. It has set (and maintained) high standards for all the others that followed. The dishes run the gamut of curry, pan-fried or deep-fried whole fish, and hot and sour. The green curry in coconut milk and vegetables prepared with strong green Thai chili pepper is the most incendiary. You can order nonspicy food and, of course, pad Thai, the famous noodle dish. A rice plate special is served at lunch.

Café Jaffa

48 Gloucester St. ☎ **617/536-0230.** Reservations not accepted. Main courses $3–$8.75. AE, MC, V. Mon–Thurs 11am–10:30pm, Fri–Sat 11am–11pm, Sun 1–10pm. MBTA: Hynes/ICA (Green Line, B, C, or D train). INTERNATIONAL.

At the far end of Café Jaffa is a piece of artwork depicting a green fish that is meant to represent the joyous quality of the food here. Young people are attracted to Café Jaffa as moths are attracted to light. The restaurant's appeal lies as much in the low prices as the excellent quality of the food. Middle Eastern cuisine predominates, but you'll also find a few Greek favorites on the menu. My favorite here is the falafel—one of the best I've ever had. I also enjoyed the baba ghannouj and hummus. Lamb, beef, and chicken kebabs are popular dishes, and they come with a Greek salad and pita bread. Try the wonderful baklava for dessert. There is a short list of available beer and wine.

BUDGET

The Original Sports Saloon

In the Copley Square Hotel, 47 Huntington Ave. ☎ **617/536-9000.** Main courses $6.50–$17.95. AE, DC, DISC, MC, V. Daily 11:30am–1:30am. Full menu served until 10pm, appetizers until closing. MBTA: Copley Sq. (Green Line). AMERICAN/ BARBECUE.

Old-time saloons had a reputation for serving good food as well as good drink; this sports saloon has the same reputation thanks to its award-winning barbecue. It was a sports bar back in 1904 when the Boston Braves hung out here. The Braves are long gone and the setup of the room has changed—11 large-screen TVs, photographs, and cartoons by the famous columnist Paul Szep. The specialty of the house is barbecued baby back ribs, a dish which takes over 30 hours to prepare. The ribs are slow cooked, using an authentic Memphis smoker, over a secret blend of hickory, ash, cherry, and apple woods. Other menu items include a Bloomin' Saloon'ion (a deep-fried whole onion) and the Larry Bird sandwich (marinated chicken breast served on a whole wheat bun with bacon, melted Swiss cheese, and honey mustard). Desserts are good, but simple.

10 Cambridge

Even if you're not staying in Cambridge, have a meal there during your sightseeing excursions. Cambridge is adjacent to Boston—most of the restaurants listed here can be reached on foot from the Harvard Square subway stop, just across the Charles River from the center of Boston. Many of your fellow diners will include members of the huge academic community that makes Cambridge one of the most exciting intellectual and international centers in the country. If you go beyond Harvard Square to Inman Square you'll find many little ethnic restaurants, including some serving Portuguese cuisine.

Very Expensive

The Harvest

44 Brattle St. ☎ **617/492-1115.** Reservations recommended. Main courses $7.50–$12 at lunch, $21.50–$28 at dinner. Dinner in cafe $7.50–$18.50. AE, CB, DC, DISC, MC, V. Lunch Mon–Fri 11:30am–2:30pm; dinner Mon–Thurs 6–10pm, Fri–Sat 5:30–10:30pm. Sat–Sun brunch 11am–3pm. MBTA: Harvard Sq. (Red Line). AMERICAN.

Purchased by the owners of Rocco's, the Harvest is a gathering place for celebrities and literati, Harvard professors, and young professionals. The menu changes daily. Main courses in the cafe might include vegetarian ravioli or a hummus platter. In the main dining room you might find a vegetarian tagliatelle with porcini mushrooms, fresh peas, and bell peppers with parmigiano reggiano in a light cream sauce. The oven-roasted pheasant breast served with pheasant leg confit, wild rice, and wild mushroom, red wine, shallot, and sage sauce is excellent, as is the pan-roasted salmon sprinkled with oats and served in a maple, saffron, and fish fumet sauce. Desserts might include a chocolate truffle cake on a praline crème anglaise or an apple-apricot compote. I generally enjoy dining in the cafe because the meals are lighter and the prices are lower, but the quality of the food is the same.

Upstairs at the Pudding

10 Holyoke St. ☎ **617/864-1933.** Reservations recommended. Main courses $8–$12 at lunch, $17–$27 at dinner. AE, DC, MC, V. Lunch Mon–Fri 11:30–2:30pm;

dinner nightly 6–10pm; Sun brunch 11:30am–2:30pm. MBTA: Harvard Sq. (Red Line). CONTINENTAL/NORTHERN ITALIAN.

You may never be asked to join the "Pudding," Harvard's famous theatrical group, but you can go for a showpiece dinner. Located above the Hasty Pudding Playhouse, it's an attractive room with forest-green walls, brass chandeliers, and flowers. There is a lovely terrace and herb garden off the dining room for al fresco dining. The menu changes daily. There may be grilled marinated Vermont quail and flat bread on lettuce, glazed with a wild mushroom port for the first course, followed by pan-steamed black sea bass with cob-smoked bacon, red onion, and citrus, served with fiddlehead ferns and boiled creamer potatoes; or grilled marinated leg of lamb, served with a plum tomato, olive, and feta relish and with fresh herbed polenta, charred tomato salad, and insalata mista. Desserts are worth waiting for. I especially like the steamed chocolate mousse cake with espresso anglaise and the lemon buttermilk budino with raspberry sauce and candied pistachios. Take time to enjoy the gallery of theatrical posters in the halls and dining room.

Expensive

The Blue Room

1 Kendall Sq. ☎ **617/494-9034.** Reservations recommended. Main courses $1.95–$7.95 at lunch, $13.50–$18.50 at dinner. AE, DC, DISC, MC, V. Mon–Thurs 11am–10pm, Fri 11am–10:30pm, Sat 5:30–10:30pm, Sun 5:30–9pm. MBTA: Kendall Sq. (Red Line). ECLECTIC.

The owners aren't singing the blues about this place, since practically from the moment it opened the Blue Room has been on the "hot" list of places to go. It's a big room with tables and booths, a bar at one end, and an open grill at the other, on which a variety of fish and meats are grilled and then prepared in many different styles—Mexican, Mediterranean, Southeast Asian. You can order entrées or a number of "small plates" in the $2 to $6 price range. Barbecue aficionados love the *tacos al carbón,* crunchy slivers of fire-roasted pork with tortillas, black bean salad, pickled cabbage, plantain, avocado, and salsa. Just roll, wrap, and eat. The soft-shell crab is excellent. Peanut-crusted, pan-seared tuna steak with grilled pineapple and tea-soaked rotisserie chicken are less spicy than the tacos and are just great. If the hot and spicy Hong Kong shrimp with a fiery Asian dipping sauce are on the menu, give them a try. An interesting dessert I had a while back was the shortbread with grilled banana, mango sauce, and whipped cream. The Blue Room has a list of flavored grappas—try the lemon fennel grappa.

Cottonwood Café

In the Porter Exchange Building, 1815 Massachusetts Ave. ☎ **617/661-7440.** Reservations recommended. Main courses $9–$16 at lunch, $13–$26 at dinner. MC, V. Lunch Sun–Fri noon–3pm; dinner Sun–Thurs 5:45–10pm, Fri–Sat 5:30–11:30pm. MBTA: Porter Sq. (Red Line). SOUTHWESTERN.

An attractive, trendy restaurant decorated in southwestern style with cacti and pottery, the Cottonwood is *the* place for "modern Southwest cuisine," a blend of Native American, Mexican, Spanish, and European cuisines. Among the specials you might find are Rocky Mountain lamb, four excellent little chops arranged on red raspberry-chipotle sauce and green cilantro pesto; salmon Colorado, a grilled fillet with smoked tomato sauce and cilantro-garlic cream; and an unusual preparation of chicken, coated with pulverized popcorn, then sautéed and served with roasted red pepper sauce and a cilantro mousse. Try the Milagro black-bean soup sprinkled with cilantro, a house specialty, or the six-chile chili, made with all meat. A great dessert is the caramel custard flan.

✪ Rialto

One Bennett St., in the Charles Hotel. ☎ **617/661-5050.** Reservations recommended. Main courses $17–$29. AE, MC, V. Sun–Thurs 5:30–10pm, Fri–Sat 5:30–11pm. Bar is open Sun–Thurs 5pm–1am, Fri–Sat 5pm–1:30am. Subway: Red Line to Harvard Square. FRENCH/ITALIAN/SPANISH.

In the past many people have avoided hotel restaurants as a rule, but today you'll find some of the country's best restaurants tucked away within a hotel. Rialto is one of those places. The dining room with floor-to-ceiling windows, rich wood trim, and plush banquettes is comfortable and inviting. Walls are hung with artwork on loan from Gallery Naga as well as some works collected by restaurateur Michaela Larson. Chef Jody Adams is a wizard with food. The way she combines taste and texture is brilliant, and you have to taste it to believe it. It was a difficult choice, but I started with the *soupe de poisson* (Provençal fisherman's soup with rouille, Gruyère, and basil oil) and I wasn't disappointed. I followed that with grilled mackerel with a tomato-caper vinaigrette and crab, asparagus, and Swiss chard bundles, and I couldn't have been happier. Finally, I had the chocolate mousse pyramid with caramel sauce and pistachio praline—fantastic! No matter what you do in Boston, you should make Rialto a first-choice stop.

Moderate

Bombay Club

57 John F. Kennedy St., in the Galleria Mall at Harvard Sq. ☎ **617/661-8100.** Main courses $4.95–$8.95 at lunch, $8.95–$15.95 at dinner. AE, DC, MC, V. Daily 11:30am–11pm. MBTA: Harvard Sq. (Red Line). INDIAN.

The owners of Kebab-'N'-Kurry (30 Massachusetts Ave., Boston) have enhanced their reputation as outstanding Indian chefs by opening this restaurant in Cambridge. The chicken, lamb, seafood, and rice specialties are the best in town. From the tandoori ovens come dishes baked to perfection in the traditional charcoal-fired clay oven. The flavorful Indian breads *tandoori roti* and *tandoori nan* are also baked there. The house specials include *barra kebab,* lamb marinated in a spicy sauce for three days and then baked on skewers, and "royal platters" combining several items. The menu includes several Indian vegetarian dishes and even an Indian barbecue Weight Watchers special.

$ Border Café

32 Church St., Harvard Sq. ☎ **617/864-6100.** Reservations not accepted. Main courses $6–$10. AE, MC, V. Mon–Thurs 11am–1am, Fri–Sat 11–2am, Sun noon–11pm. MBTA: Harvard Sq. (Red Line). SOUTHWESTERN.

Spicy, hot, flavorful southwestern cooking burst on the American scene several years ago and is still popular here at the Border Café. The menu features Cajun, Tex-Mex, and some Caribbean specialties. Choose fresh-fried tortillas, enchiladas, tacos, Caribbean shrimp (dipped in coconut and spices before frying), popcorn shrimp, or any of dozens of other interesting dishes. I liked the fajitas, served in the traditional way in a large iron frying pan smothered with onions, along with a dish of guacamole, shredded lettuce, sour cream, spicy salsa, rice, and black beans. The Border Café is especially popular with Harvard students.

Casa Portugal

1200 Cambridge St. ☎ **617/491-8880.** Reservations recommended on weekends. Main courses $7.95–$13.95. AE, DISC, MC, V. Daily 4:30–10pm. MBTA: Harvard Sq. (Red Line); from there take the Lechmere bus to Inman Sq./Cambridge St. PORTUGUESE.

The locals like this casual bistro for its hearty, inexpensive Portuguese fare and warm, inviting, casual atmosphere. Soup of the day, rice, and Portuguese fried potatoes come with all entrées. The tureens, which combine several types of shellfish, are quite popular, as is the *bacalhau assado a cuca* (codfish, garlic, peppers, and potatoes baked with olive oil). There are four items on the menu singled out as "spicy," including *grelha mista* (grilled bits of veal, pork, liver, and linguica served on a skewer).

$ Dalí

415 Washington St., Somerville. ☎ **617/661-3254.** Reservations not accepted. Tapas $2.50–$5.50, main courses $12–$18. AE, DC, MC, V. Dinner Sun–Thurs 5:30–10pm, Fri–Sat 5:30–10:30pm. MBTA: Harvard Sq. (Red Line); walk along Kirkland St. to Somerville and intersection of Washington and Beacon sts. SPANISH.

Dalí is on the Cambridge/Somerville border, a short walk from Harvard Square. Look for the corner building with the blue walls; once through them you'll imagine yourself transported to Spain. There are three separate rooms with tile tables and red walls. A long bar runs through the rooms. You can wait there for your table, sip some wine, and start nibbling your tapas—small portions of food served on small plates, allowing you to sample a variety of items. Dalí offers 18 different tapas dishes on the regular menu, along with 10 daily specials. For a complete dinner, try a soup, a tapas, and an entrée, perhaps the classic paella (a rice dish with meats, seafood, and saffron). And what better for dessert than a caramel custard flan!

Go early for a leisurely meal since the restaurant gets very crowded late in the evening. The owners of Dalí have recently opened another restaurant called **Tapeo** at 266 Newbury Street between Fairfield and Dartmouth Streets in the Back Bay. The menu is the same and the decor is equally unique.

East Coast Grill

1271 Cambridge St. ☎ **617/491-6568.** Reservations accepted only for parties of five or more Sun–Thurs. Main courses $10.50–$16.25. DISC, MC, V. Dinner Sun–Thurs 5:30–10pm, Fri–Sat 5:30–10:30pm. MBTA: Harvard Sq. (Red Line); from there take Lechmere bus to Inman Sq. to Cambridge St. SEAFOOD/SOUTHERN.

You must try the East Coast Grill—that is, if you can get in. This little restaurant is so popular that the locals line up early. It's a laid-back, friendly place with country and rock music and a grilling station in full view. Specialties are seafood, hearty soups, and southern barbecue. You have a choice of three barbecues: Texas beef, Missouri spareribs, and North Carolina pork. Barbecue platters come with baked beans, corn bread, and a slice of watermelon. Chef-owner Chris Schlesinger also features dishes from around the world, like Caribbean jerk chicken and a pasta "from Hell," a spicy dish made with "inner beauty" hot sauce. There are several antidotes for those who cannot "take the heat." Some try sugar; others like a syrup to which milk has been added. But at the East Coast Grill they suggest putting out the fire with orange Creamsicles.

Green Street Grill

280 Green St. ☎ **617/876-1655.** Reservations not accepted. Main courses $11.95–$15.95. AE, MC, V. Dinner nightly 6–10pm. MBTA: Central Sq. (Red Line). CARIBBEAN.

You shouldn't expect much here with respect to the decor, but the Caribbean food here is among the hottest and best in town. Chef Steve Cobble uses five different kinds of pepper in preparing some of his dishes. The goat stew has jalapeños, Anaheims, chipotles, serranos, and Scotch bonnets. Cobble's homemade sausages, which include a variety of peppers, herbs, and fruits, are very popular. Seafood pepper pot—a combination of mussels, lobster, Caribbean pumpkin, and eggplant in a white wine sauce—should not be missed. Grilled seafood is also done well here.

✪ Henrietta's Table

One Bennett St., in the Charles Hotel. ☎ **617/661-5005.** Reservations recommended. Main courses at breakfast $2.25–$9.50; $7.50–$10 at lunch; $9–$12.50 at dinner. AE, MC, V. Breakfast Mon–Fri 6:30–11am, Sat 7–11:30am, Sun 7–10:30am; brunch Sun 11:30am–3pm; lunch Mon–Sat noon–3pm; dinner Sun–Thurs 5:30–10pm, Fri–Sat 5:30–11pm. Market hours Mon–Fri 6:30am–10pm, Sat–Sun 7am–10pm. MTBA: Red Line to Harvard Sq. NEW ENGLAND.

The creators of Henrietta's Table describe the food as "fresh and honest country cooking." Indeed, you'll feel like you're in the country when you enter this charming place. There's a farmstand market filled with fruits, vegetables, and fresh breads adjoining the white-walled dining room. The short menu changes daily to accommodate the freshest produce, but on a recent visit for dinner I had the herb-crusted rotisserie chicken (moist and tender) and the apple wood-smoked Maine salmon with a beach plum vinaigrette (the fish was flaky and flavorful). The lunch menu features sandwiches, Yankee pot roast, and baked scrod, among other items. And at breakfast you can get hotcakes, waffles, cereals, and farm-fresh eggs. In case you were wondering, Henrietta is the hotel owner's 1,000-pound pig who lives on Martha's Vineyard.

La Groceria

853 Main St. ☎ **617/547-9258** or 876-4162. Reservations not accepted. Main courses $3.95–$7.95 at lunch, $9.95–$15.95 at dinner. Early bird special $9.95.

Children's menu $4.95–$5.95. AE, DC, DISC, MC, V. Lunch Mon–Fri 11:30am–4pm; dinner Mon–Thurs 4–10pm, Fri–Sat 4–11pm. Sun 1–10pm. MBTA: Central Sq. (Red Line). ITALIAN.

With its stucco archways, tile floors, and colorful artwork, this restaurant off Central Square could easily be off a main square in Bologna. For lunch, start out with the antipasto fantasia (an assortment of hot and cold vegetables, baked clams, salami, and prevolina cheese). Salads play a large role on the lunch menu. Sandwiches, such as the sirloin strip sandwich (grilled marinated sirloin with roasted tomatoes, peppers, onions, and provolone cheese) and the vegetarian (grilled eggplant, tomatoes, artichokes, zucchini topped with pesto and giardiniera salad) are served on focaccia bread. The dinner menu is more substantial, featuring everything from homemade pasta to fish, chicken, and veal. I'm a big fan of the fettuccine Alfredo. If you have room, top off your meal with homemade cannoli (filled to order) and a freshly ground cappuccino. Check out the pasta machine at the entrance to La Groceria. The noodles you see may be rushed upstairs to be part of your dinner. Early bird specials, served until 6:30pm Sunday through Friday, include a main course, salad, and cannoli.

House of Blues

96 Winthrop St. ☎ **617/491-2583.** Reservations recommended. Main courses $4.95–$14.95. AE, MC, V. Sun–Wed 11:30am–1am, Thurs–Sat 11:30am–2am. MBTA: Harvard Sq. (Red Line). CAJUN/PIZZA/INTERNATIONAL.

Located in a blue clapboard house just off Harvard Square, the House of Blues is one of Boston's hottest new restaurants. Everything is blue here, and the walls and ceilings are dotted with whimsical pieces of folk art by various artists. On the ceiling near the bar area you'll find plaster bas-reliefs of great blues musicians.

The menu offers a variety of interesting dishes. You might begin with the buffalo legs (they're much bigger than your average buffalo wings), followed by jambalaya or a burger. There's a long list of pizzas on the menu (try the one topped with feta cheese and garlic) that are baked in a wood-fired pizza oven. If you love barbecue, try the hand-pulled pork barbecue sandwich. The House of Blues features live blues entertainment during the week and on weekends. The Sunday Gospel brunch requires reservations at least two weeks in advance.

Ristorante Marino

2465 Massachusetts Ave. ☎ **617/868-5454.** Reservations recommended. Main courses $6.95–$11.95 at lunch, $15–$22 at dinner. MC, V. Lunch Mon–Fri 11:30am–3:30pm; dinner Mon–Fri 4–10pm, Sun noon–10pm. MBTA: Porter Sq. (Red Line); from there take bus to Arlington. NORTHERN ITALIAN.

Ristorante Marino used to be an exceptional restaurant that specialized in healthy foods. Unfortunately, the quality of the food has slipped slightly over the past year, and prices have gone up. This isn't to say that the food is terrible; on the contrary, it's still quite good—just not as good as it used to be. The menu is based on traditional recipes from the Abruzzi region of Italy. The pasta, bread, sausages, some cheeses, and desserts are all prepared in-house. The vegetables are organically grown, and the tomato sauce is prepared with homegrown tomatoes. Marino's has its own farms and greenhouses, including Lookout Farm in South Natick, which is open to visitors. Livestock is also raised there (without exposure to hormones and other chemicals). Most dishes are prepared with cholesterol-free olive oil instead of butter. Even the wine is made by Marino's from organically grown grapes imported from Italy.

Menu selections include grilled shrimp with roasted pepper purée, rice served with an assortment of shellfish, and veal sautéed in Marsala wine, mushrooms, and lemon. Also available are 10-inch pizzas made to order. Not long ago I had the butternut squash ravioli and the roast pork, both of which were very good. The minestrone, on the other hand, left a lot to be desired. The main dining area is an atrium with glass roof, live trees, vines, and attractive fish tanks. Parking is free.

S&S Deli and Restaurant

1334 Cambridge St., Inman Sq. ☎ **617/354-0777.** Main courses $2.95–$10.95. No credit cards. Mon–Sat 7am–midnight, Sun 8am–midnight. Sat–Sun brunch 8am–4pm. MBTA: Harvard Sq. (Red Line); from there take bus no. 69 to Lechmere, which goes by Inman Sq. and along Cambridge St. DELI.

Back in the good old days when nobody watched calories, Jewish mothers would show their hospitality by urging guests to "Es and es"—Yiddish for "Eat and eat." This spot, founded in 1919 by the great-grandmother of the current owners, gives you an opportunity to do just that. On the outskirts of Boston, it is close enough to be listed here. You can find the traditional deli items on the menu: corned beef, pastrami, tongue, and Reuben sandwiches; potato pancakes, blintzes, knockwurst and beans (Boston baked beans, no less!), and lox and whitefish. But S&S is also a full service restaurant with entrées of beef, chicken, and fish, plus quiche and croissants! What would Grandma say to that?

S&S serves breakfast anytime during restaurant hours. Brunch, served Saturday and Sunday, is quite popular—plan to arrive before 10am to avoid the long lines.

Spinnaker Italia

In the Hyatt Regency Hotel, 575 Memorial Dr. ☎ **617/492-1234.** Reservations recommended. Main courses $12–$23; pizzas $12.50–$14. Complimentary champagne after noon. AE, DC, DISC, ER, MC, V. Dinner nightly 6–9:30pm; Sun brunch 10am–2pm. Bar open Sun–Thurs to 12:30am, Fri–Sat to 1:30am. NORTHERN ITALIAN.

This rotating lounge and restaurant offers a magnificent view that changes as the room moves ever so slowly (50 minutes for a full circle). Try and time your visit as day turns to night and enjoy the sunset with dinner. You can go from pizza to pasta to scaloppine to zabaglione to cappuccino, with perhaps a minestrone and antipasto before your table returns to its starting point. Order the fettuccine with fresh salmon, artichokes, and tomato mixed with the pasta; or the linguine, loaded with chopped clams. The shrimp entrée has roasted Gulf shrimp wrapped in pancetta and served with grilled peppers and a Marsala sauce.

There's an elegant Sunday brunch, served buffet style with pasta and omelets cooked to order. Parking is validated for two hours with dinner. A complimentary glass of champagne is served after noon.

Tapas

2067 Massachusetts Ave. ☎ **617/576-2240.** Reservations recommended. Tapas $1.95–$6.95; main courses $3.50–$11.50 at lunch, $4.95–$14.50 at dinner. MC, V. Mon–Fri 11:30am–11pm, Sat–Sun noon–11pm. MBTA: Porter Sq. (Red Line); from there take bus no. 77, which stops at the restaurant, or walk along Massachusetts Ave. INTERNATIONAL.

Dining at Tapas can be either a budget meal or an expensive dinner, depending on how well you resist temptation—you can order as many hors d'oeuvres or desserts as you like. There is an ever-changing choice of tapas, including ravioli, crab cakes, pumpkin kibbe, pickled shrimp, crudités, and so on—about two dozen in all. Several entrées are available as well, served in full or half portions, and you might also choose one of the soups, chowders (Nana's chowder is one of the better ones), or salad. The menu changes seasonally. Parking is available in the rear of the building.

BUDGET

Algiers Coffeehouse

40 Brattle St. ☎ **617/492-1557.** Reservations not accepted. Main courses $2.25–$7.95. No credit cards. Mon–Thurs 8pm–midnight, Fri–Sat 8pm–1am. MBTA: Harvard Sq. (Red Line). MIDDLE EASTERN.

For those of us who remember the Algiers Coffeehouse when it was a dark, smoke-filled literary hangout, the "new and improved" version (which came about as a result of a fire) is a little shocking, but nonetheless pleasant. Located in Brattle Hall, it's still one of the favorite hangouts of the literari of Cambridge, and it still serves delicious soups, sandwiches, pizzas, omelettes, falafel, and hummus. It's a great stop for a snack, light meal, or just a cup of coffee or tea (there's a rather long list of beverages available).

Passage to India

1900 Massachusetts Ave. ☎ **617/497-6113.** Reservations recommended. Main courses $6.75–$11.25. MC, V. Lunch Mon–Sat 11:30–3pm; dinner nightly 5–10:30pm. MBTA: Porter Sq. (Red Line). INDIAN.

Passage to India is a high-quality Indian restaurant, with a menu that has something to please every palate—vegetarian, seafood, chicken, lamb, and rice dishes. (No red meat is served.) An assortment of appetizers (samosas are a good choice), breads (my favorites are the poori bread and *nan*), condiments, and desserts (mango ice cream is always a good bet) make choosing dinner a very pleasurable experience. Among the favorites are chicken korma (pieces of chicken marinated in fresh cream, fine herbs, spices, and nuts and cooked in its own gravy), and *nizami biryani* (rice cooked with lamb or chicken in a blend of spices and herbs). The *lassi*, a sweet yogurt and rosewater beverage, served as dessert or to soothe the fires of the spices, is excellent. The food may be ordered mild, medium hot, or hot.

Wursthaus

4 John F. Kennedy St., at Harvard Sq. ☎ **617/491-7110.** Main courses $8–$14.25. AE, DC, DISC, MC, V. Breakfast Mon–Fri 7:30–11am, Sat–Sun 9am–2pm; lunch Mon–Sat 11am–3pm; dinner Mon–Sat 4pm–midnight, Sun 11:30am–9pm. MBTA: Harvard Sq. (Red Line). GERMAN/AMERICAN.

This famous spot is very German and very crowded. The bar with its attached eating counter is always jammed with university teachers, students, politicians, passersby, and occasional businesspersons. The Wursthaus claims to have the world's largest selection of foreign beers (128 in all) and specializes in such items as bratwurst, knockwurst, sauerbraten, and imported wieners. More than 30 varieties of sandwiches are also available.

11 Charlestown

✪ Olives

10 City Sq., Charlestown. ☎ **627/242-1999.** Reservations for parties of six or more. Main courses $15.95–$30. AE, DC, MC, V. Dinner Tues–Fri 5:30–10pm, Sat 5–10:30pm. MBTA: Bunker Hill Community College (Orange Line). ECLECTIC.

This small, informal bistro, located in the shadow of Bunker Hill, is the hottest spot in town. Because reservations are not accepted, patrons line up shortly after 5pm in order to get a table when the doors open at 5:30. If you don't get there by 5:45, there's a two-hour wait for the next seating. (You can wait in a nearby lounge if you're not too hungry.) Todd English, chef and co-owner with his wife, Olivia, has a magic touch with food; he's been honored as one of the best new chefs in America by *Food and Wine* magazine. There is an open kitchen in the rear of the restaurant with a slow-turning rotisserie and a huge brick oven. To start, try the garlicky shrimp minestrone with white bean cannelloni. My choice of the pastas would be the piccolo pumpkin "pillows" with lobster, toasted hazelnuts, and a spiced ginger *mascarpone crema.* An excellent entrée for those who love seafood is the roasted paella "olivacious" with lobster, clams, mussels, assorted fish, and saffron rice, served in an aromatic broth. Vegetarians will love the "white bean waffle" served on ratatouille with a warm exotic bean salad and grilled fennel in a roasted tomato and olive glaze. For dessert, go for the Falling Chocolate Cake with raspberry sauce and vanilla ice cream. The wine list is extensive.

12 The South End

The South End, an area known for its old brownstones and young professionals, has made its mark on Boston maps by virtue of the excellent dining offered at several highly acclaimed bistros.

Botolph's on Tremont

569 Tremont St. ☎ **617/424-8577.** Main courses $6.50–$12.95, sandwiches $6.25–$7, grilled pizzas $5.95–$9.95. AE, MC, DC, DISC, V. Daily 11:30am–11:30pm. MBTA: Back Bay (Orange Line). ITALIAN.

This young spinoff of St. Botolph Restaurant in the Back Bay is a friendly neighborhood place, open for lunch and dinner, with sandwiches, grilled pizzas, pasta, and risotto combined with meat, chicken, or fish. The pan-seared duck breast and Asian rice noodles with ginger, scallions, and Montrachet demiglace was intriguing. Among the listed pizzas you can choose a six-onion pizza with five cheeses or a broccoli, spinach, and asparagus pizza with roasted plum tomatoes and assorted cheeses. It's a small storefront restaurant, long and narrow, but the plants and paintings by local artists (which change monthly) create a comfortable ambience.

✪ Hamersley's Bistro

553 Tremont St. ☎ **617/423-2700.** Reservations recommended. Main courses $18.50–$27. Petit Bistro Menu $30. AE, DISC, MC, V. Dinner only, Mon–Sat 6–10pm, Sun 6–9:30pm. MBTA: Back Bay/South End (Orange Line). ECLECTIC.

Created by the husband-and-wife team Gordon and Fiona Hamersley, Hamersley's has been able to establish itself as one of Boston's outstanding eateries. The restaurant offers a limited number of entrées, but each one emphasizes taste and texture. For example, the roast chicken is crispy on the outside, moist inside, flavored with a marinade of garlic, lemon, and parsley and served with roast potato, roast onions, and whole cloves of baked garlic that become sweet when cooked. There are several seafood dishes, such as brook trout stuffed with a scallop-crawfish soufflé and served with a champagne sauce; vegetarian plates, the best of which is the fire-roasted stuffed red pepper served with spicy black beans and white rice; and an excellent Moroccan-inspired braised lamb with chickpeas and couscous. Chocolate lovers will enjoy the Big Warm Chocolate Brownie served with strawberries and flamed in brandy. Those with more "exotic" tastebuds should try the coconut ice cream served with a warm guava compote. The menu changes seasonally. Some excellent and expensive vintages are featured on the wine list, and wines by the glass are also available. There is valet parking.

Icarus

3 Appleton St. ☎ **617/426-1790.** Reservations recommended. Main courses $18.50–$29. Sun brunch main courses $5–$10. AE, CB, DC, MC, V. Sun–Thurs 6–10pm, Fri 6–11pm, Sat 5:30–11pm. Sun brunch 11am–3pm. MBTA: Arlington St. (Green Line) or Back Bay/South End (Orange Line). ECLECTIC.

Icarus's attractive, two-tiered dining room may be tucked away below street level, but devotees of top-level cuisine have made it a popular South End dining spot. The restaurant's stylish decor includes period furniture and dark wood trim. Chef Chris Douglass, also an owner, prepares choice local seafoods, poultry, meats, and produce in a combination of national and regional styles to create imaginative menus. Offerings may include morel and foie gras soup or baked goat cheese gnocchi in tomato and chive cream to start. Recent main courses of note were the pan-roasted pork tenderloin with dried cherries and mustard; and the grilled rabbit glazed with pomegranate, tomato, and rosemary over cannellini beans. And don't skip the desserts—they range from *gâteau chocolat* to fruit sorbets, and they're all excellent. Valet parking is available.

13 Brookline

Rubin's

500 Harvard St., Brookline. ☎ **617/731-8787.** Reservations not accepted. Main courses $8–$16.95. No credit cards. Mon–Thurs 10am–8pm, Fri 9am–midafternoon, Sun 9am–8pm. Closed Sat. MBTA: Harvard Ave. stop (Green Line, B train). KOSHER DELI.

There are some small kosher restaurants in the Brookline area, but Rubin's is the "big one," serving meat and deli entrées and some fish, as it has for more than 65 years. It maintains the highest standards of kashrut, so no dairy products are served with the meat—in fact, no dairy is served at all. But there are lots of sandwiches and salads and traditional appetizers such as knishes and stuffed cabbage. Entrées include roast brisket of beef, barbecued chicken, and roast stuffed capon. The noodle pudding makes a good dessert.

Sol Azteca

914A Beacon St., Brookline. ☎ **617/262-0909.** Reservations recommended. Main courses $9.85–$14.75. AE, MC, V. Dinner Mon–Thurs 5–10:30pm, Fri–Sat 5–11pm, Sun 5–10pm. MBTA: St. Mary's St. stop (Green Line, C train). MEXICAN.

Located at the Boston-Brookline border, the three dining rooms in this below ground–level Mexican restaurant have white stucco walls and some beautiful Mexican decorative items. But the focus at Sol Azteca is primarily on the food. There are the traditional dishes—tacos, tostadas, and enchiladas—and there are the chef's specialties that make Sol Azteca worth writing about, for example, shrimp in coriander sauce and the excellent *puerco en adobo* (a pork tenderloin dish marinated in orange juice and chipotle peppers). All entrées include rice, refried beans, and marinated red cabbage. And to cool the flames of the spicy dishes, there's a good, but not great, red sangría.

Vinny Testa's

1700 Beacon St., Brookline. ☎ **617/277-3400.** Reservations recommended for large parties. Main courses $8.95–$26.95. AE, DC, DISC, MC, V. Lunch daily 11:30am–3pm, dinner daily 3pm–closing. MBTA: Green Line, C train to Cleveland Circle. ITALIAN.

Located right on Beacon Street just outside of downtown Boston is Vinny Testa's, the area's hottest Italian restaurant. This large restaurant offers enormous portions—an order of *bruschetta* (peasant bread with olive oil, garlic, tomato, and roasted peppers) is an entire loaf of bread, a half order of pasta could probably feed a small family, and a full order is literally a whole platter. You might try the *cappellini al pomodoro* (angel hair pasta with fresh plum tomatoes, basil, garlic, and olive oil). My favorite meat dish is the *vitello al marsala* (veal scaloppine sautéed in Marsala wine with shallots and mushrooms). It's doubtful that you'll have room for dessert, but if you do, I'd recommend the caffe latte cheesecake (best to stick with the half order) or the cannoli. Espresso and cappuccino are served.

7

What to See & Do in Boston

Boston is an eminently pleasant town for leisurely sightseeing and strolling. You can take in most of the major sights in two or three days, but fitting everything in can be quite complicated (especially if you're here just for a short time). The Suggested Itineraries (below) may help you decide how to allocate your time. You may want to take one or all four of the walking tours described in Chapter 8, "Boston Strolls." No matter what you decide to do, you should try to fit in a visit to the New England Sports Museum (just a couple of years old) and consider a trip with Boston Duck Tours, a new and interesting way to see the city, both on land and in the water (see below for details).

SUGGESTED ITINERARIES

If You Have 1 Day

One day isn't much—you can only scratch the city's surface, but you can still have a lot of fun. To start, follow my first walking tour (see Chapter 8, "Boston Strolls") to Faneuil Hall Marketplace. Along the way you'll cover most of Boston's historic sights. Take the Boston Harbor lunch-hour cruise offered by the Massachusetts Bay Lines (☎ **617/542-8000**). It runs 12:15 to 12:45pm and costs only $2; the boat sails from Long Wharf, located across Atlantic Avenue from Faneuil Hall Marketplace. You can buy refreshments on board or get some take-out food at the marketplace. This cruise is available daily from June through Labor Day, and on weekends (weather permitting) in early spring and after Labor Day. If you don't take the cruise, have lunch at Durgin-Park, a restaurant in the marketplace (see Chapter 6, "Dining," for details). Then continue on the Freedom Trail into the North End. Walk along Washington Street to Downtown Crossing and shop Filene's Basement and the other stores there. Have dinner in one of the city's fine restaurants and then enjoy a panoramic view of Boston by night from the John Hancock Observatory or the Prudential Center Skywalk. If you still have any energy, you might like to end the day with dancing, a drink, and a fabulous view of the city in the lounge at the Top of the Hub restaurant on the 52nd floor of the Prudential Center.

If You Have 2 Days

Spend the morning and early afternoon of the second day at the Museum of Fine Arts. Have lunch at the museum—it has three restaurants at different price levels—or at the cafe at the Isabella Stewart Gardner Museum. Take the "T" to Arlington Street, enjoy the Public Garden, and explore Charles Street and the rest of Beacon Hill. Or perhaps you'd rather spend your day shopping on Newbury and Boylston streets.

If You Have 3 Days

Spend the first two days as suggested above. Then, on the third day, begin to explore the major sights in the Greater Boston area. If you have a car, drive to Cambridge; you can park at the underground garage at the Charles Hotel. Explore Harvard Square and Harvard Yard. Have lunch in Harvard Square, then drive to Lexington and Concord and visit the Minuteman National Historic Park. You might then return to Cambridge for dinner. If you still have energy, browse the book and record shops, and then head to the House of Blues for some live entertainment.

If You Have 4 Days

Follow the suggestions above for the first three days. On the fourth day, visit one of Boston's interactive museums—the Computer Museum, the Children's Museum, or the Boston Museum of Science. If you choose the Computer Museum or the Children's Museum, you will be near Long Wharf, where you can take the 55-minute Inner Harbor/ *USS Constitution* sail. Boat trips are scheduled between 10:30am and 4:30pm. If, on the other hand, you visit the Boston Museum of Science, take a boat trip when leaving the museum up the Charles River from the museum, or from the nearby CambridgeSide Galleria shopping complex, which is also home to the New England Sports Museum.

If You Have 5 Days

Select from the above suggestions for the first four days. On your last day, perhaps you'd like to take a trip outside Boston (see Chapter 11). You might drive north to Salem to explore New England's maritime history at the museums there, then continue to Gloucester and Rockport for scenery and seafood. Or you might go south, to Plymouth and Plimoth Plantation and to the old New England village of Sandwich on Cape Cod. If you don't have a car, you can sail to Provincetown at the tip of the Cape. A boat leaves from Commonwealth Pier in Boston at 9:30am and returns at 6:30pm, with a three-hour stopover in Provincetown. When you return, you'll dock near some of Boston's great seafood restaurants. Treat yourself to a special dinner to top off your visit to Boston.

1 The Top Attractions

Boston's most popular attraction is the Quincy Market and Faneuil Hall Marketplace complex—it draws 14 million visitors a year. The

Boston Attractions

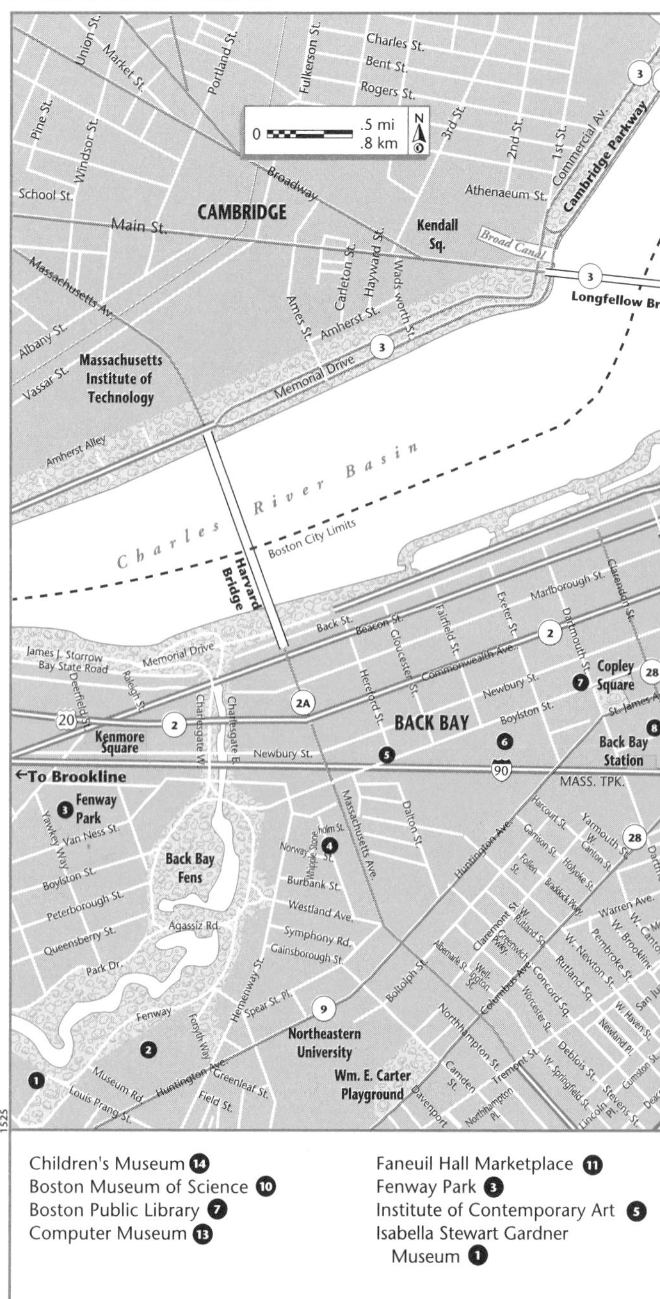

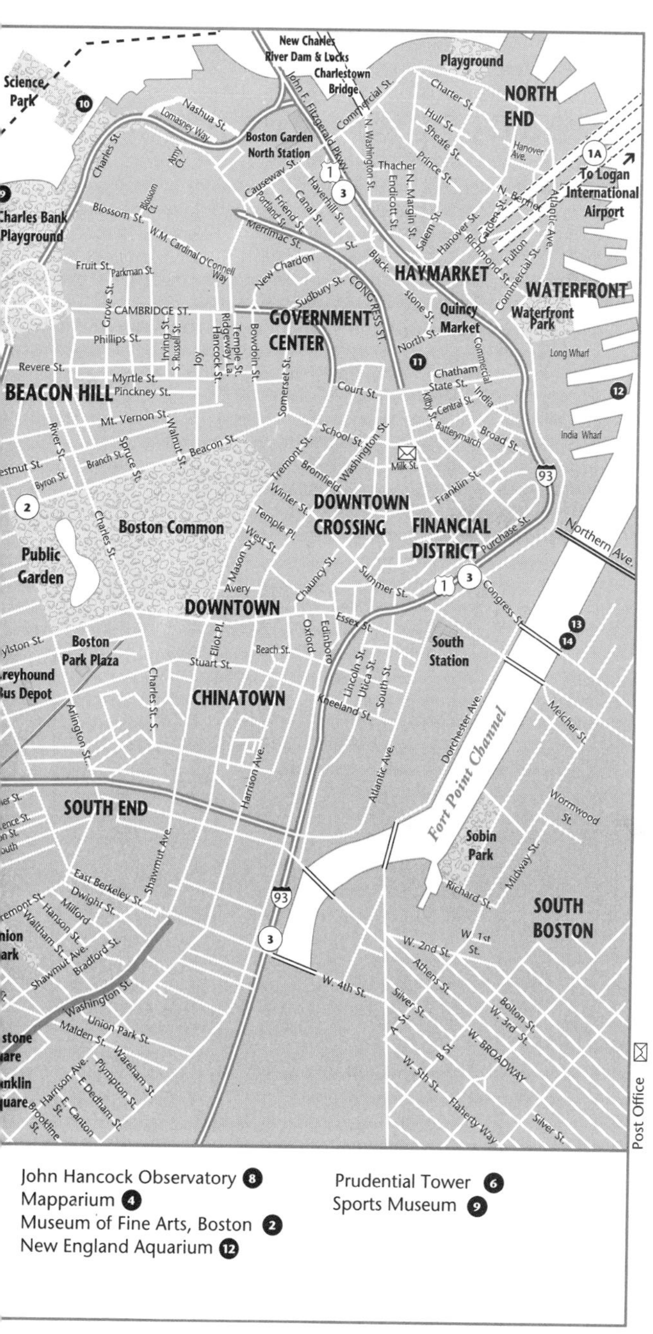
New Charles River Dam & Locks
Charlestown Bridge
Playground
NORTH END
Science Park
Nashua St.
Lomasney Way
Boston Garden North Station
John F. Fitzgerald Pkwy.
Commercial St.
N. Washington St.
Charter St.
Hull St.
Sheafe St.
Prince St.
Hanover Ave.
To Logan International Airport
Charles St.
Amy Ct.
Causeway St.
Friend St.
Portland St.
Canal St.
Haverhill St.
Thacher
Endicott St.
N. Margin St.
Salem St.
Hanover St.
Richmond St.
Garden Ct.
N. Bennet
Fulton
Atlantic Ave.
Charles Bank Playground
Blossom St.
Blossom Ct.
W.M. Cardinal O'Connell Way
Merrimac St.
New Chardon
Black- stone St.
HAYMARKET
Commercial St.
WATERFRONT
Waterfront Park
Fruit St.
Parkman St.
Grove St.
CAMBRIDGE ST.
Sudbury St.
CONGRESS ST.
GOVERNMENT CENTER
Quincy Market
Phillips St.
Irving St.
S. Russell St.
Joy
Temple St.
Ridgeway La.
Hancock St.
Bowdoin St.
North St.
Commercial
Long Wharf
Revere St.
Myrtle St.
Pinckney St.
BEACON HILL
Somerset St.
Court St.
Chatham
State St.
Kilby St.
Central St.
India
Mt. Vernon St.
Walnut St.
School St.
Washington St.
Batterymarch
Broad St.
India Wharf
River St.
Spruce St.
Beacon St.
Tremont St.
Branch St.
Bromfield
Milk St.
Franklin St.
Chestnut St.
Byron St.
Winter St.
DOWNTOWN CROSSING
FINANCIAL DISTRICT
Purchase St.
Northern Ave.
Boston Common
Temple Pl.
West St.
Mason St.
Public Garden
Charles St.
Avery
Chauncy St.
Summer St.
Congress St.
DOWNTOWN
Essex St.
Boylston St.
Boston Park Plaza
Eliot Pl.
Beach St.
Oxford
Edinboro
South Station
Greyhound Bus Depot
Stuart St.
Lincoln St.
Utica St.
South St.
Charles St. S.
CHINATOWN
Kneeland St.
Arlington St.
Harrison Ave.
Atlantic Ave.
Dorchester Ave.
Fort Point Channel
Melcher St.
SOUTH END
Wormwood St.
Shawmut Ave.
Sobin Park
Midway St.
East Berkeley St.
Dwight St.
Milford
Tremont St.
Hanson St.
Waltham St.
Shawmut Ave.
Bradford St.
Richard St.
SOUTH BOSTON
W. 1st St.
W. 2nd St.
Athens St.
W. 4th St.
Washington St.
Silver St.
Bolton St.
W. 3rd St.
A St.
B St.
W. BROADWAY
Union Park St.
Malden St.
Wareham St.
Plympton St.
Harrison Ave.
E. Dedham St.
E. Canton St.
Brookline St.
W. 5th St.
Flaherty Way
Silver St.
Post Office
John Hancock Observatory 8
Mapparium 4
Museum of Fine Arts, Boston 2
New England Aquarium 12
Prudential Tower 6
Sports Museum 9

What's Special About Boston

History

- The Freedom Trail, which will acquaint you with some parts of Boston's rich trove of colonial and Revolutionary War history.

Architecture

- Massachusetts State House (1798), the gold-domed masterpiece of Charles Bulfinch.
- Old North Church (1723), with its beautiful steeple, where the lanterns were hung on the night of April 18, 1775.
- Christian Science Center, with the Mother Church and tower dramatized in its reflecting pool.
- John Hancock Tower (1974), the mirror-glass tower designed by I. M. Pei and his firm.
- The 19th-century Federal-style homes on Beacon Hill.

Museums

- Museum of Fine Arts, Boston, ranked one of the best in the country. Noted for its Impressionist paintings and Egyptian and Nubian collections.
- Isabella Stewart Gardner Museum, an authentic copy of a Renaissance palace, with valuable art and a glass-roofed courtyard with seasonal displays of flowers and shrubs.

Public Parks and Gardens

- Public Garden, with its lagoon and swan boats.
- Arnold Arboretum, acres of trees and plants from around the world. Famous for Lilac Sunday in May.

Special Events

- First Night, a New Year's Eve celebration with ice sculptures, performances, street music, parades, and fireworks.
- Boston Marathon, run on Patriot's Day (third Monday in April)—26 miles from Hopkinton to Boston's Copley Square.

For the Kids

- Children's Museum—it's fun for adults, too.
- Boston Museum of Science, with hands-on scientific and technical exhibits.
- Computer Museum, chock-full of wondrous machines and a huge walk-through computer.
- Boston Tea Party Ship and Museum, where everyone gets a turn throwing a chest of tea into the harbor. (They're attached to ropes so they can be retrieved.)
- The New England Aquarium, from which you can take whale-watching cruises.

Freedom Trail—covered at length in Chapter 8, "Boston Strolls"—is second, tallying about 5 million visitors a year. It's followed by the

Museum of Fine Arts, the Boston Museum of Science, and *Constitution,* each attracting about 1 million people annually.

Boston's museums are among the finest in the United States and will please a wide variety of interests, including art, science, history, transportation, plants, aquatic environments, and animal life. Many of these museums include free tours with the price of admission. Such tours are usually given by docents (volunteers trained as guides)—call ahead for tour times so you can plan the rest of your day.

✪ Faneuil Hall Marketplace

Between North, Congress, and State sts. and I-93. ☎ **617/338-2323.** Marketplace Mon–Sat 10am–9pm, Sun noon–6pm; but some restaurants open early for Sun brunch and remain open until 2am daily. MBTA: Orange Line or Blue Line to State St., Orange Line to Haymarket, or Green Line to Government Center.

An exciting part of the Boston landscape, Faneuil Hall and environs is a miniature city in itself, jam-packed with shops, restaurants, exhibits, food markets, entertainment, and a swinging nightlife. The three-building complex, which is linked to Faneuil Hall by walkways and a plaza of brick, cobblestone, and granite, is in the National Register of Historic Places, but this place is *living* history—people of all kinds mingling, shopping, and eating in a bazaarlike atmosphere that still feels a little like a market in old-time Boston. The main structure, a three-level Greek revival–style building, opened on August 26, 1976, 150 years after Mayor Josiah Quincy opened the original market. The South Market Building opened on that date in 1977, and the North Market Building on the same date in 1978.

The copper-domed **Quincy Market Building** is packed with dining choices. Check out the unique items on the **Bull Market Pushcarts,** located under the North (and South) Canopy of Quincy Market. Over 100 New England artisans and entrepreneurs sell their wares here. And don't forget to buy some flowers at the stalls or in the **Greenhouse,** open 24 hours.

After a quick breather you might opt to try the **South Canopy** on the other side of the promenade—with expensive gift stores, high-fashion boutiques, and home-furnishing shops adorning its three levels, as well as an information booth (see Chapter 9, "Shopping," for details). There you'll find **Seaside Restaurant** (no view of the sea) and the bustling **Cricket's Restaurant** with its glass-canopied "Palm Court." At night the promenade between the Quincy and South buildings glitters with lights illuminating the shops, flower boxes, trees, and young entertainers who offer music, mime, and juggling.

The **North Market Building** has posh retail stores, offices, and the famous **Durgin-Park Restaurant,** where brusque service is not only expected, but thoroughly enjoyed by the clientele.

There are parking lots nearby, and multilevel parking garages at Dock Square, Haymarket Square, the Aquarium, and Post Office Square.

✪ Museum of Fine Arts, Boston

465 Huntington Ave. ☎ **617/267-9300.** Adults $8 when the entire museum is open, $6 when only the West Wing is open. Students and senior citizens $6 when

the entire museum is open, $5 when only the West Wing is open. Children age 6–17 $3.50 when the entire museum is open, $3 when only the West Wing is open. Children under 6 free. There may be an extra charge for special exhibits. Free admission for all, Wed 4–9:45pm. No admission fee for those visiting only the Museum Shop (there is also a holiday Museum gift shop located in the Copley Place shopping galleries at 100 Huntington Ave.), restaurants, library, or auditoria. Entire museum, Tues and Thurs–Sat 10am–4:45pm; Wed 10am–9:45pm; Sun 10am–5:45pm; West Wing only, Thurs–Fri 5–9:45pm. Closed Mon and major holidays. MBTA: Museum of Fine Arts (Green Line, E train).

Like the Metropolitan Museum of Art in New York (to which it ranks second among all the great museums of the country), this museum is enormously popular, usually drawing long-line crowds for its special exhibits. But even without anything special going on there is enough here to hold your attention for days—or at least many hours. The century-old museum is famous for its Asian and Old Kingdom Egyptian collections, medieval tapestries, and Buddhist temple, as well as American and European art. Some particular favorites are the Americans: Whistler, John Singer Sargent, and Childe Hassam, whose superb portraits and paintings recall the early days of the colony and the country as well as lovely old Boston.

The main entrance to the museum is in the **West Wing,** a contemporary granite I. M. Pei structure that contrasts sharply with the original building. A 200-foot-long curved skylight extends the length of the wing, which has climate-controlled galleries, an auditorium, gift shop, and an atrium with a tree-lined sidewalk cafe. The glass-walled **Fine Arts Restaurant,** on the second floor of the West Wing, has fine gourmet cuisine. The **Galleria Cafe** serves light meals, and there is a cafeteria on the premises as well. Pick up a floor plan at the information desk or take one of the free guided tours. (There's free coat and package checking just off the main lobby.)

The museum is located between Huntington Avenue and the Fenway. If you're driving, you can park in the garage or lot off Museum Road.

Boston Museum of Science

Science Park. ☎ **617/723-2500.** To either the exhibit halls or the Mugar Omni Theater, $7 adults, $5 children age 3–14, free for children under 3. To the Hayden Planetarium or the laser theater, $6 adults, $4 children age 3–14, free for children under 3. Tickets to two or three parts of the complex available at discounted prices. Daily 9am–5pm (until 7pm in the summer and on certain holidays), Fri until 9pm. Closed Thanksgiving Day, Christmas. MBTA: Science Park (Green Line); the North Station commuter rail stop is a 10-minute walk from the museum.

This museum complex has something for everyone. Young children, teenagers, adults—everyone seems to be fascinated by the engaging, exciting hands-on exhibits at the Museum of Science. You can, for example, pat a reptile, confront a live owl or porcupine eyeball to eyeball, "stop" a water drop in midair, weigh yourself on a scale—in moon measurements—or climb into a space module. Exhibits run the gamut from a giant chicken-egg incubator to a life-size replica of a tyrannosaur to a gargantuan magnifying glass. "The Big Dig" exhibit takes museum-goers on a tour of Boston's Central Artery project. The exhibit, planned and executed in conjunction with state and federal transportation officials, includes cutaways of vehicles, a computer program that allows visitors the opportunity to "work" as highway planners or crane operators, a simulated elevator ride into an excavation site, and several other interactive exhibits. There's also a brand-new preschool "Discovery Center" to help children become interested in science early in life.

There are fascinating "shows" at the museum, too. The **Thomson Theater of Electricity** produces artificial lightning twice daily and has an exhibit on the human brain where you can test your brain's reactions to external stimuli. The **Charles Hayden Planetarium** takes you through the New England sky and across the cosmos with daily star shows. On weekends the planetarium hosts rock 'n' roll laser programs. The **Mugar Omni Theater,** one of only 17 in the country, is the biggest show in town. That is, it has the world's largest film format, 10 times larger than the conventional 35mm film; a four-story domed screen 76 feet in diameter; and a sound system with 84 speakers inside the screen. Images wrap around on all sides of the viewer, creating a "you are there" sensation, whether it's cavorting with penguins under Antarctic icebergs or whizzing through outer space. The films change every four to six months.

Since the capacities of the theaters and planetarium are limited, I suggest you buy your show tickets (they cost extra) when you enter the museum, even if it's quite some time before the performance. That way you'll be sure to get a seat. It's a good idea to call ahead for reservations. The museum is also host to national and international traveling exhibitions. Check to see what's featured when you're in town. The museum has its own parking garage.

✪ Isabella Stewart Gardner Museum

280 The Fenway. ☎ **617/566-1401.** $7 adults, $5 seniors and college students with valid ID, $3 youths ages 12–17 and college students on Wed, free for children under 12. Tues–Sun 11am–5pm and some Mon national holidays. Closed Mon. MBTA: Museum stop (Green Line, E train).

Walking into this museum is like stepping back 100 years into a Venetian *palazzo* out of a Henry James novel. Mrs. Gardner, the wife of a wealthy Bostonian, lived in this house for 22 years and oversaw its design; much of the art collection within was chosen with the help of her friend Bernard Berenson. The *pièce de résistance* is a breathtaking interior skylit courtyard filled year-round with fresh flowers (lilies at Easter, chrysanthemums in the fall, poinsettias at Christmas). Each floor is filled with Isabella Gardner's treasures: Whistlers, Sargents, Matisses, and Titians; Italian religious masterpieces (including Raphael's *Pietà*); stained-glass windows; and exquisite antique furniture. A new special exhibition gallery, which opened in September 1992, features three or four changing exhibitions a year.

Try to come for one of the concerts given in the magnificent **Tapestry Room,** with its heavy-beamed ceiling, superbly tiled floor, and priceless tapestries. They're given at 1:30pm on Saturday and Sunday, from September through May. Concert prices (in addition to museum admission) are $4 for adults and $2 for seniors and students.

Lunch and desserts are served in a small cafe, and a variety of unique gifts are available in the museum's gift shop.

✪ New England Aquarium

Central Wharf. ☎ **617/973-5200.** $8.50 adults, $4.50 children 3–11, $7.50 senior citizens. Children under 3 free. $1 off for everyone on Thurs 4–7:30pm and on Wed in summer. Mon–Tues and Fri 9am–6pm, Wed–Thurs 9am–8pm, Sat–Sun and holidays 9am–7pm. Winter hours vary, so call ahead. Closed Christmas Day and Thanksgiving Day. MBTA: Aquarium (Blue Line).

This aquarium will fascinate the whole family. Buy an exhibit guide. While you're looking it over, you can watch the ground floor's resident penguin family. Then work your way up on the ramp alongside the four-story, 200,000-gallon, glass-enclosed **Giant Ocean Tank**—one of the largest cylindrical saltwater tanks in the world, with a Caribbean coral reef.

Five times daily you can watch scuba divers feed the main tank's huge sharks, turtles, and moray eels. Other exhibit tanks are stocked with more than 7,000 specimens of mammals, reptiles, amphibians, fish, and invertebrates. The penguins and harbor seals are always fun to watch; and at the hands-on exhibit "Edge of the Sea," visitors can pick up tide-pool animals, including sea stars, horseshoe crabs, and sea urchins. The 1,000-seat floating amphitheater, **Discovery,** has marine mammal presentations five times daily. The aquarium's newest exhibit, "Jellies," offers a close-up and highly educational view of many different types of "jellyfish."

Note: The aquarium sponsors whale-watching expeditions daily from mid-April through mid-October. They take you several miles out to sea to the Stellwagen Bank, feeding ground for the whales as they follow their migratory paths from Newfoundland to Provincetown. Rates are $25 for adults, $20 for senior citizens and college students, $18 for children age 12 to 18, and $17 for children age 3 to 11.

The Computer Museum

300 Congress St. ☎ **617/426-2800** or 423-6758 for the "Talking Computer." $7 adults, $5 students and senior citizens, free for children under 5. Tickets are $5 on Sun 3–5pm. Fall, winter, and spring Tues–Sun 10am–5pm; summer daily 10am–6pm. For tour schedules, call Talking Computer. MBTA: South Station (Red Line). Walk north on Atlantic Ave. and make a right on Congress St.

It's hard to believe that computers have been around long enough to have a museum dedicated to them, but these marvels of technology have a fascinating past. This museum, located next to the Children's Museum at Museum Wharf, has more than half an acre of displays, 125 hands-on exhibits, and three theaters—one offers a robot show. Visitors can make movies and music on a personal computer, design a car on a graphics terminal, have a conversation with a talking computer, or test their deal-making skills against a computerized strawberry vendor. Of interest to the harried parent might be the "Direction Assistant," one of the museum's 25 "smart exhibits"—it calculates the shortest route between any two points in Boston. And to discover the inner workings of a computer on a really big scale, you can take a stroll within the world's only **Walk-Through Computer™,** a working model 50 times actual size with a giant keyboard programmed for the visitor to operate. A major technical upgrade was completed in October of 1995, for the Walk-Through Computer's fifth anniversary. "Tools & Toys: the Amazing Personal Computer" is a 3,600-square-foot, $1 million exhibit, with 30 interactive stations offering applications on a variety of computer systems used by people with special needs. In November of 1994 the museum opened a global computer networks exhibit, "The Networked Planet."

Call the **Talking Computer** for a listing of special programs and events. And pick up some chocolate "chips" and microchip jewelry in the **Museum Store.**

Institute of Contemporary Art

955 Boylston St. ☎ **617/266-5152.** $5.25 adults, $3.25 students, $2.25 seniors and children under 16; free for everyone on Thurs 5–9pm. Thurs noon–9pm, Wed, Fri–Sun noon–5pm. Closed major holidays. MBTA: Hynes/ICA (Green Line, B, C, or D train).

Across from the Prudential Center, this handsomely remodeled Richardson-style building showcases 20th-century art, including painting, sculpture, photography, and video. The institute also offers a rich variety of activities—films, lectures, music, video, poetry, and an educational program for children and adults.

Mapparium, Christian Science Publishing Society

1 Norway St. ☎ **617/450-2000.** Free. Tues–Fri 10am–4pm. "A Light Unto My Path" exhibit Sun 11:15am–2pm, Wed–Sat 10am–4pm. Closed Thanksgiving Day, Christmas Day, and New Year's Day. MBTA: Symphony (Green Line, E train).

You can zoom out of the world at the planetarium, but if you want a chance to walk right *inside* the world and view it from a new perspective, visit the Mapparium. It's located in the complex of Christian Science buildings near the intersection of Huntington and Massachusetts avenues. You'll find yourself in an enormous room the exact shape of a globe, illuminated from the outside and explored via a bridgeway, under, above, and around which are various parts of the globe. Aesthetically, it's a delightful experience; the colors are done in the style of old European stained glass. The acoustic quality is distinctive—the hard surface of the room does not absorb sound, and one's voice bounces off. Various characteristics of the world are pointed out: where the international dateline falls, which are the deepest parts of the ocean, and much more. There is also a Bible exhibit, "A Light Unto My Path," the only one of its kind. It features a 20-minute film and slide program, an audiovisual time line, and 12 journeys of great figures of the Bible that you can follow on a sculptured map as you listen to the descriptions.

Call ahead for information on guided tours of the Mapparium and the Mother Church.

Boston Public Library

666 Boylston St. ☎ **617/536-5400.** Free. Mon–Thurs 9am–9pm, Fri–Sat 9am–5pm. Sun (Oct–May only) 1pm–5pm. Closed Sunday and legal holidays. MBTA: Copley Sq. (Green Line).

The Boston Public Library, known to locals as the BPL, is really a museum and historic building as well as a library. First opened to the public in 1852, the original Italian Renaissance–style building, with

On the Waterfront

Boston's history is tied to the sea—early fortunes were made by the clipper ship route, and colonial commercial life centered around the waterfront. While Boston was rebuilding, it turned to the source of its origins for inspiration. A small city within the city took shape as the old wharves were rebuilt and ramshackle warehouses transformed into chic restaurants, condos, and offices. In Boston society today, you have "arrived" if you have a waterfront address.

One good place to check out the waterfront rebirth is **Waterfront Park.** The walks are paved in brick, cobblestone, and granite, and there's a "tot lot" with a wading pool. You can sit on the terrace steps facing the harbor. Buy a picnic lunch and perhaps a bottle of wine from the shops in nearby Faneuil Hall Marketplace or the Haymarket.

To get there, your **MBTA** options include the Aquarium stop (Blue Line) and Government Center (Green Line), the latter involving a pleasant walk to the sea via City Hall Plaza and Faneuil Hall Marketplace.

facade windows modeled after the St. Genevieve Library in Paris, is joined to a very functional modern building added in 1972. Both maintain the same roofline and have the same pink granite facade. The older building (the **Research Library**) is a registered National Historic Landmark and contains murals and artwork by Daniel Chester French, John Singer Sargent, and John Singleton Copley. There is also a tranquil courtyard where you can read, relax—or hold a secret rendezvous. In the 1972 addition (the **General Library**), nine skylights in the Great Hall form a central core extending the full height of the library. The library has more than 6 million books and more than 11 million other items, such as prints, photographs, films, and sound recordings. Look for your hometown paper in the newspaper room.

2 More Attractions

ART GALLERIES

The big museums are the beginning, but no means the end, of the lively Boston art scene, which is concentrated in two distinctive areas: Newbury Street and the South Street area.

Several elegant blocks of **Newbury Street** between Arlington and Exeter streets are home to more than two dozen of the finest contemporary galleries in America. Plan to spend an afternoon taking a leisurely stroll to see the paintings, sculpture, and prints at these impressive galleries.

The **South Street** area, across the way from South Station and near the theater and financial districts, is a newer art center. There are about a dozen galleries now, but more dealers are planning to move to the area, which some compare to New York's SoHo. While there, look for a little restaurant at 150 Kneeland Street, called the **Loading Zone BBQ.** The name refers to the fact that the space was previously a loading zone; today the restaurant's tables—that's right, tables—are covered with works of art that you can purchase or just enjoy.

BREWERIES

Commonwealth Brewing

138 Portland St. ☎ **617/523-8383.** Free. Sun–Thurs 11:30am–midnight, Fri–Sat until 1am (food is served until 10 and 11pm, respectively). Free tours, Sat at 3:30pm, Sun at noon. MBTA: North Station or Haymarket (Green or Orange Line).

The brewing equipment here is in the basement, and guides explain the whole process, from hops to ale. On the street level is a restaurant and bar, so you can buy a glass of their English-style brew right where it is made. Commonwealth Brewing is also a popular nightspot.

Mass. Bay Brewing Co.

306 Northern Ave. ☎ **617/574-9551.** Free. The brewery offers tours (no charge) Fri–Sat at 1pm. MBTA: South Station (Red Line).

This company brews and bottles Harpoon Ale in small batches without preservatives. Visitors can sample the beer and see the various stages of processing, including the bottling and labeling of this handcrafted beer. It's best to drive here, since parking is available and the nearest MBTA stop is a mile away.

Boston Beer Company

30 Germania St., Jamaica Plain. ☎ **617/522-9080.** $1 requested for guided tour; proceeds go to charity. Tours are offered Thurs at 2pm, on Sat at noon and 2pm. MBTA: Stony Brook (Orange Line); you will exit onto Boylston St. Turn left, walk two blocks, and look for the Samuel Adams sign.

Named for the famous founding father, a brewer as well as a statesman and patriot, Samuel Adams Boston Lager has been served at the White House and is the only American beer allowed to be imported and served in West Germany. The Boston Beer Company is where Samuel Adams beer is brewed. Varieties include Samuel Adams Boston Lager, Samuel Adams Double Bock Beer, Samuel Adams Summer Wheat Beer and Samuel Adams Dark Wheat Beer. The brewers have a 1/2-hour-long guided tour in which the history and process of brewing are explained. Free tastings are offered to those who can prove they're old enough, and the brewery has a souvenir shop. If you plan to drive here, call the brewery first; they will provide the rather complicated directions. You may also call **617/522-9080** for recorded directions.

CAMBRIDGE

The relationship between Boston and Cambridge is somewhat similar to that of Berkeley and San Francisco. It's just a short ride on the MBTA's Red Line from the Park Street Station across the Charles River to Harvard Square Station in the center of Cambridge, and every visitor should see it.

To get an overall picture of Cambridge, stop first at the **Cambridge Discovery, Inc.** booth at the Harvard Square subway entrance. The blue information booth is staffed by trained volunteers who will give you maps and brochures and answer questions about the city. From June through mid-October, it is open from 9am to 6pm Monday through Saturday and the rest of the year until 5pm. Hours on Sunday are 1 to 5pm. Also from mid-June through Labor Day there are guided tours that include the entire old Cambridge area. Check at the booth about rates, meeting places, and times, or call them (☎ **617/497-1630**). If you prefer to sightsee on your own, you can purchase an old Cambridge or East Cambridge walking guide prepared by the Cambridge Historical Commission for $1. If you would like to arrange a special tour, write to Cambridge Discovery, Inc., P.O. Box 1987, Cambridge, MA 02238.

Spend a little time exploring **Harvard Square.** Here you can buy a newspaper from almost anywhere in the world and shop at the big Harvard Coop (rhymes with "soup"). Then wander along **Brattle Street,** with its great little bookstores and boutiques; perhaps have tea and pastry or lunch at the charming Blacksmith House near the spot where Longfellow's Village Smithy once stood. Farther along, at 105 Brattle Street, is **Longfellow House** (☎ **617/876-4491**), where the books and furniture have remained intact since the poet died there in 1882; the house also served as Gen. George Washington's headquarters in 1775–76. It's open Wednesday to Sunday from 10am to 4:30pm, except Thanksgiving Day, Christmas, and New Year's Day; tours are offered at 10:45am, 11:45am, 1pm, 2pm, 3pm, and 4pm. Admission is $2 for adults, free for children under 16 and seniors.

On adjoining Mount Auburn Street, you might want to see **Mount Auburn Cemetery,** where Longfellow, Oliver Wendell Holmes, and Mary Baker Eddy are buried. It is also noted for its beautiful flowering trees and shrubs, as well as its large indigenous bird population—a lot of birdwatchers come here. And opposite Cambridge Common, north of the square, is the 18th-century **Christ Church,** which was used as a barracks during the American Revolution.

HARVARD

You will, of course, want to explore **Harvard Yard,** which you can do by walking about on your own or by taking a free guided tour available through the **Information Center,** Holyoke Center, 1350 Massachusetts Avenue (☎ **617/495-1573**).

Some of the university's architectural highlights include the ultra-space-age **Carpenter Center,** designed by Le Corbusier, which manages to be both circular and square at the same time; the **Science Center,** an enormous structure modeled after a Polaroid camera; **Memorial Hall,** with its breathtaking stained-glass windows and vast ceilings; the eight residential houses for undergraduates, styled in Georgian tradition with domes and bell; the imposing **Widener Library** with its 3.4 million books (one of the largest libraries in the country), built by Mrs. Widener in memory of her son who was lost with the sinking of the *Titanic.* (The tours do not go into the libraries, in order not to disturb the readers. You can visit Widener on your own; for the other libraries, you need a Harvard ID.) You may also want to visit Yamasaki's **Center for Behavior Sciences.** Take the elevator up to the 15th floor for a spectacular view of Cambridge. Also worth seeing are the **Loeb Drama Center,** home of the American Repertory Theater, and the **Gutman Library** at the School of Education (across the street from the Loeb), the recipient of many architectural awards. You can also obtain maps, illustrated booklets, and self-guided walking-tour directions at the Information Center.

The **Harvard University Museums of Cultural and Natural History** (24 Oxford St.; ☎ **617/495-3045**) are four famous museums under one roof: The Museum of Comparative Zoology, the Botanical Museum, the Geological and Mineralogical Museum, and the Peabody Museum of Archeology and Ethnology. They offer a wonderful range of exhibits from pre-Columbian art to dinosaurs, including rare gems and the famous "glass flowers." Hours are Monday to Saturday from 9am to 4:15pm, Sunday from 1 to 4:15pm; the museums are closed New Year's Day, July 4th, Thanksgiving Day, and Christmas. Admission is free on Saturday mornings from 9 to 11am. At other times the admission charge is $4 for adults, $3 for students and seniors, $1 for children 3 to 13, children under 3 free. One charge covers admission to all the buildings.

Most unusual of the museums in this complex is the **Botanical Museum**; you don't have to be a botanist to appreciate it. The highlight here is the stunning Ware Collection of Glass Flowers**,** the most unusual—and durable—flower garden in the world. At first glance it's almost impossible to tell that the flowers and plants are not real; even when you *know* they're not, you still want to bend over and sniff the perfume. The flowers are considered the finest example of decorative glasswork every created; they are the masterpieces of two Germans, a father and son named Leopold and Rudolf Blaschka, hired by Harvard to work at their home near Dresden, Germany, from 1887 through 1936. Since Rudolf's death in 1939, no one has been able to duplicate the artistry of the Blaschkas, who "combined the mind of naturalists and the skill of artists in glass."

One of the newest galleries at the **Peabody Museum of Archeology and Ethnology** is the Hall of the North American Indian, where 500 Native American artifacts representing 10 different Indian cultures are dramatically displayed. They range from four imposing totems to miniature dioramas and include woven rugs, longbows, masks, and war bonnets.

The **Harvard University Art Museums**—the Fogg, Arthur M. Sackler, and Busch-Reisinger museums (☎ **617/495-9400** for information on all three)—house some 150,000 works of art in their collections. These distinguished teaching museums are near Harvard Yard and just a short walk from the Harvard Square MBTA station. The art museums are open Monday through Saturday from 10am to 5pm and Sunday from 1 to 5pm; closed major holidays. Admission to the museums is $5 for adults, $4 for senior citizens, $3 for students, and free for children under 18. Admission is free to all on Saturday mornings. One-hour guided tours are available every weekday.

The **Fogg Art Museum,** 32 Quincy Street at Broadway, is best known for its collection of British and American 19th-century paintings and drawings, French paintings and drawings from the 18th century through the Impressionist period, and late medieval Italian paintings.

The **Arthur M. Sackler Museum,** 485 Broadway at Quincy Street, houses Harvard's collection of Asian, ancient, and Islamic art. Included are ancient Chinese jades and cave reliefs, Korean ceramics, Japanese woodblock prints, Roman sculpture, Greek vases, and Persian miniature paintings and calligraphy.

The **Busch-Reisinger Museum** in Werner Otto Hall (enter through the Fogg at 32 Quincy St.) opened in 1991 and is the only museum in the Western hemisphere devoted to the art of northern and central Europe. It is particularly noted for its early 20th-century collections, including works by Klee, Feininger, Kandinsky, Beckmann, and artists and designers associated with the Bauhaus.

Besides Harvard Yard, there's **Radcliffe Yard,** with its own special charm, brick buildings, and stately trees.

MASSACHUSETTS INSTITUTE OF TECHNOLOGY (MIT)

If you'd like to visit the Massachusetts Institute of Technology campus on the Cambridge side of the Charles River, you're perfectly welcome to wander around on your own. Ask for the "Walk Around MIT" map/brochure at the **Information Center** (77 Massachusetts Ave., Cambridge; ☎ **617/253-4795**), which describes the environmental sculpture collection and outstanding architecture. If you have time, take one of the student-guided tours of the campus (about one hour long, at 10am and 2pm from Monday through Friday, starting at the Information Center). You'll see the two Saarinen buildings on Kresge Plaza, the **Nautical Museum, Hayden Library,** and several buildings designed by I. M. Pei.

To get to MIT, take the MBTA Red Line to the Kendall Square station. If you're driving, follow Storrow Drive to Cambridge, or cross the Longfellow Bridge at Massachusetts Avenue and you're at MIT on Memorial Drive. Continue along the drive to your left for the scenic approach to Harvard, or drive straight ahead from the bridge through the traffic of Massachusetts Avenue for the stores/restaurants/theater approach.

GOVERNMENT CENTER

If you remember your history, you know that "Old Boston" was once considered quite revolutionary. So just consider "New Boston" as following tradition when you visit the cluster of buildings in downtown Boston that form the hub of city government, typified by **Boston City Hall,** which overlooks the Faneuil Hall Marketplace. The main approach is across an 8-acre red-brick plaza, comparable—in size only—to St. Peter's Square in Rome. There are fountains at one end, good for foot-dunking in hot weather, and steps for sitting. But there are no trees or benches. The plaza comes alive at times with music and dance performances sponsored by the city—and with demonstrations and protest rallies not sponsored by the city. City Hall itself is regarded as both "one of the great civic buildings of the 20th century" and as a cold, concrete-and-brick monstrosity, depending on whether you're talking to architects or to plain Bostonians. Its critics have called it the "Aztec Tomb," and office workers and visitors say they get lost in the huge connecting passageways; in contrast, designers extol the high lobby with its exhibition areas, the huge glass doors, the light shafts, and the imaginative use of space and irregular shapes and surfaces. There seems to be general agreement that the balcony outside the mayor's office is a great place for royalty—like the ultra-successful Boston Celtics basketball team—to greet the cheering throng below. Form your own opinion by taking one of the free guided tours given weekdays from 10am to 4pm. The building is open from 9am to 5pm, and at times there are worthwhile art and photo exhibits in the lobby. To reach Boston City Hall, follow Tremont Street from the Boston Common to Government Center or take the MBTA to Government Center.

Facing City Hall across the plaza are two more new government buildings: the 26-story **John F. Kennedy Federal Office Building** and the **Center Plaza,** one of the country's longest office buildings.

Take a good look at the gleaming aluminum tower at 600 Atlantic Avenue, opposite South Station. It's the center of operations for the **Federal Reserve Bank of Boston.** One of the most striking features in Boston's cityscape, the 604-foot tower has a dramatic glass-curtain wall and landscaped plaza leading the visitor to the display area on the ground floor.

In the business wing, glass walls allow tour groups to view coin, currency, check-collection, and data-services operations. Tours are usually arranged for groups, but you might be able to join one. Call 617/973-3464 for information.

FOR HISTORY BUFFS

MUSEUMS & ARCHIVES

Boston Tea Party Ship and Museum

Congress Street Bridge. ☎ **617/338-1773.** $6.50 adults, $5.20 students, $3.25 children 6–12, free for children under 6. Ship and museum, Mar 1–Nov 30 daily 9am–dusk (about 6pm in summer, 5pm in winter). Closed Dec 1–Feb 28 and Thanksgiving. Directions: Take the Red Line subway to South Station, walk north on Atlantic Ave. one block past the Federal Reserve Bank, turn right onto Congress St. and walk one block to the water. You'll see the ship there at the Congress Street Bridge.

The events recalled here are very much a part of colonial Boston's struggle for independence. What you'll see is the brig *Beaver II,* a full-size replica of one of the merchant ships emptied by the "Indians" on the night of the tea party raid, and a museum with exhibits outlining the "tea party." You'll get to dump your own bale of tea right into the waters of Boston Harbor. At the nearby Tea Party Store you can buy some tea to take home, and complimentary tea (iced in the summer, hot in the winter) is served.

✪ John F. Kennedy Presidential Library and Museum

Columbia Point on Dorchester Bay. ☎ **617/929-4567.** $6 adults, $4 seniors, $4 students with ID, $2 children age 6–16, free for children under 6. Daily 9am–5pm. MBTA: JFK/U. Mass. (Red Line). Closed Thanksgiving, Christmas, and New Year's Day. Free shuttle bus, which runs every 20 minutes, runs from the station to the library on the hour and the half hour. Directions: From Boston, drive south on the Southeast Expressway (I-93/Route 3) to Exit 15, which is marked "JFK Library," and follow the signs. There is a large parking lot. If that is full, on weekends you can use the adjoining University of Massachusetts lot.

Camelot lives on in this combination library, museum, and educational research center. The concrete-and-glass memorial expertly captures the charisma of the Kennedy years. Perched on a hill overlooking Boston Harbor, the $12 million I. M. Pei architectural masterpiece is home to a maze of documents, photographs, recordings, and film clips that commemorate the life and items of the 35th president of the United States. In addition, all the memorabilia and the historic papers are carefully arranged to give the visitor insight into the American political process and the nature of the presidency.

From the entrance on the mezzanine level, visitors get their first concept of the dramatic tone of the building—the view across the soaring glass-walled pavilion to the sea. That is followed by a poignant 30-minute documentary film evoking the spirit of Kennedy's "New Frontier" years. The exit from the theater leads to the exhibition area, an artful arrangement of galleries organized around a central area that is a replica of the Oval Office in the White House. There are Kennedy's rocking chair and desk, just as he left them when he went to Dallas on November 22, 1963. The exhibits include some 3,000 items and 750 photographs, encompassing the civil rights movement, the Peace Corps, the space program, and the 1960 presidential campaign. Dramatic events are depicted: the Cuban Missile Crisis, the Bay of Pigs, the Berlin Wall visit. You'll also find political cartoons, favorite books, letters, and audiovisuals with the voices of JFK and his mother, Rose Kennedy. To finish your visit dramatically, the exit corridor echoes with taped sounds of the ocean and gulls and leads you out to the spectacular atrium.

Outside the building, JFK's boyhood sailboat, *Victura,* is on a strip of dune grass between the library and the harbor. Behind is the Archives Tower, nine stories of papers, books, films and oral histories of JFK and his brother Robert. The material is available free to scholars and anyone interested in research. There is also a fascinating Ernest Hemingway collection in the tower.

You can spend as much time viewing the exhibits as you wish, but count on at least two hours to see all the highlights. The last film begins at 3:50pm.

Note: A nice way to get to the museum is to take a water taxi from Long Wharf; the taxi, which leaves Long Wharf every 90 minutes from midmorning to late afternoon, takes 40 minutes and costs $2 each way. Call **Boston Harbor Cruises** (☎ **617/227-4321**) or **Bay State Cruises** (☎ **617/723-7800**).

John F. Kennedy National Historic Site

83 Beals St., Brookline. ☎ **617/566-7937.** $1 adults; free for children under 16 and seniors over 62. Wed–Sun 10am–4:30pm. Closed Thanksgiving Day, Christmas, and New Year's Day. MBTA: Coolidge Corner (Green Line, C train); then walk four blocks north on Harvard St.

A few miles away from the Kennedy Library, in Brookline, is the home where Kennedy was born. Restored to the way it was during his early years, it's pure nostalgia for anyone who grew up in the 1920s and 1930s, or for anyone interested in the roots of the family. Guided tours of the house are given at 10:45 and 11:45am and 1, 2, 3, and 4pm by a National Park Services ranger (this is the only way to see the house).

Massachusetts Archives

220 Morrissey Blvd., Columbia Point. ☎ **617/727-2816.** Free. Mon–Fri 9am–5pm, Sat 9am–3:30pm. Closed legal holidays. MBTA: JFK/U. Mass. (Red Line).

Looking for passenger lists of ships that arrived in Boston between 1848 and 1891? Census schedules for Massachusetts dating back to 1790? All that information is on hand here. You can also research old documents, maps, and military and court records going as far back as the Massachusetts Bay Company (1628–29). Knowledgeable staff members are able to help researchers by mail or phone.

The building is also home to the **Commonwealth Museum** (☎ **617/727-9150**), which has videos, slide shows, and other interactive exhibits on the people, places, and politics of Massachusetts. Exhibits change frequently; recently covered topics include witchcraft, the state's labor history, and birds native to Massachusetts.

This interesting complex is adjacent to the Kennedy Library.

The Sports Museum of New England

CambridgeSide Galleria, 100 CambridgeSide Place, Cambridge. ☎ **617/57-SPORT.** $6 adults, $4.50 seniors and children 4–11, children under 4 free. Mon–Sat 10am–9:30pm, Sun 11–7pm. The museum occasionally closes early for private functions, so you might want to call ahead before setting out. MBTA: Walking distance from Lechmere stop (Green Line); shuttle bus from Kendall Square station (Red Line).

The Sports Museum of New England houses a collection of memorabilia from outstanding moments in New England sports history. There are the bats, balls, skates, and sneakers (some at size 15 1/2) that belonged to the superstars of sports. Larger-than-life statues of Larry Bird, Bobby Orr, Eusebio, and Carl Yastrzemski stand by the cases displaying jerseys, baseball cards, programs, and printed articles. Visitors can watch sports highlights in minitheaters modeled after Fenway Park, Boston Garden, and Harvard Stadium. There are nine interactive exhibits, including "Catching Clemens," "In the Net," and "Stump Haggerty" (a sports trivia contest). Newest exhibits include "Boston Bruins: Saluting 70 years of Boston Bruins Hockey History"; and two more interactive exhibits, "Treadwall" (learn how to climb rock walls) and "The Exploder" (measure your vertical leap).

HISTORIC HOUSES

If you're feeling nostalgic, you'll enjoy visiting some of the old houses of Boston that are still standing; here you can get a sense of what life was like among the 19th-century aristocrats and upper middle class—from the inside. One of the most pleasant of these is the **Gibson House Museum** (137 Beacon St.; ☎ **617/267-6338**). Admission is $4, and afternoon tours are given at 1, 2, and 3pm. The museum is open Wednesday through Sunday from May to October, on weekends only from November to April, and is closed on major holidays. It has the kind of Victorian curios that our great-grandparents found essential: petrified-wood hat racks, a sequined pink-velvet pagoda for the cat, a Victrola, and gilt-framed photographs of every relative. What must be one of America's oldest telephones is mounted on a second-floor wall, supplementing the internal network of wired bells once used to summon servants from any part of the house.

Two homes designed by the renowned 18th-century architect Charles Bulfinch (who also designed the Massachusetts State House and the U.S. Capitol) are open for tours and are well worth seeing. **Nichols House Museum** (55 Mount Vernon St.; ☎ **617/227-6993**) is an 1804 Beacon Hill home with beautiful antique furnishings. It's open Tuesday through Saturday with the first tour at 12:15pm, the last tour at 4:15pm (open hours vary, so call ahead). Admission is $4. After the first tour at 12:15pm, they continue every half hour on the quarter hour. The **Harrison Gray Otis House** (141 Cambridge St.; ☎ **617/227-3956**), was the home of the mayor of Boston in 1796 and has been carefully restored to show how a family lived in the early years of the republic. It is close to the Charles Street, Bowdoin Square, and Government Center "T" stops and is open from Tuesday through Friday from noon to 5pm and on Saturday from 10am to 4pm. Tours are given on the hour (the last tour Tuesday through Friday is at 4pm, on Saturday it's at 3pm). Admission is $4 for adults, $3.50 for seniors, $2 for children 12 and under.

The Federal-style Otis House is also the headquarters for the **Society for the Preservation of New England Antiquities (SPNEA).** SPNEA owns and operates 34 house museums and study properties throughout New England. Write or call the society at 141 Cambridge St., Boston, MA 02114 (☎ **617/227-3956**), for brochures, visiting hours, and admission fees to the many historic house museums in the area.

NEIGHBORHOODS

BEACON HILL

Beacon Hill is a historic area that's delightful to stroll through. Located on the northern side of the Boston Common, the neighborhood is rich in architectural gems from the 19th century, especially the gold-domed **State House.** The old brownstone and brick houses are almost exactly as they were when Louisa May Alcott lived at 10 Louisburg Square, Edwin Booth at 29A Chestnut Street, and Julia Ward Howe at 13 Chestnut Street. Happily, the area has now been designated a National Historic Landmark and is safely beyond the reach of developers. One of the oldest black churches in the country, the **African Meeting House,** is on the Hill at 8 Smith Court.

The quaint narrow streets have red-brick sidewalks (a second revolution almost occurred when the city dared to suggest repaving in concrete), gaslight-style lamps, and, in spring and summer, flowering window boxes on most of the town houses. Fashionable **Louisburg Square,** the famed turf of the Boston Brahmins, with its cluster of 22 homes and a beautiful central park, is still home to the old money. The iron-railed square is open only to residents with keys.

When you explore this area, be ready for a lot of walking and climbing. **Charles Street,** with restaurants and boutiques, is at the base of the hill, and everything else goes up. Tourist buses don't make the rounds there—they could probably never turn the narrow corners—and a parking space is impossible to find.

CHINATOWN

Home and shopping center for many of Greater Boston's Chinese families, Chinatown is a tiny, 3-block-long, 12-block-wide area, bounded by the expressway, the downtown shopping district, and the Tufts University medical complex. Take the Green Line to Boylston Street and walk one block to Stuart Street; you can also reach it from the Boston Common area by following Stuart Street to Harrison Avenue and Kneeland Street, through the garment district. (You can drive to Chinatown following this same route, or take the Chinatown exit from the Massachusetts Turnpike extension. Use the parking garage at the Tufts-New England Medical Center on Harrison Avenue. Your landmarks will be red phone booths with pagoda tops and bilingual street signs.)

The best place for window shopping is along Beach, Tyler, and Hudson streets, and Harrison Avenue. Start on Beach Street and walk through the ceremonial **Chinatown Gateway,** which marks the formal entrance to the business district. The gate with its four marble lions was a bicentennial gift from the government of Taiwan. As you browse, look for the poultry stores with live chickens in coops. Go into one of the food stores, examine the exotic wares, perhaps choose some "thousand-year-old eggs" or packaged bird's-nest soup.

You can stop for a snack at **Wai Wai Ice Cream** on Oxford Street and indulge in an iced litchi or iced lotus-seed drink and some almond paste or grass jelly. They also serve chicken, fish bits, and rice dishes. Or you can have Chinese-style brunch at most restaurants. It's called dim sum and consists of assorted Chinese hot hors d'oeuvres. You might like the **Imperial Seafood** (70 Beach St.; ☎ **617/426-8439**); get there before 11am if you want to avoid a long wait. Treat yourself to a winter melon dumpling with a delicious creamy filling, steamed sponge cake, or moon cakes at **Ho Yuen Bakery** (54 Beach St.; ☎ **617/426-8320**), open from 8am to 7:30pm. They'll even bake a birthday cake for you! You can browse in gift shops or relax at one of the many good Chinese restaurants (see Chapter 6 for details).

If you're in Boston at the time of the Chinese New Year (January or February, depending on the moon), join the crowds to watch the traditional festivities, including the dragons weaving up and down the streets amid Chinese music and loud firecrackers. In August, try to see the Festival of the August Moon, a local street fair. Call the **Chinese Merchants Association,** 20 Hudson St. (☎ **617/482-3972**), for information on special events. The bronze bas-reliefs on this building represent the eight immortals of Taoism, and there are mirrored plaques along Oxford Alley to ward off evil spirits.

Ming's Oriental Super Market, at 85-90 Essex Street (☎ **617/338-1588**), is where the locals shop for daily fare, including live fish and imported delicacies such as litchi nuts, preserved strawberries, and

Chinese teas. They also have small gifts, including teapots, bowls, spoons, and mats, at reasonable prices. **Sun Sun Market** at 18 Oxford Street is another good food market. Buy some Chinese noodles, spices, or hot sauces to try at home.

PARKS & GARDENS

Boston's gardens rate a sightseeing trip of their own— give yourself time to relax and enjoy them. The **Boston Public Garden,** adjacent to the Boston Common, is one of the prettiest public flower gardens anywhere, especially in the spring, when thousands of tulips and pansies burst into bloom. It's ideal for resting, people watching, or enjoying a ride in the famed swan boats (☎ **617/522-1966**) that move gently along the pond, under the bridge, around the island, and back from 10am to 6pm. The cost is $1.25 for adults, 75¢ for children and $1 for seniors.

Not noted for flowers, but for its trees, the **Boston Common,** America's first public park, was founded in 1634. The Common's beautiful shade trees are identified with botanical fields.

The most spectacular garden of all awaits you at the **Arnold Arboretum** on 125 Arborway, in Jamaica Plain, one of the oldest parks in the United States. Opened in 1872 and often called America's greatest garden, it is open daily from sunrise to sunset. A National Historical Landmark, it is administered by Harvard University in cooperation with the Boston Department of Parks and Recreation. You can have a great time here wandering through some 265 acres containing more than 6,000 varieties of ornamental trees, shrubs, and vines typical of the Boston area. In the spring, the air is perfumed with the scent of dogwood, azaleas, rhododendrons, and hundreds of varieties of lilacs, for which the arboretum is especially famous. Lilac Sunday is in May. This is definitely a place to take a camera. There is no admission charge; if you'd like information on what's in bloom, call 617/524-1718. To get to the arboretum, take the MBTA Orange Line to the Forest Hills stop and follow the signs to the top of a small hill. The Visitor Center is open from 8:30am to 4pm weekdays and from 10am to 4pm weekends.

3 Especially for Kids

Sometimes it seems that Boston was made for kids—there's just so much for them to see and do. They'll love the performers and the sweets at Faneuil Hall Marketplace, the sharks and seals at the New England Aquarium, and all the hands-on exhibits at the Museum of Science and Hayden Planetarium (see "Top Attractions," above). Boat trips—from cruising the waterways of the Public Garden in the swan boats to looking for Leviathan during a whale watch—make for lots of fun. Sports fans of all ages will love a ball game at Fenway Park (see "Outdoor Activities," below). For whale-watching tours and a company that offers special tours for children, see "Organized Tours," below.

Two Boston institutions that are guaranteed to please the young are the Franklin Park Zoo and the famed Children's Museum.

Did You Know?

- Martin Luther King, Jr., studied at Boston University and left it many of his important papers.
- The Boston subway system, which opened in 1897, was the first in the Western Hemisphere.
- The Boston Red Sox sold Babe Ruth, who was their pitching star, to the New York Yankees in 1919 for $100,000.
- Susan B. Anthony was arrested in Boston in 1872 for trying to vote in the presidential election.
- Kahlil Gibran, the Lebanese-American poet who wrote *The Prophet,* grew up in Boston's South End.
- The toothpick was first used in the United States at the Union Oyster House. The owner hired Harvard boys to dine there and ask for toothpicks as a way to promote his new business.
- The first school in America, attended by John Hancock and Benjamin Franklin among others, was located in Boston. You'll find a plaque marking the spot on School Street.

✪ Children's Museum

300 Congress St., on Museum Wharf. ☎ **617/426-8855**. $7 adults, $6 children age 2–15 and seniors, $2 toddlers age 1, free for infants under age 1. Fri 5–9pm, $1 for all. Sept–June Tues–Sun 10am–5pm, Fri until 9pm; June–Aug daily 10am–5pm, Fri until 9pm. Closed Mon during school year, except Boston school vacations and holidays; New Year's Day, Thanksgiving Day, and Christmas. MBTA: South Station (Red Line); then walk across Congress Street Bridge. Directions: Drive across Congress Street Bridge from South Station and park in one of the museum's reduced-rate lots.

You'll recognize this museum by its unmistakable landmark: a 40-foot-high red-and-white milk bottle standing in the waterfront park next to the building. But this museum isn't just for children. Adults have just as much fun as the kids in this special place, where everyone is encouraged to touch the exhibits. It's set up so that parents as well as kids can be on their own enjoying an unstructured experience, wandering randomly from one participatory exhibit to another.

The range of exhibits is fascinating. "El Mercado del Barrio" immerses children in Spanish culture, surrounding them with Spanish newspapers, ethnic food products, and salsa music. It's a replica of a Boston Latino neighborhood market. "Under the Dock" is a wonderful environmental exhibit that teaches young people about Boston and its seaside ecosystem. "Climbing Sculpture" is a giant puzzle-piece climbing maze designed especially for children. "Giant's Desk Top" is a fantastically huge replica of Mom or Dad's desk with a Touch-tone phone whose receiver acts as a slide and a coffee mug so big your child can hide in it, and there's even a pair of sunglasses big enough to hide behind.

"The Kids' Bridge" uses interactive videos to "take" visitors to Boston's ethnic neighborhoods and speak about multicultural issues and ways to combat racism. The "Science Playground" turns kids on to science with innovative physical science exhibits, including "Salad Dressing Physics" and a "Tinkerer's Workshop" with metal and woodworking shops and a resource area. The exhibit "We're Still Here" offers a look at Northeast Native Americans and their traditions and features a wigwam.

There are two excellent exhibits on Japan: "Teen Tokyo," which introduces American teenagers to the latest in Japanese contemporary life; and an authentic two-story house transported to the museum piece by piece by Boston's sister city of Kyoto (Boston and Kyoto have an extensive cultural-exchange program), where kids can take off their shoes, walk through, and experience ancient customs and ceremonies.

If you want a great bargain in craft supplies and materials for toys and games, stop at RECYCLE, where you can buy bags of industrial leftovers at its Resource Center that can be recycled in many ways. Admission to RECYCLE and the Resource Center is free.

Note: When the kids get hungry, try the ice cream and sandwiches served from the good stand in the Hood "milk bottle" or go to the McDonald's adjoining the museum gift shop.

Franklin Park Zoo

Northeast section of Franklin Park, Dorchester. ☎ **617/442-2002.** $5.50 adults and children age 12 and up; $3 children 4 to 11; $4 seniors, military personnel, and students with ID; free for children under 4. Free admission for all Tues 9–10am and Sun 10–11am. Mon–Fri 9am–4pm, Sat–Sun and holidays 10am–5pm. MBTA: Forest Hills (Orange Line).

This zoo's African Tropical Forest covers 3 acres, indoors and out. More than 50 species of animals, including western lowland gorillas, live in the climate-controlled tropical building. They lope around in a natural habitat of rocks, waterfalls, and plants—no bars or cages in sight. There are hundreds of examples of tropical plants and wildlife to enjoy and study. Also at the zoo is a Victorian-style aviary, a seasonal petting zoo for children with New England farm animals, and a waterfowl pond.

Blue Hills Trailside Museum Visitor Center

1904 Canton Ave., Milton. ☎ **617/333-0690.** $3 adults, $1.50 children age 3–15, free for children under 3 and Massachusetts Audubon Society members with a valid membership card. Wed–Sun and Mon holidays 10am–5pm. Closed New Year's Day, Thanksgiving Day, and Christmas.

Another outdoor spot the kids will love is the Blue Hills Trailside Museum, at the 6,000-acre Blue Hills Reservation, just a short drive south from Boston on Route 138. There's room to hike, climb "mountains" (hills, actually), and enjoy the exhibits, which are designed to reproduce the natural habitats of the Blue Hills. There is a lookout tower; a crawl—through logs; a Native American wigwam; and live animals, including owls, honeybees, mammals, snakes, and turtles. Children can feed the ducks and deer. A wall of glass overlooks an outdoor pond, beautiful—and safe. Weekend activities for children of all ages include story time (11am), live "mystery" animal presentation (12:30pm), family hour (2pm), and the Naturalist's Choice (3:30pm).

Special events change with the seasons and include Maple Sugaring in early spring, Honey Harvest in the fall, and Owl Prowls in January and February.

Puppet Showplace Theatre

32 Station St., Brookline. ☎ **617/731-6400.** Tickets $6.

Puppet Showplace performs programs of favorite fables, ethnic legends, and folk and fairy tales from around the world. These are produced for children, year-round, by professional puppeteers in a charming theater that seats about 120. Historic puppets and puppet posters are on display, and you can buy toy puppets for the kids. Call ahead for the current schedule.

4 Special-Interest Sightseeing

FOR TRAVELERS INTERESTED IN AFRICAN-AMERICAN HISTORY

The **Black Heritage Trail** covers sites in the Beacon Hill section of Boston that are part of the history of the 19th-century black Boston. You can take one of the two-hour-long guided tours given by the rangers at the **National Park Visitor Center** (46 Joy St.), or you can go on your own, using a brochure that includes a map and descriptions of the buildings. These include sites of the Underground Railroad, homes of famous citizens, the first integrated public school, and the **African Meeting House** (below). If you'd like specific information on sites, call the **Boston African American National Historic Site,** at **617/742-5415.**

One of the most interesting sites is the 182-year-old **African Meeting House** (8 Smith Court in Beacon Hill), the oldest standing black church in the United States. It was there that William Lloyd Garrison founded the New England Anti-Slavery Society and Frederick Douglass made some of his great abolitionist speeches. Following extensive restoration work, the Meeting House offers an informative audiovisual presentation, lectures, concerts, and church meetings. Another must on the Black Heritage Trail is a visit to the **Museum of African-American History at Abiel Smith School** (46 Joy St.; ☎ **617/742-1854**). The museum has the most comprehensive information on the history and contributions of blacks in Boston and Massachusetts, and is open Monday through Friday from 10am to 4pm. Admission is free.

If you feel like heading out to Roxbury, there is another museum you might like to see. The **Museum of the National Center of Afro-American Artists** (300 Walnut Ave., Roxbury, MA 02119; ☎ **617/442-8614**) promotes, collects, and exhibits the works of African-American artists from all over the world. Admission is $1.25 for adults. Children and seniors pay 50¢. The museum is open Tuesday to Sunday from 1 to 5pm October through May, and Tuesday through Sunday from 1 to 6pm June through September. To get there, take "T" bus 22 (Ashmont-Ruggles) or "T" bus 44 (Jackson Square-Ruggles) to Walnut Avenue and Seaver Street.

FOR TRAVELERS INTERESTED IN WOMEN'S HISTORY

The **Boston Women's Heritage Trail** is a relatively new walking trail with stops at the homes, churches, and social and political institutions where 20 dedicated women lived and/or made great contributions to society. These include famous women such as Julia Ward Howe, Dorothea Dix, and others whose names are well known. Others include Phyllis Wheatley, a slave who became the first African-American published poet, and Lucy Stone, a feminist and abolitionist. Since the trail is quite new, maps may be necessary. Guides can be purchased in local bookstores and at historic sites, such as **Old South Meeting House.** For detailed information, call **617/522-2872.**

5 Organized Tours

GUIDED WALKING TOURS

If you prefer guided walking tours to hoofing it on your own, **Boston By Foot** (77 N. Washington St.; ☎ **617/367-2345** or 367-3766 for 24-hour recorded information) conducts architectural tours of Beacon Hill and other areas of interest May through October. The guides, or docents, have completed a special instructional program and are quite knowledgeable about the architecture and history of the city. The 90-minute tours are given rain or shine. The "Heart of the Freedom Trail" tour starts at the statue of Samuel Adams in front of Faneuil Hall on Congress Street, Monday through Saturday at 10am and Sunday at 2pm. Tours of Beacon Hill begin at the foot of the State House steps on Beacon Street Monday through Friday at 5:30pm, Saturday at 10am, and Sunday at 2pm. Other tours and meeting places are: Copley Square Tour, Trinity Church at noon on Friday and Saturday; the Waterfront Tour, at the statue of Samuel Adams in front of Faneuil Hall on Congress Street, Sunday at 10am; and North End Tour, at the statue of Samuel Adams at Faneuil Hall, Saturday at 2pm, Sunday at noon. Rates are $7 for adults and $5 for children; reservations are not required. Tickets may be purchased from the guide at any time of the tour.

Special theme tours may be arranged if there are enough requests. Included in the request tours is the Boston Women's Heritage Trail, which covers areas in the North End, downtown, Chinatown, and Back Bay.

An especially noteworthy offering (also by Boston By Foot) is **Boston By Little Feet,** geared to children from 6 to 12 years old. The guide will present a child's-eye view of the architecture on the Freedom Trail and of Boston's role in the American Revolution. Children must be accompanied by an adult, and a free explorer's map is provided. Tours meet at the statue of Samuel Adams in front of Faneuil Hall on Congress Street, Saturday at 10am, Sunday at 2pm, rain or shine, and the cost is $5 per person.

Historic Neighborhoods Foundation (2 Boylston St.; ☎ **617/426-1885**) offers several walking tours that focus on neighborhood landmarks, including Beacon Hill, North End, Chinatown, the waterfront, and financial district. The "Make Way for Ducklings" tour, very popular with children and adults, includes a ride on the swan boats in the Public Garden.

Schedules change with the season, and the programs are based on themes, such as social history and topographical development. Write or call the Historic Neighborhoods Foundation for current schedules and meeting places.

You can't pick the flowers, but you can have a wonderful time on the **Boston Park Rangers'** free guided walking tours of Boston's "Emerald Necklace," a network of green spaces tying the city to the suburbs designed by landscape architect Frederick Law Olmstead. This tour covers outstanding parks and gardens, including Boston Common, Public Garden, Back Bay, Commonwealth Avenue Mall, Muddy River in the Fenway, Olmstead Park, Jamaica Pond, Arnold Arboretum, and Franklin Park. The full six-hour walk includes a one-hour tour of any of the sites. For hours and schedules, call **617/635-7383.**

TROLLEY TOURS

A narrated tour is a good way to see the town. Take a trolley and sit back in comfort while you see the points of interest and listen to guides relate the history of Boston. Trolley companies are identified by the colors of their trolley cars. **Old Town Trolley** (329 W. Second St.; ☎ **617/269-7010**) has the orange-and-green cars; **Boston Trolley Tours** (☎ **617/TROLLEY**) takes visitors about in blue cars (it's often called the Blue Trolley); and the **Red Beantown Trolleys** (439 High St., Randolph; ☎ **617/236-2148**) are in red, of course. They each offer a 90-minute tour through Boston's historic areas and include free reboarding if you want to visit any of the sites. The Blue Trolley has ramps to make it handicapped-accessible, and the Red Beantown Trolleys are the only ones that stop at the Museum of Fine Arts. Rates on all of them are between $12 and $16. Old Town has a family pass and is the only one to stop at the Boston Tea Party Ship and Museum. Boarding spots are at hotels, historic sites, and tourist information centers. The guides have a great many anecdotes to add to the historical facts.

SIGHTSEEING CRUISES

Now, if you'd like a change of pace in your sightseeing, try one of the many cruises available. They range from a half-hour lunch trip through the harbor to a cruise to Provincetown or Gloucester.

Boston Harbor Cruises (1 Long Wharf; ☎ **617/227-4321**) offers narrated cruises of Boston Harbor. The BHC ticket office is the white booth on Long Wharf. You can choose their 90-minute historic sightseeing cruise, which departs every two hours beginning at 11am, or the 45-minute *Constitution* cruise, which docks at Charlestown Navy Yard so you can go ashore and visit the USS *Constitution.* These tours leave every hour on the half hour from Long Wharf, and on the hour from the navy yard. The John F. Kennedy Library Cruise leaves every two hours beginning at 10am. The cruise departs from JFK Library at 10:45am, 12:45pm, 2:45pm, and 4:45pm. The 90-minute historic sightseeing and JFK Library cruises cost $8 for adults, $6 for seniors, and $4 for children. The Constitution cruise is $5 for adults,

$4 for seniors, and $3 for children. And every evening at 7pm a sunset cruise is offered. It takes 90 minutes and features the lowering of the flag and a cannon blast at sunset. Admission is $8 for adults, $6 for seniors, and $4 for children. It's a great sail for the whole family.

Also on Long Wharf, at the red ticket office, the **Bay State Cruise Company, Inc.** (☎ **617/723-7800**) offers several inner and outer harbor cruises. Ninety-minute cruises to Boston's Outer Harbor with an optional visit at George's Island State Park depart several times a day; the price is $6.50 for adults, $5.50 for seniors, and $4.50 for children under 12. A 55-minute cruise of Boston's Inner Harbor is also available with the option of going ashore at the Charlestown Navy Yard; adult fare is $5, seniors $4, and children $3. In addition, cruises to Provincetown and Cape Cod, and Whale Watches (see below), are also available. Call for exact dates and schedules, as they change.

The **Charles River Boat Company** (☎ **617/621-3001**), offers scenic, historical cruises along the Charles River or in Boston Harbor. Boats depart from both the Boston Museum of Science and the CambridgeSide Galleria; price is $7 for adults, $6 for seniors, $5 for children; check at the Galleria or call the above number for information and reservations.

And for a full day at sea, Bay State runs the *MV Provincetown II* (☎ **617/723-7800**), which sails from Commonwealth Pier daily from mid-June to Labor Day, and on weekends in May and September. It's "anchors aweigh" at 9:30am for the three-hour trip to Cape Cod's picturesque Provincetown. The return trip leaves at 3:30pm, giving you a few hours for shopping and sightseeing. Same-day round trip fares are $29 for adults, $22 for senior citizens and children. It will cost $5 extra each way if you bring along your bike.

Another day trip is offered by **A.C. Cruise Line's** *Virginia C II*, which sails to Gloucester from Pier 7 (290 Northern Ave.) daily from late June through Labor Day at 9:30am, returning from Gloucester at 5:30pm. The round-trip charge is $18 adults, $14 for senior citizens. You'll have time for lunch or browsing at Gloucester's Rocky Neck Art Colony. Call **617/261-6633** or 800/422-8419 for details.

The *Spirit of Boston*, Bay State Cruises (☎ **617/457-1499**), a sleek 192-foot harbor-cruise ship, offers both a New England lobster clambake luncheon cruise (daily from noon to 2:30pm) and a dinner/dance cruise (nightly from 7 to 10pm). It sails from 60 Rowes Wharf near the Boston Harbor Hotel. Call for reservations.

WHALE WATCHING

If you have the time and inclination check out BHC's **Whale Watching Safaris** (☎ **617/227-4321**), leaving from Long Wharf at 9:30am (returns 2:30pm). Tickets, sold at the white ticket center on Long Wharf, cost $16 for adults, $13 for seniors, and $10 for children under 12. From mid-June to Labor Day, cruises depart daily; before June and after Labor Day, cruises take place on weekends only. Call ahead for reservations.

Boston Harbor Whale Watch's 100-foot *Majestic* charges out to sea at over 20 knots, promising you more time watching whales than trying to find them. Tours depart from Rowes Wharf beginning

> **By Land and By Water**
>
> The newest way to see Boston is with **Boston Duck Tours,** 64 Long Wharf (☎ **617/723-DUCK**). It also happens to be the most unusual way to see the city. Board a "duck," an authentic, renovated World War II amphibious landing vehicle, right in front of the New England Aquarium. From there you'll be taken on a ride that takes you by the Old State House, Back Bay, the Boston Public Library, Boston Garden, the North End, Faneuil Hall, and the New England Sports Museum as well as on a short ride down the Charles River. Call ahead for schedules and rates.

June 3. From that date until June 26 they're scheduled only for Friday, Saturday, and Sunday, but from July 1 to September 5 service is daily. Departure times are Monday through Friday at 10am, Saturday and Sunday at 9am and 2pm. Expect to spend about $4^1/_2$ hours on the boat. For adults the cost is $18, for seniors and children 12 and under it's $15. Call **617/345-9866** to confirm rates and schedules.

For **Bay State Cruise Company, Inc.,** whale watching begins on May 7, weekends only. From June 22 to September 5 tours depart Wednesday through Sunday. After that, until October 10, cruises are scheduled again on weekends only. They depart from Long Wharf (at 8:30am) or Commonwealth Pier (at 9am) and return at approximately 3:30pm. Passage for adults is $18, and for children and seniors it's $12. You can make advance reservations by phone by calling **617/723-7800.**

A.C. Cruise Line also has a Whale Watch cruise Wednesday through Sunday, leaving at 10:30am and returning at 5pm. The fare is $16 for adults and $14 for seniors. Call ahead (**617/261-6633** or 800/422-8419) for reservations and information.

6 Outdoor Activities

BEACHES

Although Boston is situated right on the water, people don't come here for surf and sand. There are several beaches in South Boston (Castle Island Beach, M Street Beach, Pleasure Bay, Carson Beach, and City Point Beach, off Day Boulevard) and Dorchester (Malibu Beach, Tenean Beach, and Savin Hill Beach, off Morrissey Boulevard); however, they're not the nicest of spots, so I'd recommend that you look beyond the greater Boston area for a day at the beach. You might take an hour's drive south on Route 3 or take a boat to **Nantasket Beach,** a large, well-equipped public beach in Hull. Or you can go farther south to **Duxbury** near Plymouth for a clean, quiet, 9-mile beach with dunes. The beach is located off Routes 3A and 139. Public parking is at the north end. Going north from Boston, try **Revere Beach,** which has an expanse of sandy beach and a gentle surf. Parking along the beach is free. Or take the MBTA to the Revere Beach or Wonderland station, 20 minutes from downtown. If you have a car, drive up to the end of the beach, near Point of Pines and the General Edwards Bridge, for less crowded swimming. Even more spacious, with clear, cold water for swimming, is **Nahant Beach,** about 3 miles north. (I should warn you that the temperature of the water at the North Shore beaches is apt to be quite low; they're not as cold as the beaches of Maine, but not as warm as those on the South Shore and Cape Cod.) If you're going to Nahant, get there early in the morning, especially on the weekends, since parking is just $1 and spaces fill up fast.

You could also take a one-day trip to Salem, where you can explore old houses and some outstanding museums, swim at Salem Willows, or take a boat ride to historic Marblehead, home of the American navy and now host to the chic yachting set, a great place to walk around, with its quaint streets, vintage houses, and fun shops; continue on to Gloucester, home of the fishing fleet; and to the picturesque artists' colony at Rockport. But for the very best swimming on the North Shore, you should drive (a little more than an hour from the city) to Ipswich's beautiful **Crane Beach,** with its picturesque dunes, miles of white sand, and crisp, cold water. Admission is $6.50 during the week, $10 on weekends, but it's worth it, since many of the other North Shore beaches are for residents only. The drive, incidentally, will take you through what is called "John P. Marquand country"— those elegant little villages where the Boston Brahmins have long escaped the summer heat.

If the parking lot at Crane is full (get there by 10am), try some of the other North Shore beaches. There are two fine places in Gloucester. **Wingaersheek Beach,** just off Route 128 (Exit 13), has beautiful white sand, a fantastic view, and sand dunes for climbing or hiding behind to seek privacy. It's open through Labor Day and there's also a charge for parking. Stage Fort Park, Route 128 (Exit 13), is at Gloucester Harbor and has 100 acres of oceanfront with sheltered beaches, playgrounds, picnic and cookout areas, and an old fort site for the kids to explore. If you'd like a stretch of several beach areas with magnificent dunes and a strong surf (surf fishing is allowed), take Route 1A to Newburyport and **Plum Island,** which is part of the Parker River Wildlife Refuge, with nature trails, observation towers, and wildlife. There is no admission or parking charge, but the small lots fill up early—sometimes cars are turned away at 9am.

Just a word of warning: Wingaersheek, Plum Island, and Crane beaches are host to greenhead flies as well as swimmers for a few weeks in late July and early August. Bring insect repellent with you. These beaches have lifeguard services and bathhouses.

Other fine area beaches include **Salisbury Beach** (Route 1A, south of the New Hampshire border), which has spectacular surf; and **Good Harbor Beach,** Gloucester, also with a fine surf, on Thatcher Road off Route 127A.

HARBOR ISLAND EXPLORATION

The **Boston Harbor Islands** are treasures that the locals like to keep to themselves. There are 30 islands in the outer harbor, some of which are open for exploring, camping, or swimming—great spots for the day-tripper. **George's Island** is the most popular, with an old fort built in 1834; it's open for guided tours and is rumored to have a resident ghost! There is a visitor's center, refreshment area, fishing pier, place for picnics, and a wonderful view of Boston's skyline. From there, free water taxis run to **Lovell, Gallops, Peddocks, Bumpkin,** and **Grape islands,** which have picnic areas and campsites (permits are required—call **617/740-1605** for permits). **Lovell Island** has a sandy beach and is the only one with supervised swimming. Boats leave from Long Wharf and Rowes Wharf. The islands are part of the Boston Harbor Islands State Park.

BIKING

Boston is a great city for biking, whether on marked bike paths or not. The **Dr. Paul Dudley White Charles River Bike Path** is a 17.7-mile course that begins at Science Park (near the Museum of Science) and will take you through Boston, Cambridge, and to Watertown Square. You'll ride along both sides of the river if you take this path. There are multiple entrances along the way. It's managed and maintained by the **Metropolitan District Commission (MDC).** Another good bike path is the **Southwest Corridor Linear Park Bikepath.** It runs alongside the MBTA's Orange Line and it's four miles long. Pedestrian and bike paths are separate in this park. The 11-mile **Minuteman Bicycle Trail** follows the route of an old railroad track (it's actually in the railroad bed) and runs from the Alewife "T" station in Cambridge through Arlington, Lexington, and Bedford. The **Greenbelt Bikeway** runs along the 8-mile perimeter of the "Emerald Necklace," a famous Boston chain of parks that includes Boston Common and Franklin Park. In addition to the bikepaths listed above, on Sundays, from 11am to 7pm, Memorial Drive along the Charles River is closed to traffic—bicycles are allowed.

For additional information on Boston bike paths, call the MDC at ☎ **617/727-5114,** ext. 555, or the **Boston Area Bicycle Coalition** (☎ **617/491-7433**).

Bicycles are allowed on the subway system (except the Green Line) during off-peak hours, and you can generally get away with riding on the sidewalk as long as you're careful of pedestrians.

For rentals, repairs, and general help, try **Earth Bikes** at 35 Huntington Ave. (☎ **617/267-4733**). You can take an organized or self-guided tour with Earth Bikes, and they'll supply you with a bike lock and helmet with your rental. Other bike shops to try are **Back Bay Bicycles** (333 Newbury St.; ☎ **617/247-2336**) and **Community Bike Shop** (496 Tremont St.; ☎ **617/542-8623**).

BOATING

You should try to take at least one turn around the lagoon at the Boston Public Garden on the most famous ride of all—the **swan boats** (☎ **617/522-1966**). Built in the shape of a swan, with graceful neck and outspread wings, these pedal-powered boats still look the same as they did when first created in 1877, except that now they're made out of fiberglass instead of wood. Oliver Wendell Holmes called them "as native to Boston as baked beans." Sailing along with the real swans and ducks in the lagoon, they operate from mid-April until the last Sunday in September (weather permitting). Hours are 10am to 6pm (and from noon until 4pm after Labor Day). The fare is $1.25 for adults, 75¢ for children, and $1 for seniors.

If you're looking for something a little less tame, you'll have several options. **Community Boating, Inc.** (21 Embankment Road; ☎ **617/523-1038**) offers sailing lessons and boating programs for children and adults from April to November. **Courageous Sailing Center** (☎ **617/635-4505**) in the Charlestown Navy Yard offers youth program lessons year-round. **Boston Sailing Center** (54 Lewis Wharf; ☎ **617/277-4198**) offers lessons for sailors of all ability levels. The center is open all year.

For those who prefer kayaking or canoeing**, Charles River Canoe and Kayak Center,** located at 2401 Commonwealth Avenue in Newton (☎ **617/965-5110**), rents canoes, kayaks, and sculls at their dock. Lessons are available.

If you brought your own boat and are looking for a place to launch it, call the **Metropolitan District Commission (MDC)** at **617/727-1300.**

Pleasure boating is allowed on the Charles River and Boston Harbor. The MDC will inform you of regulations.

FISHING

Freshwater fishing is permitted at **Turtle Pond** in the Stony Brook Reservation in Hyde Park, as well as on the banks of the **Charles River.** For offshore saltwater fishing, the **Harbor Islands** are a good choice. You might also try heading out to South Boston to the pier at **City Point,** and the **John J. McCorkle Fishing Pier.** Both are located off Day Boulevard.

For information about fishing around the state, contact **Massachusetts State Parks** (100 Cambridge St., Room 1905, Boston, MA 02202; ☎ **617/727-3180** or 800/831-0569).

GOLF

There's a large number of golf courses (both public and private) located around Boston. A few of the courses you might like to try are the **Fresh Pond Golf Course** (691 Huron Ave., Cambridge; ☎ **617/354-8876**), **the George Wright Golf Course** (420 West St., Hyde Park; ☎ **617/364-0679**), and the **Newton Commonwealth Golf Course** (91 Algonquin Rd., Brookline; ☎ **617/244-4763**).

The **Massachusetts Golf Association** (190 Park Rd., Weston; ☎ **617/891-4300**) represents over 270 golf courses around the state and will send you a list of courses. Call or write the above address. In addition, **Tee Times** (199 Wells Ave., Suite 9, Newton, MA 02159; ☎ **617/969-0638**) organizes golf outings.

HIKING

The **Metropolitan District Commission (MDC)** (☎ **617/727-0460**) maintains hiking trails at several reservation parks throughout the state, some of which are within short driving distance of the city. They include the **Blue Hills Reservation, Beaverbrook Reser-**

vation, Breakheart Reservation, Hemlock Gorge, Middlesex Fells Reservation, and **Belle Isle Marsh Reservation.** Call the above number for information on how to get maps. You might also try **Stony Brook Reservation** in Hyde Park.

The **Boston Harbor Islands** also offer great hiking. Contact **Boston Harbor Island State Park,** 349 Lincoln St., Building 45, Hingham, MA 02043 (☎ **617/740-1605**).

ICE-SKATING

If ice-skating is more your speed, there are several options. Try **Steriti Memorial Rink** in Boston (☎ **617/727-4708**); **Simoni Memorial Rink** in Cambridge (☎ **617/727-4708**); **Porazzo Memorial Rink** in East Boston (☎ **617/662-8370**); **Veterans Memorial Rink** in Somerville (☎ **617/727-4708**); and **Bajko Memorial Rink** in Hyde Park (☎ **617/727-6034**).

IN-LINE SKATING

A favorite spot for in-line skaters is the **Esplanade.** In addition, on Sundays in summer, **Memorial Drive** in Cambridge is closed to traffic, and rollerbladers from all over the city take to the street. If you didn't bring your own skates to Boston, try the **Beacon Hill Skate Shop,** located at 135 Charles Street South (☎ **617/482-7400**).

If you have access to the internet and want to know what's hot on the in-line skating scene before you get to Boston, go to **Inline Online:** http://www.sk8net.tiac.net/users/sk8man/icb.html.

JOGGING

City residents love to jog along the Charles River. Other sources of information on jogging include the **Metropolitan District Commission (MDC)** (☎ **617/727-1300**) and the **Bill Rodgers Running Center,** located in Faneuil Hall (☎ **617/723-5612**). In addition, virtually every hotel in Boston provides jogging maps for hotel guests.

TENNIS

There are public courts available at no charge, throughout the city. They are maintained by the **Metropolitan District Commission (MDC).** To find the one nearest you, call the MDC at **617/727-1300.**

7 Spectator Sports

The love affair carried on by the people of Boston with the city's professional sports teams is unlike anything you'll find in other American cities. In addition, there are several colleges in the area that play a good game of football or hockey.

Whenever you go to Boston, you'll find an incredible array of scheduled sports events.

MAJOR SPORTS VENUES

Fenway Park

24 Yawkey Way. ☎ **617/267-9440** for information, 617/267-1700 for tickets. Lower boxes $18, upper boxes $14, grandstand $10, bleachers $7. Games often begin at

7:30pm on weeknights and at 1 or 2pm on weekend afternoons. MBTA: Kenmore Sq. (Green Line, B, C, or D train).

Ancient, stale-smelling, and much-beloved Fenway Park opened in 1912 (it's the oldest ballpark in the country) and has been the place to see the everyday face of Boston ever since. Not to mention a baseball game. The dimensions and architecture of the park create a feeling not found in the uniform stadiums or domes of most other cities—in Fenway, the game is played on a field of real grass and dirt, bounded by walls that jut out at weird angles and, in the case of the famed Green Monster, climb to bizarre heights. The fans closely ring the field in a narrow cordon—the cramped seats aren't all that comfortable, but you'll love the feeling of sitting right on top of the game. Eat a hot dog, watch the numbers change on the old hand-operated scoreboard, listen to the cheesy organ and the deafening shouts of the vendors, and enjoy the game—Fenway Park hasn't changed all that much since the early 1900s, and baseball is a game that improves with history and tradition.

Fenway is a small park and the Red Sox have a loyal following. Whether the home team is winning or losing as you plan your vacation, call as far in advance as possible if you'd like to see a game. Seating for the disabled and nonalcoholic sections are available.

FleetCenter

150 Causeway St. ☎ **617/624-1000** (for recorded events) or 617/931-2000 (for Ticketmaster). MBTA: North Station (Green or Orange Line).

At presstime, the hallowed but decrepit Boston Garden was scheduled to be replaced by a gleaming, new sports arena, the FleetCenter, on September 30, 1995. The Garden's steep seating, cramped visitors' locker room, and the irregular bounces of its parquet-style basketball floor will be nothing more than memories when you read this.

The Celtics and the Bruins, legends in their respective sports of basketball and hockey, will have a new home in the brand-new, five-story FleetCenter, which will house considerably more spectators. The Bruins haven't won the Stanley Cup in recent years, but historically they're one of the NHL's most successful franchises, and the Celtics have won a great many NBA championships.

The FleetCenter is located right next to the Boston Garden.

BASEBALL

The **Boston Red Sox** play at Fenway Park (see above) from early April to early October (as long as nobody is on strike). This American League team hasn't won a World Series in 78 years. You can get tickets while you're in Boston or in advance by calling Ticketron or Bostix. For Red Sox information, call **617/267-1700.**

BASKETBALL

The **Boston Celtics** is the city's famed professional basketball team. The Celtics, who play at the new FleetCenter (see above), have won 16 NBA Championships since 1960. Following the baseball season, basketball season runs from early October to May. For information, call the FleetCenter at 617/624-1000; for tickets, call Ticketmaster at 617/931-2000.

FOOTBALL

The **New England Patriots** play football (not very well in recent years) during the fall and winter out at Sullivan Stadium (☎ **800/543-1776**) in Foxboro, about a half-hour drive south of the city. You can drive or catch a bus from the entrance of South Station, the Riverside "T" station, or Shopper's World in Framingham (west of the city).

College football is played by **Boston College** (Alumni Stadium, Chestnut Hill; ☎ **617/552-3004**), **Boston University** (Nickerson Field, Commonwealth Ave.; ☎ **617/353-2872**), **Harvard University** (Harvard Stadium, N. Harvard St., Cambridge; ☎ **617/495-2206**), **Northeastern University** (Parsons Field, Kent St., Brookline; ☎ **617/373-2672**).

HOCKEY

Boston Bruins hockey games are always exciting, but if you're lucky enough to be in town when they're playing Montreal, you're in for a treat. Tickets for all their games (held at the FleetCenter, see above) sell out early. For tickets, call 617/624-1000 or call Ticketmaster at 617/931-2000.

Colleges with hockey teams include **Boston College** (Conte Forum, Chestnut Hill; ☎ **617/552-3004**), **Boston University** (Walter Brown Arena, 285 Babcock St.; ☎ **617/353-2872**), **Harvard University** (Bright Hockey Center, 60 JFK St., Cambridge; ☎ **617/495-2206**), and **Northeastern University** (Matthews Arena, St. Botolph St.; ☎ **617/373-2672**).

DOG RACING

If you're a greyhound fan, there's racing at **Wonderland Park** in Revere (☎ **617/284-1300**), reached via the "T" on the Blue Line.

MARATHON

Every year on Patriots Day (the third Monday in April), the **Boston Marathon** is run from Hopkington to Copley Square in Boston.

ROWING

Another celebrated annual event is the **Head of the Charles Regatta.** It's held in October, and over 800 crews from all over the world participate. Shells leave the Boston University Boathouse every 10 seconds or so. It's a major social event as well. Thousands of people gather along the banks of the Charles River to picnic and watch the shells glide by.

TENNIS TOURNAMENT

The **U.S. Tennis Championship at Longwood** is held every year in July at the Longwood Cricket Club (564 Hammond St., Brookline). Call **617/731-4500** for tickets and information about the week-long event.

8

Boston Strolls

"A visit to Boston is a must for every American," say the historians, "for without Boston there would have been no free American life." Boston is a marvelous city for soaking up history—and other sights—on foot. It's compact and it contains many different neighborhoods, each with its own distinct charms. To help you immerse yourself in the streets of Boston, I've created four different tours for you. Remember to wear comfortable walking shoes.

WALKING TOUR 1
DOWNTOWN BOSTON AND BEACON HILL

Start: Boston Common.
Finish: Faneuil Hall
Time: Between two and three hours depending on how long you spend in shops and at various attractions.
Best Times: Early morning to mid-afternoon.
Worst Times: Mid-afternoon, when you will be rushed to see the sights before closing time.

Everyone who visits Boston for the first time should take a walk along the **Freedom Trail,** which consists of 16 numbered historical sights. However, it's a three-mile walk that takes approximately 6 hours to complete, so I've split the Freedom Trail into two complete walking tours (with a few unofficial stops as well) to make it more manageable. The Freedom Trail has been expanded and rerouted since the original one was established. There are now two loops—one through downtown Boston and the other through the North End—making the trail easier to follow. This is the way I've split it up for your convenience. Although the new "official" start is at the City Hall Visitor Center, this tour begins at the Boston Common. Either way, there are trailblazer signs and a red sidewalk line to mark the trail. You'll be able to acquaint yourself with 2½ centuries of important American history during these two walks.

From Park Street Station, exit at the easternmost corner of the:

1. **Boston Common.** An integral part of Boston's past and present, it is the oldest public park in the country (1634). It's a place where cows once grazed, soldiers drilled, witches were hanged,

Walking Tour 1—Downtown Boston & Beacon Hill

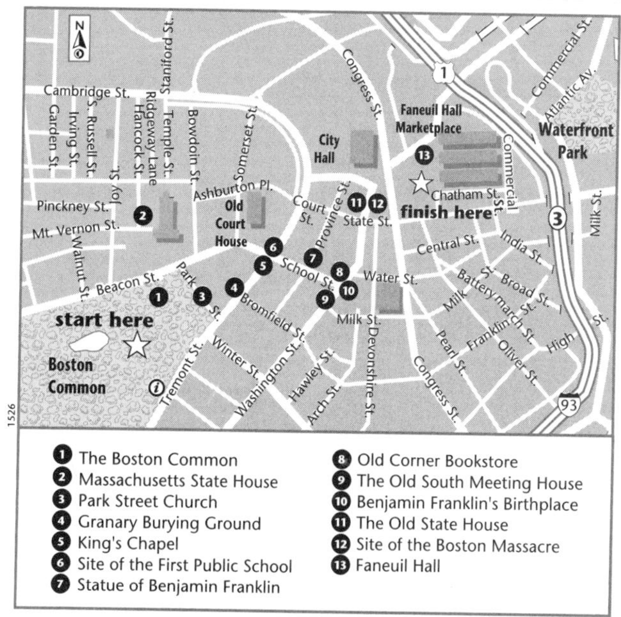

and "common scolds" were dunked in the Frog Pond (now used for wading and ice-skating). Today the original pasture ordinance is still in effect; however, you'll find no cows grazing here. Instead, you'll find concerts, sidewalk musicians, demonstrations for or against almost anything, a playground for the young, park benches for the elderly, Bostonians eating picnic lunches, flowers and ancient trees, and street people asking for handouts. Now that you've got your bearings, proceed to the:

2. **Massachusetts State House** (☎ **617/727-3676**). The "new" State House, with its great gold dome (visible for miles), is one of many masterpieces created by Charles Bulfinch. Although the building is called "new," it was actually built in 1795 to replace the smaller "old" State House (which you'll see later). Samuel Adams laid the cornerstone. The original dome was first made of wood shingles and whitewashed; later it was covered in copper purchased from Paul Revere, and finally, it was covered in gold leaf as it is today. This is where the Massachusetts General Court sits today; in its Archives (open to the public) are interesting historical documents that relate to the Massachusetts Bay Colony and the early republic. Also located within the Statehouse is the famous Sacred Cod, a woodcarving of a codfish given to the legislature in 1784 by merchant Jonathan Rowe to remind them of the importance of the fishing industry to the Massachusetts economy. The Sacred Cod is located on the third floor in the

House of Representatives gallery. The less attractive wings you see were added later to the original building.

Heading down one side of five-sided Boston Common, from which the British troops set off for Concord in 1775, the trail then passes the:

3. **Park Street Church,** at the corner of Park and Tremont Streets. Built in 1809, it was described by Henry James as "the most interesting mass of bricks and mortar in America," with its white steeple and original exterior designed by Englishman Peter Banner. The church is rich in its associations: The song "America" was first sung here on Independence Day in 1832 and William Lloyd Garrison gave his first antislavery address here on July 4, 1829. Incidentally, the site on which the church stands has long been known as "Brimstone Corner." Some think that's because of all the preaching that was done here, but others argue that it got its name because during the War of 1812, gunpowder (made from brimstone) was stored in the church's basement. From late June to August, the church is open from 9:30am to 4pm Tuesday through Saturday. It is an active congregation. Services (Congregational) are on Sunday morning at 9 and 10:45am and Sunday evening at 6:30pm.

    Just to the left of the church on Tremont Street is the:

4. **Granary Burying Ground.** This cemetery was once part of the Boston Common; later it was the site of a public granary. Pause for a moment and pay tribute to some illustrious Americans who are buried here: John Hancock, Samuel Adams, Paul Revere, Benjamin Franklin's parents, the victims of the Boston Massacre (five colonists shot in the fracas with British troops on March 5, 1770), and the wife of Isaac Vergoose, otherwise known as "Mother Goose" from the nursery rhymes of the same name. But don't try any gravestone rubbing. Once a popular pastime, it has been prohibited in Boston's historic cemeteries since the rubbing process began to wear off the engraving on the tombstones. Open daily from 8am to 4pm.

    Next on the tour is:

5. **King's Chapel.** Royal governors used to attend services at this chapel built in 1754, the first Episcopal church in Boston. George III sent gifts, as did Queen Anne and William and Mary, who presented the communion table and chancel tablets (still in use today) before the church was even built. The Crown's religion was never too popular with the colonists; after the Revolution this became the first Unitarian church in America. Unitarian/Universalist services are now conducted here. The chapel is open Tuesday through Saturday from 10am to 2pm. Buried in the adjacent graveyard are John Winthrop, the first governor of the Massachusetts Bay Colony; William Dawes, who rode with Paul Revere; and Mary Chilton, the first woman to step ashore on Plymouth Rock.

Now follow the red-brick line to School Street next to King's Chapel, where you'll find a folk-art mosaic marking the:

6. **Site of the First Public School,** where Adams, Franklin, and Cotton Mather were students. Although the building that once stood here is gone, the school survives as the Boston Latin School, and it is now located in the Fenway area of Boston.

Nearby is the:

7. **Statue of Benjamin Franklin,** the first portrait statue erected in Boston. Most people remember the story of an impoverished Franklin getting off the boat in Philadelphia to begin his illustrious career, but few remember that he began his journey in Boston, where he was born (1706) and spent his childhood. The statue was crafted by Richard Greenough in 1856 and stands in front of Boston's old city hall.

Next on the trail, at the corner of School and Washington streets, is the building that once housed the:

8. **Old Corner Bookstore** and the publishing house of Ticknor & Fields. This was the literary center of America, where such Boston literati as Longfellow, Lowell, Thoreau, Emerson, Hawthorne, and Harriet Beecher Stowe used to gather in the 19th century. It is now the Globe Corner Bookstore (3 School Street), specializing in travel and adventure books as well as maps.

Next on your walk is:

9. **The Old South Meeting House,** at 310 Washington Street, corner of Washington and Milk streets (☎ **617/482-6439**). This structure was used by the early colonists for both religious and political meetings, overflowing from nearby Faneuil Hall. In 1770 an angry crowd met here to wait for Governor Hutchinson's promise to withdraw British troops after the Boston Massacre. Here also, on December 16, 1773, several thousand citizens sent messengers to the governor demanding that the newly arrived tea be removed from the harbor and sent back to England. When they were informed of the governor's refusal, a whoop went up from the citizens disguised as Native Americans, who then rushed to the docks to begin the famous Boston Tea Party. Today the meetinghouse is a fascinating museum of revolutionary history, with its ground-floor pews, centuries-old clock, and multimedia exhibit, "In Prayer and Protest: Old South Meeting House Remembers," which highlights Old South's history. Look for the sign that reads "The Boston Tea Party started here December 16, 1773," and the vial of tea that washed up on shore the next day. Old South also offers special activities and events to highlight American history. Call for schedules and times. Basic admission is $2.50 for adults, $2 for seniors and students, $1 for children 6 to 18; children under 6 are admitted free. Old South is open daily April through October from 9:30am to 5pm, and November through March from 10am to 4pm (5pm on weekends).

Around the corner on Milk Street is:

10. Benjamin Franklin's Birthplace. In a little house at 17 Milk Street, Ben Franklin was born in 1706, the 15th child of Josiah Franklin. Ben may have made his fame and fortune in Philadelphia, but he learned his trade as a printer in Boston during an apprenticeship under his older half-brother, James. You'll find a plaque on the side of a skyscraper marking the site of the house (long since destroyed).

Backtrack on Washington Street past the Globe Center Bookstore and you'll reach:

11. The Old State House, at Washington and State Streets (☎ **617/720-3290**). It was built in 1713 and restored to its original elegance in 1991–92. The Old State House was the seat of the colonial government of Massachusetts before the Revolution and the state's capitol until 1797. From its balcony the Declaration of Independence was first read to the citizens of Boston in 1776. In 1789 George Washington, as president, reviewed a parade from the building. The Old State House is an impressive building, with a beautiful facade adorned by a large American eagle and a gilded lion and unicorn that represent British rule in America. (The entrance to the State Street MBTA station is under the building.) Inside there is a magnificent spiral staircase leading to the Bostonian Society's museum exhibits. There's an introductory video on the history of the building. Exhibits on Boston during the Revolution and collections documenting the 375-year history of the city, its people, and its neighborhood are also featured. The Old State House is open daily from 9:30am to 5pm. Admission is $2.75 for adults, $2 for seniors and students, $1.50 for children 6 to 18, and free for children under 6.

Outside the Old State House, a ring of cobblestones marks the:

12. Site of the Boston Massacre, March 5, 1770, an event that helped consolidate the spirit of rebellion in the colonies. Colonists, angered at the presence of British troops in Boston, stoned (with snowballs) a group of redcoats, who panicked and fired into the crowd, killing five men.

Continue following the trail to the next important stop:

13. Faneuil Hall, at Dock Square. Built in 1742 (and enlarged by Charles Bulfinch in 1805), it was given to the city of Boston by the merchant Peter Faneuil; it became known as the "Cradle of Liberty" because of the frequent protest meetings that took place here, while orators such as Samuel Adams exhorted the crowd against the British. The upstairs is still used as a meeting hall for state and local civic and political groups and the downstairs area is still a market, all according to Faneuil's will. On the top floor military enthusiasts can examine the weapons collection of the Ancient and Honorable Artillery Company of Massachusetts. The National Park Service gives free half-hourly talks and operates a handicapped-accessible visitor center there.

TAKE A BREAK You can continue along the Freedom Trail with the next tour, but before doing so you might want to stop here and visit the Faneuil Hall Marketplace (see Chapter 7, "What to See & Do in Boston," for complete information), which is next to Faneuil Hall. This also might be a good time to try Durgin-Park (see Chapter 6) for a New England-style dinner. If you prefer Tex-Mex, you'll enjoy Zuma's Tex-Mex Café. For a light lunch, sandwich, or a "frozen hot chocolate," there's Serendipity 3. And you can have anything from pizza to Chinese food at the food stalls in the Bull Market or outdoors. Or fruit drinks, fruit salad, or coffee at the Coffee Connection, freshly ground and brewed.

WALKING TOUR 2
THE NORTH END AND CHARLESTOWN

Start: Faneuil Hall Marketplace (subway: Green Line to Government Center).
Finish: USS *Constitution* (Old Ironsides) in Charlestown.
Time: Two to three hours, depending on how much time you spend touring the historic houses and shopping at the Haymarket.
Best Time: Any time.

From Faneuil Hall Marketplace, cross North Street and walk up Union Street past:

1. **Ye Olde Union Oyster House,** at 41 Union Street (☎ **617/227-2750**). This place, the oldest restaurant in Boston that's still in operation, was first opened in 1826.

   Continue walking north, then turn right. If it's Friday or Saturday you'll be right in the midst of:

2. **The Haymarket.** This open-air market appears every Friday and Saturday. Merchants sell fresh fruits and vegetables to locals and tourists alike. To get to the North End from here, look for the pedestrian passage beneath the Central Artery (Fitzgerald Expressway). *Note:* The massive Central Artery construction project may have changed the face of this area by the time you arrive, so look for Freedom Trail signs or signs for Paul Revere's House. Soon you'll find yourself in Boston's

3. **Little Italy.** Italian American culture is still very much alive here—there's a profusion of Italian restaurants, and you'll see old men playing boccie, hear the language of the old country, and, just maybe, experience the unique fun of an Italian street fair.

   In the 1600s the North End *was* Boston—the surrounding area was water and brush, reclaimed only after the passage of many years. The North End was home to Irish immigrants before the Italians arrived—Rose Kennedy, mother of John, Robert, and Ted Kennedy and daughter of John "Honey Fitz" Fitzgerald, a legendary Irish American Boston pol, was born in a house here.

Take in the sights as you enter the neighborhood, and soon you'll come to North Square and:

4. **The Paul Revere House** (☎ **617/523-2338**). It was about 90 years old when Revere bought it in 1770, and it's still standing today at 19 North Square. The $2^1/_2$-story wooden clapboard structure, the oldest in downtown Boston, is filled with 17th- and 18th-century furnishings and artifacts and is one of the major landmarks along the Freedom Trail. Revere, a brilliant silversmith as well as a patriot, was well trained for his famous ride of April 18, 1775; he had been hired on several occasions by the Committee of Correspondence to carry news and resolutions to other parts of the colonies. In 1774, for example, he bore dispatches to Philadelphia and New York calling for a congress; the year before, he spread the news of the Boston Tea Party to New York.

   The Paul Revere House is open from November through April 14 9:30am to 4:15pm, and from April 15 through October 9:30am to 5:15pm; it's closed Mondays in January, February, and March, as well as Thanksgiving Day, Christmas, and New Year's Day. Admission is $2.50 for adults, $2 for seniors and students, and $1 for children 5 to 17.

   At the beginning of the little cobblestone street on which Revere's house stands is the home of his Hichborn cousins, the:

5. **Pierce-Hichborn House.** This is a rare example of 18th-century middle-class architecture. Guided tours are designed for those interested in the architecture and home furnishings of that period. It is open the same hours as the Revere House. A few blocks up is:
6. **James Rego Square (Paul Revere Mall),** a pleasant little park with an equestrian statue of Paul Revere. Here also is:
7. **St. Stephen's Catholic Church,** the only Charles Bulfinch-designed church still standing in Boston. It was dedicated in 1804, and the next year the congregation purchased a bell from Paul Revere's foundry for $800. Completely restored in 1965 (the chandeliers, red carpets, white walls, and gilded organ pipes were the result), St. Stephen's is now an active Catholic church.

   Walk into the park, past the fountain, and emerge at the famous:

8. **Old North Church,** Salem Street at Paul Revere Mall. A thoroughly beautiful structure that dates back to 1723, it is modeled in the style of Sir Christopher Wren's buildings, with its red-brick facade and tall steeple. It was from this steeple, of course, that Revere had arranged for Robert Newman to hang two lanterns ("One if by land, two if by sea"), the signal that the British were on their way to Lexington and Concord. The Revere family attended this church (you can still see their plaque on Pew 54); other famous visitors who have attended services at Old North include Presidents James Monroe, Theodore Roosevelt, and

Walking Tour 2— The North End & Charlestown

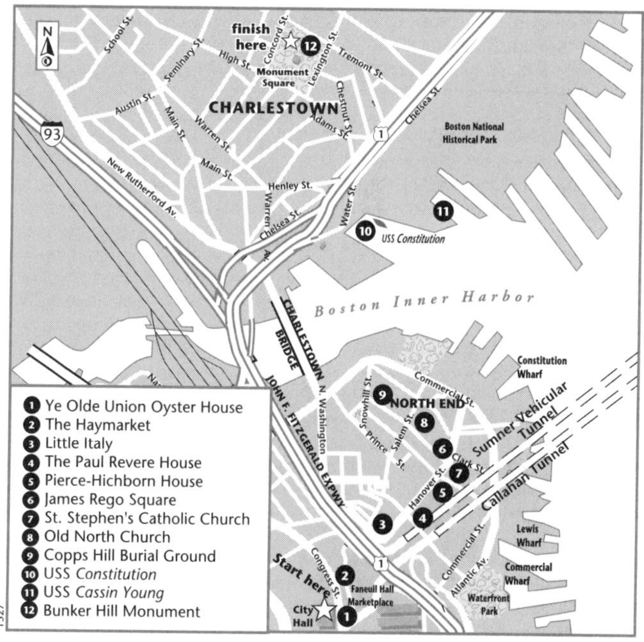

Franklin D. Roosevelt. And, more recently, there were Gerald R. Ford and Her Majesty Queen Elizabeth II. Have a look at the interior of the church: note the pulpit shaped like a wine glass, the ancient chandeliers, and the organ. Then stop at the museum shop next door, also in an old building, where you can buy maps of Paul Revere's ride, pewter, and silver, as well as general items like maple sugar candy. Proceeds are used to support the church. This is the oldest church building in Boston (1723), and is today officially known as Christ Church in the City of Boston. There are some lovely gardens on the north side of the church that are open to the public. Be sure to read the memorial plaques set into the walls there. Old North Church is open daily 9am to 5pm; you can attend Sunday services (Episcopal) at 9 and 11am and 4pm. There's also a gift shop open daily from 9am to 5pm. Donations are appreciated.

Go left on Salem Street until you reach Hull Street. Turn right and walk uphill on Hull Street past no. 44, the narrowest house in Boston, to find:

9. **Copps Hill Burial Ground,** the second oldest cemetery (1660) in the city. Used by the colonists as early as 1659, this is where Cotton Mather and his brother are buried along with other early Bostonians. On this ground, once the site of a windmill, were planted the British batteries that destroyed the village of

Charlestown during the Battle of Bunker Hill, June 17, 1775. Open daily from 9am to 5pm.

From the heights of Copps Hill you can see across the river to Charlestown, spotting the masts of the USS *Constitution.* To reach the ship (see below) you must walk over a mile, across the Charlestown Bridge and to the right; you might want to take a taxi instead.

10. **USS *Constitution.*** "Old Ironsides" of War of 1812 fame was built at a cost of $302,718 (a lot of money back in 1797), and since it never lost a battle, this must have been one of the biggest naval bargains in history. First used to help drive the French privateers from West Indian waters, the *Constitution* terrorized the British fleet during the War of 1812, participating in 40 engagements and capturing 20 vessels without ever being beaten. The ship is now preserved—"not only as a monument to its glorious past, but as a symbol of the spirit which established our nation."

The *Constitution* is now in dry dock in preparation for its 200th birthday in 1997, so no one is allowed below deck. However, the USS *Constitution* Museum, just inland from the vessel, has several exhibits that highlight the ship's achievements. The museum is open daily 9am to 6pm. Admission is $3 for adults, $2 for children 6 to 16, and free for children 5 and under. Also at the navy yard is the:

11. **USS *Cassin Young,*** a World War II destroyer that has been refurbished and is now open to the public. It is docked near the USS *Constitution.* Admission is free. Call **617/242-5601** for tour hours.

The Freedom Trail then heads inland to the heart of Charlestown, where you will see:

12. **Bunker Hill Monument** (☎ **617/242-5644**), a 220-foot Charlestown landmark built in honor of the men who died in the Battle of Bunker Hill, which took place June 17, 1775. Although the colonists lost the battle, it speeded the events that eventually pushed the British out of America. Unless you want to climb 295 steps—there is no elevator—it's best to observe the tower from a distance.

In the lodge at the base of the monument there are exhibits and talks given by National Park Service rangers from 9am to 5pm. Open daily from 9am to 4:30pm. Admission is free.

That concludes your tour of the North End and Charlestown. A fun way to return to Boston from Charlestown is to take the MBTA's water shuttle from Charlestown Navy Yard to Long Wharf. The 10-minute trip costs $1 and leaves every half hour from 6:45am to 8:25pm on weekdays (every 15 minutes during rush hour) and from 10:15am to 6:15pm on weekends. A shuttle bus from the USS *Constitution* will take you to the pier.

WALKING TOUR 3
THE WATERFRONT

Start: Old State House.
Finish: Boston Tea Party Ship and Museum.
Time: Approximately two hours to walk without stops; around five hours if museum stops are included.
Best Times: Morning.
Worst Times: Evening rush hour.

A stroll around the waterfront combines history, museums, and a chance to feel the ocean breeze and see the harbor views. Begin at the:

1. **Old State House,** a fixture of government in Boston since pre-Revolutionary War days. (It's a stop on the first walking tour, as well.)

   From the Old State House walk past the Boston Massacre Marker and follow:

2. **State Street** toward the waterfront. In Boston's early days, this street was called the Great Street to the Sea. In fact, Faneuil Hall was once directly on the waterfront, and clipper ships docked at the North and South Market buildings (now in Faneuil Hall Marketplace). But as the harbor filled with silt and garbage, wharves were built farther east, and then on pilings, until it became impractical to use any more fill to create new land.

   The block of State Street between Congress and Kilby Streets became the center of finance in the 19th century. There sea captains and businessmen invested in textile and railroad industries and created the financial institutions for which Boston and modern State Street are known nationally. One landmark you'll see is:

3. **The Exchange Building,** at 53 State Street. Built in 1887, it was at one time home to a signal tower, part of a system of towers that used flags to signal the arrival of ships in Boston Harbor. This enabled merchants to learn that their ships—and fortunes—had arrived.

   Next stop is the:

4. **Bunch of Grapes Tavern,** at the corner of State and Kilby Streets; this was a gathering place in the 18th century for Bostonians opposed to British taxes.

   On State Street where Merchants Row and Kilby Street meet is the:

5. **Shore Line of Colonial Boston.** The construction of Long Wharf began here in 1710; this was the main wharf of Boston, extending 800 feet into the harbor—hence the name.

   At the corner of State and India Streets is the:

6. **Custom House,** built from 1837–47. Ship captains made their first stop at this landmark building to pay duty on their cargoes. The tower, added in 1913, was for many years the tallest

structure in town, and it had an observation deck open to the public. The building and its tower are closed now, but the four clocks in the tower, facing north, south, east, and west, all tell the same time—something new in Boston's history. They make an attractive sight illuminated against the night skyline.

Near the Custom House Tower you will cross:

7. **Broad Street,** developed in 1805 as part of the plan to improve Boston's waterfront. The renowned architect Charles Bulfinch helped design the brick warehouse here. Many buildings from Boston's port are still standing here.

Now that you've taken the historic approach to the waterfront, the next step is to cross the busy John F. Fitzgerald Expressway to actually reach the harbor. With the Customs House on your right, I would suggest taking a left off State Street toward Faneuil Hall Marketplace and crossing at the traffic light near Atlantic Avenue.

TAKE A BREAK You can't go anywhere near Faneuil Hall Marketplace without stimulating your appetite. Some offbeat ways to satisfy it at this stage of your walk include buying a sandwich or tacos and a beverage and hoofing it over to Christopher Columbus Park for a picnic; sitting at a table under a colorful umbrella at the outdoor cafe at the Marriott Long Wharf (the Marriott also has good indoor dining with a view at the Harbor Terrace Restaurant). And since the waterfront's, and Boston's, fortunes were for so long tied to the China trade, how about trying Sally Ling's Gourmet Chinese Restaurant, at 256 Commercial Street, across from Lewis Wharf? They'll prepare lobster for you in 10 different ways. You can also combine lunch with a half-hour cruise from Long Wharf (see "Organized Tours" in Chapter 7, "What to See & Do in Boston").

After lunch and some people and boat watching at Christopher Columbus Park (on the waterfront side of the expressway), it's time to explore:

8. **Long Wharf,** Boston's principal wharf since 1711. When it was built, the town mandated that the public have access to it. Near the end of the wharf is a granite building, dating from 1846, that was used by Customs' appraisers. Now it houses offices and residences. At the very end of the wharf is a small park with free telescopes for viewing the harbor and Logan Airport. As you will notice, this is the embarkation point for many inner harbor and harbor islands cruises, as well as the Charlestown ferry.

Just one wharf away is:

9. **Central Wharf,** home of the New England Aquarium. A walk around the aquarium provides a fine view of East Boston and the harbor. The aquarium itself, of course, is one of Boston's great attractions (see Chapter 7, "What to See & Do in Boston").

Walking Tour 3—The Waterfront

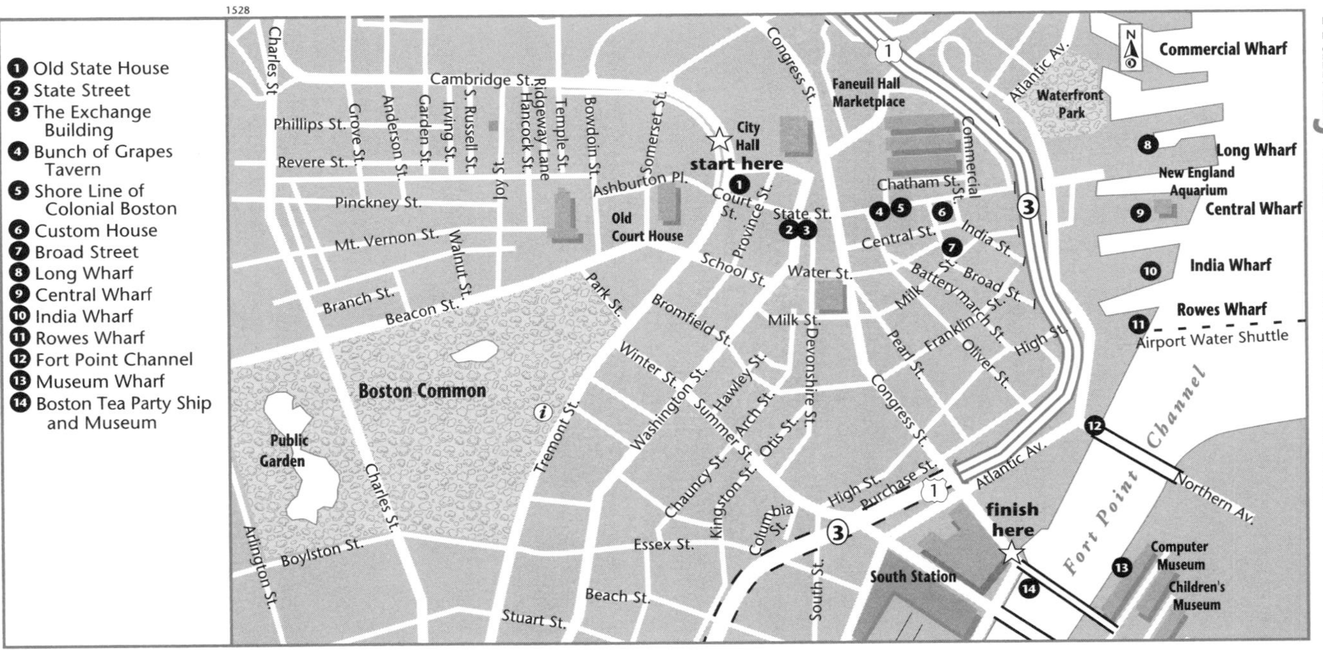

Next is:

10. **India Wharf,** flanked now by two large apartment towers. This used to be abuzz with the ships and activity of the East Indies trade; ships do not sail from here today, but if you walk between the two towers, across the boardwalk and through the archway, you'll be at:

11. **Rowes Wharf.** This is the site of the luxurious Boston Harbor Hotel, but the docks are open to the public. The wharf was constructed in the early 1760s, and many vessels have anchored there for more than two centuries, including the ferries from East Boston that connected with the Narrow Gauge Railroad that went to the North Shore. Today, the Airport Water Shuttle still ferries passengers to East Boston, this time around to Logan Airport.

Now continue to the Northern Avenue Bridge, which crosses:

12. **Fort Point Channel.** You will pass the First District Headquarters of the U.S. Coast Guard. The *Massachusetts,* the first commissioned revenue cutter, was based here. (Revenue cutters were the forerunners of the U.S. Coast Guard.) John Foster Williams, a local naval hero of the Revolutionary War, was its captain. The little white building nearby is the National Oceanographic Tide Gauge Station, where tide levels are continuously recorded.

During the 1890s thousands of commercial boats passed through Fort Point Channel. Today you can see lobster boats along the docks and cruise ships on the far side of the Northern Avenue Bridge, an iron-turntable bridge built in 1908. The channel at one time extended 1$^1/_2$ miles and was used to carry freight to various parts of the city. Major railyards were also located here.

The next wharf is:

13. **Museum Wharf,** which takes it name from the two major museums located there: the **Children's Museum** and the **Computer Museum.** (See Chapter 7, "What to See & Do in Boston," for details on both.) The wharf was once the site of a wool warehouse that supplied the once-prosperous New England textile industry.

At the Congress Street Bridge near Museum Wharf is the:

14. **Boston Tea Party Ship and Museum.** Climb aboard the brig *Beaver II,* a full-scale replica of one of the three ships involved in Boston's famous tea party of 1773. Visit the adjoining floating museum in which the story of the tea party is told through various exhibits and multimedia presentations. And if you really want to get into the spirit of the rebellion, costumed guides can help you throw chests of tea into Boston Harbor (later retrieved by rope harnesses). There is also a gift shop featuring unique "tea party" accessories. The Tea Party Ship is open from 9am to 5pm in the spring and fall, and 9am to 6pm in the summer. It is closed between December 1 and March 1. Admission is $6 for adults,

$4.80 for seniors and students, $3 for children 5 to 12, and free for children under age 5. Reduced rates are available to those on the Old Town Trolley tour.

This is the stopping point on the tour; if you've got to race off to another quarter of Boston, South Station's MBTA Red Line is just across the Congress Street Bridge on the inland side. If you're ready for a substantial meal, Northern Avenue on the Fish Pier harbors a number of restaurants serving great fish dinners, including Anthony's Pier Four, Jimmy's Harborside, Jimbo's Fish Shanty, and the Daily Catch. (See Chapter 6, "Dining," for details.)

Stalwart walkers who are enjoying the waterfront might retrace their steps back through Christopher Columbus Park to Commercial Wharf, where you can have a good look at the marina; Lewis Wharf, where the huge granite warehouses of the old days have given way to expensive condominiums; or Battery Wharf, a large shipping pier that houses the Bay State Lobster Company. When you've finished poking around, you'll find the pastry shops and restaurants of the North End close at hand.

WALKING TOUR 4
CAMBRIDGE

Start: Harvard Square "T" stop
Finish: Weld Boat House
Time: Two to four hours, depending on how much time you spend in shops and museums.
Best Time: Any time.

A walk through Cambridge will take you to Harvard University, some interesting museums, historic buildings that date back to the 17th-century, as well as to some wonderful little shops and cafes.

Take the Red Line to Harvard Square. On exiting the station you'll be right in the heart of:

1. **Harvard Square,** home of Harvard University. The area around you will no doubt be teeming with students and tourists when you arrive. There's great shopping here as well, and when the weather is nice you'll probably come across a street performer or two. One great place to visit here is **Out of Town News,** located right next to the "T" station. Here you can find newspapers and magazines from all over the world. Of course, no trip to Harvard Square would be complete without a stop at the **Harvard Coop,** located behind you at 1400 Massachusetts Avenue (see Chapter 9, "Shopping" for more details). Also here is the **Cambridge Discovery Inc.** kiosk, where you can pick up all sorts of information about the area.

Across Massachusetts Avenue you'll see the:

2. **Wadsworth House** (1341 Massachusetts Avenue). You'll know it by its unmistakable yellow facade. It was built in 1726 as a residence for Harvard's fourth president, and its biggest claim to fame is that George Washington actually slept within its walls.

Cross the street and go left along the red-brick wall to the beautiful Johnson Gate (great for photographs), the entrance to:

3. **Harvard Yard.** Known today as this country's top ivy league college, Harvard University was originally founded as a men's college for training in the ministry. The college seal, inscribed with the Latin *Veritas,* meaning "truth," was adopted in 1643. Harvard became a private institution in 1865 and has expanded to include 10 graduate schools located in over 400 buildings around Boston and Cambridge. After you enter Harvard Yard, go left and you'll be standing amidst some of the:

4. **Dormitories. Massachusetts Hall** was built in 1718 and is listed as a National Historic Landmark. The other two buildings you'll see here are **Stoughton and Hollis halls. Holden Chapel,** built in 1742, is the architectural highpoint of this early quadrangle. The facade of this little Georgian chapel has undergone a multitude of changes in the past two hundred years, losing some of its authenticity, but it still remains an enchanting part of the Harvard campus.

Backtrack a bit and go left between the buildings to the center of Harvard Yard. On your right you'll see:

5. **Widener Library.** This imposing building (1913) was built to house the college's ever-increasing collection of books. Today the library holds over 3 million volumes. Designed by architect Horace Trumbauer of Philadelphia, the library is a memorial to one-time Harvard student Harry Elkins Widener, who met his demise on board the *Titanic.* An interesting note is that Trumbauer's primary design assistant was architect Julian Francis Abele, who was a student of architecture at the University of Pennsylvania and the first black graduate of L'Ecole des Beaux Arts in Paris. He worked with Trumbauer for over 30 years.

Facing the library is:

6. **Memorial Church,** built in 1931. Seeming to shrink in the shadow of the massive Widener Library, this Georgian Revival–style church is, nonetheless, the focal point of the college campus.

Head across the center of the yard to the building that sits between Widener Library and Memorial Church. Known as:

7. **Sever Hall,** it was built between 1878 and 1880 and is the work of H. H. Richardson. Notice the gorgeous brickwork that includes roll moldings around the doors, and the fluted brick chimneys. An interesting aspect of this building's design is the "whispering gallery." If one person stands on one side of the

Walking Tour 4—Cambridge

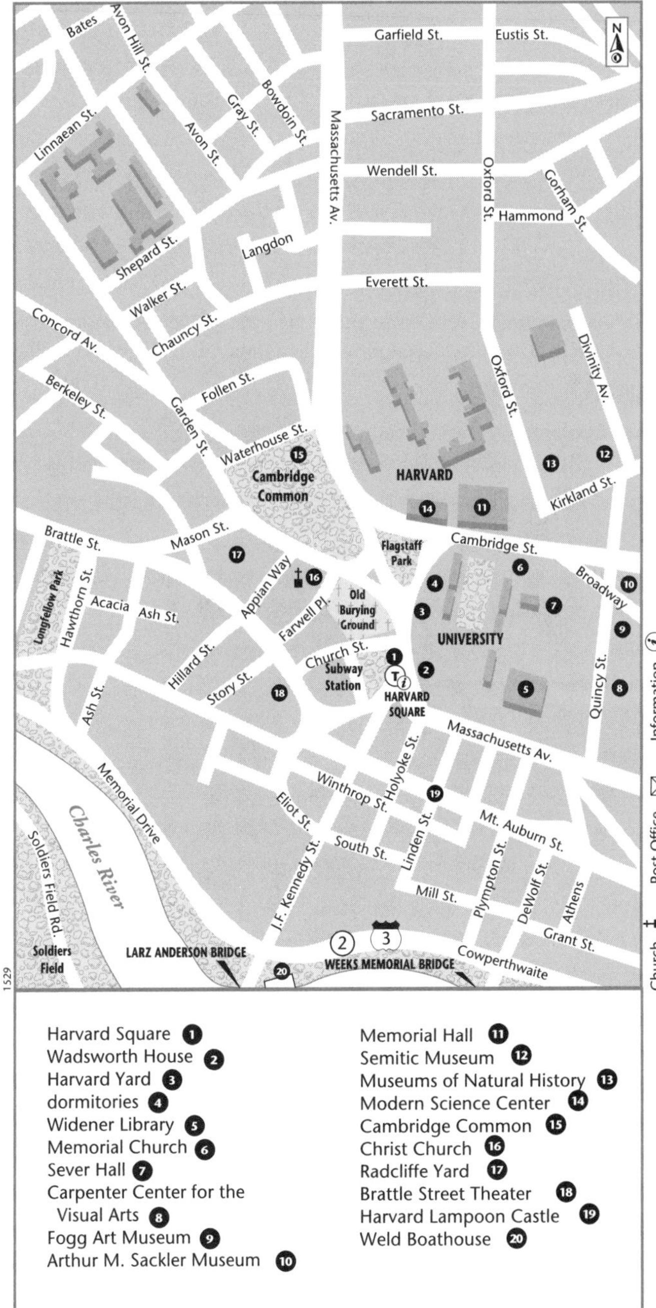

- Harvard Square 1
- Wadsworth House 2
- Harvard Yard dormitories 3 4
- Widener Library 5
- Memorial Church 6
- Sever Hall 7
- Carpenter Center for the Visual Arts 8
- Fogg Art Museum 9
- Arthur M. Sackler Museum 10
- Memorial Hall 11
- Semitic Museum 12
- Museums of Natural History 13
- Modern Science Center 14
- Cambridge Common 15
- Christ Church 16
- Radcliffe Yard 17
- Brattle Street Theater 18
- Harvard Lampoon Castle 19
- Weld Boathouse 20

entrance arch and whispers, a person standing on the opposite side will clearly hear what is being said. Try it.

Go around Sever Hall and follow the path that leads out of Harvard Yard onto Quincy Street. If you look to your right you'll see the:

8. **Carpenter Center for the Visual Arts,** a concrete and glass structure. It was constructed between 1961 and 1963 and designed by the well-known French architect Le Corbusier, along with the team of Sert, Jackson, and Gourley. It happens to be the only building in the United States designed by Le Corbusier. Go left and you'll soon come to the:

9. **Fogg Art Museum,** Harvard's oldest art museum (founded in 1891). There's a collection of French Impressionist work, as well as some British (Whistler) and Italian paintings (Fra Angelico). The museum's decorative arts collection is also quite good. See Chapter 7 for a more complete listing.

After visiting the museum, go right and follow Quincy Street to the:

10. **Arthur M. Sackler Museum,** also on your right at 485 Broadway (☎ **617/495-9400**). If you're interested in Asian art, this is the place to stop. You'll find an incredible collection of Chinese jades as well as an exhibit of Japanese woodblock prints. Special exhibits are also held here.

Next along Quincy Street you'll come upon Harvard University's:

11. **Memorial Hall,** a Victorian structure built in 1874. Harvard graduates William Ware and Henry Van Brunt won a design competition for the building, which was constructed for a total cost of $390,000 (most of the money was donated by alumni). Though it has the aura of a great church, it has never been used as such. Inside you'll find all sorts of treasures, including marble busts, tablets listing students who perished in the Civil War, stained glass, gargoyles, catwalks, vaulted ceilings, and mazes of dark, wood-paneled rooms. **Sanders Theater,** located within, has been used as a lecture hall and theater. Performances in Sanders have run the gamut from Elizabethan drama to John Cage concerts. **Alumni Hall,** located just across from Sanders, was the university dining hall until 1925.

Exit Memorial Hall back onto Quincy Street and continue in the direction in which you were headed before you stopped at Memorial Hall. When you reach Kirkland go right and make your first left onto Divinity Avenue. On your left at number 6 you'll see the:

12. **Semitic Museum.** Founded in 1889, this interesting museum (☎ **617/495-3123**) holds photographs and archaeological artifacts, most of which came from the museum's trips to the Near and Middle East. The museum was closed during World War II and didn't reopen until 1982. Open hours are Monday through

Friday from 11am to 5pm. Call to find out what exhibits are up when you're there.

Backtrack to Kirkland and go right. Take your first right up Oxford and follow it along until you get to the:

13. Museums of Natural History. All four are Harvard University museums dedicated to the study of zoology, botany, and archaeology. One of the high points here is the **Botanical Museum**'s glass flowers collection. All were handblown by Leopold and Rudolph Blaschka in Dresden, Germany. Unfortunately, the secrets of their trade went to their graves with them. Also here are the **Mineralogical and Geological Museum,** the **Peabody Museum of Archaeology and Ethnology,** and the **Museum of Comparative Zoology**. See Chapter 7 for a full listing and open hours.

Backtrack to Kirkland again and go right. Along the way you'll pass the:

14. Modern Science Center (on your right), also part of the university. This interesting building is the largest on campus. In front of the Science Center is **Tanner Fountain,** which is a group of 159 New England field boulders set in a combination of grass and asphalt. The boulders are great for sitting and on sunny spring days you'll almost always find Harvard students relaxing here in the sun. Don't worry about getting wet; the fountain sprays a fine mist, which begins slowly—you'll have ample warning.

Continue along Kirkland and go left over the overpass and then right. You'll come to the intersection of Peabody Street and Massachusetts Avenue. Cross here and you'll end up in:

15. Cambridge Common. Not much to look at now, it was, like Boston Common, once the grazing ground for local cows. It was also the site of General George Washington's main camp from 1775 to 1776.

Across Garden Street from Cambridge Common is the:

16. Christ Church at Zero Garden Street. Designed by Newport architect Peter Harrison (the first trained architect in the United States), it's the oldest church in Cambridge. Note the square wooden tower. If you go inside the vestibule you can still see bullet holes made by the British. At one time the church was used as the barracks for Connecticut troops. During their stay, they melted down the organ pipes to make bullets.

Facing the church on Garden Street, go right to Appian Way and make a left. Take your first right into:

17. Radcliffe Yard. Radcliffe College was founded in 1879 as a women's college and was named for Ann Radcliffe, Harvard's first female benefactor. It was Harvard's sister school until 1975, when admissions requirements and standards were made equal for men and women. Today, Radcliffe remains an independent corporation within Harvard University and has its own president, though its degrees, classes, and facilites are all shared with Harvard

University. Take some time walking through the yard and then head out to Brattle Street and go left. Cross Hillard Street and, if you like, it's time to:

TAKE A BREAK **The Blacksmith House Bakery & Cafe,** on your right, is one of my favorite places to stop for a cup of coffee and some pastry. My favorites are the Sacher torte and the linzer torte. If you're here around lunchtime, the Blacksmith House Bakery & Cafe also offers full meals.

After your break head back out onto Brattle Street and go right. Continue walking (and browsing through the wonderful shops as you go) and you'll soon come to the:

18. **Brattle Street Theater,** on your right at 40 Brattle Street. Opened in 1890 as Brattle Hall, it was founded by the Cambridge Social Union and was used as a venue for cultural entertainment. In 1953, due to increasing financial difficulties, it was converted to a movie house and quickly became known as Cambridge's center for art films. The Brattle Street Theater is one of the oldest independent movie houses in the country.

Back on Brattle Street, continue along and make a right to Mount Auburn Street and then follow it along to the right. You'll cross JFK Street, Dunster Street, Holyoke Street, and Linden Street before you get to the:

19. **Harvard Lampoon Castle,** designed by Wheelwright & Haven in 1909. Listed on the National Register of Historic Places, this is the home of Harvard's undergraduate humor magazine, the *Lampoon.* The main tower looks like a face, with windows as the eyes, nose, and mouth, topped by what looks like a miner's hat. In 1953, the members of the Harvard Lampoon kidnapped the Sacred Cod from the Massachusetts State House. It was returned, only to be stolen again in 1968. Since then it has remained at the State House.

Note that the famous **Harvard Bookstore** is to the left down Plympton Street at the corner of Plympton Street and Massachusetts Avenue.

Make your way back to JFK Street, taking advantage of the opportunity to browse the boutiques and bookstores in the area, and then go left. Follow JFK Street all the way down to Memorial Drive. On your left is the:

20. **Weld Boathouse,** home of Harvard University's women's sculling crew. Directly in front of you is the Charles River, where crowds gather each year for the Head of the Charles Regatta.

9

Shopping

When you shop in this city, you're benefitting from the secrets of Boston's success: its chic, contemporary sophistication and its centuries-old tradition of shrewd Yankee trading. As a result, Boston has some of the finest specialty and department stores, some of the most imaginative boutiques, and—in particular—some of the greatest bargains to be found anywhere.

1 The Shopping Scene

There are, roughly, three major shopping areas in Boston, as well as others close by. The first is Downtown Crossing, the large, traffic-free pedestrian mall along Washington, Winter, and Summer streets, near Boston Common. (The MBTA has special shuttles to take shoppers around the district. Taxis are permitted after 7pm.) This is where you find the major department stores—Filene's and Jordan Marsh—and the little bargain emporiums. Most stores are open every evening until 7pm. The second major district is the Back Bay area, long famous for its specialty shops and art galleries. Lord & Taylor and Saks Fifth Avenue have branches here. The mammoth Copley Place, with a three-story Neiman-Marcus showpiece and 100 chic shops in its two-level shopping mall, is also in this area. The third district is Faneuil Hall Marketplace, where you'll find everything from chic boutiques to pushcarts.

A 10-minute subway ride to Cambridge takes you to a colorful, boutique-filled shopping world in and around Harvard and Charles squares. And if you're visiting historic Salem, Marblehead, Gloucester, or Lexington, you can conveniently detour at several remarkable discount and bargain establishments and shopping malls.

Note: Massachusetts has no sales tax on clothing (priced below $175) and food. All other items are taxed at 5%. Restaurant meals and food prepared for take-out are also taxed at 5%.

Keep in mind that Massachusetts law still prohibits most stores from opening before noon on Sunday—possibly a remnant of the Puritan ethos.

2 Shopping A to Z

ANTIQUES

✪ Boston Antique Co-op I & II

119 Charles St. ☎ **617/227-9810** and 227-9811.

These two cooperatives are jam packed full of antiques from Europe, Asia, and the United States. You'll have a lot of fun browsing through vintage clothing, jewelry, tableware, and other unique items. This place is heavily trafficked and does a high volume of business. If you see something and you like it, get it—it might not be there when you return.

Bromfield Pen Shop

39 Bromfield St. ☎ **617/482-9053.**

If you're a collector of antique pens, you shouldn't miss Bromfield Pen Shop—they have a wonderful collection. Bromfield also sells new pens, including Mont Blanc, Pelikan, Waterman, and Omas.

Danish Country Antique Furniture

138 Charles St. ☎ **617/227-1804.**

Owner James Kilroy specializes in Danish antique furnishings dating from the 1700s onward. There's also some great folk art, crafts, and wonderful rugs.

James Billings Antiques

34 Charles St. ☎ **617/367-9533.**

If you're looking for the perfect piece of 18th-century English country furniture to finish off your house, stop in to this incredibly beautiful store and have a look around.

✪ Shreve, Crump & Low

330 Boylston St. ☎ **617/267-9100.**

A Boston institution, Shreve, Crump & Low (in business since 1800) sells new jewelry, china, silver, and crystal, but it also has an antiques department that specializes in 18th- and 19th-century American and English furnishings, British and American silver, and some lovely Chinese porcelains.

ART

Alpha Gallery

14 Newbury St. ☎ **617/536-4465.**

Owner Alan Fink exhibits contemporary American and European paintings and sculpture.

The Artful Hand

Located in Copley Place, 100 Huntington Ave. ☎ **617/262-9601.**

Showing only the work of American artisans, The Artful Hand specializes, as its name suggests, in handcrafted items, including jewelry, pottery, wooden boxes, and sculpture.

Artsmart

272 Congress St. ☎ **617/695-0151.**

Artsmart isn't your traditional art gallery—you can touch everything here. Nearly 200 New England craftspeople are represented, and works include furniture, sculpture, jewelry, hand-painted picture frames, and even hats.

✪ Barbara Krakow Gallery

10 Newbury St. ☎ **617/262-4490.**

This prestigious gallery, in existence for more than 30 years, specializes in contemporary art. It's located on the fifth floor.

Copley Society of Boston

158 Newbury St. ☎ **617/536-5049.**

Founded in 1879, this is the oldest art association in the United States. Among its illustrious membership were Sargent and Whistler. Today, the majority of members come from the New England area, and shows are held regularly. It's worth stopping in—you might discover a new talent.

Gallery NAGA

67 Newbury St. ☎ **617/267-9060.**

Located in the Church of the Covenant, Gallery NAGA exhibits contemporary works, including painting, photography, and sculpture, as well as some beautiful glasswork.

Haley & Steele

91 Newbury St. ☎ **617/536-6339.**

If you prefer more traditional prints to contemporary art, Haley & Steele is the place for you. You'll find everything from maritime and military prints to botanical and historical prints and a whole lot more. When you've found the perfect piece for the bedroom or living room, you can have it framed here in the gallery's custom frame shop.

Robert Klein Gallery

38 Newbury St. ☎ **617/267-7997.**

For 19th- and 20th-century photography, there's no better place than Robert Klein Gallery. Among the artists represented are Diane Arbus, Robert Mapplethorpe, Man Ray, and Ansel Adams. The gallery is located on the fourth floor.

Nielsen Gallery

179 Newbury St. ☎ **617/266-4835.**

Owner Nina Nielsen hand picks young, talented artists and shows their work in her gallery (which has been here for almost 30 years). Much of the work she exhibits has a particularly spiritual quality to it.

Pucker Gallery

171 Newbury St. ☎ **617/267-9473.**

Like many of the other galleries on Newbury Street, Pucker Gallery also exhibits contemporary art, some of which is the work of local artists, but the specialty here is Israeli art.

Vose Galleries

238 Newbury St. ☎ **617/536-6176.**

Even if you're not interested in 18th-, 19th-, and early 20th-century American painting, you might want to stop in here just for the history of the place. Vose Galleries was first opened in 1841 and is considered the oldest continuously operating gallery in the United States. The Vose family (now in its fifth generation) has sold paintings to major American museums, and they like to show the work of the Boston School, as well as American Impressionists and the Hudson Valley School.

BOOKS

The Harvard Coop (discussed below under "Department Stores") is certainly worth a book lover's attention.

Avenue Victor Hugo Bookshop

339 Newbury St. ☎ **617/266-7746.**

This shop buys, sells, and trades new and used books and estate libraries. Although they stock books on all subjects, they are science-fiction specialists. If you're a fan of periodicals, Avenue Victor Hugo also carries back issues of many magazines. With the recent opening of a second floor, Avenue Victor Hugo Bookshop now has over 125,000 volumes of browsable stock, making their stock of general fiction titles the largest north of New York City.

Barillari Books

1 Mifflin Place, Cambridge. ☎ **617/864-2400.**

This store at Harvard Square has a large selection and great discounts—some titles are on sale for 25% and 31% off listed prices.

Brattle Book Store

9 West St. ☎ **617/542-0210** or 800/447-9595.

This bookstore buys and sells old titles. Owner Kenneth Gloss will give you a free appraisal if you happen to be traveling with a collection of rare old books that you would like to sell.

Charlesbank Bookstore

660 Beacon St. ☎ **617/236-7442.**

Advertised as the largest bookstore in New England, this Kenmore Square shop has three floors of general, academic, and technical books. Boston University students shop here. There is free two-hour validated parking on Deerfield Street.

✪ Schoenhof's

76A Mt. Auburn St., Cambridge. ☎ **617/547-8855.**

The specialty here is foreign-language books in all subjects, including children's picture- and wordbooks.

Waterstone's Booksellers

26 Exeter St. ☎ **617/859-7300.**

Located next to Friday's Restaurant at the corner of Exeter and Newbury streets, Waterstone's is a British import occupying three floors of the old Exeter Street Theater. It is properly British—subdued and geared to nonrush shopping. But it is intellectually lively, with weekly author readings and programs for book lovers. There's also a colorful children's corner and periodic storytime. Carrying more than 150,000 titles, Waterstone's is the largest bookstore in New England.

✪ WordsWorth

30 Brattle St. ☎ **617/354-5201.**

WordsWorth is one of my favorite Boston bookstores. It has an enormous inventory (over 100,000 volumes), and everything is sold at discount prices. There's a great selection of children's books. If you don't get a chance to shop at WordsWorth while you're in Boston, you can use their on-line service on the internet, which will search for books by title and author. You don't have to use your credit card number on-line if you'd rather not. You can call or fax them instead. WordsWorth's internet address is: http://www.words-worth.com/.

CHINA, SILVER & GLASS

La Ruche

168 Newbury St. ☎ **617/536-6366.**

The scent of Agraria greets you as you enter La Ruche (which translates as "beehive"). It features unusual decorative accessories, French and Italian faience, silk flower arrangements made to order, hand-painted furnishings, china and glassware, potpourri, and scented candles. Specialties of the boutique include hand-painted furniture, European and American pottery (including the complete line of Mackenzie-Childs majolica ware), garden ornaments, and architectural birdhouses. Open Monday through Saturday, 10am to 6pm.

Stoddard's

50 Temple Place ☎ **617/426-4187.**

Selling quality merchandise since 1800, this is the oldest cutlery shop in the country. The variety of items is amazing. You can choose from about 100 types of sewing scissors and 25 styles of nail scissors. Stoddard's also sells shaving brushes, binoculars, fine fishing tackle, and fly rods. (Their Swiss army knives make lovely Christmas gifts.) The Temple Place store is open Monday through Saturday, 9am to 5:30pm; the Copley Place branch (☎ **617/536-8688**) is open Monday through Saturday from 10am to 7pm and Sunday from noon to 5pm.

Villeroy & Boch

288 Boylston St. ☎ **617/542-7442.**

Synonymous with elegance, Villeroy & Boch sells fine European china and crystal (many of this country's best restaurants use Villeroy & Boch china). At this shop you'll also find gift items, artwork, and home furnishings.

DEPARTMENT STORES

✪ The Coop

1400 Massachusetts Ave., Cambridge. ☎ **617/492-1000.**

This is the famous Harvard Cooperative Society, a complete department store where you can buy everything from stationery (with

Harvard insignia) to clothes, fine-art prints, graphics, electronics, music, and stereos. And, of course, books. The Coop annex has three floors of books, including the required texts for Harvard classes. The store is just across from the Harvard Square subway station.

✪ Filene's Basement

426 Washington St. ☎ **617/542-2011.**

To look at Filene's building—a calm, pleasant department store—you would never guess what goes on beneath the first floor. But just go downstairs to the basement level and pow! It seems as if every shopper within a 500-mile radius of Boston is there. The reason, of course, is that the "Original Basement" is famous the world over. When the most fashionable stores in the country—for example, Neiman-Marcus, Bergdorf Goodman, Bloomingdale's, and Saks Fifth Avenue—need to clear out their overstock, when a store goes out of business, or when manufacturers have extra merchandise, they sell the lot to Filene's Basement. The result is one of the Basement's famous specials, advertised in advance in the Boston papers. There they are—lots of Nieman-Marcus $500-and-up women's dresses each about $100; $200 pants suits from Saks at $80; $50 name-brand bathing suits at $25. Men's quality leather shoes may be $49 a pair. Children's $15 slacks are $7. Wedding and evening gowns are especially good buys. And so it goes: clothing for everybody, luggage, purses, lingerie, cosmetics, linens, a miscellany of items at phenomenal savings. And the automatic markdown policy keeps lowering the price of all remaining merchandise over a 35-day period; whatever is not sold by the end of that time is given away to charity. Look for the automatic racks for your best values. The crowds are fierce, the competition keen, and the race is not for the fainthearted. Get there early, sharpen your elbows, and good luck! By the way, there are dressing rooms, but nobody minds if you slip things on over your clothes. And—an unusual policy for a discount store—everything is returnable; you can even mail the merchandise back!

Founded in 1908, Filene's Basement began to expand to the Boston suburbs and beyond in 1978. The company now operates 52 stores in the Northeast and the Midwest. But none of them can compare to the original, where 15,000 to 20,000 shoppers pour through the doors each day. Filene's Basement leases its space from Filene's, the department store upstairs, but the two stores are no longer affiliated.

Jordan Marsh Company

At the corner of Summer and Washington sts. ☎ **617/357-3000.**

In the heart of Downtown Crossing is New England's largest store. Inside the handsome brick facade you can find ready-to-wear and designer fashions, gift boutiques, housewares, furniture, unique gifts, and a fashion basement, too.

FASHIONS

Men's

Brooks Brothers

46 Newbury St. ☎ **617/267-2600.**

Brooks Brothers is the place for perfectly tailored clothes. It's essential to the "proper Bostonian," and has been for generations. And it has fine outfits for women, too.

Louis

234 Berkeley St. ☎ **617/262-6100.**

This ultraprestigious men's store, housed in a building that was once the Museum of Natural History, sells $1,500 suits that can be coordinated with handmade shirts, silk ties, and Italian shoes. There is also a Louis for Women division at the same address that caters to an elegant female clientele. Louis also has a cafe on the premises, where you can have a "power" breakfast or light lunch.

WOMEN'S

Clothware

52 Brattle St., Cambridge. ☎ **617/661-6441.**

This specialty shop sells a contemporary line of women's dresses, lingerie, and fun accessories. They also have their own private label.

Laura Ashley, Inc.

83 Newbury St. ☎ **617/536-0505.**

Laura Ashley features a line of fresh, innocent, country-style dresses, blouses, shirts, and accessories.

FOOD

Cardullo's Gourmet Shop

6 Brattle St., Cambridge. ☎ **617/491-8888.**

A gourmet's delight, Cardullo's carries fine food specialties from all over the world. If you can't afford the truffles, buy some imported crackers or cheeses.

✪ Le Saucier

Quincy Market Building, North Canopy. ☎ **617/227-9649.**

You'll be amazed at the number of sauces available here. They come from over 25 different countries and range from hot sauces to dessert sauces.

Paul W. Marks Cheese Shop

Quincy Market Colonnade. ☎ **617/227-0905.**

This place has an amazing selection of imported and domestic cheeses, as well as pâté and caviar.

GIFTS & MISCELLANY

Blackstone's of Beacon Hill

46 Charles St. ☎ **617/227-4646.**

Looking for some decorative reproduction items for your home? Blackstone's is a good place to start your search. You'll find everything from stained-glass picture frames to candle snuffers.

Peabody Museum Gift Shop

11 Divinity Ave., Cambridge. ☎ **617/495-2248.**

A short distance from Harvard Square, this shop sells folk art and handmade crafts from all over the world, from primitive African sculpture to delicate Chinese porcelain, all at excellent prices. Open Monday to Saturday 10am to 4:30pm, Sunday 1 to 4:30pm.

Peacock Papers

200 State St. (in Marketplace Center). ☎ **617/439-4818.**

I love browsing through novelty shops like this one. You'll find everything from giftwrap to greeting cards, T-shirts, and desk toys here.

✪ Women's Educational and Industrial Union

356 Boylston St. ☎ **617/536-5651.**

Here you'll find beautiful pottery, jewelry, handmade children's clothes, toys, and needlework. This nonprofit educational and social-service organization has been part of the Boston scene since 1877.

MALLS/SHOPPING CENTERS

CambridgeSide Galleria

100 CambridgeSide Pl., Cambridge. ☎ **617/621-8666.**

This major shopping mall has three large department stores—**Filene's, Lechmere,** and **Sears**—and more than 100 specialty stores. Also found at this three-level mall is a food court and the **New England Sports Museum** (see Chapter 7, "What to See & Do in Boston," for more information). The Galleria's business center provides office services such as fax machines and typing. Strollers and complimentary wheelchairs are available. To get to the Galleria, take the Red Line to Kendall Square, then take the free shuttle bus, which runs every 10 minutes Monday to Saturday from 9am to 10:30pm and Sunday from 11am to 7pm. If you're driving, you can park in the garage beneath the mall.

Charles Square Complex

Bennett and Eliot sts., Cambridge. ☎ **617/491-5282.**

The stores at Charles Square (just look for the colorful flags) are a shopper's delight. Fashionable boutiques for clothing, gifts, novelties, and accessories are clustered around an atrium. An adjacent courtyard is used for dining, concerts, and festivals. Favorites here include the quality fashions at **Talbots** (☎ **617/576-2278**), which has a wonderful store for petites; the greeting cards and stationery at **Papermint** (☎ **617/492-0289**), and the travel and safari clothing at **Banana Republic** (☎ **617/497-8000**). There's an enclosed parking garage with validated parking for 700 cars under the central courtyard. Open Monday through Friday, 10am to 9pm; Saturday, 10am to 6pm; and Sunday, noon to 6pm.

✪ Copley Place

100 Huntington Ave. ☎ **617/375-4400.**

If you start your shopping excursions here, you may never leave, for there is also an 11-screen cinema complex, full-service restaurants (including a **Legal Sea Food** eatery), and several food shops. This elegant Back Bay complex appeals to the affluent shopper, who can stroll from the three-level **Neiman-Marcus** to **Tiffany, Gucci, Ralph Lauren,** and

Louis Vuitton, with perhaps a stop at **Godiva Chocolatiers** or **Williams-Sonoma** gourmet cookware. More than 100 shops radiate from a skylit atrium with a 60-foot-high waterfall sculpture circled by pink marble floors. Shop for men's and women's apparel, jewelry, music boxes, gift items, and home furnishings. For your sweet tooth there are three candy shops and **Mrs. Field's Chocolate Chip Cookies.** Escalators move shoppers (and sightseers) from level to level, and elevators are also tucked into the corners of the building.

Even if you don't plan to shop here, it's worth a visit. The six-block city within a city utilizes airspace over the Massachusetts Turnpike extension, uniting the Back Bay and the South End neighborhoods that had been split by the turnpike. The total cost of construction was more than $500 million.

The pink-and-buff stone exterior of the vast complex was designed to harmonize with the historic neighborhood of Trinity Church, the Boston Public Library, and the Copley Plaza Hotel. The complex is connected by glass-enclosed pedestrian bridges to the Westin and Marriott hotels and to the Prudential shopping center with its retail shops, as well as Lord & Taylor and Saks Fifth Avenue—and from there to the Hynes Convention Center.

Copley Place is open Monday through Saturday from 10am to 7pm, Sunday noon to 5pm. Some stores have extended hours, and the cinemas and some restaurants are open through late evening. The MBTA will take you to the Copley stop on the Green Line. An underground connection from the Orange Line and from Amtrak's Back Bay Station is also available. If you're coming in by car, take the Copley Place exit eastbound from the Massachusetts Turnpike. Park in the Copley Square garage on Huntington Avenue, corner of Exeter Street. If that's full, use the John Hancock garage or one of the nearby hotel garages. But since they're all expensive, and you'll probably want to spend your time and money shopping, public transportation may be a better choice.

Faneuil Hall Marketplace

Between North, Congress, and State sts. and I-93. ☎ **617/338-2323.**

In addition to Faneuil Hall Marketplace's appeal as a food and entertainment center, it should be part of your Boston shopping experience. There are three buildings in the market, separated by brick-and-stone malls. **The Central Building** has the food stalls, pushcarts, craftspeople, small stores, and novelties. The **South and North Markets** have the boutiques and clothing stores.

The **Arcade** in the South Market is a treasure trove of small boutiques with unusual wares. For example, at **Have A Heart,** everything from jewelry, stationery, and gift wrappings to quilts, pillows, and baby T-shirts has a heart motif.

Explore the vast assortment of furnishings and kitchenware at **Crate & Barrel.** Buy soaps, jellies, or dried petals and oils to make your own potpourri at Crabtree and Evelyn; and buy original scrimshaw jewelry and accessories, ships in bottles, and Nantucket antiques at **Boston Scrimshanders-Scrimshaw.** Take time out for a fabulous frozen hot chocolate at **Serendipity 3** (it's made with 14 kinds of chocolate).

Then on to the **Boston Pewter Company** for classic style and elegance. Buy a T-shirt at **Cheers,** a store that carries items with the logo of the famous TV show.

Check out the pushcarts in the Central Building (that's where all the food stalls are), and then go to the North Market. Perhaps you might start at one end of the building and browse through, upstairs and downstairs, stopping at whatever shops catch your fancy. Have fun at the **Disney Store,** where "greeters" welcome you as you enter and thank you for coming as you leave. And don't forget **Celtic Weavers** for handmade goods imported from Ireland and elsewhere around the world. Buy a kite for flying at **Kites of Boston**; and if you know you're going to burn off the calories, indulge your sweet tooth with fine Italian pastries at **North End Bakery.** Have lunch or dinner at **Durgin-Park** (see Chapter 6, "Dining," for details).

Unfortunately, I can mention only a few of the numerous shops here. It's fun to wander through and make your own discoveries. Shop hours are Monday to Saturday 10am to 9pm and Sunday noon to 6pm.

The Garage

36 John F. Kennedy St., near Harvard Sq., Cambridge.

This is another complex of small shops and eating places. Enjoy a roast beef sandwich with Boursin cheese at **Formaggio,** and don't leave the complex until you sample a cup of fresh-ground, freshly brewed coffee at the **Coffee Connection.**

MARKETS

✪ The Haymarket

Blackstone St. between North and Hanover sts. No phone.

This wonderful, European-style farmers' market buzzes with activity every Friday and Saturday as those in search of the freshest produce for their weekend dinner parties work their way through the crowds. In addition to produce, you can also get meats and cheeses from the surrounding shops. This is definitely one of my favorite Boston experiences.

MEMORABILIA

✪ Nostalgia Factory

336 Newbury St. ☎ **617/236-8754.**

There are hundreds of items here—"treasures" rescued from attics and closets. There's a nice collection of old-fashioned sheet music as well. A great place to browse and reminisce. There are new exhibits every month.

MUSIC

HMV

1 Brattle Sq., Cambridge. ☎ **617/868-9696.**

This music superstore is really attracting the crowds in Cambridge. The decor is sleek, and there's always a disc playing to attract the shoppers.

You can also listen to your musical selections before making your purchase.

Tower Records

360 Newbury St., at Massachusetts Ave. ☎ **617/247-5900.**

This is one of the largest record stores in the country, with three floors of records, tapes, and compact discs. You'll be greeted inside by blasting stereos and neon signs.

PERFUME

Colonial Drug

49 Brattle St., Cambridge. ☎ **617/864-2222.**

It's been several years since I first discovered this shop and I'm still working my way through the more than 900 fragrances featured at the perfume counter. No fancy displays, no pressure; just a lovely place to shop.

RUGS

Decor International

171 Newbury St. ☎ **617/262-1529.**

If you're in the market for a magic carpet, or just a tapestry or handwoven rug, stop in here. This store has the finest collection of unique handwoven rugs anywhere—including antique orientals—imported from more than 40 countries. Also check out the Navajo and hooked rugs, as well as quilts, bedspreads, pillows, folk art, and ethnic jewelry.

SHOES

Helen's Leather

110 Charles St. ☎ **617/742-2077.**

You've been looking for the perfect pair of boots, something unusual, something no one else has. Your search will undoubtedly end at Helen's leather. Many of the boots here are handmade from exotic leathers, including ostrich, buffalo, and snakeskin (of many varieties). The usual boot brands, like Tony Lama and Dan Post, are also available. If you aren't in the market for a pair of boots, maybe you'll find a new briefcase, belt, or leather jacket.

TOYS

F.A.O. Schwarz

440 Boylston St. ☎ **617/262-5900.**

At this legendary store you'll find high-quality children's toys. This is a fun place, not only for kids, but for their parents and grandparents as well. A towering teddy bear marks the entrance. Inside there are trains, games, dolls, dinosaurs, cars, and books all displayed in a collage of bright colors with happy music in the background. (Well, not exactly "background.") Also check out the 22-foot-high animated clock tower.

10

Boston After Dark

All through the year there are enough activities in Boston to keep the night owls busy, from jazz and rock clubs to romantic cocktail lounges for drinks and dancing, even dinner theaters presenting Broadway musicals.

Boston, however, is not a particularly late town. Bars can stay open until 2am, but some close earlier. The drinking age is 21, and a valid driver's license or passport is required as proof of age. If you've been drinking and don't feel comfortable driving back to your hotel, keep in mind that the "T" starts to close down at midnight, and all the trolleys and buses are tucked away by 1:30am. Taxis, however, are available round the clock.

DISCOUNT TICKETS Looking for theater or concert tickets at half price? The brightly lit Bostix kiosk in the heart of Faneuil Hall Marketplace offers a "daily menu" of entertainment events. There is another Bostix kiosk located in Copley Square as well. You'll find discounts on more than 100 theater, music, and dance events, as well as museums, historical sites, and tourist attractions in and around Boston. Half-price day-of-performance tickets, subject to availability, as well as full-price advance ticket sales are featured. (There is a service charge.) Discount-coupon packets for reduced rates on museums, films, and tourist sights are also available. Credit cards are not accepted here, and there are no refunds or exchanges. Bostix is open Tuesday through Saturday from 10am to 6pm (half-price tickets go on sale at 11am), on Sunday from 11am to 4pm. The Copley Square booth is open on Monday from 10am to 6pm as well. Call **617/723-5181** for recorded information on the day's offerings.

1 The Performing Arts

CLASSICAL MUSIC

✪ Boston Pops

Symphony Hall, 301 Huntington Ave., at Massachusetts Ave. ☎ **617/266-1492.** Tickets $31.50–$36.50 for tables. Lowest price is $11.50 for second balcony.

From early May until early July, going to the Pops is a must in Boston. Everyone loves these concerts by members of the Boston Symphony Orchestra. The music ranges from light classical to show tunes to popular. The regular seats at Symphony Hall are replaced with tables and chairs, and drinks and light refreshments are served by the Pops waitresses. The name "Pops" is short for "popular," though some local music historians say the name comes from the sound of popping champagne corks during concerts. Performances are Tuesday through Sunday evenings, and a week of free concerts is given at the Hatch Memorial Shell on the Charles River Esplanade in early July, including the traditional July 4th concert climaxed with fireworks. Call for program information.

✪ Boston Symphony Orchestra

Symphony Hall, 301 Huntington Ave., at Massachusetts Ave. ☎ **617/266-1492,** 617/CON-CERT for program information, 617/266-1200 to charge tickets in advance. Tickets $20–$60. Rush seats $11.50 (on sale 9am Fri; 5pm Tues, Thurs, and Sat). Rehearsal tickets $11.50.

A child growing up in Boston is likely to think that there is only one really great symphony orchestra in the world—the Boston Symphony, of course. It's been a tradition for more than 100 years.

The symphony season runs from October through April. The BSO performs most Tuesday, Thursday, and Saturday evenings, Friday afternoons, and some Friday evenings. Except for the Friday evening performances, a limited number of "rush" tickets, priced under $11.50, are available. Wednesday-evening and Thursday-morning rehearsals, some of which are open to the public, provide both a great value and a wonderful inside look at the orchestra.

Handel and Haydn Society

300 Massachusetts Ave. ☎ **617/266-3605.**

The Handel and Haydn Society has been giving concerts in Boston since 1815. The season runs year-round with a Symphony Hall Series, a Chamber Series, a Jordan Hall Chamber Series, and a Summer Series. The society has a reputation for high excellence in its performances.

DANCE

Boston Ballet

19 Clarendon St. ☎ **617/695-6950** or 617/931-ARTS for tickets. Tickets can be purchased at the Wang Center Box Office at 270 Tremont St., Mon–Sat from 10am to 6pm. Tickets range from $14 to $65.

You might not know this, but the Boston Ballet is the fourth largest dance company in America. For over 30 years it has maintained a high standard of artistic excellence and vision, and the Boston Ballet's repertory is an eclectic mix of classic story ballets, contemporary ballets, and avant-garde works.

Ballet Theater of Boston

186 Massachusetts Ave. ☎ **617/262-0961.** Call for ticket information.

If you're interested in contemporary ballet, you should definitely check the paper for performances by the Ballet Theater of Boston. They're a small, relatively new troupe, but their performances are excellent—both original and innovative.

THEATER

Stage productions in Boston run the gamut from professional Broadway shows to improvisational and experimental works and college productions. The name theaters that often host Broadway tryouts and national tours are the **Shubert Theatre** (265 Tremont St.; ☎ **617/426-4520**); the **Wilbur Theater** (246 Tremont St.; ☎ **617/423-4008**); and the **Colonial Theatre** (106 Boylston St.; ☎ **617/426-9366**).

College performances are quite good in Boston as well. The American Repertory Theater's **Loeb Drama Center** (☎ **617/547-8300**) at Harvard, **Tufts Arena Theater** (☎ **617/381-3493**) in Medford, **Spingold Theater Arts Center** (☎ **617/736-3400**) at Brandeis in Waltham, and **MIT** (general office of the theater department, ☎ **617/253-2877**) can all be counted on for good offerings.

Two very special institutions are the Charles Playhouse and the Larcom Theatre.

Charles Playhouse, Stage II

74 Warrenton St. ☎ **617/426-5225.** Tickets $23–$28.

The play *Shear Madness* has been a show-biz institution in Boston since it opened in 1980 in this cabaret-style playhouse. It's the longest running nonmusical play in theater history. The villain may change with each performance of this comedy-murder mystery, since the audience is part of the action, which takes place in a unisex hairdressing salon. They can also question suspects, reconstruct events, and then name the murderer. Performances are Tuesday through Friday at 8pm, Saturday at 6:30 and 9:30pm, and Sunday at 3 and 7:30pm.

Larcom Theatre

13 Wallis St., Beverly. ☎ **508/927-3677.** $10–$15 per person at either theater.

Located about a half hour's drive north of Boston, the Larcom is one of two stages upon which the nationally acclaimed Le Grand David and His Own Spectacular Magic Company create its dazzling illusions. Le Grand David has received accolades from its peers and the media, and has even performed at Easter parties at the White House. Its other venue is the Cabot Street Cinema Theater, also in Beverly at 286 Cabot Street.

A MAJOR MUSIC FESTIVAL

Tanglewood

Lenox. ☎ **413/637-1940.** Music Shed $13–$65, lawn $8–$11. To order tickets call Symphony Charge at 800/274-8499 or Ticketmaster at 800/347-0808.

Tanglewood is the summer home of the Boston Symphony Orchestra. Tanglewood concerts are presented from the end of June through the end of August; they feature outstanding conductors and soloists on Friday and Saturday evenings and Sunday afternoons. The best acoustical seats are in the Koussevitzky Music Shed, but it's great fun to pack a picnic supper, bring a blanket, and buy the inexpensive lawn seating. There are open rehearsals on Saturday mornings and student concerts on certain evenings. From Boston you can drive there in 2½ to 3 hours on the Massachusetts Turnpike.

CONCERT SERIES

FREE LUNCHTIME CONCERTS

Federal Reserve Bank of Boston

600 Atlantic Ave. ☎ **617/973-3453.**

Jazz, popular, and classical music are performed by local groups, Thursdays at 12:30pm.

King's Chapel Noon Hour Recitals

58 Tremont St. ☎ **617/227-2155.**

Concerts at 12:15pm on Tuesdays. Organ and vocal solos mark a pleasant midday interlude at this historic church.

Fridays at Trinity

Trinity Church, Copley Sq. ☎ **617/536-0944.**

Organ recitals by local and visiting artists, Fridays at 12:15pm. A wonderful time to see this architecturally notable church.

MUSIC IN THE MUSEUMS

Live music played amid a setting of masterpieces—what could be lovelier? Consider planning your visit to these museums in light of their concert schedules. There are also occasional concerts at the **DeCordova Museum and Sculpture Park,** on Sandy Pond Road in Lincoln (☎ **617/259-8355**). Check the newspapers for programs and times.

✪ **Isabella Stewart Gardner Museum**

280 The Fenway. ☎ **617/734-1359.** Concert fees, including museum admission, are $15 for adults, $9 for seniors and students, $7 youths 12 to 17 years old.

This glorious museum, modeled after a 15th-century Venetian palazzo, features soloists and chamber music in the Tapestry Room Saturday and Sunday at 1:30pm, from September through May.

Museum of Fine Arts, Boston

465 Huntington Ave. ☎ **617/267-9300.** Tickets $13.

The beautifully landscaped courtyard is the setting for a series of jazz and folk concerts Wednesday evenings in June, July, and August. The performances begin at 7:30pm, but the courtyard opens at 6pm for picnic suppers. Bring your own, or buy it there. You should bring a blanket or a lawn chair because seating is not guaranteed. If you purchase your ticket in advance, you're guaranteed a seat in the auditorium if it rains.

2 The Club & Music Scene

You can enjoy just about any type of club scene in Boston until the 2am "last call." From one end of town to the other you can find concert clubs, rock, disco, rap, and good jazz for listening and dancing. The following is a sampling of some of the best.

COMEDY CLUBS

Treat yourself to a few good laughs at the comedy clubs. Some are connected with national chains and are among the best in the country. Call for hours and "open mike" nights—tryout times for new comedians.

There are more than 20 weekly comedy rooms in Greater Boston. Some of the best known are listed below.

Comedy Connection

Quincy Market, Upper Rotunda. ☎ **617/248-9700.** Cover $7–$20 depending on evening of performance.

Boston's oldest original comedy club, established in 1968, has been rated tops by *USA Today, Rolling Stone,* and *Vanity Fair.* There's a comedy munchies menu and a dinner menu. Dinner is served only before the show. Shows nightly at 8:30 with late shows on Friday and Saturday at 10:30pm.

FOLK AND COUNTRY

If you prefer a less frenetic scene and your tastes lean to folk music, or you want a cozy place for hand-holding, try one of the many coffeehouses in town.

✪ Nameless Coffee House

3 Church St. No phone. No cover.

The Nameless attracts an enthusiastic young crowd that dotes on the wide range of music presented, the storytelling, and the free refreshments—coffee, cider, tea, cocoa, and cookies. Open September to May, Friday and Saturday 7:30pm to midnight.

Passim

47 Palmer St., Cambridge. ☎ **617/492-7679.** Cover $6–$15 depending on performers.

The best-known spot for folk music is Passim, behind the Coop. It was the focus of the folk boom in the 1960s and early 1970s and still has a national reputation as an outstanding showcase for folk musicians. Concerts are presented five nights a week; otherwise, this is a charming coffeehouse that offers lunch and light meals. Alcoholic beverages aren't served here, but you can purchase artwork and jewelry. Open Monday through Saturday from 11:30am to 11pm.

ROCK

The Rathskeller (The Rat)

528 Commonwealth Ave. ☎ **617/536-2750.** Call for a schedule of events and cover charges.

The Rathskeller, locally known as "the Rat," remains loyal to its punk-rock heritage. Located in the Kenmore Square area, it is Boston's oldest rock 'n' roll bar and grill with live music Thursday through Sunday nights in the lower level of the club. The restaurant menu ranges from barbecued ribs of considerable renown to sandwiches and vegetarian meals. The restaurant is open 11am to 10pm, the bar until 2am.

T.T. The Bear's Place

10 Brookline St., Cambridge. ☎ **617/492-0082.** Call for a schedule of events and cover charges.

This is one of the few clubs that admits guests under 21. It's "18 plus" to get in, and the Bear is usually packed with young people. Entertainment is offered from 9pm on. Monday night is Stone Soup Poetry night, and on Sunday Ethiopian food is served from 3pm to 11pm. There are also two pool tables.

JAZZ AND BLUES

Boston and Cambridge are enjoying a jazz revival. Many top musicians perform regularly in lounges and clubs throughout the area. You can even listen to live jazz in the shopping malls and outdoor plazas, such as the Prudential Center in Boston and Charles Square in Cambridge. There's also a weekend Cabaret Jazz Boat from Long Wharf. (Check the newspapers for listings.)

To find out who's performing where and when, call **Jazzline** (☎ **617/787-9700**).

✪ House of Blues

96 Winthrop St. ☎ **617/491-BLUE.**

One of Boston's most popular eateries, House of Blues is also one of the city's newest music hot spots. Blues bands perform several nights a week, and often more than one show is scheduled per night. Advance reservations are highly recommended. Call the above number for tickets and show times. (See Chapter 6, "Dining," for full listing.)

Regattabar

In the Charles Hotel, 1 Bennett St., Cambridge. ☎ **617/937-4020.** Cover charge $6–$20.

Featuring local and national artists, this nightclub offers the best jazz in the metropolitan area. The large third-floor room has a 21-foot picture window from which you can see the flag plaza of Charles Square and the bustle of Harvard Square while enjoying drinks. Buy tickets at the door or in advance from **Concertix** (☎ **617/876-7777**). Open Wednesday through Saturday with performances at 8 and 10pm.

Ryles

212 Hampshire St., Inman Sq., Cambridge. ☎ **617/876-9330.** Call for schedule and cover charges.

Serious jazz fans head to Ryles for its choice of bands on two levels. Downstairs, where dinner is served, you can socialize with music as the background. (Between sets, spin a few tunes on the jukebox—it's one of the best around.) Upstairs has great acoustics and a wide variety of first-rate jazz performances. Both offer good music and a friendly atmosphere.

Scullers Jazz Club

In the Doubletree Guest Suites Hotel, 400 Soldiers Field Rd., Cambridge. ☎ **617/562-4111.** $7–$25 cover charge, depending on performers.

The Scullers Jazz Club hosts top jazz singers and instrumentalists in a comfortable room with a view of the Charles River. Shows are usually

Monday through Saturday. There's also an excellent monthly dinner/ jazz show.

Sticky Mike's Blues Bar

Boylston Pl. ☎ **617/351-2583.**

Hear live blues every night, but don't expect to get a seat. Seating is at the bar only, and there's no dance floor, but that doesn't stop everyone from dancing anyway.

Willow Jazz Club

699 Broadway, Somerville. ☎ **617/623-9874.** Average cover charge $12.

Alternative jazz is featured here daily. The Willow's proximity to Tufts University campus makes it a popular student nightspot, but the top-notch musicians who play here lure jazz aficionados from miles around.

ECLECTIC

Johnny D's

17 Holland St., Davis Square, Somerville. ☎ **617/776-2004.** Average cover charge $6–$9.

This restaurant and music club is considered the best in Boston by some. Johnny D's books musicians from national and international tours. The music here runs a wide gamut—everything from zydeco and Afropop to Celtic balladiers.

DANCE CLUBS & DISCOS

Axis

13 Landsdowne St. ☎ **617/262-2437.** Cover $6–$12.

Axis attracts a young crowd with its progressive rock music and "creative dress." Special nights for hard rock, heavy metal, and alternative rock. Open Tuesday to Sunday 10pm to 2am.

✪ Avalon

15 Landsdowne St. ☎ **617/262-2424.** Cover varies; the average is $10.

This is a multilevel club with a full concert stage, private booths and lounges, large dance floors, and a spectacular light show. The dress code calls for jackets, shirts with collars, and no jeans or athletic wear; thus, it attracts a slightly older crowd than Axis. Open Thursday to Sunday.

Hard Rock Cafe

131 Clarendon St. ☎ **617/353-1400.** No cover charge.

The Hard Rock is a lively restaurant, a shrine to rock 'n' roll, with a menu of sandwiches, including their famous "Pig" sandwiches. The bar is shaped like a guitar; stained-glass windows glorify rock stars (Elvis is there); and the room is decorated with memorabilia of John Lennon, Jimi Hendrix, Elvis Presley, and others. You can buy T-shirts and other goods at the Hard Rock store. And there's lots of taped music to keep the crowd happy. Open daily 11am to 1am for food and until 2am at the bar.

Local 186

186 Harvard Ave. ☎ **617/351-2680.**

This is a popular spot for local talent and local residents. It's usually crowded, but if you're lucky you might be able to secure one of the two pool tables.

Zanzibar

1 Boylston Pl. ☎ **617/351-2560.** Cover varies; it averages $7 on weekends.

An atrium with a tropical atmosphere and 25-foot-tall palm trees is the setting for dancing to contemporary hits. The upscale clientele can also take a break from dancing to try the club's billiard room. Open Wednesday to Saturday 9pm to 2am.

3 The Bar Scene

Many of Boston's most popular nightspots are associated with the major hotels and restaurants (see Chapters 5 and 6); however, the following deserve a separate listing.

HOTEL BARS

✪ The Bar at the Ritz

15 Arlington St. (in the Ritz Carlton Hotel). ☎ **617/536-5700.**

This bar is elegance personified. The clublike setting with rich walnut paneling, a gleaming fireplace, and a magnificent view of the Public Garden make it one of Boston's favorite lounges. The Bar has even won several national awards for the perfect martini. Open Monday to Saturday from 11:30am to 1am, Sunday from noon to midnight. Lunch is served Monday to Saturday from noon to 2:30pm.

Bristol Lounge

200 Boylston St. (in the Four Seasons Hotel). ☎ **617/338-4400.**

This is a perfect choice after the theater, after work, or any time at all. An elegant room with soft lounge chairs, a fireplace, and fresh floral arrangements, it features a fabulous weekend dessert buffet. You can relax to the keyboard harmonies of some of Boston's foremost pianists every day. An eclectic menu is available from 11am to 11:30pm.

Plaza Bar

In the Copley Plaza Hotel, Copley Sq. ☎ **617/267-5300.**

The sophisticated Plaza Bar is a splendid setting for romance. The light is dim, the chairs and couches are of soft leather, and the drinks and food are excellent. The entertainment is a cabaret-style singer-pianist. Proper dress is required. Open Monday to Saturday 5pm to midnight.

The Spinnaker

At the Hyatt Regency, 575 Memorial Dr., Cambridge. ☎ **617/492-1234.**

If you leave your table for a few minutes and it's not there when you get back—don't worry! The core of this glass-walled rooftop lounge revolves, so it will return in about 50 minutes. Catch up with your friends and enjoy the view of Boston's skyline and the Charles River over drinks—all the regulars plus such specials as strawberry daiquiris and ice-cream cocktails. Decorated in shades of turquoise and gray, the Spinnaker is open for dinner nightly from 6 to 9:30pm. Cocktails are served until 12:30am weekdays, and until 1:30am on Friday and Saturday. Sunday brunch is 10am to 2pm. (See Chapter 6, "Dining," for details.)

SINGLES BARS

Bill's Bar

7 Lansdowne St. ☎ **617/421-9678.**

As its name suggests, Bill's is a regular kind of place, but it has an incredible selection of beers. Dancing isn't emphasized here, but drinking is; occasionally someone actually sounds good while singing karaoke. Open Thursday through Tuesday, 10pm to 2am.

Black Rose

160 State St., next to Quincy Market. ☎ **617/742-2286.**

This bar harks back to Boston's Irish roots. The music focuses on ancestral tunes and ballads, and "Mother Sweeney's" food is justly famous. Open daily 11:30am to 2am.

Bull & Finch Pub

84 Beacon St. ☎ **617/227-9605.**

The most famous pub in town, the Bull & Finch inspired the TV hit *Cheers.* The outdoor scenes were filmed at this popular bar downstairs at the Hampshire House, and thousands of tourists are attracted here each year; they find good food, drinks, and plenty of *Cheers* souvenirs. Casual pub fare is served from 11am to 1:15am.

Custom House Lounge

In the Bay Tower Room, 60 State St., Faneuil Hall Marketplace. ☎ **617/723-1666.**

One of the most romantic places in town, this lounge is on the 33rd floor. The spectacular view includes the harbor, the airport, and Faneuil Hall Marketplace. There's live music and dancing from 5 to 7:30pm Monday to Thursday and from 9pm to 1am Friday and Saturday.

The Harvest

44 Brattle St., Cambridge. ☎ **617/492-1115.**

This is a most sophisticated Cambridge watering spot, attracting celebrities, young professionals, and local faculty. (See Chapter 6 for restaurant listing.) The decor features crisp Marimekko prints against light woods. The outdoor terrace, with its umbrellas and trees strung with tiny lights, is delightful on a warm summer evening.

Jake Ivory's

1 Lansdowne St. ☎ **617/247-1222.**

Jake Ivory's is where Bostonians go to hear pianists tickle the ivories. At Jake's you won't hear rock and heavy metal; instead, you'll be treated to show tunes and sing-alongs. The big draw here is the "live dueling pianos." Open Wednesday to Saturday, 7pm to 2am.

Top of the Hub

Prudential Center. ☎ **617/536-1775.**

Boasting a dramatic, panoramic view of greater Boston, this spot is perched 52 stories above the city. There is music and dancing nightly. Dress is neat casual.

4 More Entertainment

MOVIES

Cinema in Boston is alive and well. Besides the many multiplexes that give you a choice of first-run films on six or so screens, there are assorted film festivals and theaters specializing in revival and avant-garde films.

To catch all the goodies that you missed years ago, check out the **Boston Public Library** (☎ **617/536-5400**) and the **Museum of Fine Arts** (☎ **617/267-9300**). Both offer screen oldies. There is a charge for the museum's film series, while the library's films are free.

The city's colleges and campus organizations sponsor independent film programs. Most of them are open to the general public. The prices are low, and students often get special rates by showing their ID cards. Some of the colleges offering film series are: **Boston College, Boston University, Harvard University,** the **MIT Film Society, Northeastern University,** and **Tufts University.** Check local publications for weekly information on these film showings.

LECTURES

Boston and Cambridge always attract top-name celebrities to the many lecture platforms in the area. To find out who's speaking where, check the "Calendar" section of the *Boston Globe* on Thursday, the *Boston Herald* on Friday, or the weekly *Phoenix.* One of the best series in town is the one presented by **Ford Hall Forum,** the longest running public lecture series in the country. Tickets are sold on a subscription basis, but there are usually extra seats in the large lecture halls, and the public is admitted free of charge 15 minutes before the program begins. Lectures are held on Sunday evenings at 7pm at Blackman Auditorium, Northeastern University (360 Huntington Ave., near the Museum of Fine Arts); and Thursday evenings at 7pm at Old South Meeting House (310 Washington St., in downtown Boston). For advance program information write to Ford Hall Forum, 271 Huntington Ave., Suite No. 240, Boston, MA 02115 (☎ **617/373-5800**).

POOL

As an alternative to the nightclub and bar scene, Bostonians have latched on to an old sport and made it highly fashionable. They love pool—not in the old dingy pool halls, but in the classy new clubs. Many of these clubs also offer darts, table tennis, shuffleboard, video games, backgammon tables, and batting cages.

Boston Billiard Club

126 Brookline Ave. ☎ **617/536-POOL.** Weekend evenings $11 an hour for two players. Each additional person $2 an hour. Lower prices during the day and on weekday nights.

The Boston Billiard Club, decorated with hunting prints, brass wall sconces, a mahogany bar, and outfitted with 42 pool tables has been rated the number one billiard club in the United States by *Billiard Digest Magazine.* There is full liquor service at the tables. Open Monday to Saturday 11am to 2am, Sunday noon to 2am.

Jillians Entertainment

145 Ipswich St. ☎ **617/437-0300.** $10 an hour for one player of pool, and $7 for a round of golf.

The owners of Jillians revived an interest in pool in Boston. They converted a 50,000-square-foot roller-skating rink to a 56-table pool parlor. It became a fashionable choice for the dating crowd, and grew in popularity with the addition of 18 holes of miniature golf, bumper cars, a mock casino, 150-game video midway, darts, table tennis, and more. There are three full bars and a cafe. Jillians is open Monday to Saturday from 11am to 2am and Sunday from noon to 2am.

11

Easy Excursions

Outside of Boston lies a treasure trove of sights and attractions. Though they're listed separately here, Lexington and Concord can both be visited on the same day. Boston's North Shore towns and Cape Ann would fill a second day; and a full day should be reserved for Plymouth.

1 Lexington & Concord

No visit to the Boston area is complete without an excursion to Lexington and Concord, the sites where the colonists began their fight for freedom. You'll be able to visit historic buildings like Buckman Tavern—the place where the Minutemen awaited the arrival of the British troops. And, in Concord, you'll visit Minute Man National Historical Park, which encompasses all the most important sites having to do with the Revolutionary War battle at Concord. Also in Concord, you'll be able to visit the house of Ralph Waldo Emerson, and Orchard House, the family home of Louisa May Alcott.

LEXINGTON

6 miles NW of Cambridge; 9 miles NW of Boston.

Lexington has been substantially absorbed into Boston as a suburb, but it still has an incredible sense of history about it. Resembling a small country town with an open common on which stands America's oldest Revolutionary War monument (the statue of the Minuteman), Lexington is where the growing tension between the British occupiers and the independence-seeking rebels first came to a head. Paul Revere rode through town around midnight warning the Minutemen of the approaching British troops. Hard on his heels came more than 400 British soldiers; fewer than 100 American patriots stood their ground and returned shot for shot. Nobody knows who set off the first musket, but the result of the crossfire was 8 dead and 10 more wounded. The battle continued through the day and, indeed, for the next several years.

Getting There You can follow Paul Revere's route through Arlington, but there is a more direct way. From Cambridge take Route 2 through Belmont. Follow the signs to Route 4/225 into the center of Lexington. Or take Route 128 north (I-95) to Exit 44, and then to the center of town. Do not try to drive through Cambridge and on to Lexington during the morning or evening rush hour.

The MBTA runs a bus from Harvard Square marked "Hanscom Field–Harvard, No. 528." It goes to Lexington every hour during the day and every half hour during rush periods. However, there is no night or Sunday service on this route.

Essentials In Lexington the **area code** is 617. Sketch maps and information about Lexington can be obtained at the Chamber of Commerce's **Visitor Center,** at 1875 Massachusetts Avenue (☎ **617/862-1450**).

WHAT TO SEE AND DO

The first thing to do in the area is stop by the Lexington Chamber of Commerce's **Visitor Center,** across from the Village Green. Here you can see a diorama outlining and explaining the Battle of Lexington. The **Minuteman Statue** on the Green is said to be of Capt. John Parker, whose words, perhaps more than any other, provided the rallying cry that settled the nerve of the Minutemen: "Stand your ground, don't fire unless fired upon, but if they mean to have a war let it begin here!"

Apart from the Town Common, among the major historic sights in Lexington are the **Buckman Tavern,** at 1 Bedford Street (now restored to its original state), the taproom that was the rendezvous for the Minutemen on that fateful battle day. The **Munroe Tavern,** at 1332 Massachusetts Avenue, is where the British troops maintained their headquarters. The **Hancock-Clarke House,** at 36 Hancock Street, is where Samuel Adams and John Hancock were sleeping when Paul Revere arrived to warn them of the imminent arrival of British troops. This house, furnished in colonial style, was originally built in 1738 and is now a museum of the Revolution.

All three buildings are operated by the **Lexington Historical Society** (☎ **617/862-1703**), which conducts guided tours. Hours are Monday to Saturday from 10am to 5pm and Sunday from 1 to 5pm, April through October. Admission is $3 each house; $7 for a combination ticket for all three; and children, $1 per house.

At the **Museum of Our National Heritage,** located at the corner of Massachusetts Avenue and Marrett Road (Route 2A, ☎ **617/861-6559** or 861-0729), the emphasis is on the development of the United States from its founding. There are four galleries of changing exhibits on dramatic historic events and popular culture. Lectures and films are often scheduled. An exhibit entitled "Lexington Alarm'd" explains the town's pivotal role in the American quest for independence. Admission is free. The museum is open Monday to Saturday from 10am to 5pm and on Sunday from noon to 5pm. Closed Thanksgiving Day, Christmas Eve, Christmas Day, New Year's Eve, and New Year's Day. Free admission and parking. Sponsored by the Scottish Rite of Freemasonry.

WHERE TO DINE

Hartwell House

94 Hartwell Ave., Lexington. ☎ **617/862-5111.** Reservations recommended. Main courses $3.50–$12.95 at lunch, $11.95–$21.95 at dinner. AE, DC, DISC, MC, V. Lunch Mon–Fri 11:30am–2:30pm; dinner Mon–Sat 5:30–10pm. AMERICAN.

Lexington

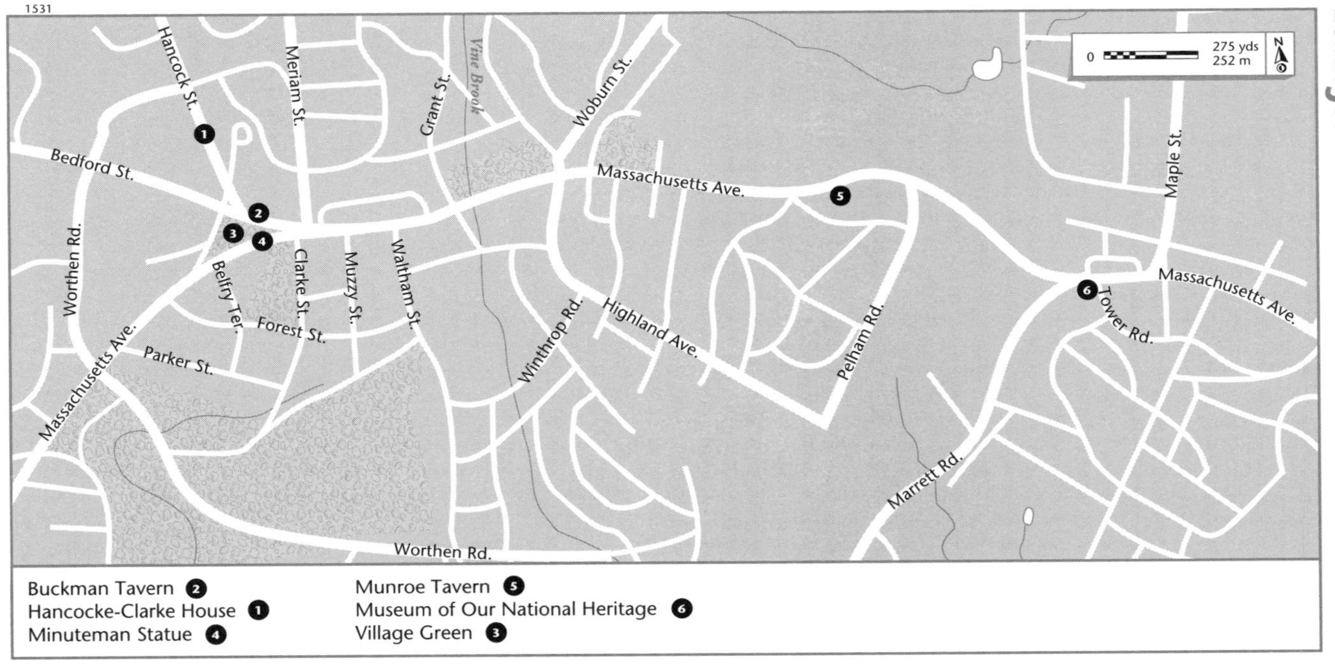

1531
0
275 yds
252 m
N
Hancock St.
Meriam St.
Grant St.
Vine Brook
Woburn St.
Bedford St.
Massachusetts Ave.
Maple St.
Worthen Rd.
Belfry Ter.
Clarke St.
Muzzy St.
Waltham St.
Forest St.
Winthrop Rd.
Highland Ave.
Pelham Rd.
Massachusetts Ave.
Tower Rd.
Parker St.
Massachusetts Ave.
Marrett Rd.
Worthen Rd.
Buckman Tavern 2
Hancocke-Clarke House 1
Minuteman Statue 4
Munroe Tavern 5
Museum of Our National Heritage 6
Village Green 3

One of the loveliest restaurants in the area, Hartwell House is located at Exit 31B off Route 128. Start your meal with an order of scallops Rockefeller (fresh sea scallops baked with seasoned spinach, Mornay sauce, and bacon) or Caribbean chicken fingers with a coconut-sesame seed crumb coating and served with a pineapple dipping sauce. As a main course, try the Oriental stir-fry or one of the fresh fish dishes. There's also a variety of pasta and meat dishes on the menu. For dessert you shouldn't miss the cappuccino ice-cream sundae. Try to get a table on the outdoor terrace, with a view of the little pond.

CONCORD

18 miles NW of Boston, 15 miles NW of Cambridge.

Getting There On your way to Concord from Lexington, take Route 2A west off of Route 4/225 at the Museum of Our National Heritage; you'll see signs reading BATTLE ROAD You'll be following the route the British took between the two towns.

There is no bus transportation to Concord, but there is a commuter train leaving from North Station in Boston that will take you there.

Essentials The **area code** in Concord is 508. Concord's **Chamber of Commerce** maintains an information booth (☎ **508/369-3120**) on Heywood Street, one block southeast of Monument Square, from April to October. It's open daily from 9:30am to 4:30pm. One-hour tours are available Saturday, Sunday, and on Monday holidays from April through October, or on weekdays by appointment.

In addition to being one of the area's most important sites in the history of the Revolutionary War, Concord was also the social center for the philosophical Transcendentalist Movement. In Concord you can visit Minuteman National Historical Park and imagine what it must have looked like in colonial days, and you can take a trip to Concord Museum, which documents the growth of the town and displays a variety of interesting artifacts. You'll also get the opportunity to visit the former homes of authors Ralph Waldo Emerson, Nathaniel Hawthorne, and Louisa May Alcott. A final stop in Concord for lovers of literature might be Sleepy Hollow Cemetery, where all of the above-mentioned are buried.

WHAT TO SEE AND DO

Minuteman National Historical Park

Monument St. ☎ **617/862-7753.** Admission to the park is free, and it's open daily (except major holidays) year-round.

The Minuteman National Historical Park encompasses many of the most important sites having to do with the first Revolutionary War battle at Concord. After the battle at Lexington, the British moved on to Concord, where the Minutemen were preparing to meet them head on. The Minutemen crossed the North Bridge (where a group of British soldiers were standing guard) and waited for reinforcements on a nearby hilltop. In Concord the British were searching homes and burning any guns they found along the way. The Minutemen saw the smoke and, thinking the British were burning their town to the ground, advanced against the men standing guard at the bridge.

The British fired at the Minutemen and the Minutemen retaliated. It was right at the North Bridge that the Minutemen fired the "shot heard round the world." While you're in the park, take a walk across the bridge (a modern version of the bridge that spanned the Concord River in colonial days). On one side you'll find a plaque commemorating the British soldiers who died in the Revolutionary War; on the other is Daniel Chester French's famous *Minuteman* statue.

You might also want to take a trip to the **North Bridge Visitor Center** (Route 2A; ☎ **508/369-6944**) which overlooks the river and the historic bridge from a hilltop location. There's a grand view from the top, and it's a great spot to view fall foliage (you can picnic in the shade of the trees, too). The North Bridge Visitor Center is open daily in summer from 9am to 5:30pm and in winter from 9:30am to 4pm.

The Old Manse

Monument Street at North Bridge. ☎ **508/369-3909.** $5 for adults, $4 for students and seniors, $3 for children 6 to 16, free for children under 6, $12 for families (three to five people). Admission includes a guided tour. Mid-Apr through Oct, Mon and Wed–Sat from 10am to 5pm and Sun and holidays from 1 to 5pm.

The Old Manse is Concord's most famous house. Built in 1769 by Reverend William Emerson, the home was occupied by his heirs and descendants for almost 170 years. That is, with the exception of the three years during which it was occupied by Nathaniel Hawthorne and his wife. During a visit to the house today you'll find mementoes and memorabilia from Hawthorne's stay, as well as from the Emerson family.

House of Ralph Waldo Emerson

28 Cambridge Tpk. ☎ **508/369-2236.** $4.50 for adults, $3 for seniors and children under 17. Guided tour $4 for adults and $2.50 for students. Mid-April to Oct, Thurs–Sat from 10am to 4:30pm and Sun from 2pm to 4:30pm.

Just a 10-minute walk from the green, the Ralph Waldo Emerson House was a meeting place for Emerson and his friends. You'll see original furnishings and some of Emerson's memorabilia.

Concord Museum

Lexington Rd. and Cambridge Tpk. ☎ **508/369-9763.** $6 for adults, $5 for seniors, $3 for students and children 15 and under, and $12 for families. Apr–Dec, Mon–Sat from 10am to 5pm and Sun from 1 to 5pm. From Jan to May the museum is open sporadically, so call for hours.

Located just across the street from the Ralph Waldo Emerson House, the Concord Museum takes visitors back to the 17th century and the founding of Concord. The various rooms and galleries depict the growth of the town from Native American habitation to European settlement, the battle of 1775 at North Bridge, and through the days of the transcendentalists and Louisa May Alcott. Interesting historical artifacts include one of the lanterns that signaled Paul Revere's famous ride; decorative arts and domestic artifacts owned by area residents or crafted by area artisans; a room arranged the way Ralph Waldo Emerson's study looked just before he died in 1882; and the largest collection of Thoreau's belongings anywhere in the world. There are changing exhibits in the New Wing throughout the year. The museum

A Local Scribe: Louisa May Alcott

Most famous for her novel *Little Women,* Louisa May Alcott (1832–1888) was educated by her father, Bronson Alcott. She was a friend of transcendentalists Henry David Thoreau and Ralph Waldo Emerson. Her first book, *Flower Fables* (1854) is a collection of stories Alcott made up to amuse Emerson's daughter, whom she cared for on occasion. In her younger years, Alcott held several menial jobs (seamstress and maid) in order to contribute to the small family income. She later worked as a Civil War nurse. During that time she wrote many letters home, which have been compiled in a collection titled, *Hospital Sketches* (1863). Because of the popularity of *Little Women* (1868), most people don't know that Alcott published her first novel, *Moods,* in 1864. Later works include *Good Wives (*1869), *Little Men* (1871), *Jo's Boys* (1886), and *Under the Lilacs* (1879), all children's books. She wrote two less successful novels for adults. The first, titled *Work* (1873) documents Alcott's early years as a working woman. The second, *Diana and Persis* (an unfinished work), is the story of the relationship between two women artists.

is currently working on an historical installation entitled "Why Concord?" to be open by April of 1996.

Orchard House

399 Lexington Rd. ☎ **508/369-4118.** $5.50 for adults, $4.50 for seniors and students, $3.50 for children ages 6 to 17 (free for children under 6), and $16 for a family (up to 2 adults and 4 children).

Heading east along Lexington Road you will come to the home in which the Alcott family resided from 1858 to 1877. Amos Bronson Alcott, father of Louisa May Alcott, a transcendentalist writer, educator, and philosopher, purchased 12 acres of land on Lexington Road and restored and joined the two early 18th-century homes that existed on the land. Mr. Alcott's life passion was to reform the educational system, but his theories of education were far too advanced to be implemented. In Concord, with the likes of Hawthorne, Emerson, and Thoreau, he found himself in excellent company and was successful in founding the Concord School of Philosophy directly behind his house. It functioned as a summer school for adults until he died in 1888. Today many educational programs are held there.

The rest of the Alcott family is equally (if not more) well known for artistic and cultural contributions. The most famous of the sisters is Louisa, author of the beloved classic *Little Women.* Anna, the oldest, was an actress, and May was a talented artist. Elizabeth died before the family moved to Orchard House. Bronson's wife was a social activist and frequently assumed the role of family breadwinner.

The Wayside

455 Lexington Rd. ☎ **508/369-6975.** The Wayside is open to visitors, but open hours and admission prices vary so call ahead.

Concord

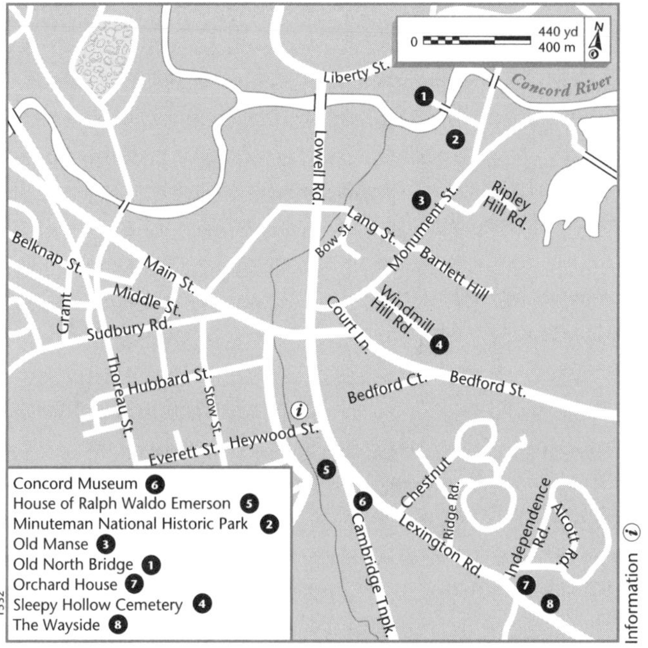

After Nathaniel Hawthorne's three-year stay at the Old Manse (1842–45), he and his wife moved to Salem, where he wrote his most famous work, *The Scarlet Letter.* From there he moved to Lenox, where he remained until 1852. That year, he returned to Concord and purchased a house known as The Wayside. Hawthorne remained at The Wayside until his death in 1864. The house is described in Louisa May Alcott's, *Little Women.* Margaret Sidney, who wrote *Five Little Peppers,* later occupied the house. Today, most of the furnishings are hers; however, there are several exhibits whose subjects are the house's famous former residents (Hawthorne included).

Sleepy Hollow Cemetery

Entrance is on Route 62 West.

One final place you might like to visit before leaving Concord is Sleepy Hollow Cemetery, which is the resting place of many of the town's famous authors, among them the Alcotts, Emerson, Hawthorne, and Thoreau. Their grave sites are located at the top of the hill in an area known as Author's Ridge. Emerson's grave, in keeping with his transcendentalist philosophy, is marked by a great uncarved quartz boulder.

WHERE TO STAY AND DINE

Colonial Inn

48 Monument Sq., Concord, MA 01742. ☎ **508/369-9200** or 800/370-9200. 54 rms. A/C TV TEL. Main inn, $125–$150 single or double; Prescott wing $85–$150

single or double; The Cottage $150–$200 single or double. AE, DC, MC, V. Free parking.

The main building of the Colonial Inn dates from 1716 and is quite small, but several new and modern additions make the inn significantly larger. Only 12 original colonial-era rooms are available to guests, and as you can imagine, they are the ones that are most sought after by visitors, so if you're interested in staying in the main inn, make your reservations as early as possible. The inn faces Concord's Monument Square.

In addition to overnight accommodations, the Colonial Inn has a restaurant offering an eclectic selection of items, including jumbo prawns, or a grilled chicken burrito at lunch. Dinner is primarily surf and turf. At dinner jackets are required for men.

2 The North Shore & Cape Ann

Cape Ann is a smaller Cape Cod, known mainly to Bay Staters and artists. This is New England's rock-bound coast, where Yankee fishermen and clipper-ship captains built their homes. Now a busy resort area, its beaches, seaports, and shops attract tourists, artists, and antiques hunters. You can drive there directly from Boston in about an hour by taking Route 128. It takes a bit longer if you take Route 1A, the winding scenic route, but it's worth it, since you can explore the North Shore towns of Swampscott, Marblehead, Salem, Essex, and Gloucester before reaching Rockport, the famous artists' colony on the tip of Cape Ann.

The **North of Boston Convention & Visitors Bureau** (P.O. Box 642, Beverly, MA 01915; ☎ **508/921-4990** or 800/742-5306) has a free 68-page guidebook to the area; you may also write directly to the chamber of commerce in the town or towns you wish to visit.

The Road North Out of Boston Since the trickiest part of getting to Cape Ann is finding your way out of Boston, some driving instructions are in order. (On summer weekends this area is incredibly crowded, by the way; try to make this trip on a weekday.) First find your way to the Callahan Tunnel by following the maze through the market district. If you take a left at the wrong place and find yourself on the Northeast Expressway instead, don't panic. Just take the Mystic River Bridge to Route 1A in Revere, where the scenic drive begins. (Take the exit marked "Revere" if you're on the bridge; the tunnel takes you directly to Route 1A.)

SWAMPSCOTT & MARBLEHEAD

Swampscott: 12 miles NE of Boston; Marblehead: 15 miles NE of Boston

Just past Lynn as you travel up the North Shore are Swampscott and Marblehead. You might like to stop here for a while; wander through "Old Marblehead," with its winding, narrow streets and 18th-century homes bordered by hollyhocks and curio shops; and then perhaps have a meal in either of the two towns. Marblehead calls itself the "Yachting Capital of the World"; in summer the boats in the inner harbor are packed together like sardines. (Marblehead fishermen specialize in

The North Shore

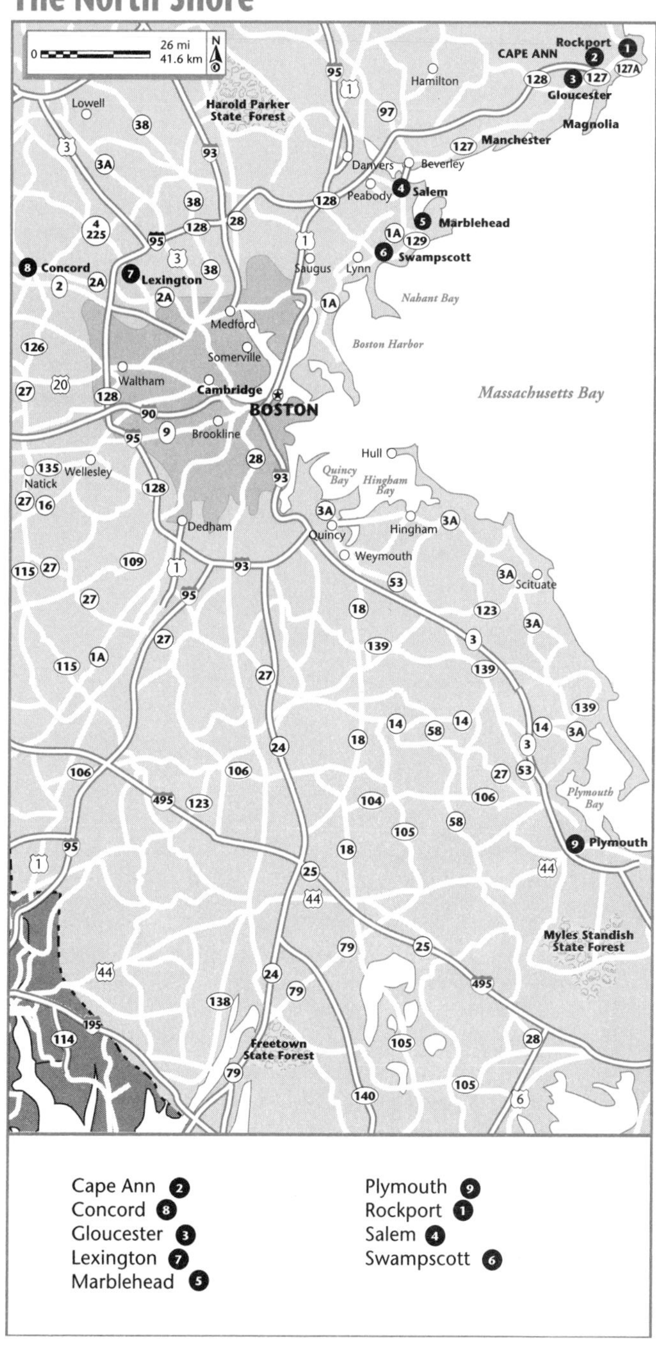

0
26 mi
41.6 km
N
Rockport
CAPE ANN
Gloucester
Magnolia
Manchester
Hamilton
Lowell
Harold Parker State Forest
Danvers
Beverley
Peabody
Salem
Marblehead
Swampscott
Saugus
Lynn
Nahant Bay
Concord
Lexington
Medford
Somerville
Boston Harbor
Waltham
Cambridge
BOSTON
Massachusetts Bay
Brookline
Hull
Wellesley
Natick
Quincy Bay
Hingham Bay
Dedham
Quincy
Hingham
Weymouth
Scituate
Plymouth Bay
Plymouth
Myles Standish State Forest
Freetown State Forest
Cape Ann 2
Concord 8
Gloucester 3
Lexington 7
Marblehead 5
Plymouth 9
Rockport 1
Salem 4
Swampscott 6

flounder, mackerel, and lobster.) In the outer harbor there is sailboat racing all summer, and the popular "Race Week" in July attracts enthusiasts from all over the country.

Marbleheaders are justly proud of their historical background. This has been a seafaring town from colonial days, deriving its name from the marblelike rock cliffs that protect it from the sea. (Walk along Front Street to Fort Sewall and you can climb right out onto the cliffs and soak up the sun and sea breezes.) Merchant ships used to sail around the world from here, and wealthy sea captains built beautiful mansions, some of which still stand.

Getting There If you're driving, head north on Route 1A through Revere and Lynn; pick up Route 129 where you see the signs for Swampscott and Marblehead.

Bus no. 441 or 442 leaves from Haymarket Square in Boston. No. 442 goes directly to downtown Marblehead, whereas no. 441 stops at Vinnin Square shopping center in Swampscott.

Essentials The **area code** is 617. Contact the **Marblehead Chamber of Commerce** (62 Pleasant St., P.O. Box 76, Marblehead, MA 01945; ☎ **617/631-2868**) for further information.

WHAT TO SEE & DO

In Swampscott, you can watch the boats in the cove at Fisherman's Beach, fish from the town pier, or go swimming right in town or at nearby Nahant Beach. You might also visit the **Mary Baker Eddy Historic House** (23 Paradise Rd., Route 1A; ☎ **617/599-1853**), open May to November, Monday to Saturday from 10am to 5pm, Sunday from 2 to 5pm; and November to January and March to May, Tuesday through Sunday from 1 to 4pm. Closed in February. Admission is $1.50 for adults, 75¢ for senior citizens and children aged 12 and over.

An interesting spot in Marblehead is the **Lafayette Home,** at the corner of Hooper and Union streets. One corner of the house was chopped off to make room for the passage of Lafayette's carriage when he visited the town in 1824.

The **Me and Thee Coffee House** (28 Mugford St., Marblehead; ☎ **617/631-8987**) has good folk music from time to time. Call to find out who's on.

Jeremiah Lee Mansion

161 Washington St., Marblehead. ☎ **617/631-1069.** $4 adults, $3 students, free for children under 10. May to mid-Oct, Mon–Sat 10am–4pm, Sun 1–4pm. Closed Columbus Day to May.

Washington and Lafayette were guests at this house, one of the finest examples of pre-Revolutionary Georgian architecture in America. Built in 1768, the mansion retains its original hand-painted 18th-century English wallpaper, elaborate architectural details, and original rococco wood carvings, and has been outfitted with period furnishings. Collections of children's furniture and toys, nautical items, military memorabilia, and folk art are all housed inside. The Jeremiah Lee Mansion is the home of the Marblehead Historical Society.

King Hooper Mansion

8 Hooper St., Marblehead. ☎ **617/631-2608.** Tour: Donation requested. Mon–Sat 10am–4pm, Sun 1–5pm. There are private parties; tours are not held those days. Call ahead.

Located across the street from the Jeremiah Lee Mansion, the King Hooper Mansion was built in 1728 (a Georgian addition was added in 1747). It was the home of merchant prince Robert Hooper, known as "King" because of his generosity to the town. Splendidly decorated and furnished, it includes a ballroom and wine cellar. This building is now the headquarters of the Marblehead Arts Association. There's free admission to the two rooms of changing art exhibits.

Abbot Town Hall

Washington Sq., Marblehead. ☎ **617/631-0528.** Admission free. Mon and Thurs–Fri 8am–5pm, Tues–Wed 8am–9pm, Sat 11am–6pm, Sun and holidays 11am–6pm.

Located high on a hill, and quite visible from the moment you enter town, is Abbot Town Hall. Stop in and find your way to the Selectmen's Meeting Room, where you'll find the famous patriotic painting *The Spirit of '76.* While you're there, take a look at the deed by which Native Americans transferred ownership of the land to the Europeans in 1684.

Where to Stay

Bed and breakfasts are a good place to stay in small coastal towns, especially if you'd like an ocean view. You can get listings from the individual chambers of commerce or through a B&B agency, such as **Bed & Breakfast Marblehead & North Shore/Greater Boston & Cape Cod.** You can contact them at P.O. Box 35, Newtonville, MA 02160 (☎ **617/964-1606** or 800/832-2632 outside Massachusetts; fax 617/332-8572).

Nautilus Guest House

68 Front St., Marblehead, MA 09145. ☎ **617/631-1703.** 4 rms (none with bath). $55–$60 double. No credit cards.

In this guest house you're really treated like a guest. It's located on the harbor, and some of the rooms have ocean views. Since it's right in the heart of "Old Town," you can easily browse in the little shops, go antiquing, and stroll the winding streets of the town. All rooms have semiprivate bathroom facilities. Reserve your room well in advance because this small Marblehead house is in great demand because of its waterfront location and its proximity to some of Marblehead's best shopping.

Spray Cliff

25 Spray Ave., Marblehead, MA 09145. ☎ **617/631-6789** or 800/626-1530. 4 rms (all with bath). Memorial Day weekend to mid-Oct $159–$199 single or double; lower rates off season. Extra person $15. All rates include breakfast. MC, V.

Spray Cliff, a large Victorian Tudor located on a cliff overlooking the ocean, changed ownership in November of 1994. Innkeepers Roger and Sally Plauché have tastefully redecorated their property, Marblehead's only oceanfront bed and breakfast. Rooms offer mesmerizing views of ever-changing ocean activity. The setting is relaxing and peaceful, and Spray Cliff is just a one-minute walk to the beach and a five-minute drive into town. A full breakfast and evening refreshments are included in the rates. Smoking is not permitted.

Where to Dine

Moderate

General Glover House

Vinnin Sq., Rte. 1A, Swampscott. ☎ **617/595-5151.** Reservations recommended. Main courses $12.95–$17.95. AE, DC, DISC, MC, V. Mon–Sat dinner only 5–10pm; Sun 12:30–10pm. AMERICAN.

This large colonial-style restaurant is run by the Athanas family, who also manage the famed Pier 4 in Boston. The specialty of the house is roast beef from the open hearth. Crudités, marinated mushrooms, and popovers are offered before dinner. There are also some weeknight and Sunday dinner specials with salad and dessert, priced from $9.95 to $12.95. The Pier 4 ice-cream pie is a fabulous choice for dessert. There is free parking in General Glover's lot.

Hawthorne by the Sea

153 Humphrey St., Swampscott. ☎ **617/595-5735.** Reservations recommended. Main courses $9.95–$24.95. AE, CB, DC, DISC, MC, V. Mon–Fri lunch 11:30am–4pm, dinner 4–10pm; Sat lunch 11:30am–4pm, dinner noon–11pm; Sun 12:30–10pm. Free parking. SEAFOOD.

Perched on a cliff overlooking the beach, this large restaurant is one of the best-known dining spots on the North Shore. The specialty is seafood—as many as a dozen different kinds are offered. As a starter try the creamy clam chowder, and top off your meal with fabulous baked Alaska. For summer dining and drinks, there's an outdoor terrace practically on the ocean.

The Landing

81 Front St., Marblehead. ☎ **617/631-1878.** Reservations recommended. Lunch $6.95–$9.95, dinner $13.95–$19.95. AE, DC, DISC, MC, V. Daily 11:30am–midnight. SEAFOOD.

The Landing, probably the largest of Marblehead restaurants, caters to the boating crowd. Within, you'll find an English-style pub and dining rooms with a view of Marblehead Harbor, as well as a deck with a view of the harbor. If you're sailing by, drop anchor at the adjacent town dock. (If you're driving rather than sailing, there's valet parking.) For lunch or dinner you can order something as simple as fish and chips, or try something on the adventurous side, like mesquite smoked duck or mahimahi. The pub section offers beer and burgers and is a favorite meeting spot of the younger crowd. The Landing is a popular singles bar at night.

Rosalie's

18 Sewall St. ☎ **617/631-5353.** Reservations recommended. Dinner 5:30–9:45pm. NORTHERN ITALIAN.

Year after year Marblehead's most popular place to dine is Rosalie's. The restaurant is located in an unprepossessing three-story brick factory building. You'll climb the stairs to the small bar, and behind the bar booths is a large, high-ceilinged dining room where polite and professional waiters glide among small tables. The eclectic decor runs the gamut from 19th-century accents to Roman columns, but the overall feeling is upbeat, elegant, and romantic. There are two other dining rooms, but the maitre d' is near the bar, so go there first.

The menu changes seasonally, but always features various antipasti, such as snails and garlic butter in mushroom caps, or shrimp with prosciutto in mustard-butter sauce. The pasta (made on premises) dishes might include lobster ravioli, cannelloni, and *fettuccine pomodoro.* Main courses include veal, chicken, shrimp, and steak prepared in interesting ways. There's *pollo Francesca,* sautéed chicken breast in a light egg batter with mushrooms in Grand Marnier; veal Giorgio with onions, Dijon mustard, and cream; lobster and shrimp fra diavola; and such specials as seafood Posillipo—shrimp, mussels, littleneck clams, and fish poached in marinara-clam sauce on linguine.

Budget

King's Rook

12 State St., Marblehead. ☎ **617/631-9838.** Main courses $5–$8. MC, V. Lunch Mon–Fri noon–2:30pm; dinner Tues–Fri 5:30–11:30pm; Sat–Sun noon–11:30pm. CAFE.

This small cafe still retains the ambience of its early coffeehouse days. Guests read newspapers and magazines from the racks and enjoy the coffees, teas, chocolate, and fancy drinks that have been a mainstay. Light entrées, pizza, and rich desserts are served here. There are over 40 wines offered by the glass.

SALEM

17 miles NE of Boston, 4 miles NW of Marblehead

Unable to live down its reputation as the city where witches were hanged, Salem has capitalized on it instead. There's a Witch House, a Witch Museum, and even a Witch Trail, with signs showing a witch on a broomstick pointing the way. Although the witchcraft hysteria of 1692 brought Salem to the attention of the world, it is famous for many other things.

Salem is one of the oldest American cities, and parts of it have retained its former characteristics. The streets are lined with 18th-century homes, some preserved with their original furnishings. Chestnut Street, with its homes of the wealthy merchants of the China trade era, is considered one of the most architecturally beautiful streets in the country, and the residents must, by legal agreement, adhere to colonial style in their decorating and furnishings.

Getting There If you're driving, head north on Route 1A and follow the signs. Drive past Salem State College and turn left at the traffic lights onto Lafayette Street, which you follow to Derby Street. Turn right onto Derby, and you're in historic Salem. Parking is available close to the **Salem Visitors Center** (2 New Liberty Street).

If you'd rather go by public transportation, take bus no. 450 or no. 451 from Haymarket Square in Boston; trip time is about 45 minutes.

The commuter train from Boston's North Station stops in Salem. If you don't like steps, skip the train, since there is a long climb from train level to street level.

Essentials The **area code** is 508. The **Salem Chamber of Commerce** (32 Derby Sq.; ☎ **508/744-0004**) maintains an information booth in Old Town Hall (32 Derby Sq). It is open Monday through Saturday from 9am to 5pm and Sunday from noon to 5pm. The **National Park Service Visitor Center** at 2 Liberty Street (☎ **508/741-3648**) has exhibits on early settlement, the maritime age, and the leather and textiles industries, as well as a free film on Essex County. It's open daily from 9am to 6pm in the summer and until 5pm the rest of the year.

What to See & Do

Twenty historic places are listed on Salem's **Historical Trail,** but there are at least twice as many attractions—cultural and recreational included—that are worth visiting. Most of them are within walking distance of each other. If you prefer to drive, however, you can get a suitable city map at information centers at Riley Plaza, the Chamber of Commerce, or Old Town Hall (32 Derby Sq.).

At the National Park Service Visitors Center (Essex Street Side) you can board the **Salem Trolley** (☎ **508/744-5469**) for a one-hour narrated sightseeing tour and shuttle service to the historic attractions. (You can also board at any of the 12 stops on the way.) Get off for shopping, sightseeing, or dining, and reboard for only one all-day ticket. Cost is $8 for adults, $4 for children age 5 to 12. In December during Salem Trolley's "Holiday Happenings Celebration," the Salem Trolley Players present Ebenezer Scrooge in a traveling presentation of *A Christmas Carol* on board the Trolley. Special performances leave from Pickering Wharf, and advance reservations are suggested.

Pickering Wharf, at the corner of Derby and Congress streets, is a delightful cluster of town-house condominiums, a yachting marina, fine ships, and restaurants in a harmonious setting between the ocean and the city. The little gift stores, bakeries, candy stores, and ice-cream parlors are charming. Pickering Wharf is a lovely place to stroll, day or evening. Take a cruise on one of the excursion boats that tour the harbor or go out to sea on a whale watch.

And for a change of pace, have a picnic at **Salem Willows,** the waterfront amusement park just a few minutes away from the center of town. Free admission and free parking.

Salem Maritime National Historic Site

178 Derby St. ☎ **508/740-1660.** Free admission. Daily 8:30am–5pm. Closed Thanksgiving Day, Christmas Day, and New Year's Day.

It might be best to begin your tour at the wharves, from which Salem's ships set off to sail the world. They are now part of the nine acres of historic waterfront representing a cross section of the commercial foreign trading port of Salem. National Park rangers provide tours and programs around the site, explaining the maritime history. Tours and buildings open to the public vary according to seasonal schedules, but they usually include the following places of interest: Derby Wharf, the

1819 Custom House, West India Goods Store, the Bonded Warehouse, the Scale House, Derby House, and Central Wharf.

The House of the Seven Gables

54 Turner St. ☎ **508/744-0991.** $7 adults, $4 teens age 13–17, $3 children age 6–12. July 1–Labor Day daily 9am–6pm; off-season daily 10am–4:30pm. Closed Thanksgiving Day and Christmas Day.

Built by Capt. John Turner, this impressive 1668 building was the inspiration for Hawthorne's novel of the same name. Inside are six rooms of period furniture and a secret staircase.

Guided tours consist of an introductory audiovisual program, a visit to the house, the period gardens, and to Nathaniel Hawthorne's birthplace (c. 1750), which is on the grounds.

Pioneer Village

Forest River Park. ☎ **508/745-0525.** $4.50 adults, $3.50 seniors and teens age 13–17, $2.50 children age 6–12. Daily Memorial Day through Halloween 10am–4:30pm. Closed Nov 1–last week in May.

This is an authentic re-creation of an early Puritan settlement from the year 1630. Interpreters wearing authentic period clothing conduct tours through the dwellings. There are also craft demonstrations and farm animals. Combination discounted tickets for Pioneer Village and the House of Seven Gables are available at Pioneer Village and the House of Seven Gables. Pioneer Village is adjacent to a beach and picnic area if you want to take time out for a swim (except on weekends).

Peabody/Essex Museum

East India Sq. ☎ **508/745-9500** or 800/745-4054. Free admission first Thurs of the month 5–8pm. To galleries, libraries, or historic houses: $7 adults, $6 for seniors or students, $4 children 6–16, under 6 free. Families $18 (2 adults and one or more children). Mon–Sat 10am–5pm, Sun noon–5pm, Thurs until 8pm. Closed Mondays from November 1 to Memorial Day. Thanksgiving Day, Christmas Day, and New Year's Day.

When a group of Salem sea captains and world travelers formed the East India Marine Society in 1799, their charter included provisions for a "museum in which to house the natural and artificial curiosities" brought back from their travels. This was the genesis of the Peabody Museum, America's oldest museum in continuous operation.

In 1824 the society and its collections moved to larger quarters at East India Marine Hall. Since then, five annexes have been added. The most recent, the highly acclaimed Asian Export Art Wing, is dedicated to decorative art pieces made in Asia for Western use from the 14th to 19th centuries.

Just about every tourist to Salem finds something of interest here: The historian of American trade and culture uses the library, nautical buffs want to see the relics of the China trade, and those interested in architecture and decoration take the tour through one or more of the institute's half-dozen Salem houses, which date as far back as 1684. Children are fascinated by the unique collection of dolls, doll furniture, and toys from earlier times.

There's a lot more here than can be seen on a day trip to Salem, but an hour spent in one of the institute's 13 buildings, particularly the main building and adjoining houses, is a must for any Salem visitor. Some of the special collections that might interest you include clocks, ceramics, military uniforms and weapons, dolls and toys, glassware, buttons, silver and pewter, lamps and lanterns, sculpture, tools, costumes from earlier centuries, and mementos from the China trade, as well as a good collection of Massachusetts works of art, including paintings and furniture. Several galleries and exhibition rooms have changing shows, so the return visitor should check to see what's new.

The museum's other collections include New England maritime history; the practical arts and crafts of the East Asian, Pacific Island, and Native American peoples; and the natural history of Essex County.

Witch House

310½ Essex St. ☎ **508/744-0180.** $5 adults, $4 seniors, $1.50 children age 5–16. Mid-March to June and Labor Day–Dec 1 daily 10am–4:30pm; July–Labor Day daily 10am–6pm. Closed Dec–March 15.

This was the home of Magistrate Jonathan Corwin, who, in 1692, conducted some early examinations of accused witches in this house, along with John Hawthorne (a member of the same family as Nathaniel Hawthorne). It's an eerie-looking dwelling that has probably changed little since those days.

Where to Stay

Coach House Inn

284 Lafayette St., on Rtes. 1A and 114, Salem, MA 01970. ☎ **508/744-4092** or 800/688-8689. 11 rms (9 with bath). A/C TV. $65–$72 room with shared bath, $72–$95 with private bath; $125–$155 suite with kitchenette. Extra person $10. AE, MC, V. All rates include continental breakfast.

Not far from Salem harbor, this charming ship captain's mansion and carriage house dates back to the middle of the last century. The elegance of that time is preserved in the furnishings, high ceilings, and lavish fireplaces, many of marble or carved ebony. The Coach House Inn is nonsmoking.

Hawthorne Hotel

18 Washington Sq. at Salem Common, Salem, MA 01970. ☎ **508/744-4080** or 800/729-7829. Fax 508/745-9842. 89 rms. A/C TV TEL. $85–$120 single, $95–$132 double. Extra person $12. Children under 16 stay free in parents' room. Senior discount. AE, DC, DISC, MC, V.

The Hawthorne is located within walking distance of the waterfront and Salem's museums. A historic hotel, it has been restored to its 1920s elegance with fine wood paneling and brass chandeliers in the lobby and restaurant. The restaurant, Nathaniel's, serves breakfast, lunch, and dinner daily, plus a Sunday brunch. Tavern on the Green offers lighter fare and entertainment.

Salem Inn

7 Summer St., on Rte. 114, Salem, MA 01970. ☎ **508/741-0680** or 800/446-2995. 31 rms (all with bath). AC TV TEL. Mid-Apr to mid-Oct $99–$169; Halloween week $140–$175; Nov to mid-Apr $89–$149. AE, DC, DISC, MC, V. All rates include continental breakfast.

Right in the heart of downtown Salem, the Salem Inn is near all the historical attractions and the shopping center. The two restored and renovated sea captain's homes (located on a busy street) may not look too impressive on the outside, but walk through the front door and the scene changes. The atmosphere is bright and cheery, and there is a secluded garden and brick terrace at the rear of the building. All rooms have king- or queen-size beds, antique furnishings and period details, whirlpool baths, and in-room coffeemakers. Some of the rooms have working fireplaces. A continental breakfast is served in the Courtyard Cafe, the on-site restaurant. There is a gift shop.

WHERE TO DINE

Salem has some excellent restaurants in all price ranges and ethnic styles, located in the center of town along Derby Street and at Pickering Wharf. In addition to the restaurants we have listed below, you might want to try **Brothers Restaurant & Deli** (283 Derby St.; ☎ **508/741-4648**), a cafeteria-style family deli with home-cooked Greek meals, inexpensively priced; or, on the more expensive side, but with a better view, the terrace at **Victoria Station,** Pickering Wharf (☎ **508/745-3400**), where you can enjoy a drink or a meal as you watch the luxury yachts in the marina.

Moderate

Lyceum

43 Church St. ☎ **508/745-7665.** Reservations recommended. Main courses $9–$18. AE, DISC, MC, V. Lunch Mon–Fri 11:30am–3:30pm; dinner nightly 5:30–10pm. Sun brunch 11am–3pm. AMERICAN.

Located one block from the pedestrian mall, near the corner of Church and Washington streets, the Lyceum was once the center of the city's cultural life, and it's where Alexander Graham Bell made his first public demonstration of the telephone. There's a fireplace in the dining room, a large glass-enclosed patio, and a pub where lunch is served. Both lunch and dinner menus feature seafood, grilled meat, and chicken. The grilled butterflied whole baby chicken with a maple glaze is quite good, as is the cracked black pepper and lemon rubbed grilled pork tenderloin (served with Yankee cranberry chutney and garlic mashed potatoes).

Roosevelt's

300 Derby St. ☎ **508/745-9608.** Reservations recommended. Dinner $8.95–$17.95 (includes salad bar); Sun brunch $9.95. AE, DC, DISC, MC, V. Dinner Mon–Fri 5–9pm, Sat 5–10pm, Sun 2–10pm. Sun brunch 11am–2pm. AMERICAN.

Roosevelt's serves moderately priced seafood, pasta, and prime rib. The salad bar is the most bountiful in the area and comes free with your dinner. (Be sure to sample the baked beans.) Early-bird specials served 5 to 7:30pm include dinner and salad bar for around $11.

Budget

Stromberg's

Rte. 1A. ☎ **508/744-1863.** Seafood platters $9–$14. Lobster is priced according to season—usually around $14. AE, DISC, MC, V. Tues–Thurs 11am–9pm, Fri–Sat until 10pm. Closed Tues on long holiday weekends. SEAFOOD.

On the bridge between Salem and Beverly, Stromberg's is one of the most popular seafood restaurants on the North Shore. The drawing card is the combination of top-grade fish and low prices. Flounder comes straight from the fishing boats. There are always several daily specials in addition to the regular menu. Stromberg's is located on the spot where Roger Conant and his followers landed in 1686 and founded the town of Salem.

EN ROUTE TO GLOUCESTER & ROCKPORT

Whether you're zipping straight to Cape Ann from Boston or you're taking the scenic route through Marblehead, Salem, and other North Shore towns, there are several places along the way you should know about. If you have time to explore, exit from Route 128 at Route 133 to **Essex,** one of the country's earliest shipbuilding centers, now known for seafood restaurants, Essex clams, and antiques shops.

On Main Street on the Causeway in Essex, you'll find some excellent places to eat, including full-service restaurants and take-out spots. For both good food and a fine river view, try **Tom Shea's** (☎ **508/768-6931**). For a good buy, the **Village Restaurant** (☎ **508/768-6400**) at the end of the Causeway is top-rated for inexpensive dinners and fried clams (there's also take-out service). The most famous of the Essex restaurants is **Woodman's** (☎ **508/768-6451**), where, according to local historians, the first clam was fried when it was accidentally dropped into heated batter. It's a rustic, self-service eatery where long lines attest to its popularity. The portions are generous: The large clam chowder can really serve two people.

Well worth a stop is **Hammond Castle,** also known as Hammond Museum (80 Hesperus Ave., Gloucester; ☎ **508/283-2080**). You reach it by following scenic Route 133 (Exit 14 on Route 128) onto Route 127 going toward Manchester. Turn left onto Hesperus Avenue and follow the road to the castle. Financed (at a cost of more than $6 million) and planned by the inventor John Hays Hammond, Jr., this medieval castle was constructed of Rockport granite. There are 85-foot towers, battlements, stained-glass windows, a great hall 60 feet high, and an enclosed "outdoor" pool and courtyard lined with foliage, trees, and medieval artifacts. Many 12th-, 13th-, and 14th-century furnishings, tapestries, and paintings fill the rooms. A pipe organ with more than 8,200 pipes is used for monthly concerts. Write for a copy of their calendar. There are guided tours of the castle every day. Admission is $6 for adults, $5 for senior citizens, and $4 for children age 6 to 12; children under 6 enter free. The museum is open daily May through October from 10am to 5pm, weekends only November through April.

GLOUCESTER

33 miles NE of Boston, 16 miles NE of Salem

Gloucester's history is poignantly summed up by the bronze statue of the ***Gloucester Fisherman,*** a memorial to the more than 10,000 fishermen who went "down to the sea in ships" and did not return. The city's history goes back to the Norsemen who skirted the coast in A.D. 1001, and to the French explorer Samuel de Champlain, who founded what is now Eastern Point. A more recent claim to fame is the invention here of the process for blast-freezing foods by Clarence Birdseye.

The fishing industry is still alive and well in Gloucester. Each morning the "fishing boats out of Gloucester" still head out to sea in the early hours of the morning. If you decide to make a stop here, you'll get to see some of the little boats festooned with nets and rigging down at the harbor. Fish packing is done right at the quayside plants as soon as the fleet returns with the catch of the day. In addition, Gloucester is one of the whale-watching centers of the eastern seaboard, and if you've been considering a whale-watching tour, this is the time to do it.

Getting There If you're driving north from the Salem area on a leisurely tour, follow Route 1A from Salem to Beverly, where you can take Route 127 up through Manchester all the way to Gloucester. If you're coming from Boston or you'd like to take a speedier trip from Salem, work your way to Route 128 heading east and stick with it; the road goes directly to Gloucester.

The commuter train from Boston's North Station runs to Salem, Beverly, Gloucester, and Rockport. Be forewarned: At some of these stops you'll have to walk a mile or more to reach the points of interest. Call the **Massachusetts Bay Transportation Authority** (☎ **617/722-5000**) for train schedules.

The **Cape Ann Transportation Authority (CATA)** runs buses from town to town on Cape Ann. Call **508/283-7916** for information.

Essentials The **area code** is 508. Information can be obtained at the **Cape Ann Chamber of Commerce** (☎ **508/283-1601** or 800/321-0133), which maintains a courtesy phone, public restrooms, and an information center with a menu rack and brochures. It's open year-round at 33 Commercial St., Gloucester, MA 01930.

What to See & Do

Gloucester still retains almost as close an association with the sea and seafarers as it did when founded about 350 years ago. It has a large Italian and Portuguese fishing colony, and their annual **Festival of Saint Peter** (at the end of June or beginning of July), the blessing of the fleet, attracts tourists from all over the country. There are parades, floats, and marching bands; and a remarkable 600-pound statue of St. Peter is carried aloft through the main streets.

The **Rocky Neck Art Colony** in East Gloucester is the oldest working art colony in the country. Primarily a working center for artists (as opposed to just a series of shops selling their wares), it's on a tiny jetty of land connected to the mainland by a causeway. About two dozen galleries are located in its colorful alleys and piers, along with fishing boats, appealing shops, and restaurants. To reach Rocky Neck, take Route 128 to East Gloucester, Exit 9, and follow East Main Street to Rocky Neck Avenue. (Rudyard Kipling worked on his book *Captains Courageous* on Rocky Neck.)

Stage Fort Park is the site of an historical fort with ancient cannons. Located on Hough Avenue (off Western Avenue), it has picnic areas and beaches open to the public. **Harbor Loop** is where band concerts are held. **Eastern Point Lighthouse** and **Breakwater** offers a magnificent view of the ocean. In nice weather you can walk to the end of the breakwater. On **State Fish Pier,** Parker Street, fishermen unload their catches every morning.

North Shore Harbor Cruises & Whale Watches

For cool ocean breezes, sightseeing, a sunset cruise, or whale watching, take an excursion boat from either Gloucester or Salem. In Gloucester, an old-time paddleboat named *Dixie Belle* sails from the Seven Seas Wharf at the Gloucester House Restaurant on the hour from 10am to 5pm, and from Rocky Neck in East Gloucester, near the Rudder Restaurant, on the half hour, for a 45-minute narrated tour. At Pickering Wharf, Salem Willows, and Central Wharf at the Derby waterfront in Salem you can choose from a variety of cruises around Salem and Marblehead harbors.

The most exciting excursions are the whale-watching trips that take you 15 miles out to sea to Stellwagen Bank, which runs from Gloucester to Provincetown. During their north-south migration, the whales feed upon the millions of sand eels and other fish that gather along this bank. The whales often perform for their audience, too, by jumping out of the water, and occasionally dolphins join the show.

Dress warmly for these cruises, since it's much cooler at sea than in town, and take sunglasses, a hat, rubber-soled shoes, and a camera with plenty of film. For some it might be advisable to take a motion-sickness pill before boarding.

Check the local marinas for sailing times, prices (around $20 for adults, less for children and senior citizens), and reservations. In Gloucester, call **Seven Seas Whale Watch** (☎ **508/283-1776**) or **Yankee Whale Watch & Deep Sea Fishing** (☎ **508/283-0313** or 800/WHALING). Or contact the **Cape Ann Chamber of Commerce** (128 Main St., Gloucester, MA 01930; ☎ **508/283-1601**) for information and brochures from the many whale-watching fleet captains.

Beauport (Sleeper-McCann House)

75 Eastern Point Blvd. ☎ **508/283-0800.** $5 adults, $4.50 seniors, $2.50 children under 12. Tours May 15–Oct 15 Mon–Fri 10am–4pm; mid-Sept to mid-Oct Mon–Fri 10am–4pm, Sat–Sun 1–4pm.

Beauport was designed by interior decorator Henry Davis Sleeper to house his vast antique collections. From 1907 to 1934 he designed more than 40 unusual rooms, of which 26 are open to the public. The most popular are the Golden Step Room, with a breathtaking view of the harbor; the Pine Kitchen, in the style of an old pioneer home; the Tower Library, with an immense collection of antiquarian books; and the Paul Revere Room.

Cape Ann Historical Association

27 Pleasant St. ☎ **508/283-0455.** $4 adults, $3.50 seniors, $2.50 students, children 6 and under free. Tues–Sat 10am–5pm. Closed Feb.

Combining an historic furnished house with a modern addition, this museum details Cape Ann's history. Exhibition areas include the Capt. Elias Davis House (1804), decorated and furnished in the Federal style with furniture, silver, and porcelains; plus the nation's single largest collection of paintings and drawings by Fitz Hugh Lane, the American luminist painter. New galleries featuring 20th-century Cape Ann art include the work of John Sloane, Maurice Prendergast, Milton Avery, and Paul Manship. The fisheries and maritime galleries feature vessels, famous solo sailors, exhibits on the fishing industry, ship models, and historic photographs of the Gloucester waterfront and fishing fleet.

WHERE TO STAY

Atlantis

125 Atlantic Rd., Gloucester, MA 01930. ☎ **508/283-0014.** 40 rms. TV TEL. Late June–Labor Day $95–$105 double, Labor Day–Columbus Day $75–$90 double, Columbus Day–Oct 31 $60–$65 double. Rates also adjusted seasonally Apr–June. Extra person $8. AE, DC, MC, V. Closed Nov–Apr.

One of the friendliest motor inns is Atlantis, in the Bass Rocks section of Gloucester. It has the charm and warmth of a guest house, yet it's a large up-to-date facility with Danish modern decor, wide picture windows, private sun decks, and a landscaped heated swimming pool. There's a coffee shop on the premises.

Best Western Bass Rocks Ocean Inn

107 Atlantic Rd., Gloucester, MA 01930. ☎ **508/283-7600.** Fax 508/281-6489. 48 rms. A/C TV TEL. April 28–June 15 $85–$99 single or double; June 16–Sept 4 $110–$125 single or double; Sept 5–Oct 22 $105–$115 single or double. Extra person $8. Rollaway bed $12. Children under 12 stay free in parents' room. All rates include continental breakfast. AE, CB, DC, DISC, MC, V. Closed Dec–Mar.

Directly on the oceanfront, this outstanding motel looks like a southern mansion, with its stately white columns and red-brick walls. The rooftop sun deck, balconies, and swimming pool all offer excellent views of the surf. The large rooms have balconies or patios. Each morning a complimentary, cold buffet breakfast is served, and each afternoon coffee and chocolate chip cookies are free to hotel guests. A billiard room and library are available, and bicycles are at the disposal of the guests. Rooms are available for nonsmokers.

WHERE TO DINE

The Gull

75 Essex Ave. (Mass. 133). ☎ **508/283-6565** or 281-6060. Reservations recommended for parties of 8 or more. Main courses $5.95–$11.95 at lunch, $6.95–$20.95 at dinner. MC, V. Daily 5am–9:30pm. Directions: Take Mass. 133 less than two miles west of the "Man at the Wheel" statue or approach along Mass. 133 eastbound from Mass. 128. SEAFOOD.

Among my favorite places to dine in Gloucester is the Gull, located at the Cape Ann Marina on Mass. 133, a mile or so from the center of town right next to where the Yankee Whale Watch boats depart. The staff here is very friendly, and the big, simple, but attractive restaurant overlooks the Annisquam River. The Gull is a favorite with boaters, tourists, families, and sailors. Seafood is the forte here, and you can have the huge, succulent lobster sandwich or a full clambake with steamers, corn on the cob, coleslaw, and a lobster. The fish and chips here are quite good also. In addition to seafood, prime rib and steak selections are also offered. The Gull has a full bar.

The Rudder Restaurant

73 Rocky Neck Ave., East Gloucester. ☎ **508/283-7967.** Reservations required for weekends. Main courses $12.95–$19.95. DISC, MC, V. Mid–Apr to Nov, daily noon–10:30pm. SEAFOOD/INTERNATIONAL.

A meal at the Rudder is not just a meal—it's a party. One look at the wildly creative menu will confirm that. Located on the water, right in the heart of the Rocky Neck Art Colony, the Rudder is jam packed, floor to ceiling, with gadgets, colored lights, antiques, photos, menus from around the world, and other collectibles. If that isn't enough, there's live entertainment, including a woman who does an invisible flaming baton twirling act. The chefs here are creative (try the shrimp farcis for an appetizer), and main course offerings run the gamut from baked stuffed sole to fried clams and chicken picatta. Brunch is served Friday through Sunday.

ROCKPORT

40 miles NE of Boston, 7 miles N of Gloucester

Over the years the small coastal town of Rockport, at the very tip of Cape Ann, has undergone a transformation from a workingman's town with an active fishery and a thriving granite excavation and cutting industry to a town whose lifeline is its popularity with tourists. It's always been a charming place, in a particularly New England way, and Winslow Homer is only one of the famous artists who have come here to capture the local color on canvas.

The **Rockport Art Association** is still an active organization, and there are many art galleries in town. You'll also find a number of interesting places to stay and some great restaurants.

Getting There If you go by car, Rockport is a few miles north of Gloucester along Route 127. If you stop at all of the North Shore spots discussed above, it will probably take you three days to drive there from Boston. On the other hand, if you do all your sightseeing from the window, your trip will take less than 90 minutes.

Commuter trains run from Boston's North Station to Rockport. The trip takes about an hour. Call the **Massachusetts Bay Transportation Authority** (☎ **617/722-5000**) for details.

The **Cape Ann Transportation Authority (CATA)** runs buses from town to town on Cape Ann. Call **508/283-7916** for details.

Essentials The **area code** is 508. The **Rockport Chamber of Commerce** (3 Main St.; ☎ **508/546-6575**), is open year-round from 9am to 5pm daily. They also operate a seasonal (mid-May to mid-October) information booth on Upper Main Street.

Since weekend parking can be a hassle, try to go on a weekday. I suggest circling the square once (meters have a two-hour limit), and if there's no place to park try the back streets, even if they're some distance from the center of town. Or use the parking lot on Upper Main Street, Route 127, on weekends. Parking from 11am to 6pm will cost about $7, and there's a free shuttle that will take you downtown and back.

What to See & Do

Even though there are many charming areas in Rockport, the wooden fish warehouse on the old wharf in the harbor stands out, since it has probably been the subject of more paintings than anything since the Last Supper. The red shack, known as Motif No. 1, is a fitting symbol for this beautiful fishing town. Destroyed during the blizzard of 1978, it has been rebuilt through donations from the local community and tourists. It stands again on the same pier, duplicated in every detail, and reinforced to withstand further northeast storms.

It's easy to see why aesthetes are captivated by the town's charm: the picket-fenced colonial houses; the narrow, winding streets; the crash of waves against the rocky shore, and the ever present squeal of swooping seagulls. Rockport's pride and joy is Bearskin Neck, a narrow peninsula of one-way alleys lined with galleries, antiques stores, and ancient houses, set so close together that neighbors could almost lean out of their upstairs windows and shake hands across the street. Bearskin Neck was supposedly named after an unfortunate bear that drowned and was washed ashore here almost 200 years ago.

Part of the fun in Rockport is shopping along Bearskin Neck, where there are about 50 little shops carrying clothes, gifts, toys, inexpensive novelties, and expensive handmade crafts and paintings. There are lots of places to snack, too; take your pick from lobster-in-the-rough to Austrian-style strudel in four delicious flavors.

Well over two dozen art galleries in town display the works of both local and nationally known artists. And the **Rockport Art Association** (12 Main St.; ☎ **508/546-6604**), open daily year-round, sponsors major exhibitions and special shows throughout the year. In October there's an Amateur Art Festival, and in the winter a live Christmas pageant, a holiday highlight that attracts big crowds.

At the Rockport Chamber of Commerce office, be sure to ask for one of its colorful maps of the town. In the bottom right-hand corner it carries the warning: "Our sea serpent visits only every 25 years." How reassuring!

If you'd like to find a way to recycle that brown bag or want some tips on what to do with old newspapers, visit the **Rockport Paper House** (52 Pigeon Hill St., Pigeon Cove; ☎ **508/546-2629**). It was built in 1922 entirely out of 100,000 newspapers—walls, furniture, everything! Every item of furniture is made from papers of a different period. Admission is $1 for adults and 50¢ for children.

Where to Stay

Moderate

Captain's Bounty Motor Inn

1 Beach St., Rockport, MA 01966. ☎ **508/546-9557.** 24 rms. TV TEL. Apr 1 to May 11 $65 oceanfront room, $68 oceanfront efficiency, $70 oceanfront efficiency suite; May 12 to June 15 $77 oceanfront room, $80 oceanfront efficiency, $85 oceanfront efficiency suite; June 16 to Sept 3 $95 oceanfront room, $100 oceanfront efficiency,

$110 oceanfront efficiency suite; Sept 4 to Oct 31 $78 oceanfront room, $80 oceanfront efficiency, $86 oceanfront efficiency suite. Extra person $10, rollaway bed $5. All rates based on double occupancy. DISC, MC, V.

For those who want modern hotel comfort and a beachfront location, this inn is the place. Ocean breezes provide natural air conditioning, since each room overlooks the water and has its own balcony and sliding glass door. Comforts such as soundproofing and ceramic tile baths with tub and shower are provided. Kitchenette units are available.

Old Farm Inn

291 Granite St. at Pigeon Cove, Rockport, MA 01966. ☎ **508/546-3237.** 10 rms. TEL. In season $88–$125 double, off season $78–$115 double. Room with kitchenette $115, two-room suite $125. Two-bedroom housekeeping cottage, $995 per week. Extra person $10. Rollaway bed $15. All rates include buffet breakfast. AE, MC, V.

The Old Farm Inn is a 1799 saltwater farm with charming antique-furnished rooms in the Inn, the Barn Guesthouse, and the Fieldside Cottage. Each room is uniquely decorated with country-style furnishings (many have beautiful quilts on the beds) and is equipped with everything you could possibly need to make your stay enjoyable and comfortable. The buffet breakfast here, which includes fresh fruit, home-baked breads, a selection of hot and cold cereals, yogurt, and juices, is excellent. All rooms, except one, have air-conditioning.

Peg Leg Motel

10 Beach St., Rockport, MA 01966. ☎ **508/546-6945.** 15 rms. $95–$110 double. AE, DISC, MC, V. Parking free. Closed Nov–Apr.

Operated by Jim and Polly Erwin, this attractive motel is on a quiet knoll overlooking Rockport Harbor and directly across the street from the public beach. The rooms are decorated with Ethan Allen furniture, some with rocking chairs or "overstuffed" comfortable chairs. All rooms are outfitted with double, queen-, or king-size beds and ceramic tile bath with tub and shower.

Ralph Waldo Emerson Inn

Phillips Ave., Rockport, MA 01966. ☎ **508/546-6321.** Fax 508/546-7043. 36 rms. A/C TEL. High season $77–$131 single, $100–$138 double. $23 extra for breakfast and dinner. DISC, MC, V. Parking free. Closed Nov to mid-May.

Somewhere in the old guest register of the Ralph Waldo Emerson Inn you might find the name of Emerson himself, for the distinguished philosopher was a guest in the old section of the inn in the 1850s. Of course, changes have been made since then in this lovely resort at Pigeon Cove, but it still retains the charm of a gracious era with furnishings like spool beds and old-fashioned toilets. The view of the ocean from Cathedral Rocks is magnificent. Guests can enjoy the heated outdoor saltwater swimming pool or the indoor whirlpool and sauna or go fishing, sightseeing, shopping, or just relax in the comfortable chairs on the veranda. Recreation rooms include areas for playing cards, table tennis, or watching the wide-screen TV.

The dining room is open to the public on an availability basis. Breakfast is served from 8 to 10am, and dinner from 6 to 8pm.

Yankee Clipper Inn (Romantik Hotel)

96 Granite St., Rte. 127, Rockport, MA 01966. ☎ **508/546-3407** or 800/545-3699. Fax 508/546-9730. 27 rms. A/C TEL. $95–$219 single or double. Extra person $25. All rates include breakfast. AE, DISC, MC, V.

Just north of town on the road to Pigeon Cove, this luxurious lodging is set on extensive lawns overlooking the sea. There are actually three different buildings, of which the inn, with its Georgian architecture, heated saltwater swimming pool, and rooms with private balconies is the most attractive. From almost all parts of the property there are excellent views of the sea, especially from the large and attractive dining room, which is open to the public. Reservations are necessary.

Budget

Inn on Cove Hill

37 Mt. Pleasant St., Rockport, MA 01966. ☎ **508/546-2701.** 11 rms (9 with bath). $66–$102 double with private bath, $50 with shared bath. All rates include continental breakfast. No credit cards. Closed Nov–Mar.

This inn was built in 1791 from the proceeds of pirates' gold found a short distance away. I don't know if any gold is hidden on the grounds, but this attractive Federal-style home, operated by Marjorie and John Pratt, is an excellent vacation hideaway. Many of the colonial features have been preserved or restored at this white three-story inn. The guest rooms have colonial furnishings, handmade quilts, some canopy beds, and fresh flowers in summer. In warm weather, a continental breakfast with home-baked breads and muffins is served on china at the garden tables; in inclement weather, breakfast in bed is served on individual trays. No smoking is allowed at the Inn on Cove Hill.

If you're coming by train from Boston, the hosts will meet you at the station; if you drive, parking is provided.

Peg Leg Inn

2 King St., Rockport, MA 01966. ☎ **508/546-2352** or 800/346-2352. 33 rms (all with bath). TV. $80–$125 double mid-June to mid-Oct. Off-season rates are lower. Extra person $10. All rates include continental breakfast. MC, V.

If you enjoy a colonial atmosphere, this inn consists of a group of five early American houses with front porches, attractive living rooms, and well-kept flower-bordered lawns. Some rooms have excellent ocean views. Guests at the inn may use the sandy beach across the road. The Peg Leg Restaurant, with its ocean view dining room and greenhouse dining room, is next door.

Where to Dine

Rockport is a "dry" community where restaurants are forbidden by law from serving alcoholic beverages, but you can brown-bag it with your own bottle.

Blacksmith Shop

23 Mt. Pleasant St. ☎ **508/546-6301.** Reservations recommended. Main courses $6.95–$12.95 at lunch, $8.95–$15.95 at dinner; breakfast $1.25–$3.95. AE, DC, MC, V. Last week of Mar–Oct 31, daily 7am–10pm. Closed Nov 1–last week in March. SEAFOOD.

Although most visitors come here primarily for the excellent food, some connoisseurs choose this fine restaurant overlooking Rockport Harbor for the atmosphere—the antique furnishings, chairs from Italy, lights from Spain, paintings in the gallery, and the old forge, anvil, and bellows preserved from the shop where Rockport's village smithy stood. The main dining room, resting on stilts in the harbor, has been enlarged many times since its establishment in 1927, and it now accommodates 200. Seafood is the specialty, and owner Larry Bershad goes to the docks every morning to select the best of the local catch. In season he brings back swordfish, halibut, and lobster from Rockport lobster pots. The menu also features meat and poultry specials. The luncheon menu, available all afternoon, has seafood specials plus sandwiches, salads, and quiche. You can also drop by in the afternoon for dessert and coffee.

My Place-by-the-Sea

68 Bearskin Neck. ☎ **508/546-9667.** Reservations accepted at dinner. Main courses \$8–\$12 at lunch, \$12–\$18 at dinner. AE, CB, DC, DISC, JCB, MC, V. Apr–Nov daily 11:30–9:30pm. Call ahead for hours during the rest of the year. SEAFOOD.

My Place, with Rockport's only outdoor, oceanfront deck, is a favorite with many locals, who personally refer to it as "my place." Located at the very end of Bearskin Neck, at the top of the hill where the cars turn around, it has a view of Sandy Bay from its two decks and shaded patio. Hanging baskets of flowers, borders of plants, and ceiling fans make this one of the prettiest places around. Menu choices depend on the daily catch, so everything is fresh. The seafood fettuccine and the wolffish stuffed with shrimp are popular items. Chicken and beef dishes are also available. And don't skip the desserts, especially the homemade fruit pies.

Peg Leg

18 Beach St. ☎ **508/546-3038.** Reservations recommended. Main courses \$4.95–\$19. AE, MC, V. In season, lunch daily 11:30am–2:30pm, dinner nightly 5:30–9pm. AMERICAN/SEAFOOD.

For lunch or dinner in a greenhouse, complete with hanging baskets, 5-foot geranium trees, and flowers all around, walk through town to the end of Main Street to Peg Leg, where both the food and the surroundings are superior. The greenhouse, very romantic in the evening with its recessed spotlights and candles, is behind the cozy and attractive main restaurant. Dinner entrées include chicken pie, fresh fish, steaks, and lobster. All baking is done on the premises, and breadbaskets always include sweet rolls and bread. The service is excellent; owner Robert H. Welcome exemplifies his name.

3 Plymouth

40 miles SE of Boston

The historic town of Plymouth (pop. 45,000) is where the United States began (in spirit—Jamestown preceded it by 11 years); it's hard not to be awed by reminders of the more than 3½ centuries of history that have accumulated there. When the Pilgrims first set up their encampment at this site in December 1620 (after a preliminary but unsatisfactory landing at Provincetown), all was bleak and uninviting. But the hardy adventurers built homes, planted crops, and established friendly relations with the natives; and the seeds they planted have, in more ways than one, endured to this day.

Cape Cod was named in 1602 by Capt. Bartholomew Gosnold, and 12 years later Capt. John Smith sailed along the coast of what he named "New England" and designated "Plymouth" as the mainland opposite Cape Cod.

The passengers on the *Mayflower* had contracted with the London Virginia Company for a tract of land near the mouth of the Hudson River in "Northern Virginia"; in exchange for their passage to the New World, they promised to work the land for the company for seven years. However, on November 11, 1620, experiencing perilous shoals and roaring breakers, with the wind howling, they had to make for Cape Cod Bay and anchor there. Subsequently, their captain announced that they had found a safe harbor and he refused to continue the voyage farther south to their original destination. They had no option but to settle in New England, and with no one to command them, their contract with the London Virginia Company became void and they were on their own to begin a new world.

Getting There By car, follow the Southeast Expressway from Boston to Route 3. Take Exit 6 to Plymouth, turn right onto Route 44, and follow signs to the historic attractions. Stop at the **Regional Information Complex** on Route 3, Exit 5, for maps, brochures, and information.

Buses operated by the **Plymouth and Brockton Street Railway** leave the Peter Pan (Trailways) terminal at 555 Atlantic Avenue (☎ **508/746-0378**), across the street from South Station. You can also make connections at Logan Airport, where buses take on passengers at all airline terminals.

Essentials The **area code** is 508. Possibly your first stop should be the town's **Visitor Center,** at 130 Water Street, across from the town pier.

If you'd like to plan ahead, call **Plymouth Visitor Information** (☎ **508/747-7525** or 800/USA-1620).

What to See & Do

The Plymouth of today is an attractive seafaring town with much to occupy your attention. The most logical place to begin your tour is where the Pilgrims first set foot—at **Plymouth Rock.** The rock, accepted as the landing place of the *Mayflower* passengers, was originally 15 feet long and 3 feet wide. It was moved on the eve of the Revolution and several times thereafter, before acquiring its present permanent position at tide level, where the winter storms still break over it as they did in Pilgrim days. The present portico that enshrines the rock was given in 1920 by the Colonial Dames of America.

You can't stay at the beautiful historic houses of Plymouth, but you should visit them to see the changing styles of architecture and furnishings since the 1600s. Costumed guides explain the homemaking details and the crafts of earlier generations. There are six homes that can be visited during a walking tour: **Richard Sparrow House** (1640), **Howland House** (1667), **Harlow Old Fort House** (1677), **Spooner House** (1749), **Antiquarian House** (1809), and **Mayflower Society Museum** (1754–1898). Combination tickets for tours of all the houses are available; inquire at the Visitor Center, discussed above, for details.

To get around town, try the picturesque open-air trolley—it runs frequently to points of interest. Trolley markers indicate the stops.

To get away from the bustle of the waterfront, you might want to relax at **Town Brook Park** at Jenny Pond, across from the Governor Carver Motor Inn. This is a beautiful tree-lined pond with ducks and swans. Across from the pond is **Jenny Grist Mill Village,** a reconstructed early American water-powered mill and a cluster of specialty shops. And they say that the fish ladder at the mill is the best place to see the spring herring run. The shops are open seven days a week from 10am to 6pm. There is plenty of parking.

You can shop at the **Village Landing Market,** overlooking the Plymouth waterfront. The specialty shops and boutiques are clustered along cobblestone walkways bordered with benches, trees, and flowers. Summer band concerts are held in the gazebo, and it's a charming place for shopping or browsing.

A combination ticket for Plimoth Plantation, the Indian campsite, and *Mayflower II* is $18.50 for adults and $11 for children 5 through 12. (Wear comfortable shoes. There's a lot of walking involved and, naturally, it isn't paved.)

Mayflower II

State Pier. ☎ **508/746-1622.** $5.75 adults, $3.75 children age 5–12, children under 5 free. Apr–Nov 30 daily 9am–5pm.

Berthed only a few steps from Plymouth Rock, *Mayflower II* is a full-scale reproduction of the type of ship that brought the Pilgrims from England to America. Although little technical information is known about the original *Mayflower,* William A. Baker, designer of *Mayflower II,* incorporated the few references in Governor Bradford's account of the voyage with other research to re-create as closely as possible the actual ship. Exhibits on board show what life was like during that 66-day voyage in 1620 on a vessel crowded with 102 passengers, 25 crewmen, and all the supplies needed to sustain the colony until the first crops were harvested.

Men and women in period costumes on board the ship talk about the ship's crossing, answer questions, and dispatch little-known but interesting pieces of information.

You will probably want to tour the ship. The vessel is owned and maintained by Plimoth Plantation, which is 3 miles south of the ship. A combination ticket for *Mayflower II* and Plimoth Plantation is $18.50 for adults and $11 for children age 5–12.

Alongside *Mayflower II* are museum shops that replicate early Pilgrim dwellings from 1620–21.

Pilgrim Hall Museum

75 Court St. ☎ **508/746-1620.** $5 adults, $4 senior citizens, $2.50 children. Daily 9:30am–4:30pm. Closed January.

The Pilgrim Hall Museum, the oldest public museum in the United States, is listed on the National Register of Historic Places. A major attraction in town, it is replete with original possessions of the early Pilgrims and their descendants. The building itself dates from 1824. Among the exhibits is the skeleton of the *Sparrowhawk,* a ship wrecked on Cape Cod in 1627, which lay buried in the sand and undiscovered for more than 200 years.

Plimoth Plantation

Rte. 3 (Exit 4). ☎ **508/746-1622.** Plimoth Plantation and Mayflower II $18.50 adults, $11 children age 5–12, children under 5 free. Apr–Nov daily 9am–5pm. Directions: From Rte. 3, take Exit 4, marked "Plimoth Plantation Highway."

Plimoth Plantation is a worthy re-creation of a 1627 Pilgrim village. You enter by the hilltop fort that protects the "villagers" and then walk down the hill to the farm area, visiting the homes and gardens along the way, which have been constructed with careful attention to historic detail. It's great fun to talk to the Pilgrims, people who, in speech, dress, and manner, assume the personalities of members of the original community. You can watch them framing a house, splitting wood, shearing sheep, preserving foodstuffs, or cooking a pot of fish stew over an open hearth, all as it was done in the 1600s. And they use only the tools and cookware available at that time. (It's a challenge to try and get them to acknowledge modern phrases such as airplane, camera, silverware, and ice cream.) Sometimes you can join in the activities—perhaps planting, harvesting, a court trial, or a wedding party.

The community is as accurate as research can make it: accounts of the original Pilgrim colony were combined with archaeological research, old records, and the 17th-century history written by the Pilgrims' leader, William Bradford, who often used the spelling "Plimoth" for the settlement. There are daily militia drills with matchlock muskets that are fired to demonstrate the community's defense system. In actual fact, little defense was needed, since the local Native Americans were friendly. Local tribes included the Wampanoags, who are represented at a homesite near the village, where the museum staff show off native foodstuffs, agricultural practices, and crafts. The homesite is included in admission to the plantation.

At the main entrance to the plantation you'll find two modern buildings with an interesting orientation show, exhibits, gift shop, "live" crafts center, bookstore, cafeteria, and nearby picnic area.

Cranberry World

225 Water St. ☎ **508/747-2350.** Free admission. May 1–Nov 30 daily 9:30am–5pm.

If you like cranberries—cranberry sauce, cranberry bread, or even cranberry salsa—you'll be fascinated by the exhibits at Cranberry World, where there are outdoor demonstration bogs, antique harvesting tools, a scale model of a cranberry farm, and film and slide shows. September and October are harvest time. In addition there are daily cooking demonstrations and free refreshments. Ocean Spray's **Visitors Center** is a 10–minute walk from Plymouth Rock.

Where to Stay

On busy summer weekends, every room in town is often taken. It is advisable to make reservations well in advance.

Moderate

Governor Bradford Motor Inn

98 Water St., Plymouth, MA 02360. ☎ **508/746-6200** or 800/332-1620. Fax 508/747-3032. 94 rms. A/C TV TEL. $76–$120 single or double in season. Extra person $10. Rates vary with season. Children under 14 stay free in parents' room. AE, DC, DISC, MC, V.

One of the finest hotels in Plymouth, this inn is beautifully situated right on the waterfront and only one block from Plymouth Rock, the *Mayflower II,* and the center of town. The rooms, each with two double beds, are attractive in a modern style, with wall-to-wall carpeting, refrigerator, and in-room coffee. There's a small heated outdoor pool.

John Carver Inn

25 Summer St. at Town Brook, Plymouth, MA 02360. ☎ **508/746-7100** or 800/274-1620. Fax 508/746-8299. 79 rms. A/C TV TEL. Apr 14–Jun 15 and Oct 22–Nov 21 $69–$89 single or double; June 16–Sept 14 $79–$99 single or double; Sept 15–Oct 21 $85–$105 single or double; Nov 26–Apr 12 $59–$79 single or double. Passport to History package $246–$298 depending on season. Senior discount. AE, CB, DC, DISC, MC, V.

This imposing colonial-style building offers excellent, comfortable, modern (and recently renovated) accommodations, a large pool, free cribs, and all the amenities. It is also within walking distance of the main attractions. A **Hearth 'n' Kettle** restaurant is on the premises. The hotel offers a special package (the John Carver Inn Passport to History Packages) that includes a two-night, three-day stay for two, four breakfast tickets to the Hearth 'n' Kettle restaurant, two $10 discount dinner tickets at the restaurant, two Plimoth Plantation or Whale Watch tickets, and two tickets to the Trolley or Wax Museum.

Pilgrim Sands Motel

150 Warren Ave., Rte. 3A, Plymouth, MA 02360. ☎ **508/747-0900** or 800/729-SANDS. Fax 508/746-8066. 64 rms. A/C TV TEL. $90–$120 double, summer; $70–$95 double, spring and Indian summer; $60–$80 double, fall; $50–$70 double, winter. Higher rates for ocean view. Extra person $8. AE, CB, DC, DISC, MC, V.

This attractive vacation spot is outside town, yet within walking distance of the Plimoth Plantation. The ultramodern units, located right on the ocean, have individually controlled heating and air conditioning, wall-to-wall carpeting, and tasteful furnishings. In the summer you can enjoy the private beach, terraces, whirlpool spa, and outdoor and indoor pools, too. Most rooms have two double or two queen-size beds. Many rooms have refrigerators. Open year-round.

Sheraton Plymouth

180 Water St., Plymouth, MA 02360. ☎ **508/747-4900** or 800/325-3535. Fax 508/746-2609. 175 rms. A/C TV TEL. Apr–Oct $90–$150 single, $100–$160 double; Nov–Mar $75–$100 single, $85–$125 double. Extra person (18 and older) $15. AE, CB, DC, DISC, JCB, MC, V.

Located at the Village Landing, this very attractive facility faces the harbor and shares the charming ambience of the marketplace with its little shops and park. The guest rooms have climate control and in-room movies. Some have balconies that overlook the indoor swimming pool and whirlpool, in a colorful garden setting. The hotel also has an exercise room and a restaurant, **Harbor Grill,** which serves a delicious Sunday brunch, and **Flix,** open on weekends for Top 40s dancing.

Budget

Cold Spring Motel

188 Court St., Rte. 3A, Plymouth, MA 02360. ☎ **508/746-2222.** 31 rms. A/C TV TEL. $51–$66 double, $58–$76 cottage in season. Lower rates spring and fall. Extra person $5. AE, DISC, MC, V. Closed Mid–Oct to Apr.

Convenient to all historic sites, this pleasant, quiet motel has rooms with wall-to-wall carpeting and private bath. There's parking at your door.

Where to Dine

Seafood, of course, is the specialty at almost all Plymouth restaurants, where much of the daily catch goes right from the fishing boat to the kitchen. And with so many restaurants in town you can choose one to fit your tastes—on the waterfront, in town, or at the Jenny Grist Mill Village.

On the Waterfront

Isaac's

114 Water St. ☎ **508/830-0001.** Reservations recommended. Main courses $6.95–$10.95, burgers and sandwiches $3.95–$5.95, Sun brunch $7.95. AE, MC, V. Mon–Sat 11:30am–10:45pm; Sun brunch 8am–noon, lunch and dinner 1–10:45pm. AMERICAN.

Isaac Allerton was the first assistant governor of the colony that later became Massachusetts. His keen business sense made him a legend in the early 1600s. This excellent restaurant, located on the waterfront and bearing his name, is also becoming a legend in its own way. It has great food, great values, and a grand view of the harbor. The prices may be moderate, but everything else is top line. And there's something for almost everyone—charcoal-broiled sirloin; fettuccine; specialties stir-fried in a wok; baked, broiled, and fried seafood; and deli and turkey sandwiches.

The dining room is on two levels separated by a brass rail, and large windows overlook the harbor. The decor is striking, with red tablecloths, accents of black, and glass walls that visually enlarge the room. Isaac's is on the second floor of a renovated building.

Lobster Hut

On the Town Wharf. ☎ **508/746-2270.** Fax 746-5655. Reservations not accepted. Luncheon specials $4.50–$7.95, main courses $4.95–$12.95 (lobster meat), sandwiches $1.75–$5.95. MC, V. Daily 11am–9pm in summer; daily 11am–7pm in winter. SEAFOOD.

Lobster Hut is a clean, shiny, self-service restaurant. Take your order to an indoor table or out on the large deck that overlooks the bay. For starters have some clam chowder or lobster bisque. Then choose from a long list of fried seafood—including clams, scallops, shrimp, and haddock. Or you might prefer boiled and steamed items, burgers, or chicken tenders. Beer and wine are served but only with a meal.

McGrath's Harbour Restaurant

Town Wharf. ☎ **508/746-9751.** Reservations recommended. Lunch and dinner $9.95–$14.95. AE, MC, V. In season daily 11:30am–10pm. Closed Mon in winter. SEAFOOD.

McGrath's is big, busy, and the choice of many families and tour groups. In addition to fish and seafood dinners, the menu features chicken, prime rib, sandwiches, and a special children's menu. Check on the clambakes, too. McGrath's has been a waterfront favorite for about 50 years.

At Jenny Grist Mill Village

Run of the Mill Tavern

Jenny Grist Mill Village. ☎ **508/830-1262.** Reservations recommended. Main courses $6–$11. AE, MC, V. Mon–Sat 11am–10pm, Sun noon–10pm. AMERICAN.

You'll find the Run of the Mill Tavern near the waterwheel at Jenny Grist Mill Village at Town Brook Path. It's an attractive setting, and the tavern offers good inexpensive meals. Appetizers include nachos, potato skins, buffalo wings, and mushrooms. Entrées are standard meat, chicken, and fish, but there are also seafood specialties with scallops and shrimp. And if you want a light meal, try a sandwich and clam chowder, or a salad.

The children's menu is a great bargain, with burgers and fish and chips at $2.50 to $3.50.

South Carver

Crane Brook Restaurant

Tremont St., South Carver. ☎ **508/866-3235.** Reservations required. Main courses $8.95–$14.95 at lunch, $18.50–$29 at dinner. AE, MC, V. Wed–Fri lunch 11:30am–2:30pm; dinner Wed–Sun 5:30–9pm; Sun brunch (Sept–June only) 11:30am–2:30pm. AMERICAN.

Crane Brook is a charming restaurant with a wood-beamed, candlelit dining room, a lounge with a wood-burning stove, and a deck with gazebo overlooking a pond for outdoor dining. Entrées include a nice selection of meat, chicken, and fish and are served with homemade rolls. Crane Brook was formerly a tearoom, but now serves afternoon tea only for groups of 15 or more. Currently, there is live piano music on Friday and Saturday evenings. The restaurant can be reached from Route 495 and Route 3. Ask for directions when you phone for reservations.

Index

Notes

Notes

Notes

The following Frommer's guides are available from your favorite bookstore, or you can use the order form on the preceding page to request them as part of your membership in Frommer's Travel Book Club.

FROMMER'S COMPLETE TRAVEL GUIDES

(Comprehensive guides to sightseeing, dining and accommodations, with selections in all price ranges—from deluxe to budget)

Acapulco/Ixtapa/Taxco, 2nd Ed.	C157
Alaska '94-'95	C131
Arizona '95	C166
Australia '94-'95	C147
Austria, 6th Ed.	C162
Bahamas '96 (avail. 8/95)	C172
Belgium/Holland/Luxembourg, 4th Ed.	C170
Bermuda '96 (avail. 8/95)	C174
California '95	C164
Canada '94-'95	C145
Caribbean '96 (avail. 9/95)	C173
Carolinas/Georgia, 2nd Ed.	C128
Colorado '96 (avail. 11/95)	C179
Costa Rica, 1st Ed.	C161
Cruises '95-'96	C150
Delaware/Maryland '94-'95	C136
England '96 (avail. 10/95)	C180
Florida '96 (avail. 9/95)	C181
France '96 (avail. 11/95)	C182
Germany '96 (avail. 9/95)	C176
Honolulu/Waikiki/Oahu, 4th Ed. (avail. 10/95)	C178
Ireland, 1st Ed.	C168
Italy '96 (avail. 11/95)	C183
Jamaica/Barbados, 2nd Ed.	C149
Japan '94-'95	C144
Maui, 1st Ed.	C153
Nepal, 3rd Ed. (avail. 11/95)	C184
New England '95	C165
New Mexico, 3rd Ed.	C167
New York State, 4th Ed.	C133
Northwest, 5th Ed.	C140
Portugal '94-'95	C141
Puerto Rico '95-'96	C151
Puerto Vallarta/Manzanillo/ Guadalajara, 2nd Ed.	C135
Scandinavia, 16th Ed.	C169
Scotland '94-'95	C146
South Pacific '94-'95	C138
Spain, 16th Ed.	C163
Switzerland, 7th Ed. (avail. 9/95)	C177
Thailand, 2nd Ed.	C154
U.S.A., 4th Ed.	C156
Virgin Islands, 3rd Ed. (avail. 8/95)	C175
Virginia '94-'95	C142
Yucatán '95-'96	C155

FROMMER'S $-A-DAY GUIDES

(Dream Vacations at Down-to-Earth Prices)

Australia on $45 '95-'96	D122
Berlin from $50, 3rd Ed. (avail. 10/95)	D137
Caribbean from $60, 1st Ed. (avail. 9/95)	D133
Costa Rica/Guatemala/Belize on $35, 3rd Ed.	D126
Eastern Europe on $30, 5th Ed.	D129
England from $50 '96 (avail. 11/95)	D138
Europe from $50 '96 (avail. 10/95)	D139
Greece from $45, 6th Ed.	D131
Hawaii from $60 '96 (avail. 9/95)	D134
Ireland on $45 '94-'95	D118
Israel on $45, 15th Ed.	D130
London from $55 '96 (avail. 11/95)	D136
Madrid on $50 '94-'95	D119
Mexico from $35 '96 (avail. 10/95)	D135
New York on $70 '94-'95	D121
New Zealand from $45, 6th Ed.	D132
Paris on $45 '94-'95	D117
South America on $40, 16th Ed.	D123
Washington, D.C. on $50 '94-'95	D120

FROMMER'S COMPLETE CITY GUIDES

(Comprehensive guides to sightseeing, dining, and accommodations in all price ranges)

Amsterdam, 8th Ed.	S176
Athens, 10th Ed.	S174
Atlanta & the Summer Olympic Games '96 (avail. 11/95)	S181
Atlantic City/Cape May, 5th Ed.	S130
Bangkok, 2nd Ed.	S147
Barcelona '93-'94	S115
Berlin, 3rd Ed.	S162
Boston '95	S160
Budapest, 1st Ed.	S139
Chicago '95	S169
Denver/Boulder/ Colorado Springs, 3rd Ed.	S154
Disney World/Orlando '96 (avail. 9/95)	S178
Dublin, 2nd Ed.	S157
Hong Kong '94-'95	S140
Las Vegas '95	S163
London '96 (avail. 9/95)	S179
Los Angeles '95	S164
Madrid/Costa del Sol, 2nd Ed.	S165
Mexico City, 1st Ed.	S175
Miami '95-'96	S149
Minneapolis/St. Paul, 4th Ed.	S159
Montréal/Québec City '95	S166
Nashville/Memphis, 1st Ed.	S141
New Orleans '96 (avail. 10/95)	S182
New York City '96 (avail. 11/95)	S183
Paris '96 (avail. 9/95)	S180
Philadelphia, 8th Ed.	S167
Prague, 1st Ed.	S143
Rome, 10th Ed.	S168
St. Louis/Kansas City, 2nd Ed.	S127
San Antonio/Austin, 1st Ed.	S177
San Diego '95	S158
San Francisco '96 (avail. 10/95)	S184
Santa Fe/Taos/ Albuquerque '95	S172
Seattle/Portland '94-'95	S137
Sydney, 4th Ed.	S171
Tampa/St. Petersburg, 3rd Ed.	S146
Tokyo '94-'95	S144
Toronto, 3rd Ed.	S173
Vancouver/Victoria '94-'95	S142
Washington, D.C. '95	S153

FROMMER'S FAMILY GUIDES

(Guides to family-friendly hotels, restaurants, activities, and attractions)

California with Kids	F105
Los Angeles with Kids	F103
New York City with Kids	F101
San Francisco with Kids	F104
Washington, D.C. with Kids	F102

FROMMER'S WALKING TOURS

(Memorable strolls through colorful and historic neighborhoods, accompanied by detailed directions and maps)

Berlin	W100
Chicago	W107
England's Favorite Cities	W108
London, 2nd Ed.	W111
Montréal/Québec City	W106
New York, 2nd Ed.	W113
Paris, 2nd Ed.	W112
San Francisco, 2nd Ed.	W115
Spain's Favorite Cities (avail. 9/95)	W116
Tokyo	W109
Venice	W110
Washington, D.C., 2nd Ed.	W114

FROMMER'S AMERICA ON WHEELS

(Guides for travelers who are exploring the U.S.A. by car, featuring a brand-new rating system for accommodations and full-color road maps)

Arizona/New Mexico	A100
California/Nevada	A101
Florida	A102
Mid-Atlantic	A103

FROMMER'S SPECIAL-INTEREST TITLES

Title	Code	Title	Code
Arthur Frommer's Branson!	P107	Frommer's Where to Stay U.S.A., 11th Ed.	P102
Arthur Frommer's New World of Travel (avail. 11/95)	P112	National Park Guide, 29th Ed.	P106
Frommer's Caribbean Hideaways (avail. 9/95)	P110	USA Today Golf Tournament Guide	P113
Frommer's America's 100 Best-Loved State Parks	P109	USA Today Minor League Baseball Book	P111

FROMMER'S BEST BEACH VACATIONS

(The top places to sun, stroll, shop, stay, play, party, and swim—with each beach rated for beauty, swimming, sand, and amenities)

Title	Code	Title	Code
California (avail. 10/95)	G100	Hawaii (avail. 10/95)	G102
Florida (avail. 10/95)	G101		

FROMMER'S BED & BREAKFAST GUIDES

(Selective guides with four-color photos and full descriptions of the best inns in each region)

Title	Code	Title	Code
California	B100	Hawaii	B105
Caribbean	B101	Pacific Northwest	B106
East Coast	B102	Rockies	B107
Eastern United States	B103	Southwest	B108
Great American Cities	B104		

FROMMER'S IRREVERENT GUIDES

(Wickedly honest guides for sophisticated travelers and those who want to be)

Title	Code	Title	Code
Chicago (avail. 11/95)	I100	New Orleans (avail. 11/95)	I103
London (avail. 11/95)	I101	San Francisco (avail. 11/95)	I104
Manhattan (avail. 11/95)	I102	Virgin Islands (avail. 11/95)	I105

FROMMER'S DRIVING TOURS

(Four-color photos and detailed maps outlining spectacular scenic driving routes)

Title	Code	Title	Code
Australia	Y100	Italy	Y108
Austria	Y101	Mexico	Y109
Britain	Y102	Scandinavia	Y110
Canada	Y103	Scotland	Y111
Florida	Y104	Spain	Y112
France	Y105	Switzerland	Y113
Germany	Y106	U.S.A.	Y114
Ireland	Y107		

FROMMER'S BORN TO SHOP

(The ultimate travel guides for discriminating shoppers—from cut-rate to couture)

Title	Code	Title	Code
Hong Kong (avail. 11/95)	Z100	London (avail. 11/95)	Z101